"HE FOUND HIMSELF SET IN SADDLE IN THE MIDST OF A CLUMP OF SPEARS."

No. 1.

BRAKESPEARE

OR

The Fortunes of a Free Lance

BY
GEORGE A. LAWRENCE

NEW YORK
GROSSET & DUNLAP
PUBLISHERS

Copyright, 1904
by
F. M. Buckles & Company

"Brakespeare"

BRAKESPEARE;

OR,

THE FORTUNES OF A FREE LANCE.

CHAPTER I.

TWENTY YEARS BACK.

RIGHT in the shadow of the wooded hills that fringed the border of the Kentish Weald, stood the ancient castle of Bever—so ancient, that, before the thirteen hundredth year of Grace, it had begun to show signs of decay; crevices bare of mortar gave rare holding-ground for moss and wallflower, and the coigns where wind and weather beat sharpest had already moldered.

Moreover, it had the evil chance to be sacked and burned in two Civil Wars. After the first of these disasters it was partly restored; but in the second, mining-powder helped fire and battering-train, and the work was so thoroughly done, that scarce a semblance of the dwelling was left among uncouth heaps of rent, blackened stone. No wonder that Dynevor, coming to his own again, should turn aside from the unlucky site, and choose to build a more modest mansion on the nearest hill-spur, where he found a fairer prospect and healthier air. Long after that, the country-folk came to the spot, as to a quarry, for such rude repairs as needed not fresh mason-work; and the ruins that were left crumbled fast under their dank shroud of ivy and lichen, till at last the sward closed smoothly over all. Fifty years ago, a careless wayfarer might have passed by, without ever noticing the low broad mounds swelling over the foundations of flanking tower, barbican, and keep, and the faint irregular hollow that traces the circuit of the castle-ditch. Nevertheless, the husbandman guesses that there is masonry enough, not a cubit below the sod, to turn the edge of the stoutest plowshare: and the antiquary—witting well that with this spot neither Briton, Roman, nor Anglo-Saxon has had ought to do—cares not to delve in soil barren of treasure-trove in clay, metal, or bone. So the old pasturage remains unbroken; neither is it likely that for many a year the South Down wethers will be troubled in their enjoyment of the short, sweet herbage on which they thrive so marvelously.

But it was a fair castle enough in its day—overlarge, in truth, for the demesnes which were its appanage; and these had been greatly narrowed early in the fourteenth century by the grant of lands made by Sir Giles Dynevor to the Cistercian Abbey of Haultvaux.

The causes of which munificence, and other matters pertaining to this tale, shall now be set forth.

Men of a certain mold must needs leave their mark on their time, even if they achieve therein no great dignity or honor; and the cool, crafty schemer is most dangerous in an age where rapine by the strong hand prevails, and the mass have neither patience to wait, nor providence to plan. Such an one was Giles Dynevor. Violent, sensual, and rapacious by nature—he kept anger, lust, and covetousness in fetters, till it was safe or profitable to let them loose; and, though his favorite sin was avarice, he would scatter gold broadcast without murmur or regret, if thereby he hoped to compass some end worthy the cost. He was possessed by that thorough-going ambition which is not devoid of simple unselfish grandeur, insomuch that it aims rather at the advancement of posterity than at profit, private and personal, for oftentimes the schemer can no more hope to reap the ripe fruit of his policy than the planter of an acorn could hope to sit under the full shadow of the oak. Nevertheless, he throve not after the measure of his merits; and, when long past middle age, his advancement would have fallen far short of his desires, had they been tenfold more moderate. Nor would the causes of this ill fortune be hard to find; though Dynevor, with all his subtlety, perceived them not. The very qualities that might reasonably have made him powerful, made him both misliked and mistrusted. The rude barons and unlettered knights, that were his fellows, felt that there was one in the midst of them whose thoughts were not as their thoughts, and shrank from the quiet, taciturn, clerkly plotter as they would have shrunk from an intruder of alien blood. Few cared openly to avoid his company, much less to provoke his enmity; but none cared to court his friendship; and many would have been well pleased to thwart his purpose, even though it clashed not with their own.

To this dislike, covert or avowed, there was one singular exception. Ivo Malpas and Giles Dynevor had been not neighbors alone, but sworn companions, from boyhood upward. They had followed the chase through the same woods; had caroused at the same table when the hunting was done; and, if all the tales were true, had wrought more evil deeds in common than need be recorded here.

In public quarrel, or private feud, these two had ever espoused the same cause; and their vassals fought, naturally, side by side, when the battle was set in array. Once, in the Scots wars, when Malpas had blundered into an ambush, like a wild bull into the toils, Dynevor had ridden in gallantly to the rescue, and brought off his brother-in-arms scathless, at the cost of a shrewd lance-thrust in his own side; for the Black Douglas, though overmatched, gave ground slowly and sullenly, turning, every now and then, to gore.

In all this close companionship, it would have been strange indeed had the weaker nature not been enslaved by the stronger; and Ivo Malpas was noted for witlessness, in a witless age. Moreover, he was given to strong drinks, to an extent rare among the Normans, who despised drunkenness as a vice of a conquered people. As time passed on, the subjection grew more complete, till at last Ivo was no more a free agent than if he had been born a villein on the fief of Bever. Two solitary virtues, honesty and courage, abode with him still; but, in despite of these, he would have turned his hand to any work, howsoever base or cruel, had his comrade so willed it.

It may be that Giles Dynevor liked the poor faithful sot, as much as it was in his nature to like any living being not of his own blood. Yet, had it served his ends, he would scarcely have scrupled to mix for the other such a posset as should have made his slumbers last till the Judgment Day. Through long years, Dynevor had kept one purpose steadily in view; and matters had not yet come to the point where Ivo's death could profit any one.

That purpose was—the alliance of their several houses.

For many rods their lands marched together; but, at a certain angle where the boundary stream tended eastward, the fief of Dynevor ended, while that of Malpas stretched its fertile length a full league beyond his neighbor's landmark. Sir Giles could scarce remember the time, when he first cast covetous eyes on the broad inheritance that seemed to dwarf, by contrast, his own domain. Certainly, before boyhood ended, he had sworn to attach it to himself by fair means or foul. For awhile the course of events seemed to run strangely in unison with his design.

After the birth of one son his own marriage-bed was barren; and, of four born to Ivo Malpas, one daughter only remained, some years younger than Dynevor's heir. True it was, that at the death of its lord without issue, the fief of Tyringham would revert to its suzerain. But, for years to come, the crown must needs be worn by a driveler, or an infant; and Sir Giles had faith enough in his own sagacity and knowledge of court tides, not to fear the result. The husband of Malpas's only daughter, being of suitable degree, might reasonably ask for the renewal of her father's seisin; and, by the time it was wanted, there should be gold enough in the family coffers to secure the intercession of any favorite by glutting his greed.

So, let Ivo only live till the night of the day that should make their houses one. Afterward—

At this stage in his musings Sir Giles's cruel face would harden and darken. Of a surety he did not reckon on his friend's enjoying great length of days.

Before Edith Malpas was well into her teens, she was solemnly betrothed to Simon Dynevor; and the plighting, by proxy, of hand and glove was celebrated at Tyringham by a mighty carouse, whence the lord of the castle was borne senseless to his couch; while the other contracting party walked slowly and steadily to his chamber, where he sat pondering late into the night.

The affianced pair grew up through boyhood and girlhood, meeting very seldom. Neither did this rare intercourse ripen their liking. The damsel was anything but pleasant to look upon; being in truth, somewhat deformed in shape, and afflicted almost from her birth with fits of the falling-sickness. Of these defects, when he sent his son a-wooing, Sir Giles made account of no more than, in choosing a war-horse, he would have objected to a coarse neck or heavy crest, where all other points were perfect. In bare justice to him it should be averred, that he would not have been a whit more delicate had the case been his own. The broad lands of Tyringham must needs be taken with an encumbrance; and he would as lief have laid the burden on his own shoulders as on those of his heir. But Dame Alice Dynevor cared for her body's health no less than for her soul's; and showed no signs of presently quitting the world whose sins she was ever bewailing. So, since better might not be, he prepared to sacrifice his first-born calmly—if not complacently—as many fathers, Pagan, Hebrew, and Christian, have done before and since his time.

Now, though all the surface looked placid and prosperous enough, there was an under-current fraught with danger and wreck to these politic plans. Though he inherited not his sire's ruthless strength of will, there was in Simon Dynevor a slow sullen obstinacy, prompting him to run counter to the bidding of any authority whatsoever, so long as he risked not open revolt. Having no ambition, and but a moderate share of avarice, he held that the fief of Bever might well suffice his needs, as it had hitherto sufficed his father's; and cared not to pay with his body for the acquirement of wealth and power that he wist not how to use, or for possible advancement to baron's degree.

He had conceived an aversion for his child-betrothed from the first moment he had heard her shrill, querulous voice, and set eyes on her white, pain-stricken face and misshaped figure. As the days drew on, this deepened into somewhat nearly akin to loathing; and the unseen fetter galled him more and more sorely. When he was of age to ride in his father's train to distant jousts, or other congresses of knights and barons, it was strange to see how his mood would change and lighten when once fairly out of sight of the watchtower of Tyringham, which was a landmark for leagues around. By the time they reached their journey's end, Simon was ready to join in revel or mischief with as keen a relish as the maddest esquire of them all; albeit there was ever a certain feverishness in his mirth. When they turned bridle again, the cloud settled down faster than it had lifted; and there passed in over the drawbridge of Bever the same sullen, silent youth that had ridden forth a week agone.

When the lords of the Western Marches rose up in revolt, Dynevor went not forth with Lancaster and his compeers. Farther, he prevailed on Malpas to bide quietly at home. Not without difficulty—for that brainless knight could never hear of brawl or battle, without coveting his share in bowls and plunder. During their brief success, Sir Giles never once repented himself of his caution, neither did he deign to answer his comrade's repeated grumblings. But, after the disaster at Boroughbridge, when the best blood in England was flowing under the doomster's knife, said Dynevor with his surly smile—

"Owest me no thanks for again saving that big carcass of thine? This last was a better turn than when I plucked thee out of Black James's grip. Were it not for me, thou wouldst be feeding crows on the same gibbet with yonder wittol of Badlesmere."

To all this Ivo gave ready assent, and thenceforth believed more helplessly than ever in the other's foresight and sagacity.

So the time for the fulfilment of the contract drew nearer and nearer, till the espousals were fixed for Edith's sixteenth birthday. It was in the year that brought a weak and wicked reign to a shameful ending —the year that saw a long debt fairly paid, when Isabella and her liegemen gave monarch and minion quittance in full.

Ere this, another feeling besides aversion was at work in Simon Dynevor's breast.

CHAPTER II.

MATCHED, NOT MATED.

In those times, many discreet and pious ladies, even of no great estate, were wont to take under their charge one or more damsels of gentle birth, whom death or other chance had deprived of their natural protectors, for the purpose of educating them till they should be sought in marriage; such education being in most cases confined to perpetual practise of tapestry work, and the hearing of homilies and saintly legends, read aloud by the chapellan of the castle.

Maude Warenne's father was but a poor knight-bachelor; and spent well-nigh all the remains of his worldly estate in the furnishing of a small clump of lances, when the King set forth for his last Scottish war; hoping, doubtless, to recoup himself by ransom of prisoners, if not by plunder. But by that ill-fated armament neither wealth nor fame was to be won. When Michael Warenne died gallantly in his harness at Bannockburn—covering the flight of the monarch who knew him not by name—he left his orphan child nearly a beggar.

Dame Alice Dynevor was a somewhat distant cousin; nevertheless Sir Giles made no objection when his wife proposed to take the maiden in charge. The hangings in the great presence-chamber sorely wanted renewing; and, for some few years to come, a deft worker in tapestry might be well worth clothing and maintenance.

Maude Warenne was a fair, delicate girl—fair enough, at least, to draw to herself whatsoever of heart the heir of Dynevor had to spare. It was the old story over again, that never lacks a new phase— the story of the Labyrinth as ancient as Time, wherein any one of ten thousand thousand paths may lead to the same fatal goal. Dame Alice, albeit the austerest and most vigilant of matrons—like other dragons—saw no danger in her own brood; and set little check on the companionship of those two. Simon Dynevor grew wondrously duteous in attendance of his mother, and fond of listening to the chapellan's long-winded readings. Then there came about meetings—brief at first, and seemingly by chance, soon of design, and perilously prolonged—in some lonely echoing corridor, through which few of the household would have cared to pass alone after nightfall; then, stolen trysts by moonlight in some shady nook of the castle garden. One morning, just a month before the day for which the Malpas espousals were set, those two strolled forth into the plaisance beyond the barbican, innocently enough; but they came not back to the nooning: and, before vespers, all at Bever wist that they had fled together.

When Sir Giles returned—he had ridden forth to a neighboring town soon after dawn—he found his household in great turmoil; and Dame Alice ill at ease, tended only by her bower-woman and mediciner.

That imperious lady stood in mortal fear of her husband, albeit her worst treatment at his hands had been cold neglect, varied by some brutal jest or savage sneer; and she preferred that he should hear bad tidings from any other mouth than hers. But Dynevor received them with singular calmness, only grumbling under his breath—

"A murrain on the hot-blooded fool! Could he not have waited for his leman till he was wived?"

He thought his son was but repeating one of the profligate adventures for which his own youth and early manhood had been evilly renowned; and guessed that the seducer would not tarry long with his victim after his fantasy was sated. Also, he knew that Ivo Malpas would be more like to laugh than be wroth at such a freak of his future son-in-law; and that the child-bride—even if it came to her ears—would not dare to murmur. So that the espousals need not necessarily be deferred. The good knight had ever a politic horror of open scandal or uproar; wherefore he caused no hue and cry to be made after the truants, and for awhile seemed content to let things bide.

But on the fifth evening one of Dynevor's foresters, coming homeward through the twilight, was accosted about a league from the castle by a stranger of mean exterior, who thrust into his hand a sealed packet, with charge to deliver it instantly to his lord; and then dived into the woodland without abiding question.

The missive, penned by Simon Dynevor himself—the youth had no mean clerkly skill—was simple enough. It told of his marriage to Maude Warenne according to the rites of Holy Church; besought his father's forgiveness; and, farther, prayed that answer should be sent to the house of a certain obscure scrivener dwelling in the borough of Southwark.

When Sir Giles had read the letter through, there came over his face a change such as no man had ever seen there; and there broke forth betwixt his grinded teeth a curse and an oath that made the chapellan, who alone chanced to be present, shiver and cross himself as though he stood in the visible presence of the Fiend. The curse was leveled at the heads of both the rebels: in the oath, Dynevor swore that, come life or come death, his will should yet be wrought out, by foul means or fair. After that first outbreak, he gave no sign either of grief or anger; only he bade the priest keep his tongue from wagging, if he would keep it in his head; and so betook himself to his chamber, where for years past he had been wont to sleep or watch alone.

In those times of rapine and misrule, few knights or nobles scrupled to thrust any obstacle out of their path with strong hand. More than once during his long night-musings, Dynevor meditated violence against the life or liberty of the new-made bride. Even if she were not done instantly to death, prisons might be found scarcely less safe and secret than the grave. But the penniless orphan was of gentle birth, and it might not be wise to crush her like a churl's daughter. Certain of her kinsfolk might be both able and willing to exact heavier *wehr-geld* for their cousin's blood than it would be convenient to pay. Notably, there was Hugh Warenne, who had won great renown in the

Scots and Irish wars, and had taken part with the King in the rebellion of the Earls—a good knight and true, but very choleric and rancorous, apt to draw sword in quarrels far less just than the redressing of a kinswoman's wrong. So malpractice behooved to be managed warily.

Sir Giles thought within himself—

"Anent such matters, good counsel is often found under a monk's cowl. I will ride to the Abbey, ere I carry these news to Tyringham. It is ill talking with Ivo, while his wits are flooded with yester-even's drink. The Abbot is naught; but Hildebrand, the Sub-prior, bears a subtle brain. I would fain have his aid in this strait, though I wis it will cost no mean fee."

Early on the morrow Dynevor went forth, without communing with any of his household, attended only by one ancient esquire whom he specially trusted; and lighted down under the porch of Haultvaux, when matins were newly done.

He was sure of welcome there, were it only for his wife's sake; for the name of that devout lady was a password to priestly favor throughout the countryside; he himself, too, had somewhat amended his ill ways of late; paid all church dues regularly; and showed courtesy, if not reverence, to frock and hood. The monks might have had many a worse neighbor. Thus, when he had told his errand, he was not bidden to wait; but the lay brother brought him into the presence of the man he sought, who chanced to be walking in the convent garden alone.

The Sub-prior was tall and spare of frame, with a face far more care-worn and deeply-lined than was warranted by his forty years. He had a swift, restless glance, and the curt, decisive manner of one who cares not to waste time in idle speech. It was not the first time that these two had conferred together, though never on matter of such grave import; and each had conceived a certain respect for the other's sagacity, even if between them there were not perfect trust.

While Dynevor told his brief tale, Hildebrand walked on silently, his head bent upon his breast; but, at the last words, he halted and looked up, with a glitter in his keen black eye—

"This comes of showing charity to beggarly cousins."

"It is ill repenting any charity whatsoever," the churchman said. "And to whom should alms be given, if not to a man's own kin? Yet I knew not the damsel was of your blood."

"Neither is she," the other answered; "but a far-off kinswoman of my dame, who must needs befriend her when the Scots slew her father; albeit there were others whom the charge better became."

"A far-off kinswoman, sayest thou? Near enough, perchance, were her lineage heedfully looked into, to be within the degrees forbidden to wed, unless by special license of the Church. There hath been loose observance of such rules of late by many godless laymen; but, I mind me, these matters were much spoken of at the last Council; and our Holy Father averred that order should be taken with such as occasion shall serve. Thus much I know of a surety, from a near kinsman of mine, who hath long been high in trust with our Holy Father; though he wears the cardinal's hat but newly."

Seldom, indeed, had Dynevor's well-trained face betrayed so much emotion as disturbed it then. His voice was unsteady as he made answer; and the fingers that gripped the priest's sleeve shook with a fierce, nervous emotion.

"By Christ's body! I did well in seeking thee in this my strait. Thou canst give good help, no less than good counsel, here. I wot well such service is costly; for each door at Avignon must be unlocked with a golden key. Now, good Father Hildebrand, say what thou requirest. I will not stand a-chaffering, though I have to give bond on the half of my possessions to Longobard or Jew."

The monk's restless eyes grew steady, as though they had been carved in jet, as they settled on the other's face.

"For myself I require nothing," he said, very coldly. "And, it may be, my kinsman will take no guerdon for serving me or mine: yet were it shame, if I let pass a chance of profiting mine Order. Lo, I will deal plainly and roundly with thee. In our chartulary there lies, as thou mayst see, a map of the lands wherewith this Abbey was endowed by the first Henry, our pious founder. Our limits are narrower now, by many a rood, than there set forth. Wottest thou why? Thou hast heard of the troubles in King Stephen's time, when those that sat in high places waxed so stubborn in their guilt, that Theobald, the Archbishop, was constrained to lay all this fair realm under ban? In those dark and evil days, many quarrels arose betwixt clerk and layman. Taking vantage of one of such, and, perchance, of some faint uncertainty in bounds, thine ancestor, Oliver Dynevor, violently ousted our vassals from all our lands lying westward of the streamlet men call the Neme ; and held them ever after by the strong hand. This iniquity King Stephen did manifestly countenance and approve ; for which misdeed, and many others, may God assoilzie him! All these things are set down in our chronicles, not without dolor and something of self-reproach, by Ingilram, our then-time abbot—a godly man, and of tender conscience —albeit, scarce made of martyr's stuff. Now—should I place in thine hand our Holy Father's rescript, utterly annulling this, thy son's marriage—wilt thou make amends for the sins of thy fathers, and restore to the Church her own? If this please thee, it is well. With the good leave of my Superior, I will aid thee to the uttermost of my power. Neither do I fear but that we shall compass our ends. If otherwise—let there be no farther words betwixt us ; but go thy way in peace ; being assured that I will not bewray thy counsel."

While Sir Giles stood silent, his brows were ominously overcast. Yet was the frown rather of thought than of anger. He knew—none better—the length and breadth of each acre he was asked to resign ; the hanging woods holding so many oaks and beeches ripe for felling ; the fair corn lands sloping to the southeast, so as to miss no gleam of morning and noonday suns ; the fat meadows, where the herbage hid the hocks of browsing kine. But, fairer and broader and richer yet, stretched before his mind's eye the domains of which one standing on Tyringham Keep could scarce see the ending. His choice was not long a-making.

"Thou art a shrewd bargainer, Sub-prior," he said, with a short, sullen laugh. "But I blame thee not for making good terms for thine Order; especially since its advancement may, one day, be thine own. 'Tis a heavy venture and a perilous: I am even as a merchant, who sends forth his mightiest argosy to trade in unknown seas. Only chances of life and death are harder to reckon than hazard of wind or waves. Nevertheless, as I said afore, I will not chaffer with thee. Do thou engage that this matter shall be managed, at thine own cost and risk, should it miscarry. On my part, I will cause to be prepared a gift-deed of every acre whereof thou hast spoken. This will I exchange with the rescript, that shall leave my son free to wed again."

On this compact, without more ado, the priest and the knight struck hands; and presently, after it had been approved by the Abbot, each swore to perform his part therein faithfully, on the most precious of the many reliquaries for which Haultvaux was famed—that enclosing a veritable morsel of the Holy Scourge.

Then, with heart and brain somewhat lightened, Sir Giles set forward to tell his tale at Tyringham.

CHAPTER III.

THE WORKING OF THE RESCRIPT.

On hearing the news, Malpas fell at the first into great wonderment and wroth; but soon sank into his wonted sullen acquiescence in his comrade's will: swearing, with a grisly oath, that "it would do the wench no harm to wait; and that, if she wedded not Dynevor's son, she might, for aught he cared, die a maid."

So the runaways dwelt for awhile, in great peace and content, in a lonely hostel without the skirts of Southwark; subsisting on moneys taken up at heavy interest by Simon Dynevor, from certain Hebrews who were ready to pleasure the heir of Bever; never dreaming that doctors learned in Church-law were even then busy with their names and lineage, and that the highest, if not the wisest, head in Christendom had been disquieted with their matters.

They began by being very timid and wary; keeping always their chamber by day, and only venturing forth after nightfall to take the air; but as time went on, bringing no answer to Simon's letter, and yet no farther cause for alarm, they waxed bolder, and crept farther afield; though they ever shunned open street or frequented highway.

Of a truth, caution was utterly wasted. In the very month of their flight, the cunning hunter whom they both so dreaded had harbored his game; and could afford to bide quiet till the fitting time came for loosing his gazehounds. Fettered in one of his own dungeons, Simon would scarce have been a safer prisoner, than where his going out and comings in were never unwatched by his father's spies.

The Sub-prior had not overrated his kinsman's authority or good-will; and fear or favor wrought more potently at Avignon than even at Rome. Before the summer was far spent, the Pope's rescript came, making utterly null and void Simon Dynevor's marriage, and bidding him put away his wife, under pain of Church's ban.

One evening, in that same week, Simon walked forth along the river-side alone; for Maude's failing health did not suffer her to go often abroad. Passing through a coppice, he was suddenly beset and overcome before he could make a show of resistance. When the mantle which both blindfolded and gagged him was removed, he found himself set in saddle in the midst of a clump of spears. None of those horsemen bore badge on helmet, or blazon on shield; but, as they sped swiftly through the summer night, the youth recognized the burly figure of Philip Kemeys, the ancient esquire who carried ever Dynevor's banner. He asked no question after that; and kept sullen silence till they brought him, some few hours later, into his father's presence.

Sir Giles was, has been aforesaid, a man of few words. If he gave the runaway no kindly greeting, neither did he waste time in reviling. When they were alone together, he set before his son a copy, fairly engrossed, of the Pope's rescript, and gave the youth time to digest it thoroughly. But, when he spoke, each slow syllable carried with it the weight of a fell, pitiless purpose.

"Hearken!" he said; "we have well-nigh done with boys' play. I have paid for yonder parchment tenfold the price that might have saved thy fool's head from gibbet or block—marry, it might have ransomed a belted earl! Shall it be for naught, that I have let pass away the lands stout Oliver Dynevor won? I tell thee, Nay. Thou art free, as thou seest, to woo and wive again. Either this night thou shalt swear, with hand on altar, to wed Malpas's daughter as soon as he and I shall deem it becoming—never stirring meanwhile beyond his domains and mine own—or, before another sundown, by Christ's body! it shall have fared with thee worse than ever it hath fared with malapert vassals. I wis, thou hast seen me deal with such ere now."

Simon Dynevor could be obstinate enough in his own saturnine way; but he had not the savage self-will and dogged courage of the old wolf who begot him. No marvel that at those last words he shivered. He felt they carried no vain threat—that he was utterly in the power of one who feared not God, neither regarded man. Moreover, it was possible that satiety had begun, though he knew it not, to sway his brutal nature. He might have been content to dwell on forever with Maude, yet she no longer seemed worth the risk of life or liberty. So, without more ado—stipulating only that fair maintenance should be insured to his divorced wife and her child, should it be born alive—he expressed himself ready to follow in all things his father's will.

That same day Philip Kemeys rode forth again bearing a letter, writ in Simon Dynevor's own hand, and a gipsire crammed with bezants. The ancient esquire had served his master not less faithfully for evil than for good, and had taken part ere now in some black misdeeds: yet he went on this errand with a great loathing and heaviness of heart, and never cared to speak of it in after-times.

During all the hours of her husband's absence. Maude had been well-nigh distraught with terror; nevertheless she took the news of her desertion and shame with singular calmness. Only, as she deciphered, painfully, the curt, cold, cruel letter, with its set forms of remorse and formal farewells, the blood ebbed out of her cheeks: while she lived, it came back no more. She made no loud moan or lamentation; neither did she send back one word or message to the man who had done her such deadly wrong. But she bade Philip Kemeys—" begone with his gold; for that her own kinsfolk, she doubted not, would henceforth grant her food and shelter; and that, were it otherwise, she would go forth into the highways, and ask alms of passers-by, rather than trust to a Dynevor's bounty." She said this without any display of passion or bitterness; yet there was a look in her bright, tearless eyes that made the esquire right willing to escape from her presence.

Sir Ralph Warenne chanced to be then tarrying at

his lodging near the Abbey Church of Westminster: before nightfall he had conveyed his cousin thither, and given her into the charge of his own sister, a discreet and charitable widow who governed his household. The choleric old soldier espoused his kinswoman's cause with great heat and rancor: nor could Maude's piteous entreaties withhold him from sending cartel to Bever, wherein he spoke of both father and son as disloyal faitours; offering to prove the same on both or either of their bodies. To which Dynevor made answer, that—

"Those two had bound themselves together without leave or license from him; and that, though he was well pleased to see them asunder, the work was not his doing, but the will of Holy Church, against the which he trusted a Christian knight would not array himself.; yet were it otherwise, neither he nor his would draw sword in such a quarrel, save to guard their own lives or goods, and would be content to underlie Sir Ralph Warenne's challenge."

This politic reply made the other chafe more savagely; but just then arose such a public turmoil, as left no man leisure for private brawls. In that September set sail from Dordrecht, Isabella the Queen, with Mortimer her paramour, and John of Hainault, her true knight; and, with three hundred men-at-arms, marched westward from Orwell Sands, till she besieged her husband with a mighty host.

Now Ralph Warenne had grown aweary of king's caprice and favorite's insolence; so he joined the advancing army readily enough, with all the lances he could muster; and after Bristol leaguer, went northward on the queen's behest, only returning to Westminster in January to see the third Edward crowned.

He had not been so moved for years as when they told him, on dismounting at his own door, that Maude Warenne had died in childbed but a week before, leaving a healthy boy. The rude, bluff soldier felt very keenly the loss of the pale, delicate woman whose existence he had never heeded till of late. He caused the child to be christened after his own name, and swore a great oath that he would some day adopt it as his own; for up to threescore Sir Ralph had found no time to wed.

Before that year's leaves were brown, the good knight's wars were ended. When they marched northward to chastise the Scotch marauders, Warenne was already greatly trusted by the young king, and attached to his household. One hot August night, as they lay on the banks of Wear, Sir Ralph had lain down to rest in his tent touching the royal pavilion— it was not his turn to keep watch—when a familiar war-cry mingled with his dreams: struggling up from under the folds of canvas and tangled tent-ropes, he found himself face to face with the Douglas. Black James in many points was the very mirror of chivalry; yet he spared not to discharge on the bare head of his old antagonist one downright mace-stroke, which settled forever their long and doubtful balance of hard blows.

The great Pendulum is often swinging steadily and evenly enough, when such as read not the dial aright deem that it keeps uncertain time. Before the motherless baby lost his second protector, there was heavy counterpoise of retribution.

When Sir Giles caused his son to swear that he would wed Malpas's daughter so soon as it was thought becoming, he knew well that there were many, even in that unscrupulous age, who would have cried shame, had the espousals been pressed on with indecent haste. He was well content to let things bide for a full year; for he did not fear that the bridegroom would again try to break trammels. So, when Dynevor—who took no part in the troubles of the autumn—deemed it politic to make a late display of loyalty by attendance at the anointing of the young king, Simon rode to Westminster in his father's train, a free man to all outward seeming. They tarried there not long—three nights only—yet long enough for the youth to hear (one of his fellow-esquires had a cousin in Warenne's household) of the birth which brought him a son, though not an heir, and of the death which made him doubly free. He received the news without any show of sorrow or surprise; only, for some days afterward, he was silent and morose even beyond his wont, and there was a deeper gloom on his downcast face.

But all this while, a certain frail life-thread, on which many hopes hung, was parting strand by strand. Edith Malpas seemed to wither as the wild flowers began to bloom: her cheeks were almost livid at times in their paleness; and she pressed her thin hand often on her heart with a low moan of pain. But of these signs none took heed, unless it were perchance the girl's nurse and foster-mother, who stood in too great awe of Ivo's drunken furies, even to whisper her fears.

It was within one week of the espousal-day. Already preparations were far advanced at Tyringham, for a

banquet that should cast past carousals into the shade.
The morning meal at Bever was done, and Sir Giles
was just starting for the neighboring town, where he
was to confer with certain cunning artificers concerning the bridal pageant. He stood waiting for his
palfrey, stirrup-cup in hand. As he raised it to his
lips, a man-at-arms rode into the courtyard at headlong speed. The great silver hanap fell clattering
down, and the good liquor flowed out far and wide;
for the horseman's visor was up, and Sir Giles guessed
from his face that he brought evil tidings.

Before the messenger had faltered out half his brief
tale, the purposes and plans of so many years were as
though they had never been. Edith Malpas must have
died soon after she laid down to rest the night before;
for that morning they found her stiff and cold.

Sir Giles answered never a word; but stood swaying
slowly to and fro, like a drunkard, whose will still
struggles against strong wine. Then the blood rushed
up brow-high in a dark crimson surge; leaving cheeks
and lips ashy white, when it ebbed again as suddenly.
He cast his hands aloft, clutching the air as men
clutch at the water in their last drowning pang; and,
with one choking gurgle in the throat, fell down right
under the horse's hoofs a helpless distorted heap. As
they bore him away, the least learned in leech-craft, of
all who stood by, guessed that their lord had been
stricken down by swift and deadly palsy.

He never spoke intelligibly after that; and showed
token of absolute consciousness once only—in this
wise.

The Abbot of Haultvaux, anxious that so large a

benefactor to the Church should not lack her last good offices, and being himself ill at ease, sent the Sub-prior in his stead with profuse messages of condolence. Father Hildebrand's nerves were not easily moved by pity or fear; yet on the threshold of the sick-chamber he shrank back appalled. Over so much of Sir Giles's writhen face as the palsy had spared, there swept an awful convulsion of hatred and loathing; and his one uncrippled hand was clenched and outstretched in feeble menace or warning. The monk read those signs of passion aright. He guessed how the memory of the broad acres, sacrificed utterly in vain, was rankling then; and felt his priestcraft powerless to grapple with the thwarted devil of avarice that glared out of those bloodshot eyes; so, with scant ceremony of excuse, he departed out of the evil Presence like a baffled exorcist; leaving the chapellan of Bever to deal with the grisly penitent.

So died Sir Giles Dynevor—scarcely in the odor of sanctity. Nevertheless, his bones were laid with great reverence and honor under the chancel at Haultvaux; and over them was built, at the sole charge of the House, a stately tomb of Sienna marble, bearing the effigy of that good knight with hands duly folded in prayer; whereon, till the eighth Henry made havoc with the Abbey and all appertaining thereto, might have been read an epitaph in fair monkish Latin, of the which the last two versicles may serve for an ensample:

MARTE : FEROX : IN : PACE : SAGAX : HUIC : ILLE : SACELLO
    E : PIETATE : SUO : MUNERA : LARGA : DEDIT.

CHAPTER IV.

THE BREEDING OF THE BASTARD.

THE heir of Bever bore the loss of his father, and his own accession to the family honors, with singular calmness, not to say indifference. Neither did it seem likely that his house would be much advanced by his care for its honor and dignity. But, in truth, had Simon been endowed with all the energy and ambition of his sire, both must needs have been cramped by the unhappy disaster which befell him, before he had been three full years in possession of his inheritance. Returning home one frosty evening, his horse floundered on the slippery stones before the barbican; and Dynevor was carried in with a broken thigh, and hip so sorely strained, that a better chirurgeon than the unskilful leech who tended him would scarce have saved the patient from halting thenceforth. While still in the spring of life, he was cut off from all share in the wars and sports of his peers; for neither in tourney, chase, nor *mêlée*, can place be found for one who may not sit saddle-fast. From courtly pageant or pastime he was yet more estranged, for out of such metal never was molded squire of dames.

The bearing of that heavy cross might perchance have warped a kindlier and more patient nature; so 'tis no marvel if Dynevor grew up to middle age, a soured and morose man—not absolutely a domestic tyrant or brutal despot; yet over-apt to vent his evil tempers in a slow, sardonic fashion, on such as were bound to endure them.

Some short while before his mishap, Simon Dynevor had sent sufficiently courteous messages to Ralph Warenne's surviving sister; thanking her for her charitable care, and proffering thenceforward to take the child in charge. To this Dame Margaret assented very readily: she was left something straitened in means, and had no mind to keep needless encumbrances. So the little Ralph was brought home to Bever, along with Gillian, his foster-mother; whose husband was slain, hard by his lord, in that night-surprise on the banks of Wear. The same Gillian was very comely to look upon, and still in her early prime: by the time her nursling could be trusted alone, she was married again to one of Dynevor's foresters, and settled in a cottage of her own, some few bowshots from the castle.

In that cottage Ralph Fitzwarenne (thus the boy, by the will of his dead godfather, had been christened) spent much of his early boyhood.

The conscience of Simon Dynevor seems to have been satisfied so soon as his son was fairly in his charge; and, after that one act of grace, the meanest of his household was not treated with more utter neglect. While she lived, Dame Alice Dynevor showed no small kindness to the child; for she had liked his mother well, in her own staid austere way, and—despite her belief in the deceased Sir Oliver's sagacity, and her reverence for Holy Church's behest—she could not but fear that Maude had been hardly dealt with. Neither could she ever wholly put aside certain vague self-reproaches for negligence, in not having stood more heedfully betwixt the dead and her own son. She did her best to instruct the boy in such simple lore as she herself had attained: but she could scarcely spell over her own missal; while monkish legends made up her History. To these long-winded discourses Ralph would sit listening gravely for hours, never once indulging in a yawn of weariness. In those days he was too grateful for any loving word or look, not to be ready to repay such by harder self-denial than this.

The orphan—for such in very truth he was—had one other ally at Bever.

Rheumatism and many old wounds had so far told on Philip Kemeys, as to make him more fit for home service than foreign wars; though betwixt the pains that ever and anon crippled him, he could wield ax, or sword, or lance, as starkly as of yore. The ancient esquire, from the day when at his dead master's bidding he carried that message to Maude Warenne, had been possessed of a vague remorse—the more strange, because his conscience carried, with much ease and comfort, the burden of many seemingly blacker deeds. He never told this to his confessor, and, perchance, never allowed it to himself. But, if Ralph had been his own son, he could not have ministered more sedulously to his caprices, or trained him more carefully in each manly sport and martial exercise for which he himself was renowned.

Before the boy was sixteen, he was left once more utterly lonely; for, in the same winter, the devout lady and the godless old *soudard* went to their several accounts; and their pupil regretted the sinner far more than he did the saint.

Some three years earlier, a great change had come over Bever. Though Sir Simon Dynevor cared little for the advancement of his house, he knew that it behooved him to wive again, if only to purvey himself with heirs-male. His choice fell on the Lady Ursula Montacute—a damsel neither fair, young, nor richly dowered; but of morals unimpeached, and stainless descent—the sister of a neighboring baron.

The Lady Ursula was born with a quick temper and shrewish tongue; and long waiting for tardy wooers had helped to sour the one and sharpen the other. She chose to rule her new household less by love than by fear—being careful only to never thwart her sullen lord. Ralph Fitzwarenne, for reasons not hard to guess, she held in special aversion, and lost no chance of stinging him with bitter words, or of bringing him under his father's displeasure: twice or thrice she caused the boy to be severely scourged by the castle chapellan; for Sir Simon himself never laid his hand upon the boy in anger. Once, in early marriage days, she ventured to hint that his very presence and maintenance in the castle was a grievous insult to herself; but she was bidden to "hold her peace, and not presume to meddle;" while an ominous look from under her husband's brows warned her she had gone too far. She broached that matter no more.

But Ralph was wondrously hard and stubborn. Of

taunts, or reproofs, or stripes, he took no more heed than of an April shower: if he was chary of smiles, and seldom laughed aloud, neither man nor woman since his early childhood had heard him wail or seen him weep. When the chiding or chastisement was over, he would betake himself straight to the cottage of his foster-mother, and bide there till curfew. Even to her he made no complaint; only at such times he was most eager to hear the only story of which he never wearied—the story of his dead mother and her wrongs. As he listened to the simple tale—varied only by some trifling incident, that most would have thought not worth recording—the boy's face, that had never changed during his own punishment, would lower and darken strangely. His big brown eyes would gleam with a malignant fire, and there broke from his lips certain muttered words that made Gillian cross herself, and aver that she would speak of these things no more. But she did speak of them again and again, and thus, unwittingly, kept alive the embers of a bitter enmity.

So the years went by, till Ralph grew into a tall sinewy youth, overtopping his sire by a full head, and looking gigantic beside the puny fractious urchin, the sole issue of the second marriage.

Sir Simon's bearing toward his first-born was somewhat perverse and inconsistent. He rather encouraged than otherwise the pursuit of those bodily exercises, in which the youth showed already a rare excellence. Ralph had always horse and hound ready to his hand, and coin enough to enable him to mingle, after a modest fashion, in the amusements of the countryside.

But, when Dynevor sent forth his vassals to war, under command of the Lord Montacute, his brother-in-law, Ralph was constrained to tarry at home, and practise at the quintain with blunted lance, while his comrades were shivering grinded spears. How he chafed under such idlesse—how his spirit burned within him when, in the long winter evenings, youths not older than himself boasted or jested of what they had done in spring or summer beyond the narrow seas—how the flaunt of banner, the sound of trumpet, and the rattle of steel, haunted his waking and sleeping dreams—may be more easily conceived than told. But he was too proud and stubborn ever to require the reason of his father's caprice—much less to pray him to change it. It may well be that Sir Simon only waited to be entreated: but he waited in vain. So betwixt these two ripened day by day an evil crop of distrust and discontent, and the harvest-time could not be long a-coming.

All this while the wars were waging in Flanders and Normandy with varying fortunes; till at last the heart of broad England leaped up as the heart of one man at the news of Creçy; when grinding taxes, rough exactions, and broken promises were all forgotten in the first great success of the brave, patient king. In the same autumn, too, was won a notable victory; the like whereof hath seldom been seen since on Rephidim the Lawgiver's hands were stayed up, till Amalek was smitten hip and thigh about the going down of the sun. Nor is it wonder if at Neville's Cross, where queen and noble, knight and yeoman, gained large store of honor, to the Church militant was given the chiefest share. For, to sound of matin song, chanted from Durham tower, the armies were set in array; monk's frock fluttered side by side in the ranks with archer's gipon; and, in the very forefront of the fight gleamed bishop's rochet, though Mowbray, Dacre, and Percy laid their lances in rest.

To the tidings of these feats of arms, when they came in due course to Bever, Ralph Fitzwarenne gave attentive ear. He spoke little at the time; but thenceforward day by day grew more taciturn and reserved, and withdrew himself from the sports and pastimes in which he had heretofore delighted; going forth alone to hawk or strike a deer; and in all ways rather avoiding than seeking the company of his fellows.

The change in the youth's demeanor escaped not Sir Simon Dynevor; and his sharp, suspicious glance, dwelt more often than was its wont on his son's face, while the other's eyes would flash back something akin to defiance. So through winter and early spring the pair lay watching each other; like wary commanders, each within his own entrenchment, waiting, perchance, the opportunity to make sally.

CHAPTER V.

ANN HAGARENE.

EARLY on a breezy March day Sir Simon Dynevor sat in his judgment-seat—a huge arm-chair, drawn into the embrasure of a window looking westward from the dais of his hall. Close to his shoulder stood the Lady Ursula—shrill and voluble in accusation—clasping to her side a sallow, hard-featured boy, some ten years old, the very image of herself, whose grief was yet more clamorous than her own invective. Only two others were in presence—the chapellan of the castle and Ralph Fitzwarenne.

While the lady's eloquence was in full tide, her husband raised his hand impatiently:

"I prithee hush, *ma mie;* thou art too distempered to tell thy tale. And, Oliver, still that fool's tongue, or thou shalt have good cause for whining. Father Clement, it seems thou hast witnessed such and such things. Speak on, in the fiend's name!"

Thus rudely adjured, the other gave his testimony with some haste and tremor. Yet in his tone there was a bitterness scarcely dissembled. Plainly the priest owed Fitzwarenne an ancient grudge, and was right ready to pay it. He averred that, reading his breviary in his chamber, he had been disturbed by a great outcry, and by the baying of the sleuth-hound bitch chained in the base-court below; that, looking forth, he had seen his young Lord Oliver haled along, not without violence, by Messire Ralph, and finally flung under an archway, where, some moments later, he, Father Clement, descending in haste, found the child making piteous moan. But the door leading into the base-court was shut and barred, and Messire Ralph had gone he knew not whither.

Then for the first time Sir Simon Dynevor's sullen glance lighted on the accused. As that youth shall be the hero of this our tale, it may be well to set down here his outward seeming.

Though his features were neither coarse nor ignoble, they were too strongly marked and roughly-hewn for beauty. It was a quiet resolute face; far too grave and stern indeed for his years, even when his brows were not bent in thought or anger. His head—fringed with short crisp hair, some shades darker than his eyes, where a reddish tinge mingled with the brown— was well set on a short clean-cut neck, and looked smaller than it really was, from his great breadth and squareness of shoulder. Though only in his twentieth spring, his joints seemed already set, and with each careless movement of the long sinewy limbs, the coils of hardened muscle showed themselves under his close hunting-dress. There was little of culprit or penitent, indeed, about the demeanor of Ralph Fitzwarenne, as he stood there haughtily erect; seeming to dwarf every other figure in that group.

"Thou hast heard," Dynevor said. "Hast aught of excuse or denial to urge; or speaks the priest truth?"

"Truth, after the fashion of his order," the youth answered. "That is—half truth, or so much as suits him to tell: yet, may be, he saw not all. He saw not yonder pretty poppet, goading Fay with a steel-shod hunting-pole, till her muzzle was all a-gore. Rare sport, i' faith; though it well-nigh came to bitter earnest. He held himself safe beyond the sweep of her chain; but, when I came, the staple was dragging from the post. Yet another minute, and Fay had avenged herself in her own fashion. This runs in her blood: when fairly wode they will turn on him that feeds them, if he come betwixt them and their wrath. Wouldst have had me dally, when I saw that the brache hearkened no more to my voice than to the voice of a stranger? Marry, when I hied back, not without ado got I leave to drive the staple home: she left her marks on me ere we were friends again."

Drawing up his doublet sleeve, he showed, a little above the left wrist, a deep row of fang marks; already black and swollen, though the skin was not broken; they were plainly the traces of a hasty chance snap, not of a grip given in pure malice.

Had the sleuth-hound's fangs been on her darling's throat, the Lady Ursula could scarce have raised louder outcry than she did, hearing of his danger. But her husband hushed her again with his hand; and in his tone, as he made reply, there was a calm more ominous than passion.

"Whence gottest thou yonder hound? And since when hast thou license to keep, under this roof of mine, brutes from whom there comes peril of life and limb? Had harm come to yonder child, thinkest thou amends had been made by the throttling of a score like thee?"

The young man's face began to darken; and that evil light, before spoken of, came into his bright brown eyes.

"She was Philip Kemeys's last gift to me. He traveled many a league to fetch her, when his mortal sickness was upon him; for from that day he sate never in saddle again. There is not her match—as all thy foresters know—betwixt Thames and the narrow seas. Moreover, she is the only thing that ever I owned, for which I was not beholden to thy charity. Her food and kennel-room she hath fairly earned: she hath saved thee many a deer. I had been right sorry had harm happened to the child; and I wot well that my life against his is, in thine eyes, like a cinder from the furnace against fine gold. Yet were it scant justice to demand of me the blood-price—seeing that for his own sport he put his neck in peril."

"The brache dies by the halter ere noon," Sir Simon said. "And now I will speak of thine own matters. Lo! I approve not what the boy hath done: but he hath been more than punished by the rough treatment he got at thine hands. Hadst thou no more reverence for him who, if he live, shall one day rule here in my stead, than to cast him aside like a mangy cur? Didst thou forget that thou, whose beard is well-nigh grown, wert dealing with a weakling child? Ay—more. Hadst thou forgotten that, what is but petulance in the heir, is mere *outre-quittance* in—"

With all his cynicism, he hesitated over the last brutal word. But the other took up the broken thread of speech quite unconcernedly.

"—In the bastard. 'Tis a simple name, and soon said: I wot not why thou didst draw second breath over it. Nay, sir, my father, I have not forgotten; neither am I like to forget. I have heard the tale often enough to tell it without halting. I know how thou didst sit with folded hands, whilst others wrought shame to thy wedded wife—'wedded,' I say, in the teeth of monks and schoolmen—and wrong to thine unborn child. I have been bred up by thy bounty—for what purpose of thine own I may not guess; since hitherto it hath not pleased thee to send me where honor or wealth is to be won, nor even to raise me to esquire's estate. Wert thou as weary of giving, as I am of eating, the bread of idlesse, thou wouldst let me fare forth to the wars, were it only as a mounted archer. It should go hard, but I would one day repay thee the charges thou hast been put to for me."

Once more Sir Simon's eyes—this time rather pensively than angrily—rested on his first-born's face.

"Thy speech lacks not reason," he said, after a long pause: "though, like thy demeanor, of late, 'tis something masterful and overbold. Grievous wrong was done before thy birth; though, by Mary's truth, I plotted it not, and would have stayed it had I been able. Moreover, I have been in fault for keeping thee in paresse here: but I cared not, by setting thee amongst mine esquires, to breed in thee hopes which might not be fulfilled; and I was something loth to send forth thy mother's son as a simple man-at-arms. These things shall be mended, and that speedily. Either thou shalt ride amongst my lances that are bound to France under my kinsman of Montacute's banner, and win advancement according as he shall report of thy deserts; or thou shalt go forth this day alone, with coin enow to purvey thee a stout horse and armor of proof, and some bezants to boot. But mark thou me. If this last be thy choice—thou hast thy portion. Whether thy fortunes be made or marred, thou comest back hither no more; for I and mine shall be held quit of thy maintenance forever."

The blood flushed up in Ralph Fitzwarenne's cheek, as he made prompt reply:

"Sir, my father, the choice is soon made. I care not greatly to ride under my lord of Montacute's banner, or to win his good word; neither hoped I better hap, than to carve mine own road to honor. I trust not to misuse thy bounty, for the which I here render duteous thanks. Give me such portion as seemeth to thee good; and let us part in peace. Thus much I dare aver—from this day, unless at thine own express behest, thou shalt look on my face no more, whether in life or death."

While his son was speaking, Dynevor's hand was laid on the silver bell that stood beside him: at the last words he rung it sharply.

"Go thou to my chamber," he said to the page who answered the summons, "and fetch me hither the steel-wrought coffer that stands near my bed's head. And bid the seneschal assemble me here mine household, and such others as chance to be within the castle, whether vassals or villeins: it is my pleasure to speak with them presently."

Sir Simon unlocked the coffer with a key he wore under his doublet on a thin silver chain, and from among certain leather bags of coin chose out one—the heaviest. Then he drew from the fourth finger of his left hand a chased gold ring, wherein was set a balas ruby; and laid ring and bag on the table before him.

"There is thy portion," he said. "Take it with my good leave; and may God and our patron saint prosper it to thee. Yon ring was thy mother's only jewel; she willed that I should wear it, the night we were wedded: it hath never left me till now."

Ralph Fitzwarenne came near; thrust the bag unopened into his gipsire; and drew the ring on his finger, speaking never a word. At that moment he liked his father better than he had ever before done; for his quick ear had caught a certain tremor in the other's measured tones, and his own heart was fuller than he cared to show.

By this time the body of the hall was filling fast with the numerous household, among whom were mingled not a few dwelling beyond the castle walls, who chanced to be within them that morning for business or pleasure. In front of these, marshaling them into something like orderly ranks, stood the ancient seneschal, bearing his chain and wand of office, while the squires and pages gathered in a knot by themselves, just below the dais. The Lady Ursula—somewhat overawed, albeit not displeased with the turn matters had taken—had withdrawn herself farther into the deep embrasure, whither her child and the chapellan followed. Then Dynevor arose and came forward, till he stood full in front of his retainers. His gait was slow, and his figure, even before the mishap which crippled and bowed him, had been somewhat ungainly:

nevertheless, his bearing was not devoid of a certain grave dignity, as he made his brief oration.

"Good friends, and liegemen, and servitors of mine, whether free or bond; I have called ye here this day, to be witnesses betwixt myself and this youth, whom ye all know to be my son, born in wedlock—albeit in wedlock which Holy Church saw fit to disallow. Ye know, too, how, up to this hour he hath been nourished and trained at my charge—if not with such honor as would befit mine heir, at least with such tendance as is not unworthy of my blood. And what I have given I have given, the saints wot, not grudgingly; nevertheless, he goeth forth this day—having received such a portion as contenteth him—of his own free will, not driven by me. Now, I hold all ye here present to wit, that, even as I discharge him of all duty and fealty to me, so do I hold myself quit of all claim and clear of all duty toward him forever. Furthermore, if any man here present, beneath esquire's rank—being of sound mind and able body—shall choose to bear him company, he shall do this with my free leave. If such an one be villein, I will enfranchise him here before you; if he be free, he shall carry with him the full wages of a foot-archer for a year and a day."

There was a sway and a stir in the little crowd that filled the body of the hall; and one came to the front who, after making obeisance, waited, as it seemed, to be questioned.

He was a short, thick-set man, with an honest heavy face, imperfectly lighted up by two pale gray eyes, and scarcely relieved by hair of the lightest flaxen, cut square across his low forehead, and close round his bull's neck. His double joints and deep chest gave promise of vast, though, perchance clumsy, strength; and as he stood there, his brawny bow-legs were planted, naturally, in the posture of a practised wrestler watching for the grip.

On him Sir Simon looked with some surprise.

"How now, Will Lanyon?" he said. "Comes the grist so slowly to thy father's mill, that thou must needs seek fortune by wandering thou knowest not whither? I warrant that before a week is past thou wilt be homesick and wearying for the clack of the hopper. Moreover, I guess thy father would scarce approve this venture of thine."

The other made answer in slow, sententious fashion, like one who, having few ideas to spare, is chary of their utterance. His voice was strangely deep and gruff for his years, which might have numbered some five-and-twenty.

"I thank your worship, trade thrives apace. Nevertheless, if he will endure my company, I am minded to go forth with Messire Ralph this day; and if I have your worship's good leave, of my father I will crave none. For his own pleasure he brought home Cloudesley's shrewish widow before my mother's grave was green; and I purpose to do mine own pleasure now, whether it like him or no. If I miss the clack of the hopper, I shall also miss the clatter of my step-dame's tongue: mayhap I shall sleep the sounder. Marry, if her tongue were all—but this morning I had taste of her five fingers, and my cheek is red-hot yet. I care not to take hard blows without chance of paying them back in kind."

"Ay, and is it so?" Dynevor said, with his hard laugh, so like his father's; in which there was much of gibe, and little of mirth. "Light cause, methinks, to make a man leave hearth and home behind: yet doth a gadfly chafe a war-horse quicker than a sore wound. I will not cross thy purpose, especially as thou art of full age, and free of aught save vassal's service; come near, and take the year's wage whereof I spoke. If thou bearest thyself as starkly under shield as thou hast done at the wrestling and cudgel-play, the King hath gained a stout archer, though I lose a trusty liegeman."

When the silver marks had been counted out in due tale, and Lanyon had fallen back into his place again, Sir Simon turned, and beckoned to Ralph Fitzwarenne. As the youth drew near, and bent one knee, Dynevor's dark face softened more than, surely, it had ever done since the days of his first wooing; and he was fain to clear his throat twice or thrice, before he could speak steadily.

"I bid thee farewell in all kindness; and do thou think of thy father as little hardly as may be in the after-time. If the blessing of a right sinful man may avail thee, thou hast it freely: counsel I have none to give. I know thee to be honest; and to one born of our blood there is no need to say—'Be bold!' I say only—'Be patient, and prosper!' In the name of the most Holy Trinity, and of St. Giles, our patron saint, so mote it be!"

Ralph Fitzwarenne laid his lips on his father's hand, scarcely with a son's devotion, but rather like a vassal paying homage to his liege lord. As he rose to his feet,

there was a mist over his own eyes, that for a second
or two made the figures in the body of the hall look
blurred and dim : yet in his bearing there was never a
sign of weakness or regret as he strode swiftly toward
the great doorway ; looking neither to the right hand
nor the left, and changing with none either word or
sign. Close to his shoulder, just as silently, followed
Will Lanyon. Not a few, as the pair passed through
their midst, wished them "God-speed" with bated
breath; but neither squire nor servitor, vassal nor
villein, presumed to stir from his place till, some
minutes later, Sir Simon Dynevor seemed to wake
from a reverie, and with a wave of his hand gave them
license to depart.

CHAPTER VI.

HOW RALPH FITZWARENNE MET A HOLY PRIEST BY THE WAY, AND WOULD NONE OF HIS BLESSING.

So, out of the crowd and shadow, those two passed through the sunlight of the empty court; till, under the outer archway, Fitzwarenne halted and spoke, looking earnestly into his follower's eyes—

"Honest Will, I pray thou mayest never repent having cast in thy lot with mine. Hearken now—if thou be minded to say farewell to thy father, or any other, do so quickly; I will tarry at the cross-roads till thou come; mine own leave-takings are well-nigh said, and I shall not draw free breath till Bever is a league behind us; but cumber not thyself with change of garment, and such like. Here is gold enow for both our furniture, if we win safe to Southwark; till we know whither we wend, and with whom, 'tis hard to tell what we may need."

"I thank thee, messire," the other answered, gruffly: "I care for leave-takings no more than thou. If Gaffer Lanyon be vexed by the news he will hear this day, he will drink another pottle or two to-night, and to-morrow 'twill be all one; and should Cicely, the tanner's daughter, be moved to shed some few tears, there are fools enow left in Bever hamlet to dry the jilt's blue eyes. I wot well that London is thy mark; so let us forward, as soon as thou wilt. The roads are heavy with the late rains: yet thou and I have compassed harder journeys than shall bring us this night to Tunbridge town."

"Then do thou set on forthwith," Ralph said. "I have yet another errand to do here; and I would speak a word to my foster-mother, whose cottage lies not a bowshot out of the way. I will overtake thee before thou comest to these cross-roads."

Lanyon nodded his head, and went forth without farther question; while the other turned aside into a vaulted passage leading to the base-court, where the sleuth-brache was kenneled.

Fay was lying outstretched in a broad bar of sunlight that fell within the sweep of her chain. She was still looking somewhat sullen and grim; but, at the sound of her master's steps, she lifted her head, and greeted him with a low whine of pleasure; she was quite conscious of having done amiss, and longed to show penitence in her own way.

Ralph knelt down by his favorite and caressed her; murmuring in her ear the while—

"Thou mayst not bear me company; and for one of thy temper homes are hard to find. Lo! I come to do thee the last good office. 'The halter'—did he say? Nay—cold steel whenever our time shall come; but no cord for me or mine. Brave Fay, stanch Fay— kiss me once more."

Slowly and half-reluctantly, as though she understood the words, and guessed what was a-coming, the great bloodhound reared herself, till her tawny jowl and black muzzle rested against his shoulder and cheek. Ralph's eyes were not misty now, but glistening wet; yet he faltered not in his purpose a whit. With his left hand thrown around Fay's neck, he felt for the pulse of her heart, while his right drew the dagger stealthily from its sheath, and drove it home—so surely that, without a howl or moan, the brache slid down out of his grasp, and, after a single convulsion, lay stone-still. No drop of blood followed, till Ralph very gently and heedfully drew forth the blade; then, despite his care, some three or four heavy gouts spirted on his wrist, leaving broad dark stains on the green sleeve of his hanseline.

And these things were so quickly done, that the foremost of those who just then came streaming forth out of the great hall, barely caught the flutter of Ralph Fitzwarenne's short mantle, as it vanished under the arch of the barbican.

Over the youth's interview with his foster-mother we here need not linger: in truth, though fond even to foolishness, on one side at least, it was soon ended. Long before Will Lanyon had fully gathered his sluggish wits out of the maze into which they had wandered, he had been overtaken by the other; and the two strode on swiftly side by side, each with hunting-pole in hand.

They might have gone some league or so, when a sharp turn in the road brought them face to face with three travelers, one of whom was mounted, while the other two followed afoot. At sight of these Fitzwarenne halted, looking to the right and to the left, as though he would fain have avoided the meeting. But the banks on either side rose steep and woody, and there was scarcely foothold on the slippery clay; so he waited, with brows clouded and overcast, till the others drew near.

The foremost personage has been painted before. It was no other than Hildebrand, sometime Sub-prior of Haultvaux—now, its mitered Abbot. Twenty years had worked little change in his keen face and lean frame; only some deep lines had grown into furrows, and the strong black hair round the tonsure had waxed thin and iron-gray; but the braced lips were resolute, and the glance restless as ever. The very mule under him was characteristic of the man. Not a sleek pampered ambler—such an one as hath been affected by all saintly dignitaries since the days when Jewish rulers rode upon white asses—but a gaunt, sinewy beast, with a red, vicious eye, whose rough action would have suited none but hardened bones—a beast that would have tired down many knightly coursers between sunrise and sundown; and its long stride—though the pace was scarce beyond a swift walk—sorely tried the wind and limb of the two sturdy lay-brethren who, with frocks girt up knee high, followed closely as they might. On high and solemn occasions few surpassed the Abbot of Haultvaux in pomp or parade; but, when bound on his own affairs, he cared for none of such vanities; and now, in his simple riding-garb, he looked rather like some staid franklin, than a spiritual peer.

Lanyon made low obeisance as the Abbot drew nigh; but Ralph barely touched his cap, as he stood aside out of the narrow roadway. Yet the churchman spoke with his wonted cool courtesy; never noticing, as it seemed, the irreverence of the youth's salute.

"We give thee good-morrow, fair son. On whose business art thou and honest Will Lanyon faring forth? On pleasure ye can hardly be bent; since 'tis no weather yet for wrestling-match or quintain-play; and thou hast with thee neither hawk nor hound. Nevertheless, thou wilt be home ere nightfall, we wot. Wilt thou save us time and trouble by delivering to our good friend, Sir Oliver Dynevor, a brief message which we will presently teach thee? For we have far to ride and much to do ere even-song."

Fitzwarenne looked full in the speaker's face—always with the same lowering on his own.

"I am forth on mine own business," he answered, "and for junketing, I have had little heart of late. Also, it will be long ere I hollo again to hawk or hound. But your lordship must seek some other messenger to Bever than Lanyon or myself; for thither do I return no more; neither will he, I think, for many a month to come."

"Is it even so?" the Abbot said, bending his brows. "Truly; we boded no good of the stubborn temper we have noted in thee of late. Hath some unhappy brawl —*Sancta Maria!* what mean those dark stains on thy sleeve?"

"There hath been no brawl," the other replied: "only the clatter of some shrill shrewish tongues; and my doublet is stained with no redder blood than that of a trusty sleuth-hound, whom I slew but now to save her from the halter. Also, I go forth with Sir Simon Dynevor's good leave—if that may advantage me—and we parted not in anger. But, I marvel that your reverence's mind should cumber itself with my matters. We, too, have far to go ere we sleep, and under your favor, we have dallied here too long."

"Nay then, we detain thee not. Draw nearer, my son, and bow thine head. Though it were more seemly for thee to crave, than for us to proffer it, thou shalt not lack our blessing."

And, as the Abbot spoke, he stretched forth his right hand.

Then Ralph Fitzwarenne drew himself yet more erect; while through the darkness of his face flashed out enmity open and defiant.

"Some six times," he said, in a low, bitter voice, "have I come to Haultvaux, since I knew evil from good—always in Simon Dynevor's company, or on his errands—but I never broke bread nor drank water there. I would liever bear the burden of mine own sins, than have them lightened by thee. Do I not know how and where the plot was hatched that robbed my mother of her good name, and me of my birthright? 'Twas not for naught, that the landmarks were shifted in that same year. Marry—seeing the manner of man he was, and how he was outwitted at the last—'tis wonder that my grandsire should rest quiet in his grave. Lord Abbot, I owe thine order a shrewd turn; may be, I shall repay something thereof ere I die. Albeit, the heaviest accompt may never be cleared—the accompt betwixt me and thee!"

The lay-brethren crossed themselves in devout horror, and Will Lanyon's ruddy cheek paled: it seemed as though all three expected that such blasphemy would draw down some instant manifestation of Heaven's wrath. But the Abbot's countenance betrayed neither anger nor surprise; and his lip curled in a cold disdainful smile.

"Thou art distraught—utterly distraught in thy folly. Granting such and such things were done in those days, how darest thou impute either the shame or the honor to me? Did not Abbot Anselm—God rest his soul!—rule at Haultvaux then? And was not I the simple Sub-prior?"

"Go to!" the other retorted. "Do not all men know that the holy man's heart was soft as his brains; but that, when it behooved to grind the poor or to oppress the weakling, there stood a wise counselor ever close to his ear? Good father; I wis, the change was more in seeming than in truth, when thou didst don alb and miter."

The monk bowed his head, in real or affected humility.

"Truly, well is it written—*Beati sunt mortui*. For not alone do those blessed ones rest from their labors, but they garner all the grain they have sown, whilst others must needs gather in the tares. Over the lintel of the fair alms-houses yonder, Abbot Anselm's name is graven; and in the prayers of twelve devout widows it will be remembered forever. Yet none guessed how patiently and long I strove with my sainted Superior, till I wrought upon him so to dispend the surplus in our treasury; rather than set another rose-window of painted glass in our church, where daylight hath trouble enough to come already. But, if aught was done in needful severity—and the Church must needs smite sometimes as well as heal—against whom murmurs all the countryside? 'Out on the Sub-prior!' they say; 'may God requite him this! Doth not his face bewray that his heart is as the nether millstone?' Had Hildebrand been a portly priest, with a moist eye and a cheerful countenance, perchance he had lacked no man's good word. But let these things pass. It is not well that thou and I speak farther together; for I can profit thee naught. Nay—more—thou mightst be provoked into uttering what might hardly be atoned for. So pass on in peace. I would say a few words to this stout follower of thine, which I trust thou wilt not hinder."

As, with another slight salute, Fitzwarenne strode slowly away, the Abbot urged his mule some ten paces forward, so as to be beyond earshot of the lay-brethren, and beckoned Lanyon to his side.

"Look not so scared, good fellow," he said; "nor think that the rash speech of yonder misguided youth hath chafed us, or that we bear malice thereat. Truly, an evil ensample were we to our flock, if we could not suffer patiently a greater wrong. Nay, I would serve thy master—for such must he be henceforward—in despite of himself; and of this shalt thou presently have proof. Do thou hold the mule's bridle: 'tis a skittish beast, and may not be left to its own devices."

With that, the Abbot undid a pouch hanging at his right side, in which were several compartments for different kinds of coin; and, farther, in the inner lining a small pocket so cunningly concealed that it might have escaped a careful scrutiny. In this were four or five broad thinnish pieces of gold; evidently bezants beaten out with a hammer, till no trace was left of effigy or legend. On one of these, with a sharp penknife drawn from another case holding writing implements, the priest proceeded to grave certain lines and dots, till the result was something resembling an ancient musical score, except that the dots were in the spaces instead of upon the lines, as thus:

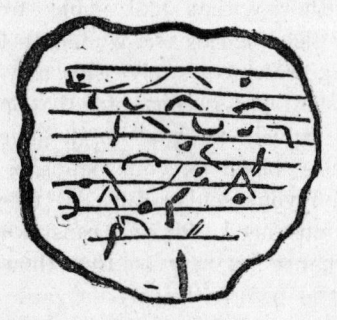

While these things were a-doing, a certain distrust mingled with the wonder of Lanyon's broad gray eyes, as though he had been watching some wizard at his work.

"It is no charm, thou simpleton," the Abbot said, scornfully, though not unkindly, as though aware of the other's suspicions. "Know that the Holy Church dealeth not in such matters, leaving spell and talisman to the misbelieving magicians. Nevertheless, do thou hang this token around thy neck ere thou sleep, and keep it—secretly as thou mayst—with no less care than if it were relic of saint or martyr; for much may it advantage thee in foreign lands, to which, I guess, ye both are bound. Thou comest of the right bulldog breed, and will never be far from thy master's heel in weather fair or foul; so that, if he lie in sore peril, thou thyself mayst be in as evil case. Now, mark. If ye be come to such a pass that there is no hope of help from man, and ye have brief time to make your peace with God, do thou show this gold piece to the priest that shall shrive thee; adjuring him, by his vow of charity, to carry it straight to his Superior, or the churchman, highest in authority, that shall chance to be near. If the token be discerned by one who hath the power of life and death, or whose intercession may avail, I dare aver that ye shall both go forth, for that once, scot-free. Ay, though—which Heaven in its mercy forfend! —there be holy blood on your hands, or the guilt of sacrilege upon your souls. But use this warily, and only at uttermost need; for thou canst not use it twice. 'Tis but a chance: it may be that thou wilt fall in brawl or battle before thy master, and yonder coin may swell some camp-follower's plunder. But all this life of ours is made up of what men call chances. What we have said thou mayst carry to thy master, if thou wilt: yet thou wilt keep thine own counsel for awhile, if thou art wise; it may be, in his stubbornness, he would reject our good offices. Should he speak of these things with better understanding in the after-time, thou mayst tell him all; and tell him, moreover, that he hath not been forgotten in Hildebrand's prayers. *Thou* art not too proud to receive our benison; take it, and go thy way with good hope and courage."

With a few muttered thanks, Will Lanyon took his humble leave, and made haste to overtake his master; while the Abbot also set forward at a much slower pace than he was wont to ride—musing, it seemed, as he went.

"What said the shaveling to thee?" Ralph asked, as the other came up.

"He gave me much good counsel, and one piece of gold," Lanyon answered.

None could have guessed at any secret behind that simple stolid face; and Ralph forbore any farther question. Indeed, right little was said during all that long day's journey; for of those wayfarers one was by nature exceeding taciturn, and the other busy with his own thoughts. But they reached Tunbridge town ere sunset; and were on their road again early on the morrow, without aught having befallen them worthy of record.

CHAPTER VII.

HOW RALPH FITZWARENNE TOOK FROM AN HONEST MAN HIS GOOD NAME.

Hour after hour those two journeyed on, compassing hill and dale, rough and smooth, with the same swift, level pace, and breaking silence only at rare intervals with some trivial question or answer. Long before noon they had risen the crest of the Westerham downs, and were deep in the beech woods that fringed—then as now—the steep chalk-hills. At midday they made brief halt by a wayside spring, to refresh themselves with the provender Lanyon carried in his wallet.

Like most other Normans of pure descent, Fitzwarenne was sparing both in his eating and drinking; his meal was finished before his companion's appetite was half appeased. After bathing hands and lips carefully in the running stream, he said—

"Will Lanyon, two things have I noted in thee, not without some wonder. Since we crossed the drawbridge yester-morn, never once hast thou turned thy face backward, were it but for a single glance over thy shoulder; and, furthermore, thou hast never questioned me concerning mine intents, or whither we wend when we set forth again from London town."

"Good faith, messire," the other answered, gruffly,

without breaking off the play of his busy jaws, " there is little cause for wonderment. Wherefore should I look back, when I leave naught behind but trouble; and wherefore pester thee with questions as to our road, when all are alike to me, so they lead not homeward again? My good lord, your father, hath bestowed on me certain wage, which I would fain work out honestly. I wot well, it will not please you to tarry idling long: beyond the narrow seas there is most a-doing; therefore I guess we shall cross them anon."

"Thou art wiser or hardier than I," Fitzwarenne replied. "If mine eyes traveled not backward, my thoughts did so oftener than I care to own. Also, thou hast guessed rightly that I am heart-sick of tilt-play. and would fain hear shivering of grinded spears, There will be naught stirring yet awhile in Borderland; for the Scots wolves lie licking their wounds, and will scarce make sally while they are stiff and sore. But King Edward still holds Calais in leaguer: from thence down to Languedoc there is work enow for all such as cry, 'St. George Guienne.' There were shrewd gaps made in many companies at Creçy; and, if we attain not to serve under Chandos or Manny, other good knights may well lack an archer and a man-at-arms. Hearken, now. I have pondered on many things during this our journey, and thus far my purpose is fixed. If thou goest to the French wars, thou goest not thither with Ralph Fitzwarenne."

Lanyon's light blue eyes opened to their widest: the blankness of utter discomfiture overspread his bluff face; then it began to lower, and his tone was hoarse and sullen.

"You will do your pleasure, messire. I force myself on no man's company ; neither do I fear but that I shall be hired readily enow. Yet would I hear what fault of mine hath brought me into this quick disfavor."

Fitzwarenne laughed a low genial laugh—the pleasanter, perchance, because it came so rarely—as he smote the speaker lightly on the shoulder.

"I take shame to myself for paltering with thee, were it but for an instant. Am I a priest, too, that I should speak in parables ? Thou hast cast in thy lot with mine, and we sink or swim together, so long as thou carest to follow my fortunes ; they will be neither made nor marred by what I purpose to do. Ralph Warenne was a good knight and a charitable—God rest his soul ! Had he lived on, I had been other than I am, and well content to wear till death the name he gave me ; but to none other of that kith and kin do I owe even a careless kindly word. Therefore, I care not to carry longer the surname that keeps alive my mother's wrong and mine : I will change it, so soon as I come across a better. If this displease thee, speak thy mind frankly and fairly ; yet, if I read thee aright, thou followest not the title, but the man."

The cloud cleared from Lanyon's countenance more rapidly than it had settled there, and he grinned in broad simple glee.

"I was wittol not to guess thou wert jesting, messire. Take what name thou wilt, so it be one that Christian may bear, or English lips speak without stumbling : I warrant I soon shall like it as well as the old one, or better. Yea, if it please the saints, others shall know it too, an' they like it not, before our beards are gray.

'Twould be rare sport should we ride through Bever hamlet in the after-time—thou a belted knight, and I thine esquire, leading a stout clump of spears."

"Tush," the other answered, half angrily; yet he smiled as he sprang lightly to his feet—" pratest thou thus to one who hath never seen color of blood shed in anger? Old Dynevor spoke sooth—' Cravens come not of our stock : ' nevertheless, I profess to thee, I would my first stricken field were over, that I might know how I shall bear myself under shield. But wishing, no more than fearing, brings the proof-time near. Let us forward : thou art ready, I see; for, if thy stomach be not full, thy wallet is empty : I would be in Southwark ere sunset."

Lanyon bent down and drank deep of the stream, lapping quick and noisily, like a thirsty hound; then he, too, arose, shaking the drops from his bushy beard, and followed the other, who had already moved some paces away.

Thenceforward, without let or stay, the wayfarers marched steadily on; but the day was waning fast as they entered the outskirts of the suburb. A chill, gloomy March evening—with threat of wilder weather yet, in the sharp, sudden gusts that brawled round gable and chimney, and whistled through the masts and cords of shipping, breaking the brown water into foamy wavelets as it met the strong ebb tide; and in the lurid western sky, against which the towers of the great Abbey stood out black and frowning—an evening that would have caused most travelers to hurry on toward roof-bield.

Yet Ralph Fitzwarenne, who had slackened his

pace gradually during the last hour, loitered more and more, as though loth to reach his journey's end. It was not the awkward uncertainty of finding himself in a place utterly strange that caused him thus to dally ; for he had ridden once forward and backward through Southwark in his father's train, on their way to and from the *herbegage* beyond Thames, where Dynevor was wont to abide ; and Ralph possessed, to a rare degree, the quick eye and tenacious memory for passing objects which, in some, form as it were a sixth sense. He had already settled that they should lie that night at the sign of the " Spur," a modest hostel of no mean repute : so he walked on slowly; heeding not the clamor, hoarse or shrill, of the wayside vagrants who had crawled forth from purlieus round the Clink to ply their trade of theft or beggary, till night should send them with less unclean beasts, to lie down in their dens. Neither did Fitzwarenne seem to notice the keen malevolent glances lighting on them as they passed certain ale-houses, round the doors of which evil-looking men were lounging, with " cut-purse," or " cut-throat," written on every line of their villainous faces ; though from these groups, more than once, two or three detached themselves, following stealthily in the track of the strangers, till a look out of Lanyon's wary eye, and a yet more significant movement of his quarter-staff, made them slink back hastily : though the game was fair, it was too fierce and big for such curs to meddle with.

The travelers might have advanced some three hundred paces up Kentish Street—so the main thoroughfare into Southwark from the country was then called

—when Ralph, who, despite his reverie, had not ceased to glance to the right and to the left, came to a full halt where the red light from a forge streamed across the already darkening roadway.

A low two-storied house, with more lead than glass in the diamond panes of its upper windows, but wealth of wood in the projecting beams and broad brown eaves, under which there was shelter from sun or shower; while a sort of pent-house shielded the forge from the full in-draught of the outer air; against the wall over this was nailed a helmet of a fashion now out of date—so dark with rust that one could only guess of what metal it was wrought; and above the lintel were carved, in rough straggling letters, these three words:—

JOHN BRAKESPEARE, ARMORER.

There was the cheeriness of light and warmth that has made the smithy the favorite resort for idlers since the time of Tubal Cain; and cheery sounds, too, came from within, as two or three voices chanted snatches of a rude ditty that chimed in pleasantly enough with the ring of hammers. But not in these sights and sounds seemed to lie the attraction that kept the youth standing there, with his eyes fixed steadfastly on the legend over the lintel.

Just then the master-armorer glanced up from his work, and guessing with quick trader's instinct at a likely customer in one, at least, of the pair that were lingering without, thrust the half-forged steel into the water-trough, and came quickly to the front. He was a broad, burly man, something past middle age, with a merry eye, and full, moist mouth, whose smile—ready, yet not a whit servile—twinkled through soot and grime.

"Give you good-even, fair sir," he said, in a deep, mellow voice, the first sounds of which made one think involuntarily of the good liquors that make glad the heart. "Doth your worship, or yon stout follower of thine, lack aught in which John Brakespeare can serve ye? These are not times in which such thews and sinews as yours lie idle. Mine own fighting days are done; yet can I tell a right man-at-arms within a bowshot—marry, 'tis no marvel; I have taken measure oft enow of such—I know naught of my craft, if ye both are not bound to the wars. I deal not in the cunning work of Milan, yet can I give ye honest ware. Prove bascinet or hauberk with axe or sword-dent; if ye can make more damage than mine hammer can amend within the hour, our bargain is naught, and I am a lying cozener."

The direction of Ralph Fitzwarenne's eyes was changed; for the last minute or so they had rested thoughtfully on the speaker's face. He seemed pleased with what he saw there, for he answered with more courtesy than was his wont—he was generally rather cold and reserved with strangers.

"Truly, good armorer, thou hast guessed partly aright, albeit thou doest us both overmuch honor. It shames me to aver that neither I nor this my comrade have as yet drawn blade in fair fight; nevertheless, it is our purpose to take service in the French wars. In such a case, I doubt not thou canst purvey me with harness such as a man may well trust unto, whose life is better worth the keeping than mine is like to be. But of this ware we will speak anon; I have somewhat else to say unto thee now. Come thou hither with me, without; I have some score of words for thine ear."

There came a great wonder, and perchance the faintest shade of distrust, on the armorer's jovial face. Yet he hesitated not to do as he was bidden; but, laying his brawny hands on the window-ledge, vaulted into the street with a nimbleness surprising for his weight and years.

Fitzwarenne took him by the arm, and led him some few paces backward from the spot, where Lanyon leaned on his quarter-staff in stolid patience, as having concern with none of these things.

"Thou seest that?" Ralph asked, pointing to the legend on which his own glance had lately been riveted. "Yon is thy name?"

"Surely I see it," the other answered—still with the same puzzled look; "and have seen it most days since first I crawled over yonder threshold. My father carved it—rest his soul! He and my grandsire—marry, my great grandsire, for aught I know—have borne the same name. It hath brought us no great wealth, God wot, and no greater honor than that of honest craftsmen living by their toil; but the good wife hath never lacked a Sunday kirtle, and the brats have meat enow to make them thrive, and I have ever a pottle of ale for a neighbor, or a cup of sack of holidays. So I know not why I should grumble or make moan. But wherefore is your worship curious concerning that poor name of ours?"

"Because I am aweary of mine own," Fitzwarenne answered, "and would fain change it. Thou knowest naught of me, and may believe or disbelieve, as thou wilt. But I swear to thee, by the Holy Rood, that not for fear or felony would I do this. Thy name caught mine eye as I passed, and it pleased me well: 'tis a fitting one to bear where hard blows are going. Lo, I proffer thee no guerdon—such things are not bought and sold—yet I dare aver that, if I bring no great credit to thy name, I will bring it to no dishonor."

He drew himself up as he spoke, with a gesture neither boastful nor defiant, but full of self-reliance and loyalty. John Brakespeare, who, in the course of his trade, had stood face to face with many knights and nobles, thought that he never had looked on a more gallant bearing: the last spark of suspicion vanished from his honest heart, but some simple wonderment still remained.

"'Tis a quaint fancy," he said, thrusting back the thick tangled hair that fell low over his brows; "nathless I wis it covers no malfeasance, and I care not to baulk it. 'Tis a tough, work-day name enough; though, I warrant me, less high-sounding than what your worship has borne heretofore. I am no wizard, to read the lines of hands or faces; yet would I wager a harness of proof against an archer's hacqueton, that no drop of churl's blood runs in your veins."

Ralph's brown cheek flushed a little as he made reply.

"Gramercy for thy courtesy. Thou shalt hear of my lineage—the more readily that thou hast asked never a question thereanent. My mother was cousin to Sir Hugh Warenne—who, in the first year of this reign, died gallantly under shield, by the hand, men say, of the Black Douglas. She was wedded, with all due rite, to Dynevor of Bever, though that wedlock the Church saw fit to disallow, on plea that they were within the degrees; and from her death up to this hour have I been nurtured as his charges. But yestermorn set me free of all duty to Dynevor, and lightened him, I trow, of a weary burden. I am adrift now, like a skiff on the deep sea, and henceforward forever I have neither kith nor kin. So—going forth to do my *devoir*, as I hope, and fighting for mine own hand —I would fain carry a name bearing not the brand of bastardy. Hast thou my meaning, or is there aught thou wouldst have made more clear?"

The armorer doffed bonnet, and made a rough obeisance.

"I thank your worship, I have learned all that I care to know. I mind Sir Hugh Warenne well, and certain inklings of yonder sad tale came to mine ears; or I had dealings with some of his household. I saw that armament set out that fared so ill in the North; and I mind well how starkly the old knight reined his destrere, as he rode close on our boy-king's right hand. Marry, there was great dolor and moan when men knew that he should come back no more. 'Bastard' —said ye? By Saint Benedict, there lives not belted earl, betwixt Thames and Tyne, that can boast of gentler blood. Take my name, sith it pleases you, and the saints send you luck therewith! Never, I wot, since my great grandsire was enfranchised, had 'Brakespeare' such chance of coming to honor."

Ralph held out his hand, which the other, though he drew back at first, took and wrung heartily.

"Then so shall it be. I lie at the 'Spur' to-night: come thou thither at thy leisure, and we will drink a stoup of right Bordeaux wine over this our bargain, which in sooth will profit thee but little. Tush, man," he broke in impatiently, seeing that the other was still oppressed by some shy diffidence—"knowest thou not that I am 'Brakespeare' for evermore, and have no more to do with Dynevor and Warenne than thou? Thou hast had many choicer boon companions, than one who has far to climb ere he reach esquire's estate. Furthermore, I would speak with thee concerning the matters whereof I shall have need so soon as I have taken service: it may be that I set forth at brief notice, and with scant time for furnishing. No more words: I shall expect thee anon."

With a wave of his hand, Ralph turned on his heel to rejoin his patient follower. The gesture was friendly and familiar enough, yet slightly imperious withal, as of one wont to see his bidding done undisputedly. And so the honest armorer interpreted it, as he stood looking wistfully after the tall figure receding fast up the dusky street.

"I may not say him nay," he muttered; "but—for all his fair words—such company is not for the like of John Brakespeare. I warrant me, I shall feel as if they had set me down at our good bishop's table above the salt. By Saint Benedict, a proper youth! Bastard or no bastard, one would have thought ne'er a father in England but would have been proud of such a son; either the wenches are blind in the Weald, or he must have left some sore hearts behind him. If God will, I shall hear great news of him ere I die. There is work enow done for the nonce: I will go cleanse me of this grime, and don my holiday doublet and hosen, so that I shame yonder gallant as little as I may."

"Mark me well," Ralph said to his companion, who walked close to his shoulder—"I am Fitzwarenne no more, but Brakespeare by surname, to thee and all others whom it may concern. Canst thou learn the trick of it, so that thou keep thy tongue from sliping?"

"I will take good heed, messire," the other answered, betraying no whit of surprise. "'Tis a simple word enough; and my tongue wags not so fast that it should babble astray."

Almost as those last words were spoken, they came to their journey's end, and strode in through a low-browed archway into the courtyard of the "Spur."

CHAPTER VIII.

OF THE COMPANY THAT RALPH, SURNAMED BRAKESPEARE, MET UNDER THE SIGN OF THE "SPUR."

Supper was over in the common room of the hostel, and the guests—not numerous, as it chanced, on that especial night—had broken up into groups; some lingering at the board where they had eaten, others clustering at small tables, drawn nearer the hearth. The logs that burned bravely were useful, otherwise than for warmth; or the great chamber, with its dusky walls and blackened beams, would have looked gloomy enough, lighted only by three or four of the clumsy oil lamps called *mertiers*, and by the rude torch-candles fixed on spikes on either side the doorway, that swirled and guttered in the frequent draughts.

In the nook formed by the outer angle of the huge projecting chimney, and so somewhat in the shadow, sat Ralph and his guest, the armorer—a mighty stoup of Bordeaux wine betwixt them; while on a settle hard by, Lanyon dozed in that half stupor that, when no care keeps men wakeful, comes pleasantly to the hardiest wayfarer after long travel and a hearty meal. The good liquor had thawed the craftsman's shyness and unloosed his tongue; so he was ready enough in answering to the best of his power the other questions, and in tendering his advice.

"An' ye would be ruled by me, messire, ye would not be hasty in taking service with the first that shall make proffer. There be some who adventure themselves in these wars, overmuch for plunder's sake; and with such little honor is to be gotten, even if they 'scape the shame. I have accointance with certain knights and barons—always in the course of trade— who might serve thy turn bravely. But right few of such, I wot, are now on the hither side of the narrow seas; for there is work enow in Guienne for all the lances that our king can spare from Calais leaguer. Truly, there is Sir Walter Rokeby—a leal knight and stalwart—who is now at his lodging beyond Thames, scarce healed of the sore hurt he gat at Neville's Cross. It may be he will be setting forth ere long; I warrant me he will tarry at home not an hour after he hath leech's leave to sit in saddle. Peradventure, my good word may profit you somewhat; for Sir Walter hath shown me no small kindness, and calls me ever his trusty armorer."

While Ralph thanked the friendly speaker, the heavy door at the farther end of the guest-chamber swung open quickly, as though thrust inward by a strong, hasty hand; causing the decent merchants and franklins, who formed the greater part of the company, to start from their grave converse or quiet games of tables to look at the newcomer. In truth he was one to whom few men, and fewer women, would have denied a second glance, if only for his marvelous beauty.

His face was a pure oval; with a complexion of clear pale olive, features straight and finely chiseled, a mouth nearly perfect in form, though not in expression, and long, lustrous dark eyes, naturally languid, but flashing out at times with animal ferocity. He was tall and powerful of frame, without the angular squareness which usually accompanies great strength; and one would hardly have guessed at the stark muscle and sinew hidden under the delicate rounding of joint and limb. His dress of rich murrey cloth was of a foreign fashion, and not disfigured by sleeves of preposterous length, or any other of the fantastic fopperies in which the English gallants of that time were prone to indulge; while the careful trimming and studied arrangement of his silky beard and wavy hair—both of intense blue-black—showed that the possessor of such rare personal advantages was disposed to make use of them to the uttermost.

He was evidently not quite a stranger to some present there; for, as he entered, there was a kind of flutter and murmur among certain of the staid burghers, betokening distrust and dislike, with perchance a shade of fear, just as you may see a whole rookery thrown into tumult by the sudden appearance of a sparrow-hawk.

It was manifest, too, that something had ruffled the newcomer's humor, as he swung up the center of the guest-chamber; glancing half insolently, half defiantly, to the right and to the left; and cast himself down on the settle, in the corner corresponding to that where Ralph Brakespeare was sitting; never deigning to notice the courtesy of the meek artisan who yielded place to him hastily. Then he called for a stoup of Muscadine; and, long before it could have been brought, cursed the drawer for dallying—in fair English enough, though with a soft foreign accent: when the liquor came, he fell to drinking, not in quick, greedy gulps, but daintily and slowly, savoring each drop as it glided over his palate.

The stout armorer glanced at the stranger from under his brows with evident disfavor.

"Whom have we here?" he grumbled. "One of a marvelous goodly presence, *pardie ;* but a ruffler, I warrant me, if no worse. Loth would I be to drink with him in the dark, and yet more loth to play with him at the dice. Yon may well be the Italian who, as I heard but yester-even, won thirty silver marks of Josselyn, the Abbot's reeve, and picked a quarrel with him thereafter. Marry, had not help been near, the wittol—besides losing his year's savings—would have brooked the stab. By Saint Benedict, I like not such company; and if my gossip, our host, were of my mind, he would have none such at the 'Spur.'"

"I am partly of thine opinion," Ralph answered, carelessly; "but I see not how he can concern us. We are not birds for his net, I trow. Go back, I prithee, to where thou brakest off talk but now, and finish yonder stoup, which is well-nigh drained. I have beckoned already to the drawer to bring hither another."

The armorer complied, nothing loth. But, as he wiped his beard, and prepared to resume converse—he was somewhat slow and deliberate of speech—the outward door swung open once more, this time timidly and cautiously, and there entered a girl, leading by the hand a white-haired man, somewhat bent with age or infirmity, who walked with the faltering, uncertain gait peculiar to the blind. There was no mistaking the profession of the pair; the threadbare cotehardie, and the gittern, or rebecque, slung round his neck, betokened the minstrel; while from her raiment of gay, contrasted colors, no less than from the instrument carried in her right hand, all knew the tymbestere.

"'Tis Gilbert the gleeman," John Brakespeare said, with a kind of gruff apology, seeing his companion's brow overcast at the fresh interruption—"with his granddaughter. It were charity to let them play out their play, an' you would have patience; for they will take no alms unless they seem to earn them. Marry, I mind him as deft an archer as ever drew clothyard shaft; in the Scots wars got he that ax-blow which hath dazed his brain ever since and left his eye darkling: he hath no mean skill on his instrument, and she dances right featly, howbeit in somewhat strange fashion. Moreover, 'tis a good wench and a chaste, as I have heard true folk aver; though it may seem likelier to find a pearl in Thames ooze, than virtue in a glee-maiden."

Ralph's face softened in contrition—as he made answer—

"I take shame to myself that I should have chafed but now. It fits me well—a poor aspirant in arms—to grudge charity to one who hath come by mischance, fighting manfully under shield. Let them play on with a good courage; I promise that, when 'tis done, they shall not lack guerdon."

To higher and holier places than hostels, in those days, minstrel, jester, and tregetour had easy access. It was clear that the entertainment about to take place was of no unusual occurrence here; and perchance, others of less reputable sort were not uncommon. After the two had made lowly obeisance, the girl had led her grandsire to a vacant bench, and moved forward herself to a clear space left in the center of the guest-chamber, where no rushes were strewn.

She looked singularly picturesque as she struck her first attitude—her lithe, elastic figure, set off by a trim blue bodice quaintly broidered, drawn back, and poised firmly on the right foot—whirling the timbrel on one finger of the hand raised above her head; the firelight gleaming on her light hair, braided with gay ribbons and glittering coins, and on her pretty, mutinous face, whose natural fairness of complexion had not altogether yielded to the tanning of sun and wind; while the short, striped skirt gave liberal glimpses of a neat ankle and shapely leg, cased in scarlet hosen. After a brief prelude, the gittern-player broke into a wild, fitful measure—slow for the most part, but sometimes quickened abruptly—with which chimed in the jingle of the bell sewn to the dancer's dress, and at irregular intervals the clash and rattle of the timbrel.

The performance differed materially from those of the same class then in vogue, and rather resembled those practised by the Moriscoes on the Continent, but little known in England, the chief characteristics of which have probably been preserved by the modern Gitanas. There were none of the violent feats of activity, or displays of posture-making, in which the tymbesteres were prone to indulge; and, though some of the gestures were provocative enough, none were coarse, immodest, or unseemly. Such as it was, the dance was a complete success: long before it was ended, the soberest spectators were ready to applaud, and to open their purse-strings. Before it had fairly begun, the dark stranger, who sat drinking alone, had roused himself from his reverie, and was watching the performer with something more than idle curiosity. As the last rattle of the rebecque died away, the girl made another obeisance, lowly and gracefully, and went round for such alms as it pleased the audience to bestow, beginning at the lower end of the long chamber. She passed on, her timbrel growing heavier with silver esterlings and groats, till she reached the angle of the chimney where the Italian sat. As he thrust his hand into his gipsire he glanced at the heap of small silver coins, and laughed contemptuously.

"Is that all the largess thou hast gathered hitherto from churl and trader, *poverina mia?* Here is a new broad florence for thee; and, if thou wilt kiss me twice betwixt the lips, I will e'en double the guerdon."

As he spoke, his right arm was thrown suddenly round the tymbestere's waist, and he half drew her on his knee. She was no countrybred wench, to start at a rude jest or innocent freedom; and the shyness of maidenhood perchance was gone before her cheek lost its bloom; but there was a look in those evil, handsome eyes that made her shrink back with an instinctive dislike and fear.

"I pray you, set me free, fair sir," she said, trying to veil her terror under a seeming of mirth. "I deal not in such wares as you would chaffer for, and it were flat robbery to take your florence, sith a groat overpays our pains."

He smiled, half in amusement, half in scorn, but his

and advancing yet a few steps, stood face to face with his adversary. He was by some two inches the taller of the twain, but far lighter of frame; of all the bystanders Lanyon alone, perchance, doubted that the result would be other than they wished; for a mere youth was pitted against one in the flower of his strength, and from the way in which the Italian took up his position, the judges of such matters saw in him a practised wrestler.

Without another word spoken on either side, they grappled. At first, as they swayed to and fro, the foreigner's superior weight did tell, and it seemed as though his opponent must needs be borne down, or uprooted from the floor. But not for naught had Philip Kemeys's pupil studied under a master whose name had been for a quarter-century the boast and terror of the countryside: at the very moment when Ralph seemed to bend and yield under the other's grip, with a quick side-twist he brought his own hip under the other's groin; then, before any could guess how it was done, the Italian's feet, struck clean from under him, flew high in air, and he came to the ground with a dull, ominous crash, flung fairly over Brakespeare's shoulder.

No wonder that for some seconds' space he should have lain there half stunned and motionless; not twice in a lifetime will a heavy man rise from such a fall on hardened ground without scathe to life or limb; but, before the murmur of applause called forth by the unexpected feat had died away, the Italian gathered himself up slowly, and stood upon his feet.

His handsome face, deformed as it was by pain and malice, had not wholly lost its beauty; but it was so fearfully transfigured that a painter, limning some old saintly legend, might have no apter semblance for tortured or baffled Belial. The brutal lust that lately gleamed in his eyes was supplanted by a keener desire —the acrid thirst for blood: he plucked from its sheath a long, keen poignard, on whose dark-veined blade there were stains not a few, and drew himself together halfcrouching, like a savage panther about to spring.

And in Ralph Brakespeare's eyes there was the evil light spoken of before; and his face was set as a flintstone, dark and pitiless, as he bared his own huntingknife, and, without giving a hair's breadth of ground, waited warily for the onset. All present there wist that none could come betwixt those two without sore risk to his own life; yet Lanyon started forward with some such intent, while the armorer shouted lustily for the watch, and the host wrung his hands helplessly, and the tymbestere shrieked in her terror, and many called on the combatants in God's name to forbear. Intercession or interference must have been equally vain and the watch could only have come in time to carry a corpse away, had it not been for an incident on which none had reckoned.

A side door leading into a small inner chamber opened, and, through all the bustle and uproar, a single voice made itself heard.

"What! brawling again, Gian Malatesta? Will those hands of thine never be quiet till they are in the gyves?"

A very calm, quiet voice—not raised a whit above its wonted tone—yet marked with an indescribable accent like that of one fated some day to hold authority over his fellows, even if his turn for command hath not come yet. The first syllables acted on the Italian's wrath, like a necromancer's spell on a rebellious familiar: he thrust back his dagger into its sheath, and, as he turned toward the speaker, the ferocity on his face changed to the sullen confusion, which, with natures like his, replaces shame.

The newcomer deserves to be somewhat carefully portrayed, for that age, rife though it was with names of mark, bred few more notable worthies.

CHAPTER IX.

HOW RALPH TOOK SERVICE UNDER SIR JOHN HAWKWOOD.

There stood on the threshold of the open doorway this manner of man.

Something over the middle height; of a complexion rather florid than pale; with hair and beard of rich dark chestnut; and features cast in keen aquiline mold; the face was too calm and resolute to be ignoble, and marked by too decisive a character to be vulgar; yet certainly it wanted the stamp of birth and breeding that gives a charm to many more commonplace visages. His attire was plain even to meanness; consisting of a close jerkin, or cassock, of coarse dark russet cloth, with nether garments and hose of the same color, all frayed and stained with pressure of hauberk, cuissard, and steel boot.

Such an one at the age of thirty, or thereabouts, was John Hawkwood—son of the tanner of Sible Hedingham, and whilom prentice to the tailor in Chepe—then, a simple man-at-arms; till, within this very year, for wight service at Creçy he took from King Edward's own hand the knightly accolade. He held in his right hand, sheathed, one of the short swords, called *coutels;* and with the other beckoned the Italian toward him.

The other obeyed without a word, though, as it seemed, rather sullenly and reluctantly; and in another second, the door of the inner chamber was closed behind them.

Then there broke forth again a stir and murmur in the guest-chamber, but now of merriment rather than of fear; for there was not one present whose heart was not gladdened by the sight of the foreigner's handsome head laid low. Several gathered round the conqueror, pressing on him their simple gratulations, while loudest among them rose the voice of the honest armorer. Lanyon, when he saw that help was no longer needed, had cast himself down again on his settle, and had already relapsed into stolid placidity. In the midst of the hubbub, none noticed the disappearance of the glee-maiden and her grandsire. Hastily, though not uncourteously, Ralph broke through his admirers; and, plucking him by the sleeve as he bustled past, drew the host aside.

"I fain would learn the name and degree of him who entered but now," he said, "if thou knowest them, and there be no special reason for thy silence."

"There is none such, fair sir," the other answered readily. "Men call him Sir John Hawkwood now; but a year agone, as I have heard, he rode a simple archer in the Lord Neville's train. I warrant him a good lance and a bold, yet very straitened in his means, I fear me. He hath been at no charges, save for needful meat and drink, the three days he hath lain in my private chamber. Marry, had it not been for his follower—yonder roysterer, with whom your worship dealt so roundly but now—the 'Spur' had gained little by their custom. Nathless, I grudge him not house-room, God wot. 'Tis a fair-spoken knight, and a kindly; and mayhap he will tarry here some day, when he hath gotten both wealth and honor."

As they spoke, the armorer had approached, unobserved, and struck in with scant ceremony.

"And is that Sir John Hawkwood? I am well pleased to have foregathered with him. My good wife hath kinsfolk in the parts where he was born and bred. It was but the other day that her cousin told us of the wonderment and gladness at Hedingham, when they heard that their neighbor's son had won his spurs. 'Tis pity that the honest tanner lived not to look on his boy's face again; but he was in mortal sickness when the news came, and the great joy may well have hasted his end. The knight hath started fair, certes; yet he hath a brave long race yet to run, and there will be prizes worth the winning for such as keep him company. Had I to choose my service, I swear by Saint Benedict, I had liever ride under his pennon than under the broadest banner that flaunts in Flanders or Guienne."

Just then the inner door opened again, and the Italian re-entered the guest-chamber. On his smooth brow there was no vestige of cloud; and none but a very keen observer would have detected in his smile a cover sneer.

"I crave pardon of this goodly company," he said, in a soft voice, " for having broken off their drink and troubled their mirth. I did but jest with the demoiselle after my rough foreign fashion; and, had she not fled so suddenly, else had I made her amends before you all. I will take good heed so to offend no more. To you, gentle sir,"—he bent low as he turned toward Ralph Brakespeare—"would I make special excuse in presence of Sir John Hawkwood, the knight I follow, if it will please you to visit him in his chamber."

Ralph bent his head; and, with a sign of intelligence to the armorer, went out with the Italian.

They came into a small chamber, dimly lighted by a single oil-lamp, and scantily furnished with a few rude lockers for arms and wearing apparel; two bed-places let into recesses in the wall, after the fashion still prevalent in parts of Scotland; and a heavy oaken table strewn with parchments and writing materials, near which sat Sir John Hawkwood. As he arose to greet his visitor, there might have been noticed in his courtesy the stiffness and constraint of one who has had little practise in social forms and ceremonies: neither did he waste many words in preamble.

"It shames me much, fair sir," he said, "that the ill conduct of follower of mine should have drawn you into unseemly brawl; albeit you have dealt him a sharp lesson, for the which I thank you heartily. I know no more than it hath suited him to avow; but I guessed what happened, when I saw the glee-maiden cowering there. Sathanas needs but to take the shape of a dainty paramour, and Gian Malatesta will wend lightly wherever it lists the fiend to lead. Nevertheless, I have told him roundly that, if he proffer not such excuse as it may fit you to receive, he and I part this night. 'Twere a sorry jest if I, who but lately stood bareheaded in presence of captains, should suffer insolence toward their betters in such as ride with me."

'Tis scarce worth while to set down at length the

Italian's apology; more especially as it imposed not altogether on him to whom it was addressed. Indeed, a vague feeling of dislike and distrust rather increased than abated in Brakespeare's breast; he cut the glib speaker short, so soon as he could do so without manifest discourtesy.

"I pray thee be less liberal in excuse, messire: enough has been said and to spare. Perchance little harm was meant; and, as it chanced, none hath been done. 'Tis a fashion in my country to strike hands after a tough wrestling bout, in token that no bad blood rankle; here is mine, if ye list to take it."

With great show of eagerness the Italian accepted the proffer; but their fingers were barely locked before they unclasped again, and Ralph turned away somewhat hastily—

"There are graver matters concerning which I would speak to this knight, at his good leisure."

"There is no better time than now," Hawkwood answered. "Leave us, Gian Malatesta; but go not far away, and keep thy brain as cool as thou canst; I may need thy help with this scrivener work ere I sleep."

When they were alone, Ralph stated his wishes briefly and bluntly; proffering for himself and Lanyon to take service in the French wars as man-at-arms and archer, while Hawkwood listened, leaning his brow on his hands, and half shading his face.

"How are ye called?" he asked, without looking up.

When he heard the answer, he dropped his hand, and gazed steadily on the youth with his small, piercing eyes.

"Brakespeare?" he said, doubtfully. "'Tis an

honest yeoman name, certes, like to the one I bear: yet right seldom worn by those of the degree to which, if I err not, thou belongest by birth, if not by fortune?"

Ralph met the fixed look without blenching.

"I say not that they christened me so," he answered; "but to none other name have I better claim, and by none other will I henceforth be known, whether I speed with you, sir knight, or no. Also, ye do greatly err in imputing to me higher estate than my name imports: there are merchants and franklins not a few in yon guest-chamber who, if right were done, might sit higher at the board than I."

Sir John's lip curled with a quaint smile, sarcastic, yet not unkindly.

"Good sooth, I marvel how the great folk of thy country apparel themselves, and what manner of gimmals they wear, when on the finger of yeomen's sons shine fair balas rubies! Nay, be not wroth," he went on, in a grave voice, marking the quick flush on Ralph's cheek—"I have no title to question thee. Rather take thou this my counsel: if on light incitement thou hast left thy home, repent thee in time; so shall thy fortunes not be marred in peevish fit; but, if there be weightier causes, and thou art in truth utterly adrift, then take service with some knight or baron of higher repute and larger means than I. Ill will it suit such as from youth upward have lain soft, and lived delicately, to ride with plain John Hawkwood, whose worldly wealth—the accompt of which lies under mine hand—may scarce suffice for the furniture of three men-at-arms."

"Let that be no hindrance," Ralph answered, with eagerness unwonted in him; "I bear gold pieces enow in this gipsire to purvey myself and my follower yonder, both with horse and armor. Nay, for that special purpose were they given to me. As for choosing another leader, the honest armorer whose surname I bear—albeit, I profest not to be of his kin—said, speaking of your worship but now: 'He hath a brave long race yet to run, and there will be prizes worth the winning for such as keep him company. Had I to choose my service, I had liever ride under his pennoncelle than under the broadest banner that flaunts in Flanders or Guienne.' Even so say I. Yet will I thrust my service on none, and I may not gainsay your pleasure; so, if ye will have none of me and mine, I will cumber your time and chamber no more."

Now, John Hawkwood, though imbued with many of the high and generous qualities which are part and parcel of the heroic character, was by no means a hero of romance, either in disinterestedness or disregard of his own advantage—to which, indeed, as his later history shows, he had a marvelously keen eye. Here was a rare chance before him; and he was scarce likely to let it slip. Rising up, he laid his hand on the other's arm, as it were with a sudden impulse, which, if not natural, was excellently feigned.

"Nay, fair youth, we part not thus. It may be I have been over-nice in this matter—especially since the king, our master, stands in sore need of thews and sinews like thine: thy follower, I guess, was yon brawny carle I saw but now, so eager to thrust himself between thee and harm at his own life's peril. Sith ye will have none of my counsel, I will take your frank proffer as frankly; and ye both shall be enrolled this night—thou as man-at-arms, he as archer. If ever I thrive, so as to maintain a household, we may speak of thine advancement to esquire's degree. In such a case, were it set to the proof, baseness of birth, I warrant me, would not be thy bar; though I choose not to pry farther into what concerns me not nearly. Write thyself down as it lists thee: a man may fight well, God wot, under a worse name than thou hast chosen."

"Nay, not so," the other made answer; "if you, sir knight, scruple not to attach to your person an unknown runagate, I were a very churl to be more niggardly of trust. Hearken, an' it please you, though 'tis scarce worth your while."

Then, very briefly and simply, for the second time that day, Ralph Brakespeare told his story to a stranger. But Hawkwood evidently thought it not wasted time, as he listened with marked interest: when it was ended, he shook his head with a compassion that may well have been real.

"'Tis a sad tale," he said. " I know but little of the ways and fashions of knights and nobles; yet often hath it seemed to me that they deal with their own flesh and blood more hardly than they deal with us of low estate. For what thou hast done I blame thee not now; nay, by the Rood, I think thou hast chosen thy part both wisely and well. I am right glad that all lies fair and open betwixt us two; thou dost not fear I should bewray thy secret? There is yet another matter troubles me: I know not how thou and Gian Malatesta will agree. Forsooth, I myself like him not hugely, and trust him no farther than I would trust a sworn dicer and drabber; yet is the knave useful manywise. He speaketh three tongues indifferently well, and, with good skill at all weapons, hath a special gift for ambushments and stratagems of war; moreover, when in the humor, or hardly pressed, he will fight like a very fiend; also never a clerk or shaveling of them all can read and indite more deftly: indeed, though he babbles not much concerning himself, even in his drink, from certain words he hath let drop, I guess him to have been cloister-bred, and to have broken bounds. Chiefly to this end did I yield to his desire, and suffer him to come hither in my company. I needed help in dealing with all this gear "—he pointed to the table strewn with parchments—"for scrolls are but sealed books unto me. I have been seeking to turn into gold pieces the slender heritage that came to me but of late: marry, when the charges of my journey and the cost of these parchments are paid, my gipsire will be heavier by scarce a score of nobles. It may be that the Lombard and scrivener are cozening me, and the Italian is in league with both; but I have no patience to dally longer here. Yet another three or four days, and we will be clear of English air: not on light cause, I wis, will I breathe it again."

"Let not that trouble your worship," Ralph answered, cheerily, yet with a touch of scorn. "It is not like, indeed, that Messire Malatesta and I shall knit brotherhood in arms; nathless might we drink at the same board, and couch in the same tent, and ride under the same pennon for many a year, without either looking askance at the other. For all that you have seen to-night, I am not, in very truth, given to brawling, nor have I thus far found men hasty in picking quarrel."

"That can I well believe," Hawkwood replied, smiling slightly; "and, though Gian Malatesta be a rank brawler when crossed or in drink, I have noted in him a certain shrewd wit in choosing such as may be safely overborne. Thou art not of these, as he has found out at cost of a rib's-ache; I dare aver he will mell with thee no more. Go now, I prithee, and send that same varlet hither to me: I must get forward with these matters to-night. And come with thy follower early to-morrow, that I may enroll your names, and give ye handsel of King Edward's wages. Then will we speak of purveying thee with horse and armor: in these times there is no lack of such gear ready to all men's hands."

With an obeisance that marked that he already held himself bound by new duties, Brakespeare went out; and, after delivering his message to the Italian, sat down to tell Will Lanyon and the armorer how he had sped.

The first-named took the news with his wonted placidity, it was indeed, to him, of singularly small importance under whom he served, so long as he parted not company with the one man whose fortunes he had chosen to follow. The armorer, who by this time had nearly rendered an account of the second stoup, was voluble in congratulation and approval; perchance his satisfaction was in nowise lessened by reflection on the custom that the morrow would bring him. But John Brakespeare was no late roysterer, and had a character to keep up both at home and abroad; so, when the flagon was finished, he rose to go, resisting manfully all temptation of another. Ralph went out with him, for his head felt heated—not with wine, of which he had been sparing, but with excitement of diverse kinds—and he longed for a draught of fresh air, free of fume of food or wood-smoke.

Besides the great gates of the archway leading into the courtyard, which were now closed, the inn had another door opening into the street, beyond which a heavy porch projected some three yards. Against the outer angle of this Ralph leaned and watched the burly armorer as he strode away, planting each solid footfall with a studied deliberation, as though bent on dissembling even to himself a certain unsteadiness of gait.

It was a black boisterous night, with dreary glimpses of a watery moon through the rifts in the tossing cloudrack; and every gust brought closer the chillness that foreruns heavy rain; but there the youth lingered, loth to return to the heat and bustle of the guest-chamber, and not sorry for awhile to be left to his own musing. His right hand was thrust into the breast of his doublet, while the other hung listlessly at his side. Suddenly he started, for on that left hand there came first the faintest pressure, then it was lifted gently till two soft lips were laid on the palm: glancing downward in his wonder, his eyes looked full into those of the tymbestere, gleaming out of the shadow where she knelt.

With the liking that most men feel for any helpless creature whom they have defended not unsuccessfully,

CHAPTER X.

HOW RALPH BRAKESPEARE RODE AFTER SIR JOHN HAWKWOOD TO SANDWICH.

VERY early on the morrow, Ralph held brief converse with Lanyon, which resulted in a certain change of plan. When they presented themselves before Hawkwood, Brakespeare prayed that his follower might be enlisted as a *hobelar*, or mounted archer of the inferior, or light armed class. To this the knight gave ready assent. Neither, indeed, could he have objected with any good grace, seeing that both recruits were to be equipped at their own expense. Gian Malatesta welcomed his new comrades in a fair set speech, to which Ralph made answer, courteous, and cold; though in his heart he made light of the Italian's compliments, he gladly availed himself of the other's proffered aid in the purveyance of horse and harness.

First, was provided a strong, active gelding, well fitted for the lighter weight he had to carry; for Lanyon's defensive armor consisted only of a bascinet, hacqueton, and gantlets; his weapons were spear, coutel, and knife. Ralph's destrere was chosen with much more trouble and care. Indeed, though the weight of metal had been lessened by the gradual replacement of chain-mail by plate, it was still a sore task for ordinary horseflesh to bear a rider armed *cap-à-pie* through a long day of march or battle. At length they fixed on a powerful roan stallion—something heavy in the crest and shoulder for our modern notions, but with the short broad barrel that promises hardiness no less than strength, and with rare loins and limbs. John Brakespeare had not vaunted his wares unduly; and, if the Italian's critical eyes—used to judge the work of Florentine or Genoese—found something now and then to cavil at, it was rather at want of finish in the fashion than at defect in the quality of steel. By nightfall the equipment was complete; and, more weary with busy excitement than he had ever been with exercise on foot or saddle, Ralph Brakespeare sat down to supper. His gipsire was sorely shrunken from its fair round proportions of yester-even; but this troubled the youth not a whit: he was full of hope and health, and knew that his soldier's pay would suffice his moderate desires; so 'tis no marvel if he felt himself wealthy with the few gold pieces that yet jingled under his girdle. Right glad, too, was he to hear that Hawkwood's own business was done, and that on the morrow they would set forth to Sandwich, whence they would take ship.

There are few but would have lingered to look at the small group gathered the next morning round the porch of The Spur, in the level rays of the late risen sun.

Of the three horsemen armed *cap-à-pie*, Hawkwood himself was, perhaps, the least imposing in exterior: there were shrewd dints, both in his bascinet and breastplate; neither was his harness so carefully polished as that of the Italian, whereon certain bosses, and other attempts at ornament, gave token of a leaning toward martial foppery. Both of these were well mounted; though their cattle were somewhat low in flesh, as from long travel or campaigning, and made contrast with the high condition of the roan destrere, pawing and curveting impatiently under the strong, skilful hand that reined him. In very truth, Ralph Brakespeare was a gallant sight as he sat there—square and erect, yet swaying to each movement of his charger, easily, as though his limbs had been cumbered with nothing weightier than silk or serge—his eyes flashing under his raised vizor, and a genial smile upon his lips, which were apt to be somewhat too set and stern. Will Lanyon had backed too many wild colts to feel timid in saddle: but he lacked the grace of an accomplished horseman, and was evidently something ill at ease in his new caparison; his vast breadth of shoulder and corded muscles showed to advantage, even under the heavy hacqueton; and looking at the grip of his brawny thighs, you guessed that trying to bear such an one down—so long as his horse kept its footing—would be like tilting at a tower. Glancing at the pair with a keen, soldierly eye, Hawkwood thought that he had gotten for the king, if not for himself, a rare bargain.

Close by the knight's rein bowed the host of The Spur, stirrup-cup in hand, with the smug satisfaction on his face of one whose reckoning has just been paid without wrangle or close inquiry: a pace or two off stood the honest armorer, come to take a last look at his own handiwork, and to wish his namesake Godspeed. Hawkwood barely touched the hippocras with his lips, and Ralph was nearly as temperate; but the Italian drank deep in his own deliberate fashion; and Lanyon drained the huge beaker to the dregs, muttering something as he wiped his beard about "the sin of wasting good liquor."

The brief farewells were soon said, and then came the clash and rattle of steel, as the small cavalcade moved slowly away; the knight riding alone in front, his two men-at-arms following abreast, while the archer brought up the rear, leading the single packhorse laden with their scanty baggage. Shading his eyes, John Brakespeare watched them till they disappeared round the sharp corner of Kentish Street; and then, with a half sigh and a muttered benison, he turned into the hostel, to comfort himself with a liberal morning posset.

Through that day, and the next, and the next, Hawkwood and his followers rode steadily onward; making the best speed they could, without distressing their cattle, along the main road to the southeastern coast, through Rochester, Sittingbourne, Charing, and Canterbury. No incident worthy of record befell them, till, on the fourth afternoon, from a crest of rising ground, they saw the old Roman walls of Richborough, rising like a rocky islet out of the dreary marshland; and, beyond this, houses clustered on either side of a harbor estuary; and, farther yet, gleams of wet sand and a broad selvage of foam. And two of the wayfarers felt the mingling of pleasure and wonderment common to all who for the first time draw into their nostrils briny air, and, for the first time listen to the language of the sea.

Very few, riding through so long a march side by

side with Gian Malatesta, would have been proof against the fascination of his manner, when, as now, he wished it to be winning. His glib tongue never seemed to weary as he told stories of adventure in many lands, racy and picturesque and stirring enough, yet not so redolent of rapine as to shock or revolt the listener; while, throughout, he had the tact to avoid egotism and affect modesty—hinting at, rather than avowing, the share that he himself had borne in orgie or broil. Ever and anon, too, his rich, round voice would break out into snatches of melody—English drinking ditty, French *rondelai*, or, more frequently, a *canzonet* of his own land; specially in these last, the veriest stranger, to whom the words were meaningless, might have guessed that he sang of love—love, not of the heart, but of the senses—not a high romantic devotion, but passion, half selfish and wholly sinful. At each hostel or wayside inn where they made halt, the Italian had banter or admiration ready for every buxom face or trim figure that crossed his path; but he carried not his jest to the verge of licentiousness, and refrained from all undue excess in liquor. Altogether, it would have been difficult to find a pleasanter fellow-traveler, and Ralph could not but own that the way was made shorter by his company.

Despite the genial and generous feelings pervading his nature—like gold damasking iron—the youth was imbued with that hard, stubborn obstinacy which the Northmen express by the one word "dour"; he was of the stuff of which stanch friends and stanch haters are made, and changed neither his likes nor dislikes lightly. On the fourth day of their society, the vague distrust and aversion which he had felt at his first meeting with the Italian, were little if anything abated. It was not that he showed himself in anywise churlish or sullen; he smiled at the other's jests, listened to his stories with unfeigned interest, and praised his songs, whether he understood them or no. Once the other spoke of the brawl which had so nearly ended fatally, still marveling on his own discomfiture.

"I served long ago," Malatesta said, "with one Michael Tregarva, who averred himself to have kept the ring for a year and a day in the barbarous country wherein he was bred—Corn-ou-alle, I think he called it. He was but a clumsy lubbard, and a lying braggart to boot. With him I practised many an idle hour, till I had learned, or thought I had learned, each foin and foil that he could teach; but that sleight of foot and hip which laid me low so deftly, is utterly strange to me. I would be much beholden to your courtesy an' ye would bestow on me a lesson at fitting season."

"'Tis a simple trick enough," Ralph answered, "though the foil is something harder to learn; and I will do mine endeavors cheerfully to make ye perfect in both."

So, in fair outward show of amity, if with no great heart-kindness, they rode in together to Sandwich town.

CHAPTER XI.

BEFORE CALAIS.

THERE was in Sandwich no lack of means of transport; for never, surely, before or since, hath the high water-way across the Straits been furrowed by so frequent keels. Almost daily, fresh supplies or munitions were needed for the mighty host with which the English King held Calais in leaguer; also many merchants and chapmen flocked thither, sure of a quick and profitable sale of their wares; for French gold was plenty in the *Ville de Bois*, specially since the return of Derby's armament laden with the plunder of Gascony and Poitou. That same night Hawkwood parleyed with the master of a carrack then ready for sea; before dawn, he and his followers were bestowed aboard, and they sailed out of Sandwich with the morning tide.

Slowly the huge, clumsy craft forged ahead, pitching and wallowing from sheer top-heaviness—though the swell was moderate, and the breeze fair—to the dire discomfort of Lanyon and others making their first essay of seafaring. Ralph Brakespeare fared better, for long temperance and hard exercise made him proof against qualms; yet his brows throbbed, and his eyes swam painfully; so he was right glad when, toward close of day, Cape Grisnez loomed nearer and nearer; and more glad still when they cast anchor, in as shoal water as they dared, on the outskirts of the throng of vessels—some transports, some ships of war—that clustered round and blockaded the harbor. Before it was quite dark, the carrack's boats had landed the passengers, their arms and caparisons; and the horses, forced one by one through a vast square port-hole in the after-hold—half swimming, half wading—had come safely to shore.

In the after-years, full at they were of varied adventure, Ralph never forgot the first night he spent on foreign soil. He remembered how they dried and cleansed their chargers, in presence of Hawkwood, there on the sea-sand, till the beasts were fit to bear caparison; and then, mounting, rode in the same order as they marched before, over the bridges of the double ditch forming the outwork of the English entrenchments; and passed through more than one long street of broom or straw-thatched huts, till they came into the broad market-place, where the knight bade his followers halt till he had spoken with the camp-marshal, who could allot them quarters. He remembered how, sitting there in saddle, he had listened to the babble of many and divers tongues till his ears grew dizzy; and how the lonely feeling of isolation overcame him more and more as the darkness closed in; and how, glancing round at his companions to mark how they bore themselves, he envied Lanyon the stolid indifference into which the archer's face had settled, so soon as the throes of seasickness left him in peace; and how he envied yet more Gian Malatesta his experience and evident familiarity with the scene, as, ever and anon, the Italian exchanged a nod or careless word of greeting with some passer-by. He remembered how close, and dark, and stifling their huts seemed to his eyes, used so long to chambers lofty and groined; and how through the night he tossed restlessly on his pallet, listening to the tramp of the sentinel, till, near daybreak, he fell into a broken sleep, troubled—for the first time since he set forth thence—with feverish dreams of his old home.

But the feeling of novelty soon wore off; and he fell into the groove of daily duty with the quick aptitude of a born soldier; before a week had passed, the grayest veteran there was not more thoroughly at home than Ralph. Neither was his life weary nor monotonous; by Hawkwood's order, he was ever seeking to improve himself in the martial exercises in which he already rarely excelled; he took his turn regularly with the outposts, who rode forth to watch and check the foragers of Boulogne, St. Omer, and Guisnes; but week after week passed, without Brakespeare's crossing lance in earnest. Sport and duty brought him into contact with new comrades, more to his taste than Gian Malatesta: and, though he was not of those who make friends fast, he was popular rather than otherwise; and where he was liked he was trusted. Looking at the quiet, resolute face, and eyes—frank, though somewhat stern, men felt that it would be easy to find a blither boon companion, but hard to light on a better backer in mortal quarrel.

Sir John Hawkwood seemed much of this opinion. Albeit, reserved and taciturn, he showed toward the youth marked favor in his grave fashion; and not seldom vouchsafed word or gesture of approval to

Lanyon, who toiled at his training in arms with a dogged perseverance that well replaced adroitness.

Ralph's idle hours, too, were fully amused. Pleasant it was, after Lent was done, to watch the pomp and pageantry, while the great lords of Flanders, Hainault, Brabant, and Germany streamed in with their long trains to render homage to the prosperous king and the victress of Neville's Cross; and, last of all, came Robert of Namur, with the tan of Syrian sun on his fair young cheek, to proffer himself as their true and loyal liegeman. Pleasanter yet—to watch the sheen of velvet, the glimmer of jewels, and the glitter of brocade, as the dames or demoiselles, who waited on or followed Philippa, swept, with flutter of veil, sleeve, and *contoise*, through the Ville de Bois on their palfreys, or tripped daintily forth from the thatched pavilions, where dwelt the knights and barons of their kin.

Very often, in the midst of this gayety, the youth fell a-wondering as to how it fared with those within the gray ramparts that—seamed and scarred with dint of battering-engine—still frowned defiantly, like some old warrior, who having gotten a mortal wound, braces himself for yet another onset.

In very truth, the condition of the Calaisois was such as might have stirred pity in a harder heart than Ralph Brakespeare's; slowly and surely, hour by hour, they were forced to watch the lines of blockade tightened around them; till their case might be likened to his who, mured in the Italian torture-chamber, saw inch by inch the walls and ceiling slide together, that one day should crush him out of shape of humanity.

After that desperate night-sally in which Arnold d'Andregha and his fellows carried havoc and fear up to the very portals of the royal pavilion, they had no distraction of their long agony in the excitement of hand-to-hand combat. At regular intervals, less and less frequent, were heard creak of trebuchet, the whistle of espringal, the rattle of pateraros, the roar of bombards; but they guessed that this was ordained rather for display or practise of the English artillery than with any serious intent of making breach; for their foe, with a malign patience, forbore all assault—not choosing to waste the services of so potent an ally as famine. No lighter pangs had the garrison now to endure; seventeen hundred had long ago departed whom Edward, with somewhat ostentatious charity, dismissed with food and alms; since then, another detachment had been thrust forth; but the mercy of the besieger was spent, and five hundred corpses of women, weaklings, and dotards—slaughtered outright by cold and hunger —made hideous and noisome the space betwixt camp and town. And still too many mouths remained to feed.

And after Warwick scattered with sore loss and shame the Genoese flotilla, there was no hope of open succor by sea. Besides the galleys that patroled the Straits, and Northampton's war-ships anchored near shore, the men-at-arms and archers in the great wooden castle set up over the harbor-mouth kept such jealous watch and ward, that scarcely under cover of the darkest night could a light skiff slip out or in—even were it manned by Marant and Mestriel, the skilful mariners whose deeds of *hardiesse* have found place, not unworthily, among the feats of arms of that age. To make their own straits more keenly felt, in their ears were ever sounds of revelry from without, and signs of unstinted plenty in their eyes; the provision alone, that they saw wasted in the market-place of the Ville de Bois, would have been as a royal banquet to them. Each morning, faces more gaunt, and wan, and wild, looked toward the rising sun in search of the rescue which never came. Yet still faith and loyalty held their own bravely. If men gnashed their teeth and groaned within their own dwellings, none murmured in public; and whoso should have spoken of lowering the Ancient, that still floated vauntingly as ever on the topmost tower, would have died a traitor's death.

No marvel if the great heart of John de Vienne sickened within him, at sight of sufferings that he could not lighten, and of despair he could not cheer; till, after taking counsel of his peers, he tried one last appeal to their master. He himself indited that letter —so piteous in its rude simplicity—of which a copy is still preserved:

Sachez, tresdoute Seignieur, que nous Gentz in Caleys ont mangez Chevals, Chiens & Ratz & n'est remit rien pour leuc vivre sinon chescun mange aultre. Par quey treshoneurable Seigneur, si nous ne eymes hastife Succoure, la ville est perdue; & nous sommes toutz accordes, si nous ne eymes eyde, de ysser & mourir sur nous ennemies au Honneur, plus tost que dedens mourir pur defaulte. Et Dieu vous deigne de rendre al nous & nos Heirez nostre Travaile.

Close under the town ramparts, and protected by their artillery, there lay a swift Genoese galley; the master of which—half soldier, half trader, and, on occasion, whole pirate—was one of those who—appraising life and liberty at a certain sum of gold—are ever ready, for sufficing recompense, to risk either. This man the governor called into his presence, and with a rich bribe persuaded him to carry out the letter; promising farther, on his knightly honor, that the guerdon should be trebled when it reached King Philip's hand. Soon after midnight, on a strong ebb tide, with the wind blowing freshly from shore, the Genoese put out; having as his pilot one of those Abbeville mariners whose luck in such ventures had hitherto been miraculous. Past the castle at the harbor's mouth, unchallenged by the sentinels, whose eyes were blinded with rain and spray, the galley glided like a ghost; but the meshes of the toils beyond were drawn too closely to let through even such a light-winged skimmer of the seas; before long she was encompassed beyond hope of escape. The Genoese was no hare-brained gallant to fight to the death against desperate odds; inured to changes of fortune, he was cool and honest enough to act at once as he thought best, both for himself and his employer; weighting the precious letter with an ax-head, he cast it overboard, just before he lowered his sail, and cried out to be surrendered.

The shoal water stretches far out on that coast; and the letter sank not so deep but that some keen eyes in a patrol-boat, when the sun was risen and the tide was low, caught the glitter of steel and parchment on the dark-brown sea-weed. So John de Vienne's missive was opened by King Edward's hands ere noon. He read it heedfully; and then, with that grim irony of which traces are found in so many of that monarch's words, letters, and actions, forwarded it straightway to its address; adding thereto a brief taunting message of his own. He might have done this in wariness or subtlety; and, confiding in the strength of his own position, might have wished to provoke his enemy to give him battle at disadvantage. If this were so, Edward reckoned not ill. Philip of Valois—lacking both skill in warfare and firmness of purpose—was neither so craven nor cold of heart, as to be patient under insult of a foe or death-peril of a friend.

The tenor of the intercepted letter had spread, as such things will do, through the English camp; and none marveled when, soon after, there came certain rumors that the Oriflamme of France was cast to the winds once more, and that Philip had bidden all who owed him vassalage to rally round it at Amiens, by Whitsuntide; having sworn a deep oath that, by the grace of God and Saint Denis, he yet would break Calais leaguer.

CHAPTER XII.

HOW RALPH BRAKESPEARE RAN A COURSE WITH A FRENCH KNIGHT, AND SLEW HIM.

For the nonce, this chronicle has less concern with the fortunes of Kings and Kaisers, than with a certain personal adventure which befell Ralph Brakespeare. It happened in this wise.

From the English camp, as has been aforesaid, were made constant excursions; either for the purpose of foraging, or to check the scattered lances who rode forth from such fortresses of Artois and Picardy as still held out, or from the armament with which John of Normandy sought to harass the besiegers. On this service Hawkwood was often employed; for the Earl of Lancaster, who had special charge of the scurriers, held the knight in high esteem, both for tact and courage, and loved to see him in command of a clump of spears.

On a certain May day, Hawkwood pricked forth, at the head of some score of men-at-arms, and half the number of demi-lances; turning past Courgaine to the north, whence incursions had been most frequent of late. Noon was long past, and they had seen no trace of enemy nor of plunder worth the harrying; for the country had been so drained and desolated that it could scarce provide victual for its own scanty inhabitants. It was wearisome travel for barded chargers through white drifting sand, or through black marshy loam; so Hawkwood, ever loth to distress men or cattle needlessly, halted by a rivulet in a little hollow, overgrown with alders; first detaching in diverse directions several pickets—as they would now be termed—each consisting of a man-at-arms and a hobelar, to guard against the possibility of surprise, or of an enemy passing unchallenged. For this duty Brakespeare was selected, having Lanyon as his companion.

As Ralph was about to depart, the knight beckoned him aside, and thus bespoke him:

"Canst guess why I have bestowed on thee this charge, rather than on an elder and better soldier? It is because I like thee so well, that I would be loth thou shouldst lose occasion of advancement, though at thy proper peril. Also I wot thou hast chafed inwardly of late, at having thus far proved thy manhood by no feat of arms. Nevertheless, it behooves thee to consider that thou art no knight-errant, seeking adventure wheresoever it may be found; but a sworn liegeman—even as I am—of our lord the King, to whom, rather than to thyself, thy life, and horse, and armor belong, so that thou art bound to endanger or endamage none of these save on sufficient cause. Wherefore, if there be occasion, bear thyself rather warily than rashly this day. Ride not far beyond the sound of our trumpet; covering yourselves as much as may be, and halting in some convenient spot, whence ye may see without being seen. Ye will, doubtless, give timely notice if the foe show himself in force—retiring yourselves speedily, yet not disorderly. If, as seems not likely, ye come suddenly on stray foragers not exceeding three, I bid ye not turn bridle: but deal with them as ye list, and God and Saint George give you good-speed! Go now and give heed to what I say; for I warn not twice, neither do I trust, if warning be slighted, or trust bewrayed."

The manner and tone of the speech were somewhat austere; but the youth felt it was kindly meant; so he promised obedience cheerfully, and rode off with a gladder heart under his breastplate than had throbbed there for many a day.

Some half league or so from the spot where Hawkwood had halted, the sand-hills trended inward from the coast, breaking up the ground into low irregular hillocks, through which wound a single track, beaten down and worn by broad-wheeled wains, in many places sunken feet below the surface of the soil. Here Ralph judged it best to post himself; for beyond this the country grew flat and open again, and an armed man would have far to ride before he found other chance of cover. So he dismounted, and leaving Lanyon with the horses in the hollow way—where they were perfectly concealed—couched down himself under the crest of a sand hillock, whence he had far view around—bareheaded, lest the eye of some wandering scout should catch the glitter of his bascinet. There he lay hour after hour, till weary disappointment replaced the hopeful excitement with which he had set forth: and glancing toward the west, where the clouds were reddening already, he began to listen for the note of recall which he knew Hawkwood's trumpets would sound before sundown. Suddenly, as he gazed mechanically back in the direction where he had watched, his heart stood still for an instant, then leaped up with a fierce joy.

Above a stunted thicket of alders and willows that fringed the track some two furlongs off, came the sparkle of spear-heads, and a second later a broader glimmer of steel, as a knight, fully caparisoned, with pennon on his lance, appeared, followed by another horseman, whom, even at that distance, Ralph's keen eye made out to be more lightly harnessed. With a mighty effort the youth mastered his impatience, and lay quite still till he was certain that the pair were not forerunners of a more numerous enemy; a long sigh of relief broke from his lips as he withdrew his head cautiously, only rising to his feet when he was well under cover of the sand-hill. Lanyon, roused from a half doze by the rattle of harness, knew by the other's look that something was afoot, before he crouched down to catch the hurried whisper—

"Now, our Blessed Lady be praised! They come straight hitherward; and we have leave to deal with them as we list, sith they are but two against two."

The yeoman's gray eyes flashed eagerly, though he uttered never a word; and a faint reflection on his broad, bluff features of the battle-light gleaming on the Norman's face showed that his slower Saxon blood was fairly stirred.

Some few yards from the spot where they stood, the roadway turned a sharp corner, and then ran on quite straight and level for near a hundred yards, between banks, on either side, about stirrup-high; here, too, the ground was tolerably sound, though sandy. At this angle Ralph took post, with vizor down, and his lance at the carry; having Lanyon some yards to his rear Ere they had waited three minutes, there came through the still evening air a smothered clash of steel, and the low clear notes of a mellow voice, chanting a *virelay*, in the musical *langue d' Oc;* and the foremost rider came into view round the opposite angle of the road to that where Brakespeare sat. He reined up abruptly when he saw his path barred in front. If surprised, he was in no wise disconcerted by the presence of an enemy; but trolled out the last line of the verse he was singing to the full as gayly as he had begun it.

The knight's vizor was up, and Ralph was struck by the beauty of his face, enhanced by the soft, rich coloring peculiar to the south of France. The perfect workmanship of his armor made it, perhaps, seem lighter than it really was: yet, with its fanciful graving and ornament, it appeared more fitted for tourney or pageant than the rough usage of a *mêlée*. Round his neck was slung a triangular shield, the bearings of which were somewhat defaced, like the blazonry of his surcoat. The brown Limousin, which he bestrode, though lacking not power in its fine sinewy limbs, looked somewhat light and small compared to Ralph's great roan destrere. His helmet was not a plain bascinet or camail, but rather molded in tilting shape, bearing both crest and plume; and under the crest was twined securely a long hawking-glove, curiously wrought with silk and seed pearls, that must have been worn only by a delicate woman's hand.

Ralph brought his lance down quickly from the carry to the rest; but the French knight kept his own pennoncelle pointed upward, and waved his hand, in token that he wished to parley. There was an easy grace in the gesture that made the youth half ashamed of his own eagerness, as he recovered his weapon, and, raising his own vizor, advanced to meet the other, who had already ridden some paces nearer.

"*Beau sire*," the stranger began, in good Norman-French, when he was fairly within earshot, "before we come to mortal arbitrament, may I crave of your conrtesy to anwer me two brief questions? First, I would know how far is this spot from the English camp, from which doubtless you have lately sallied forth?"

"Hard upon three leagues, as I should guess," Brakespeare answered, with a look of some surprise.

"Not near enough by half," the Frenchman muttered, biting his handsome lip. "Unless worse chance befall him, Raoul hath gotten within sight of the trenches ere now. So I am constrained to ask farther, do ye two hold this pass alone, or are there other of your lances near in force?"

Brakespeare hesitated, doubting whether he were right thus to parley with an enemy; but something in the French knight's manner forbade suspicion of treachery. So he answered after awhile—

"It is even so. There are none of our folk that I wot of nearer than half a league, where Sir John Hawkwood, whom I follow, halts with the residue of his lances."

The other smiled, as though well pleased.

"It is as I thought, then. And now, *beau sire*, lest my questions appear to you unseemly, I have you to wit that yester-even I, Loys de Chastelnaye, did devise, with Raoul de Mericourt, my brother-in-arms, concerning certain matters which, in fair Provence, are judged only in the court of love; and, in all amity, there was great debate betwixt us; so that at the last we agreed to ride forth this day—each with a single esquire—and, unless put back by a force of four at the least, to prove which of us could carry his lady's gage closest to Calais gates. '*Las*, my *destrier* cast a shoe, and with sore trouble, after hours' seeking, did we light on a smith; for you brave English have frightened Jean Picard, till he hath become shy as a field-rat. Wherefore if, as I guess from your bearing, ye purpose not to yield me passage peaceably, it is needful that I pass on in your despite. This place, too, is marvelously well fitted for running a course. But, good youth, under thy favor, I had rather than a hundred crowns that thy spurs, if not golden, had been silver at the least; for perchance thou has had scant tourney practise, and so can little honor accrue to me from the encounter. If thus it be with thee, avow it frankly. Lo, I will forego the lance, and engage with mace and sword."

Brakespeare's temper was rising fast under the Frenchman's self-confidence and easy condescension; but he curbed it, and answered very calmly—

"This is no tilt-yard, where none can joust unless of lineage approved by the heralds; and in these times none can say how soon he shall change the metal of his spurs. *Beau sire*, your nobility must e'en abase itself to contend with one of my degree; for an' ye were willing to turn bridle, I, for my part, am not willing to let you go in peace. It may be I have better skill with my weapon than ye deem. So, set on and spare not, looking for the like measure from me."

The Frenchman's face never lost its gay good humor, as he bowed his head courteously.

"I am fitly reproved," he said, "for I spake over-presumptuously. *De pardieu*, all true men are equal under shield. Let us take ground speedily; for the light is waning fast, and one of us will have a moonlight ride. Call on your patron saint when ye are ready to do your devoir, and I will answer with the name of my fair lady. *Marguerite, ma Marguerite!*"

Long afterward, Ralph Brakespeare remembered how lovingly the speaker's lips lingered over that last word, as though—all familiar as it must have been—they were loth to let it pass. Within a few moments each had regained his own station. The Frenchman, seeing that his adversary bore no shield, drew off his own, and handed it to his esquire, saying something the while with a light laugh; Ralph, too, as he clasped his vizor and settled himself firmer in the saddle, driving his feet well home in the *sautoirs*, found time to say some hurried words over his shoulder to his follower, who was in a state of unwonted excitement.

"Honest Will, I trust well to lower yonder gay plume; for I have vantage in weight if not in skill; but, if it be otherwise, since I purpose not to take mercy, thy tarrying here will naught avail. So I charge thee, in such case, to hie thee back to Sir John Hawkwood at speed; and tell him that I thanked him heartily for this chance of approving myself, though it pleased God that I should fail."

Then Ralph Brakespeare laid lance in rest; and

AT THE FIRST SHOCK BOTH HORSES SUNK ON THEIR HAUNCHES, BUT ONE ONLY
RECOVERED HIMSELF.

getting his horse well in hand, cried lustily, " St. George Guienne!" and drove the sharp rowels in; clear and mellow through the still air came the answering war-cry, " *Marguerite, ma Marguerite!* " The dust flew far and wide under the savage plunge of the roan distrere and bound of the swifter Limousin; and just about midway the two hurtled together.

At the first shock both horses sunk on their haunches, but one only recovered himself. The Limousin, fairly overborne, rolled over sideways and backward, till he lay helpless athwart the roadway, crushing his rider against the bank. Nor was this all; the Frenchman's lance struck full and fair on Ralph's breast, and was shivered to the vamplate; but the Southwark armorer had put better metal into his spear-head; it pierced sheer through the gay corselet and the habergeon beneath, just above the gorget, and the tough English ash only broke off at last close to the embedded steel. Before the sand-cloud had cleared away, Ralph had sprung from saddle, and holding his *misericorde* to the throat of his fallen foe, bade him " Yield, rescue or no rescue! "

No answer came, save a low moan of intense, half-conscious agony, as dark red drops oozed not only from the breast-wound but through the bars of the vizor. A strange chill horror overcame Brakespeare as he felt himself for the first time in presence of death—death, too, dealt by his own hand. Enmity of race, the fierce delight of battle, the flush of a maiden triumph, were all swallowed up in a deep pity nearly akin to remorse. He beckoned, first to Will Lanyon, then to the French squire, to come to aid the fallen knight; while he himself held down the Limousin's head, lest in struggling to rise he should do his lord farther hurt. Slowly and painfully the three succeeded in disentangling the dying man—for that he was dying none doubted; and propping him against the road-bank, they loosened helmet and gorget. Ralph would have given much to have undone his work, as he gazed on the countenance whose marvelous beauty he had marred. The features were already pinched and drawn; the rich color of the cheeks had faded to dull ashen gray; and through the rigid lips a thin dark stream was welling. The Gascon squire showed his grief after his impassioned southern fashion; wringing his hands, and speaking fast in a dialect that Ralph could scarcely comprehend. Even on Lanyon's rugged face were manifest signs of compassion, as he stood holding the bridles of the loose horses; for by this time the Limousin had scrambled up, seemingly none the worse for his fall.

"Bring water," Ralph said to the French squire; and, kneeling down, he rested the knight's head on his own shoulder. The pool was not three roods off; but, before the water came, Loys de Chastelnaye had begun to revive. The flow of blood from his mouth abated; and, as he looked up and saw who supported him, his lips relaxed into a faint semblance of their old pleasant smile; when his face had been laved, and he had drunken twice or thrice, he spoke—almost in a whisper, but quite calmly and clearly—

"*Pardie*, I was the veriest vantard but now, and I am rightly served: nevertheless, I take no shame to myself to have gone down before so strong a lance. Scant time have I for parley; *beau sire*, this my esquire, no less than I, are at your mercy; but Aymery, my good cousin and heir, will, I know, ransom him speedily. Gilles, I charge thee, so soon as thou art free, make all speed to Hacquemont; and deliver into the white hands of the demoiselle Marguerite this her gage. Say to her that I have done it no dishonor; but have borne it ever so forward as I might, turning bridle before no single foe, till thus in loyal combat was I slain: furthermore, by my hopes of mercy do I aver, that since she kissed these lips of mine they have been virgin of woman. So do I earnestly entreat of her pity, to grant unto no living man favor—be it ever so small—for the space of one year and one day; after that she shall be assoilzied of her troth-plight. Let her grace with her dear love some knight, worthier and more fortunate than this her poor servitor; and may the saints send to both long life and *liesse*."

"Nay, not so," Ralph broke in, so soon as the weak voice ceased. "Of ransom will I have none; and this your squire is free to set forth when he will to carry his message of dolor. I wis not what maketh me so heavy of heart; but, gentle sir, I had liever have miscarried in this my first proof of arms, than have won honor at the cost of your fair life."

A brief gleam of pleasure shot across the other's face, darkening already with the death-shadow.

"Ay, so?" he murmured. "Long since, in truth, from your manner of speech might I have guessed that I dealt with no common *routier*. To God and to the holy saints do I give thanks, that by no churl's hand was Loys de Chastelnaye sped. For this your kindness may—"

The benison, if such was meant, was choked in mid utterance by a fresh gush of blood, coming now in sharp, quick jets; and when it abated, the pulse had nearly ceased to beat. Once only in that last quiet minute of life—for death-struggle there was none—the white lips moved; and Brakespeare, bending down his ear, caught what may have been an appeal to the Virgin-mother's mercy; but Ralph always believed it was a woman's name.

For some brief space after all was over, the youth never stirred; suddenly he started and shifted very gently the corpse from his shoulder to the ground beside him, for he heard Hawkwood's trumpet sounding the recall. All his soldierly instinct came back at once, and he was a man-at arms again, ready and willing for any duty: he laid his hand almost roughly on the shoulder of the Gascon squire, who seemed still well-nigh distraught with grief.

"Waste not time in wailing here," he said, "thou knowest what thou hast to do; set about it speedily. First,—it behooves thee to see thy lord's body carefully bestowed, where it may lack no due rite or funeral observance; there is a *moustier* in yon wood to the right; I heard its bells chime but now. That rich armor will ensure the monks their guerdon, if they grudge free masses to such a knight's soul. His *destrier* wends with me; but thou mayst keep thine own, which I perceive tarries for thee there. For the rest—I have set thee free, that thou mayst do thy lord's bidding to the uttermost: if thou fail therein, or linger by the way, the shame of broken trust is thine."

So—with one more look at the face which waxed

beautiful again as it settled into the death-calm—Ralph picked up his headless lance from where it lay; and, after glancing heedfully over both the chargers so as to be sure that neither had suffered from the encounter, mounted and rode slowly back by the way that he had come; followed by Lanyon, leading the Limousin by the bridle. It was characteristic of the yeoman that, while they were alone together, he troubled his leader with no word of gratulation or triumph: whether this silence is to be set down to rough natural tact, or to the trouble and confusion of his simple mind, would be very hard to determine.

CHAPTER XIII.

HOW RALPH BRAKESPEARE DONNED SILVER SPURS.

The other scouts had all rejoined the main body before Brakespeare and his follower appeared; and none brought tidings, or had seen traces of an enemy; so there was wonder, and perchance a little envy, among some of Hawkwood's followers when they saw how Fortune had favored the youngest of their band. On their leader's usually reserved face there was frank pleasure, as he rode out some paces to meet Brakespeare, and bent his own head in acknowledgment of the other's salute.

"Where leftest thou thy lance-head, my son?" he said. "For well I wot it was not idly wasted. And how comest thou by yon gallant war-horse? Those clean limbs and high crest never were nurtured on thin Normandy pastures; but, I dare swear, near the banks of Garonne."

"Scarce some half hour ago," Ralph answered, "a French knight came to where I was posted, with his squire, and would have passed on in my despite, not —as I judge from our brief parley—with purpose of plunder or of espial, but rather in discharge of some chivalrous vow. I gainsaid him, as in duty bound; and we ran a fair course, wherein it was my evil hap to wound unto death as proper a *gentilhomme* as mine eyes have ever looked on. He called himself Loys de Chastelnaye."

A half-incredulous murmur spread among the men-at-arms who sat within earshot, and Hawkwood himself raised his eyebrows slightly, as he made answer—

"Now lift thy vizor, good youth, that I may read in thy face if this be jest or vaunt. Dost thou come back to tell me, thus sadly, that thou, a raw youth, hast, in thy first tilt with grinded spears, slain outright the Vicompte de Chastelnaye, whose prowess all we who fought in Gascony or Guienne have seen? By the Rood! if thou sayest sooth, thy valiance is less wonderful than thine unconcern."

Ralph did as he was bidden, and all could see that the heaviness on his countenance was not feigned.

"I speak as I was told," he answered simply, "and men seldom fable in the death-throe. Moreover, on the housing of his destrere there is blazonry to witness if I lie."

At the word Lanyon wheeled the charger that he led, so as to bring full into view the escutcheon on the *cointise*. The three gold chevrons on a sable field, not a few there present had seen before—had seen them borne on a broad banderol, in the forefront of a charge, when England was sore put to it to hold her own. There arose another murmur, this time of honest applause.

"I did wrong to suspect thee," Hawkwood said— "though it seems passing strange; at another time I will hear how it all befell. Loys de Chastelnaye bore himself ever as a true knight; and died not cravenly, I dare avow—God rest his soul! The esquire seeing his lord's misadventure, doubtless made haste to fiee?"

"Nay," Ralph answered, "he was no recreant; but abode to the last, giving such aid as he might, having surrendered himself prisoner at our mercy. Nevertheless, that he might care for the bestowal of his lord's body, and bear certain messages of import to the demoiselle whom that knight served loyally, I judged it best to let him go free. Meseems I did not wisely."

In truth, the change in Hawkwood's countenance showed that he was ill-pleased by what he now heard. He was, as has been aforesaid, no chivalrous hero of romance, but a patient, hard-working soldier, with talents and energy enough to compensate for his poverty and lowly birth, not apt to be overcovetous or mean in his dealings, yet not ashamed to avow that he fought for livelihood no less than honor. However, the knight recovered himself quickly, and cleared his brow as he answered—

"I cannot chide thee to-day, my son. Howbeit, hereafter forget not that, by all laws of warfare, the harness and arms, no less than the person of the vanquished, are retained for the profit of the conqueror; and that none under knight's degree may relinquish such advantage, or deal with such at his pleasure, save by special leave of his superior. The ransom of De Chastelnaye's body-esquire should not have been cast down like a minstrel's largess; and messages to dame or demoiselle should be borne by their own minion pages, not by *gens d'armes*. Thou wilt not so err again; and thou wilt be wiser, too, ere long, than to call such chance as hath befallen thee—'evil hap.' None the less will I care that thou art rewarded after thy deserts; needy though I be, I may still dare to maintain a single esquire; as such shalt thou serve henceforth, by the king's leave, unless thou preferrest to enter some more notable household. Then I will speak in thine behalf to my good Lord of Lancaster, who has shown me some favor of late. Make not thy choice in haste, but soberly, and without fear or scruple: churl were I, to begrudge parting with thee for thine own manifest advancement. Now, let us set forward; I love not night marches for naught, and these roads are ill traveling in the dark."

The youth bent almost to his saddle-bow as he muttered some words of thanks; and fell into his place in the column, by the side of Gian Malatesta, as it moved off. He was so busy then, and for some while afterward, with his own reflections, that he noticed not the malignant fire gleaming in the Italian's eyes.

Every wayfarer through this world must needs encounter certain points in his journey where the main track divides. For awhile the two paths may run so near to each other that they may seem still almost one; but they will diverge more and more till, ere they end, their issues lie as widely apart as those of good and evil, light and darkness, life and death. So was it now with Ralph Brakespeare. Had he availed himself of Hawkwood's really unselfish kindness, and attached his fortunes to those of some powerful noble, there is little doubt but that the change would have been both to his profit and honor. Men of martial desert rose high and quickly in those stirring times; and perchance Brakespeare's name might have been recorded with those of Chandos and many others, who forced open the gates of wealth and renown with the points of their good swords. But the stubborn hardihood, ingrained in his nature, stifled the suggestions of prudence and ambition; when he cut himself adrift from family and friends, and cast his very name behind him, he severed himself, in intent, no less decisively from the class in which he was born and bred than if, as a novice, he had taken upon him the vows of humility and poverty. With a scrupulousness, surely somewhat fantastic, he was not ashamed of his *nom-de-guerre* while he followed John Hawkwood, the lowly-born, self-made adventurer; but he cared not to wear it in the train of one who might possibly claim kinship, however distant, with the houses of Dynevor or Warenne, and among esquires of gentle blood who might once have been reckoned his peers. Moreover, he had conceived a certain kindness and respect for his commander; and having once embarked his hopes in that modest craft, he was minded to see the voyage out, through fair weather or foul, rather than shift to the deck of any one of the statelier caravels sailing in their company. So, late in the evening, Brakespeare, after rendering duteous acknowledgments of the choice proffered to him, declared himself willing to serve on as Hawkwood's esquire, rather than to enter the household of the Earl of Lancaster himself.

Sir John was more pleased than he cared to show; for, sooth to say, since his offer was made he had more than once reproached himself for his own generosity; viewing it in the light of an extravagance he could by no means afford. Yet perhaps there was nothing feigned in the emotion, apparent both in his voice and manner, as he laid both his hands on Ralph's shoulders; saying, simply and earnestly—

"My fair son, I trust well that ye may never have cause to rue those gentle words of thine. It may be one day poor John Hawkwood may have somewhat better than thanks wherewith to repay such as follow him loyally. Keep thou with me; and do thy devoir, even as thou hast done this day: then—if my will shall be equaled by my power, and I forget thee—call recreant and mansworn."

So, with a few more words, it was settled; and that night the youth shifted his quarters; thenceforth it it was his duty to abide under the same roof as the knight whom he served as esquire. Perchance it was for his own weal or another's that he did thus change; for, in the breast of one who lay in the other tent, festered such jealousy and malice, that there might have been ill work ere morning.

"*Bestie!*" the Italian muttered through his grinded teeth. "See how these English swine cleave together. May the black pest rot them, body and bone! here is a springald dropped from none knoweth whence—a foundling or a bastard, belike—who, for one lucky lance-thrust in his first encounter, hath gotten advancement such as in years of service, wherein I have spared my own life no more than other men's, hath never befallen me—me, in whose veins run the right *sangue azurra*."

He broke off for an instant; laughing his low, peculiar laugh, so full of insolent devilry.

"True it is, that my own house would have hunted me to the death, for having made mine uncle taste my dagger: but of this the fools hereabout know naught. *Per Dio!* I would this same hilt came not ever so cursedly ready"—his lithe, white fingers were caressing it longingly. "Had he lain here to-night, with his broad breast open under the moonshine, I doubt if I could have foreborne it: ay—though I had to flee again before the avengers of blood. I owed him one shrewd turn before; and to-day the debt is doubled. If I pay not all the score one day in full, then were I no true Malatesta, and—"

It were better not to render, even faintly, the volley of bitter blasphemy that rounded off the speech. But with no better orison the Italian lay down to rest; and, after awhile, slept soundly as ever did monk betwixt matins and prime. To him, as to better men, the night brought counsel; and on the morrow he was able to congratulate his late comrade, suavely and monotonously; mingling with the warmth of his manner the slightest shade of respect, too delicately conveyed for suspicion of irony.

And so, while spring waxed into summer, matters went on smoothly enough, no special incident breaking the routine of siege warfare.

CHAPTER XIV.

HOW CALAIS WAS WON.

ON the eighteenth day of July, the Earl of Derby set forth with a sufficient force of men-at-arms and footmen, intending to make descent on a great cattle fair, then appointed to be held in the neighborhood of Amiens. But on the third day of march, when he had advanced some ten leagues into the enemy's realm, a scout spurred in with the news that a mighty French host was already moving forward from Amiens, where it had been gathering since Whitsuntide. So the Earl—being a commander no less politic than valiant—judged it best to fall back on the English entrenchments, driving before him five thousand sheep and two thousand beeves. True, the old *soudards* who had rioted in the plunder of Poitou, scorning to cumber themselves with aught less precious than gold, and gimmals, and plumes of knightly crests, thought scorn of such humble booty; but it was very welcome in the Ville de Bois, where supplies had grown less plentiful since the country round had been laid waste.

It was no false rumor that the foragers brought back. The sluggish spirit of Valois was at the last fairly stirred by the piteous wail for help and vengeance that had gone up—not from Calais alone, but from all Artois and Picardy; the unhappy peasants cried aloud they could endure their misery no longer, and would rather submit themselves as liegemen to the English king, than endure at close quarters the extremity of his anger. Neither did the greatness of the armament misbeseem the urgency of the need; few of those who owed vassalage to France were absent on the muster-day. Normandy, Bourbon, Foix, Burgundy, Hainault, Savoie, Armagnac, and Valentinois, headed the long roll of those who saw the Oriflamme unfurled: and there marched forth from Amiens to Arras not less than two hundred thousand of all arms, covering, from vanguard to baggage-train, three full leagues of ground.

From the very first, doubt and difficulty beset Philip's advance. Free passage to the northward was barred by the sturdy Flemings, who had of late waxed so bold in the cause of their English ally as to lay siege to Aire, and carry fire and sword to the gates of St. Omer and Tournay: to the southwest, betwixt him and Calais, lay leagues of marshes, only to be traversed by narrow causeways—ere this, doubtless, well guarded by the foe. Yet still he moved forward—perchance without any definite plan of attack—through Hesdin, Wissant, and Falkenberg, till his tents were pitched on Sandgatte, within view of the beleaguered town. Eyes that never by night or day wearied in their watch from Calais walls, caught the flaunt of banner and the play of moonbeams on steel and canvas; and the hearts of the famished garrison leaped up in a rush of joy; even as the hearts of castaways at sea, who—their last morsel spent, and their last beaker drained—see sails swelling against the sky to windward. All at once, on the topmost tower, sprang up a tongue of flame, and the beal-fire blazed till long after dawn; then flaunted in the sight of the besiegers, not the Ancient of France alone, but the banners of many puissant barons, whom the Calaisians guessed to be coming to the rescue; and all through early noon horns and trumpets rang out alarms and flourishes of defiance.

Yet was it but a very mockery of rescue after all. Hour after hour, day after day, the gorgeous armament lay encamped at Sandgatte, achieving no worthier feat than the destruction of a puny wooden fortalice and a few skirmishes of outposts; for their marshals, after survey of the country, brought back ever the same heavy tidings, that to Calais there was no way, save by the Downs, under the full fire of the English fleet's artillery; or by the marshes, that no barded horse could pass; or by narrow causeways leading to the Bridge of Neuillet, that none might hope to force in the teeth of Derby and his men-at-arms. Vainly, too, did Philip, in the bitterness of his disappointment, strive to tempt forth his wary foe from his entrenchments to trial of force in the open plain; King Edward had proved his courage so often and fairly, that he could now afford to despise knight-errantry. So, to Eustace de Ribeaumont and those other three who brought Philip's challenge, he replied in some such words as these:

"Messires, I perfectly understand the request you have made me from my adversary, who wrongfully keeps possession of my inheritance, which weighs much upon me. You will therefore tell him from me, if you please, that I have been on this spot near a twelve-month. This he was well informed of, and, had he chosen it, might have come here sooner; but he has allowed me to remain so long, that I have expended very large sums of money, and have done so much, that I must be master of Calais in a very short time: I am not, therefore, inclined in the smallest degree to comply with his request, or to gratify his convenience, or to abandon what I have gained, or what I have been so anxious to conquer. If, therefore, neither he nor his army can pass this way, he must seek out some other road."

Not less vain were the good offices of the pious cardinals, mediators for peace sent by Pope Clement from Avignon, to stand, if it were possible, betwixt the living and the dead, and stay the plague of war. King Edward held in his iron glove the fair prize for which he had waited so patiently, and paid so dear; if force of arms could not unlock his grip, he was little likely to relax it in obedience to the voice of the Holy Church; ay, though if, instead of meekly whispering intercession, she had spoken in thunder.

One morning, at dawn, the hill of Sandgatte loomed dim through thick smoke-wreaths: Philip had fired his tents, and now was falling back, to hide his shame and disband his vassals within the walls of Amiens. And soon, of all that great host, no traces were left save the blackened ruins of their encampment; and dismantled wains, surrounded by frequent corpses of stragglers, that lay along the road nearly up to the city gates, showed how mercilessly the English horsemen had harassed the rear of the retreat.

No marvel if the tough hardihood of Calais was fairly

broken at last—no marvel if John de Vienne, still sick of his sore wounds, yielded to the prayer of the weak, piping voices, and wild, hollow eyes that encompassed him. Nay, who shall blame those unhappy citizens if, in agony of spirit, they trampled under foot the banner they had upheld so long, while they hoisted the English ensign in token of surrender.

Then ensued one of those famous passages wherein history treads so closely on the verge of romance that the two seem for awhile as one. But that scene in the conquerors' pavilion—the six noble hostages kneeling humbly, yet not cravenly, in the midst; the shame and anger of Manny and his peers, whose intercession had been denied; the King, with his dark, passionless face set in the same cold smile as it wore at Creçy, when he would send no help to his first-born at his sorest need, but bade him win his spurs alone; the pale, beautiful Queen—paler yet with languor of imminent travail—whose pleading at the last prevailed; all these things have been portrayed so often by pen and pencil that they shall not be touched here.

One word only. There have been raised since grave historic doubts whether all this be not a flattering legend, designed to embellish the fairly-written volume that Jehan de Froissart laid at Philippa's feet. Yet surely those who caviled not at the honor of Leonidas, Decius, and Maccabee, might have been content not to meddle with the wreath that posterity has hung over the ashes of Eustace de St. Pierre and those other five who laid down their lives so royally. Was it worth while to undergo the shame of the halter, the sorrow of the parting, and the long bitterness of anticipated death—only to find matter for some pragmatical schoolman, or critic who would thrive on literary infidelity?

Howsoever these things may have been, in some kind or other Calais paid her heavy accompt. Yet the mercies of her conqueror were very cruel: of all that he found alive within the walls Edward suffered none to abide, save some three or four graybeards, whose knowledge of the place was useful for the establishment of the new colonists; for the rest, such as bore arms, when they were fit to travel, betook themselves to Guisnes; the others were fain to seek for a livelihood and home as best they might, if they chose not to ask alms by the wayside. Very soon the streets, through which lately only a few gaunt, famine-stricken shadows had wandered, begun to be thronged with bluff English faces. For not only from London came at the King's behest twoscore citizens of substance and repute, with their families, 'prentices, and craftsmen; but Kent sent over her wool-staplers, curriers, yeomen —sturdy saplings who cared not a whit for transplanting, so their roots were wet with the golden stream.

On a certain day, it chanced that Sir John Hawkwood went to wait on Sir Walter Manny—under whose immediate command he was then placed—taking with him his esquire. As the two turned a street-corner, they came full on a decent-looking burgess, evidently one of the newcomers. As the knight passed, the man just lifted his hand to his cap; but when he came close to Ralph Brakespeare, who walked some paces in the rear, he doffed it and louted low, muttering some words of salute. Much to the other's discomfiture, the youth passed on, taking no more heed of the courtesy than if he had been deaf or blind. While the honest currier lingered there with a blank look of angry surprise on his face, he was accosted by Gian Malatesta; who, loitering in the sun—as was his wont when not on duty, or over the wine-cup—had witnessed what had passed from the other side of the street, and crossed over unperceived. The Italian was too wary at once to broach the subject of his curiosity; so he began with some commonplace question as to the whereabouts of a cordwainer of some repute, intimating that he judged from the other's appearance that he spoke to one of the trade; when he had been satisfied on these points, or sufficiently so for his purpose, Malatesta, with glib and courteous thanks, turned as though to depart; but suddenly, as if recollecting himself, he said carelessly—

"If I err not, worthy sir, there is some acquaintance betwixt thee and yonder fair youth, albeit he did strangely slight thy greeting."

The bluff burgess shook his head rather sorrowfully; for his short-lived anger was passed.

"I have good reason to know him," he answered. "Was I not nurtured within a mile of the castle of his father—erst time my very good lord? Marry, I was right loth to lose sight of Bever keep, when mine uncle would have me to Sandwich to help him in his trade. Though, I thank the saints, I have thriven since not ill. I mind him, from the time when he scarce could sit astride on a war-saddle, till he grew up into a proper stripling, well-nigh as tall, though not so stalwart as he now is. Then, though he was seldom merry of mood, and brooked no license, he had ever gentle word and kindly look both for vassal and villein; and, if we wended the same road, he thought not scorn of my poor company. I marvel what hath changed him. Right sure I am that he knew me when our eyes met, though 'tis years since we foregathered."

The Italian's black bushy brows were bent as if in thought or displeasure.

"How callest thou the lord his father? And canst expound unto me, wherefore the heir of a noble house taketh service and wage of a simple man-at-arms?"

"Sir Simon Dynevor begat him," the other made answer—"but I said not Messire Ralph was the heir. The knight was duly wedded in his early youth to a daughter of Warenne, whose blood to the full matched his own. But Holy Church disallowed the marriage, for that those two were over-close of kin; and the poor lady died, as I have heard, in her first travail; so the child was cheated of his heritage. What name he chooses now to bear, I know not; but in old times they ycleped him ever Fitzwarenne."

Malatesta's lip curled slightly, though his brow lowered still.

"A bastard, I fear me," he said, smoothly, "in the eyes of the law, though 'tis a hard case and a piteous. Yet I blame Ralph Brakespeare—such is his title now, —in that he demeaned himself so haughtily toward thee but now. True it is that he hath lately been advanced to be esquire to Sir John Hawkwood, under whom I, too, serve as vintenar. 'Tis a way of the world, as doubtless hath not escaped thine experience; new honors make men forget old friends."

"Nay, not so," the other returned sturdily. "Messire Ralph is none of such time-serving coistrels.

Neither is advancement to esquire's estate such credit to his father's son, that he should wax misproud thereafter. He changed not his title, I dare be sworn, for shame or fear: and for his demeanor anon he had reason good. If he speak not next time we foregather, I will not chafe thereat, neither will I accost him; but only, under my breath, wish him God-speed."

The Italian's smile waxed insolent and bitter.

"A most Christian currier," he said; "such as one as hath scarce been seen since St. Paul wrought at thy trade. Heaven keep thee in such holy frame! With which benison I dismiss thee to thy sport or business."

So, leaving his companion more puzzled than he had found him, Malatesta strode away, muttering through his beard as he went—

"No beggar's brat, after all, but nobly born: so nobly that—but for a priest's juggle—he might have carried his head as high as he listed. By the blood of Bacchus! I hate him threefold more than I did yester-even; and that is no light word."

CHAPTER XV.

THE BATTLE ON THE CAUSEWAY.

The bustle and turmoil of arrival and departure was over at last. Queen Philippa—after safe deliverance of a daughter—sailed for England with her consort; in Calais were left only the new settlers, with the strong garrison in which Hawkwood and his followers were numbered; and, while autumn passed into winter, all in the town rested as men love to rest after long and sharp toil, never witting that they were as those who keep watch on a wall well-nigh already mined. For Emeric of Pavia, governor of the castle—whom King Edward trusted as his own right hand—had been tempted by the French, and was in covenant to open the gates, at a fitting time and season, to Geoffrey de Chargny, who held command at St. Omer. Before the treason was complete, tidings thereof were brought to Windsor; and the wary monarch—disdaining to wreak his anger on one head, howsoever guilty—contrived to turn the plot to his own advantage: the shameless Lombard was only too ready to purchase his own safety at the price of a double treason.

The last day of December saw Edward and his son back again at Calais. They sailed into the harbor, not as they had gone out—with flourish of trumpet and flaunt of standard—but under cover of a black winter's night, in a lull betwixt storms. On that very night Emeric of Pavia had covenanted to open the Boulogne gate to De Chargny and his men-at-arms. But first the blood-money was to be paid; and paid it was—no less punctually than the pieces of silver to the most famous of traitors fourteen centuries before. Scarcely had Odoart de Renty and those who bore the gold lightened themselves of their base burden, when they found themselves hopelessly trapped, with no choice but to render themselves to Edward's mercy. Half an hour later the Boulogne gate was cast wide open in the face of De Chargny and his company, and the dark arch vomited forth a torrent of spears. In the fore front of the column floated the guidon of Manny, and behind it came the banners of Suffolk, Stafford, Montacute, Beauchamp, and Berkeley; only the standard of the master of them all was not displayed, for it was the King's will to fight that night unknown.

Now Geoffrey de Chargny was a hardy knight and loyal, though he had come thither on a disloyal mission; and, when the first surprise was past, he and all his company bore themselves right worthily. They felt themselves indeed in desperate case; in their front was the enemy, whose strength must needs overmatch their own; and on either flank the hungry morass waiting for its prey, wounded or dead; and miles of the narrow, darkling causeway must be traversed ere they could hope to fall back on their rear-guard. It may be, too, that De Chargny guessed that the crossbowmen of St. Omer and the knights of Picardy, who held Neuillet Bridge, would, ere long, be sore put to it to hold their ground. Howsoever this may be, when the French had rallied from their first panic, none spoke of flight or surrender; they lighted down from saddle, and drove their destreres away; and then, entrenching themselves behind the fence of their shortened lances, awaited the English onset. They had not long to wait, for Edward—though he neglected no duty of generalship, and at once sent off a detachment to take the foe in rear—cared not to defer his vengeance. Yet, when he saw the attitude of the gallant little company, he, too, judged it best to dismount his followers; and so advanced to the encounter.

Amid all the war-pictures of that stirring time, there are few more striking than this one—few more vividly marked with the stamp of the pure and romantic chivalry that began under Charlemagne and ended under Charles the Emperor.

First under the darkness, then under the gray, chill dawn, the combatants wrestled together, locked hand to hand and foot to foot; neither side, for awhile, giving or gaining ground—like mighty stags countering on a narrow hill-track. There, under Manny's banner, Edward and his son did their devoir as simple knights; but with every sweep of the king's sword rang out his favorite war-cry, "Ha, Saint Edward! Ha, Saint George!" And many stout English hearts waxed stronger, as they knew that their liege—even as themselves—was bearing up the burden of the battle.

In this his first hand-to-hand encounter, Ralph Brakespeare demeaned himself not amiss. Glancing aside sometimes as he fought, Hawkwood found his esquire ever at his shoulder, laying on lustily with a ponderous mace; but suddenly the knight heard a crashing blow close behind him; and, when he turned, Ralph Brakespeare was down. It was well for the youth that he had listened to Hawkwood that night—who, looking for sharper work than usual, had bidden him put on his camail under his bascinet—otherwise, surely he would have been sped. As it was, the dint was so sore that it brake the outer steel, and for a brief space the esquire lay under trampling feet as one dead: his armor shielded him from farther injury. After awhile, the mellay surged forward past the spot where he had fallen; so that, when Ralph struggled up with swimming eyes and dizzy brain, he was able to breathe freely. But his was one of those hardy natures that never know when they are beaten, and take ordinary rough usage as a matter of course, if not of health. So soon as the first faint numbness passed away, Brakespeare shook himself till his harness rattled again, and gripping his mace—which he had never let go—tighter, plunged once more into the press.

The fury of the battle was abating fast; for the French, pressed back by sheer weight of numbers, were forced to give ground, not without sore loss of knights slain outright on the causeway, or thrust over the brink to perish miserably in the morass. Nearer and nearer in their rear rang out the English trumpets; and De Chargny knew that Neuillet Bridge had been forced, so that they were hemmed in on all sides now. To fight longer would have been very madness of self-sacrifice; and this Eustace de Ribeaumont felt, to whom was given the palm of prowess, where so many deserved well. Twice that night—little witting of the prize so nearly in his grasp—he had stricken King Edward to his knee, and now to him delivered his sword; knowing nothing more of his enemy's quality than that he had shown himself worthy to receive it. This was the sign for a general surrender.

So Emeric of Pavia kept his word, after the fashion of Sathanas with his dupes. He had indeed opened the Boulogne gate to Chargny and his company; and such of them as were left alive thereof did sup that New Year's night in Calais castle. For King Edward —being one of those whose hearts are softened rather than hardened by victory—was jocund of mood, and feasted as he fought, right royally; entreating both friends and foes with the like frank courtesy: only Eustace de Ribeaumont was set in the chief place of honor.

This converse took place in Hawkwood's quarters, while his esquire helped him to doff harness:

"Fair son," said the knight, "this day, for the second time, thou hast doughtily approved thy manhood; wherefore give God thanks as is due. There be many who rush hotly to their first encounter; but few so steadfast therein as not to lose somewhat of their vantage at weapons. I was not so busy but that I had leisure to mark thy bearing; and I perceive that thou lackest coolness no more than courage; yet never, since first I drew sword, have I seen sharper passage of arms than yonder. Give thanks, too, for thine escape. Once I thought thou hadst gotten thy death-wound; and trust me, I was right heavy of heart; though, had I stooped to succor thee, I myself had been sped."

"'Twas a shrewd dint," Ralph answered with a light

laugh, "and 'tis no marvel if mine ears are singing still. Marry, I owe it to your worship's wisdom that my brain-pan is whole; for it went sheer through the bascinet and scored the camail."

Hawkwood took his esquire's helmet from the settle whereon the other had cast it down, and looked upon it, at first with an idle curiosity: but as he looked, his countenance changed.

"A swashing blow," he muttered at last, "yet a cravenly withal, and felonly delivered. Seest thou not, from the slant thereof, that it must needs have been dealt from behind thee?"

"Nay, I had not noticed," Brakespeare answered, indifferently. "Nathless, I see not how it could be. My memory is somewhat dazed; yet I mind not to have heard any cry 'Saint Denis' behind me: besides, as your worship knows, the French were then somewhat giving ground. 'Twas a chance blow from one of our own side mayhap, meant for another: the light was doubtful even then, and the mellay rude."

Hawkwood shook his head. He was one of those who—coming not hastily to conclusions—are exceeding obstinate in maintaining them.

"That was no chance blow, nor a glinting one; neither was it aimed at any life save thine. Wottest thou with what manner of weapon was it delivered?"

"With mace or gisarme, I should guess," Ralph replied. But this time his carelessness was rather assumed than real, and his cheek flushed slightly.

"Ay, or with curtal-ax," the other said darkly. And as the eyes of the two met, each knew what thought was in the other's mind. Such a weapon of curiously damasked Milan steel hung ever at Gian Malatesta's saddle-bow.

With an angry impatience most unusual in him, Hawkwood cast the bascinet crashing down; and strode backward and forward twice or thrice through the chamber, muttering under his breath—

"By the Mother of Mercy! if this can be proven— Canst thou help me to the truth? It is thy bounden duty so to do; I charge thee, on thine oath, neglect it not. Have we then fouler traitors among us than Emeric of Pavia? A malison on these false Lombards, say I: no true man's life is safe in their company."

As the knight stood still waiting for an answer, his esquire bent the knee before him reverently.

"I do beseech your worship," he said, "to grant me this—the sole grace that I have asked at your hands since you overpraised my poor deserts, and make no farther inquiry into this matter. I aver on mine honor, that proof have I none, and shame it were that any, on bare suspicion, should underlie your disfavor. There is no reason, that I wot of, why any should practise against this poor life of mine. But, if such there be, 'Forewarned is forearmed,' quoth the proverb: I fear not but I shall hold mine own."

Hawkwood's heavy frown relaxed, as he leaned one hand on his esquire's shoulder; looking down into his face with something like fatherly kindness.

"I may not deny thee, fair son: thou hast thy will. I pray that neither thou nor I repent having let this matter sleep. If hereafter thou comest by foul play, I swear not to sit at board with knights till the misdeed be avenged, and till by fast and penance I have cleared my soul of blood-guiltiness. But from such evil hap Christ sain us! Do thou disport thyself for the rest of this day and night amongst thy fellows: right well have ye all earned your pastime. For me, I am boune to sup in the castle to-night, where our good lord the King hath deigned to require my company."

On the morrow, when his little troop paraded, Hawkwood's brow grew dark again, as he saw a mace hanging at Malatesta's saddle in place of the curtal-ax.

"Hast thou lost thine Milan weapon?" he asked, curtly and sternly.

Not a muscle of the Italian's well-trained face stirred as he made answer.

"Yea; for the first time it played me false yestermorn. The handle shivered in my grasp, early in the mellay; so that I was forced to betake me to estoc and dagger. I searched for the head when the causeway was clear; but some prowler had been beforehand with me, and I found it not."

In very truth, he who should have lighted on that good piece of armorer's work, must have dived a fathom deep into black marsh ooze. Gian Malatesta was no clumsy criminal—to miscarry by leaving such proof of his guilt as might have been furnished, by fitting edge of curtal-ax to cleft in bascinet.

CHAPTER XVI.

HOW RALPH BRAKESPEARE FARED AT CASTING THE DICE.

There was rare revelry that New Year's night throughout Calais town. In the presence-chamber the vanquished did honor to the feast—to all outward seeming—not less frankly than the victor. There, Emeric of Pavia caroused with that desperate merriment not uncommon to men already within the shadow of doom; for, despite his brazen assurance and cynicism, the Lombard was ill at ease. Ever and anon over the wine-cup he caught glances of hungry hate, and he could not mistake their bitter promise: before the gold for which he bartered his honor was half spent, that promise was fulfilled.

There was much mirth and jollity too in the ale-houses and taverns scattered through the streets and clustered round the port; and chiefly in a certain hostel of greater pretensions than its fellows, on whose sign the Red Cross had lately replaced the Lily Flower. This had of late been the favorite resort for the esquires and better sort of men-at-arms; who on certain occasions mingled freely together, especially at seasons like the present, when barriers of degree were, to some extent, broken down, and few were disposed to stand overmuch on their dignity.

In the common room of the Red Cross there was a motley crowd, and a very Babel of tongues. But the loudest talk and the closest press were in a certain corner, whence, in the lulls of clamor, came the sharp crack of the dice-box and the rattle of the dies. Gamester succeeded gamester in quick succession at the small round table, as each was satisfied with his gain, or weary of forcing ill luck. But one man had kept his seat there, as if determined to encounter all comers; neither giving nor taking quarter. In truth Gian Malatesta's *veine* seemed almost supernatural in its persistency and duration; for a full half hour the tiny pile of coins with which he had begun had gone on swelling into a fair heap of gold and silver. Sometimes— when the stake was trifling—he lost; but so soon as it became of real importance, he was sure to sweep the board.

In the ring of lookers-on stood Brakespeare, chained there by a fascination that he was ashamed to own to himself. The youth was not moved, like his fellows either to admiration or envy of the successful gambler; but his loathing and hatred of the smooth, smiling face waxed hotter every instant; the low, mocking laugh grated on his ears intolerably; and he thought he could discern in the black, bright eyes, as they met his own, the insolent challenge that he had read therein on the first night of their meeting. Furthermore, though Ralph had not gone far beyond the bounds of temperance, he had drunk more deeply than was his wont; and the Burgundy grape had a greater effect on a brain not yet fully steadied from the rude shock of the morning. At length, he could no longer resist the temptation to oppose himself personally to Malatesta. A German esquire had just thrown for his last cast; and as Wilhelm von Falkenstein arose—growling out a curse on his own ill luck and folly—Brakespeare dropped into his vacant place.

Certain of the bystanders, almost strangers to the two, were struck by the expression of the Italian's glance as it lighted on his fresh adversary. For an instant it blazed out with a savage eagerness, and then sparkled in mockery—the mockery of one who knows his triumph is sure. Some, too, noticed that the face of the younger man was strangely set and stern for one sitting down to a friendly cast of the dies.

"I scarce had reckoned on this honor, fair sir," the Italian said, in his silkiest tones, "so 'tis the more welcome. Never, since we two have served together, have I known you court Dame Fortune—or any other demoiselle, *pardie*—therefore have I esteemed you as a pearl of continence, no less than of valor. Sith for this one night you condescend to make merry with us *ribauds*, for what stakes is it your pleasure that we play?"

Ralph did not seem to notice the taunt, as he drew forth some half dozen gold pieces and cast them on the table, without speaking a word. And so the game began—the very simple one called *paume carie*, in which only a pair of dice were used.

The esquire's gipsire was indifferently well furnished, for his habits were frugal and his expenses few; so that the small store he had brought with him over the sea was not quite spent: furthermore, he had received his full share of the price at which the Limousin destrere was valued. But coin after coin went to swell the Italian's winnings, till not one remained at the bottom of the pouch.

Brakespeare bit his lip till the blood sprang. Besides the feeling of personal enmity, he was infected for the first time in his life with the real gambling fever; his brain grew dizzy again with passion; for a second or two, he saw everything as through a mist, and the murmured exclamations of those who stood close around him, came to his ears like a vague distant drone. But he saw there was no help for it: he was preparing to rise mechanically, when the Italian spoke —this time without a touch of sarcasm.

"It grieves me, gentle sir, that you should have fared so ill in your maiden essay; and, by the body of Venus! I can afford to be generous to-night. See, now; I will set these forty golden crowns, and my sorrel, against your destrere. 'Tis an honest brute enough, though he lacks fire: but I have ever fancied the roan since we chaffered for him in Southwark. How say you? Ye can deal with the horse as ye list. Was he not bought with your own broad pieces?"

The other nodded his head hastily, as though afraid of giving himself time to think. The chances of the die did not change. In two minutes more the gallant beast—who was to Ralph Brakespeare a dear friend, since they ran their first course together—had passed away from him to the one living man whom the youth hated, to be used or misused according to the other's caprice.

One of the swift revulsions of feeling which dispel, as though by magic, clouds of anger or strong drink, happened to Brakespeare then. Suddenly his brain became so cool and clear, that he could smile, in utter scorn of his late foolish passion. As he prepared to yield his place to another, his hand leaned on the table, in the act of rising; and the light of the sconce, hung overhead, fell full on the ring that never quitted his finger.

"Stay yet an instant," Malatesta said eagerly, his eyes gleaming with avarice and exultation; "'tis ill quitting play with a stake left you worth all we have cast for, and more. None but fools risk all on one cast; yet I care not. Lo! I will set every piece I have this night won, and thy roan destrere to boot, against yon balas ruby that sparkles so bravely."

Ralph had a hard battle with pride, and prudence, and conscience besides, ere he brought himself to consent to what he afterward repented as a branding shame. Was it not disgrace enough that his good destrere should be backed by Malatesta, without periling his dead mother's ring—to be flaunted, perchance, as a bait to covetous harlotry? Yet, as has been aforesaid, his brain was quite clear now; and, with one of those inspirations by which fortunes are made and marred, there mingled a certain suspicion which decided him.

"So be it," he said, speaking, for the first time since he sat down, in a hard, unnatural voice. "Win or lose, I swear by Holy Rood this shall by my last cast while I live."

A hush of expectation fell on the circle of bystanders that deepened and narrowed round the table; while the Italian pushed forward, somewhat ostentatiously, the great pile of his winning, and Ralph laid down over against it the ruby ring.

"Hold an instant," Brakespeare said, just as Malaesta was preparing to throw. "Ye may call it superstition, or what ye will; but this cast will I not risk, unless some one of this fair company place the dies in the dice-box for us both."

The youth, you know, was very keen of sight. He had noticed that in his companion's casting, one die came up almost invariably a six; and the ivory of this one he fancied to be somewhat lighter in hue than the others—a difference not apparent when he himself used them; also he had noticed that the other, after casting, almost invariably replaced the dies in the box before passing it over.

Gian Malatesta's face grew black as thunder, and livid streaks showed themselves under his clear olive skin; but one glance at the faces round them told that he could not refuse without exciting suspicion, both shameful and dangerous. Scant mercy would cogger of dice have met with at the rough English hands that would have dealt with him.

The secret of his success was very simple. By a palming sleight familiar to modern sharpers, he substituted, when his turn came to cast, a die weighted to throw high, for one loaded on the reverse principle; changing them again as he passed the box to his opponent. But the Italian was too thorough-paced a gambler to be proof against the temptation of playing for a great stake on even chances; though he infinitely preferred to control fortune.

"A strange fancy, fair sir," he said sneeringly.

"But losers have large license, and I see not why I should balk it. Who, now, will it please you, shall do this office for us both?"

In the circle of bystanders stood Wilhelm von Falkenstein, watching the play with the sullen envy peculiar to the ruined gamester. Ralph's eye lighted on this man, and he pointed him out without speaking. Malatesta nodded assent, also silently. So the German came forward, and dropping the dies into the box, pushed it toward Malatesta; muttering something under his heavy blond mustache that was anything rather than a benison. The dies rattled loud and long, and came down with a crash at last. The numbers were seven—no such great throw after all; and so evidently thought Von Falkenstein, as he did his office again with a grim smile.

Ralph threw quickly and carelessly; and the dies, after rolling over twice or thrice, as though to tantalize the lookers-on, came up the double quatre.

With a blasphemy, so ghastly that it made some start and shiver who understood not one half its meaning, the Italian sprang to his feet; while at the same instant rolled out the German's guttural "*Gott sei Dank!*" With the first natural impulse of passion Malatesta's hand glided to his dagger-hilt; but he was not mad enough to attempt violence at such a place or time. After one hungry glance at the glittering heap of his lost gold, and another of unutterable hate leveled at his opponent, he thrust his way rudely through the ring of bystanders, most of whom, as well he knew, rather gloried in his disaster, and cast himself down on a bench in a remote corner, shading his face with his hand.

Ralph Brakespeare indulged in one long breath of relief; and drew the ring on his finger once more. He seemed in nowise elated by his success; as, pulling the heap nearer toward him, he began counting it out deliberately. Not a few of those whose sympathies had hitherto been wholly with the English esquire, were both surprised and chagrined at seeing him now bear himself rather like a trader reckoning his gains than a free-handed gamester. Ralph continued his occupation quite unconcernedly, till he had counted out the precise number of coins that he had owned when he sat down to play.

"These come back to me," he said, as he thrust them back into his gipsire. Then looking round, he called to the host of the Red Cross, who had pressed forward with the rest to watch the last cast decided. "Hark thee here, Jenkyn; canst thou furnish me presently with canvas bag, wax, and twine?"

When the matters he asked for were brought, Ralph swept the rest of the gold and silver by handfuls into the bag; and fastening its mouth carefully, stamped the wax laid over the knots with his ring, the curious chasing of which, though the stone was not graven, made a very sufficient seal.

"It is not that I doubt thine honesty, good mine host," Brakespeare said, "but yon gold, which I deliver to thy keeping here in presence of this fair company, is Holy Church's now, not mine. To-morrow, before noon, the almoner of St. John's Priory will visit thee; to him shalt thou render thy charge. Every broad piece there shall buy a mass for the souls of those who died unshriven in the battle of this New Year's morning.

The hands of anointed priests make pure things howsoever foul or unholy; mine are sullied enough already with this night's work, without meddling more with dicer's gold.

There was a slight stir of surprise in the small crowd which still surrounded the speaker; but most of his hearers were more inclined to applaud than deride. Acts of lavish generosity and self-sacrifice were not uncommon in those days, when knights, in achievement of their vow, rode half blindfold into the fight; or, having impoverished themselves forever to win the barren honors of the tournament, cast down their last broad pieces in largess to herald. So, though not a man present would probably have followed Ralph's example, few were disposed to cavil thereat, or even greatly to wonder.

But another black drop was added to the bitterness already seething in Malatesta's breast, as he guessed at the truth—guessed at the scornful loathing which caused the other to shrink from touch of his gold as though tainted with plague. From that time, and long after, the Italian yielded to a kind of sullen despair whenever he thought of Ralph Brakespeare. Though he made mock of religion, and would have pledged his paramour in a chalice from the altar, he was superstitious after the fashion of his birthland, where spells, philters, and charms have been rife since the days of Canidia. He had come to believe that the youth's star was more powerful than his own; so that only at a planetary conjunction, such as had not yet appeared, could he hope to prevail. Thenceforward he treated the Englishman coolly and cautiously; never failing in the deference due from vintenar to esquire; but making no pretense of cordiality, and avoiding the other's company whensoever it was possible. With the patient ferocity of the great tropical snake—that will lie coiled near the pathway for hours and days, till there passes by fitting prey for its repast—he was content to bide his time.

There was some talk on the morrow in Calais town of the doings at the Red Cross the night before; and they came at the last to Hawkwood's ears. Though the knight shook his head gravely, and read his esquire a long lecture on the sin of gaming, he was, perchance, not ill pleased at heart. Will Lanyon rubbed his hands and laughed in noisy triumph.

"By'r Lady, Messire Ralph," the archer said, "I had rather than any miracle-play have seen the clipping of yonder gay gled's wings. Set England against Italy in sport or earnest—if they do but play or fight fair— and it will be hard if Saint George keep not his own."

CHAPTER XVII.

HAUTE JUSTICE AT ST. OMER.

About this time, other causes, besides the ceaseless intercession of the good old peacemaker at Avignon, so wrought upon the rival kings as to incline them to make a truce; which, in form, though not in substance, endured for some years. It was not that either was weary of warfare, or ready to abate one jot of his pretensions; but the treasury of France was well-nigh drained, and all the plunder brought from over the sea scarcely lightened the tax-burdens that galled the necks of Edward's Commons. Moreover, though the name of England was terrible abroad, the hand of heaven was heavy on her at home. In the autumn of 1348, the ghastly enemy, whose coming had been foretold by the astrologers of Oxenford, and heralded by portent, comet, and earthquake, showed himself in bitter earnest. The small cloud, that rose out of the sea on the Dorset coast, spread and darkened till it overshadowed all the length and breadth of the land. And from town and hamlet, hall and homestead, went up wails of lamentation, or shrieks of terror; while all who had not strength or means to flee, cowered helplessly before the approach of the Black Death.

The walls of castle or abbey were not always safe

fence against the plague; though, like its antitype of modern times, it raged most pitilessly in the close, noisome dwellings of the poor. On a certain wet night in early spring, a minstrel craved and found shelter at Bever. The traveler brought with him the taint of pestilence: he himself was a corpse before noon; and, ere the month was out, Sir Simon Dynevor was wifeless and childless. Childless—for, brooding there alone, he knew that the yearning and repentance of his desolate heart were utterly without hope. He knew that that other son—on whom he might have leaned, as on a fair, strong pillar in his sore trouble—was divided from him now and for evermore, no less than if the grave lay betwixt them. Yet his grief slew him not: he was endowed with that strange vitality which seems to savor rather of curse than blessing, when it attaches to those who have little cause to love life; even the plague, clutching eagerly at younger and healthier frames, would have naught to do with the gaunt, sallow cripple. The punishment of his youth's misdeeds was upon him; yet he turned not to heaven in his distress —bearing his heavy cross doggedly and silently. But with Simon Dynevor's sins and sorrows, this chronicle hath naught farther to do: neither was it till long after that any of these things came to the knowledge of Ralph Brakespeare.

During all this season of panic and misery, when churches stood empty for lack of ministrants, and churchyards were full to overflowing, the King— whether from policy or recklessness it were hard to say —abated naught of pomp or revelry. In the spring of 1349 was founded the famous Order that commemorates a world's wonder: for this once, by the balance of testimony, did courtly virtue come triumphant out of royal siege. Later, too, though the pest had more than decimated his land, Edward found time and forces wherewith to chastise the Spaniard's insolence in the great sea-battle off Sluys; where, after sore peril of his own life and his son's—for John of Lancaster bore down but just in time to take both from their sinking ship—a signal victory was won, under the very eyes of Philippa, and the other dames, who, from Winchelsea heights, looked upon the deeds of their kinsfolk, husbands, and lovers.

Beyond the seas, too, restless spirits were at work. In Gascony and Guienne, the truce was broken almost daily; and John of Normandy, when he went thither in person, did naught to check the disorders on his own side; nay, he scrupled not to head divers incursions, taking fortified places not a few with the strong hand, and making others underlie his challenge. Also in those troublous times sprang up apace, like ill weeds, hardy marauders such as Bacon and Croquart; who so throve on blood and rapine as to maintain a state equal to a crown-vassal's till it became worth a king's while to purchase their allegiance.

The heart of Edward grew hot within him when he heard how the English, from Bretagne to Languedoc, were daily put to despite and distress; so, calling to him the man whom, next to his own son, he loved and trusted—his cousin of Derby, late made Earl of Lancaster—he bade that wise captain go forth with all speed, to be his lieutenant in Poitou, and all the marches thereof.

All this while, Hawkwood and his following had abode in garrison at Calais, under command of Sir John Beauchamp, then time governor of the castle and town. During this time a strange adventure befell Lanyon. The honest hobelar had been rather out of luck's way in this respect heretofore; for he had seen no pitched battle, or even sharp skirmish; and, for reasons good, had not been present at the combat without the Boulogne gate.

On a certain day there came to Calais, over channel, Sir Henry Audley, with a strong force of archers and spearmen. That knight was near of kin to John Beauchamp, and had come thus far out of his way—being bound for Brittany—to confer with his cousin on family affairs of grave import. It chanced that their discourse turned on the French lords then held on parole in England. Now Henry Audley had been much in their company of late; and was loud in praise of their gentle demeanor in tilt-yard, hall, and bower: among other names of note that came up was that of Geoffrey de Chargny.

"A courtly knight and *debonnaire*," said Audley. "Never but once did I mark him look sadly or angrily. It was when some one—witting not that he was near —spake in his hearing of Emeric of Pavia. Then the Lord Geoffrey's countenance was possessed with a black rancor such as I mind not to have seen on any man's face afore; and he muttered certain words, crossing himself the while, which I take to have been some form of vow. I dare aver, that he will one day even himself with that felon knight. Marry! soon we may hear news of the twain; for, while I was at Nottingham, I heard that De Chargny was put to ransom. He must have crossed the seas ere now; and I marvel that he passed not this way, where doubtless he would have been entreated by thee with all fitting honor."

These words set the governor a-pondering. He was a politic courtier, no less than a famous soldier, albeit he himself held Emeric in no great respect or love, he knew, despite of all that had passed, the Lombard had not lost King Edward's favor, who would be right sorry to learn that he had come to harm; moreover, the Lombard was an ancient comrade, and he had often admired the other's prowess in old time. True there were foul stains now on Emeric's escutcheon, and he had doubly deserved traitor's doom; yet Beauchamp could not resist giving him another chance for life. So, incontinently on rising from table, he indited a brief message, in some such terms as these:

"JOHN BEAUCHAMP TO THE LORD EMERIC OF PAVIA, AT HIS CASTLE OF FRETUN, SENDS GREETING:

"SIR:—By these presents I have you to wit that within short space the Lord Geoffrey de Chargny hath been put to ransom, and is now, as I well believe, within the realm of France.

"He scruples not, as I farther understand, to aver that he holdeth you in mortal feud, purposing, if it be possible, to get you into his power. Wherefore, being avised of all this, it behooves you to make such provision against surprise as may seem in your wisdom best, if it please you not to remove to some more distant country, or some place of greater security than where you now abide. And so God have you in his holy keeping. JOHN BEAUCHAMP.

"Given at the King's Castle of Calais, on the eve of the blessed Saint Anthony."

Beauchamp chanced to encounter Hawkwood as he came forth from his private chamber, and to him the governor delivered the letter; charging him to seek out a messenger who would convey the same without loitering by the way. The knight's choice fell on Lanyon, whom he held in higher esteem for trustworthiness and sobriety than many others of quicker parts.

The hobelar did, in truth, make good speed too, for he felt rather proud of his mission, though he liked not the place whither he was bound; and the *haquenée* that bore him was both active and willing: but the traveling was heavy, and it was past sundown when he came under the walls of Fretun.

"By Saint Bridget, the knaves keep careless guard," the Kentishman grumbled, as he marked, even at that late hour, the drawbridge down. His simple notions of discipline were still more shocked when, at the sound of hoofs under the archway, there staggered out of the gatehouse a warder, whose swollen features and blinking eyes bore traces of sleep and recent carouse. With some difficulty Lanyon made this official comprehend the object of his coming; after some minutes, delay he was committed to the charge of a passing page, and conducted into the presence-chamber, where—at the head of a long table, crowded toward the lower end with dissolute-looking retainers—the castellan had just begun his evening meal.

Emeric of Pavia was tall and portly of person, with a handsome—rather sensual—face, of the Venetian type, and profuse black hair, lightly flecked with gray. His small, bright eyes had always been searchingly cunning, and of late he had gotten a habit of glancing often over his shoulder—scarce timorously, but warily—like one who travels along a path beset with peril; also his temper, which had been singularly suave and even, had waxed uncertain, and he drank deeper than was good for his health. Though he went seldom abroad, and right few of his peers visited Fretun, he indulged none the less in pomp of attire and domestic display, which have ever been the national weaknesses of his country. Nevertheless, the Lombard's own rich dress was quite cast into the shade by the apparel of the lady who sat on his right hand; a superb blonde—with broad blue eyes, flashing like sapphires, and a dazzling white skin, that shamed her pearls. With such a bait, in truth, hath the Red Fisherman angled for, and caught, the souls of many better men than was her Lombard paramour before he sold himself to shame.

When the letter was placed in Emeric's hand he gazed sharply for a second or two in the messenger's face, as though he would have guessed its import before breaking the seal. But he might as well have peered into a blank wall; neither did the archer's stolid face betray the faintest curiosity nor surprise, though before and around him there was paraded such wealth of plate and jewels as he could never have seen, even in his dreams; so the castellan was fain to read the letter through. At first his brows were slightly bent; but, as he ended, there broke out on his lips a scornful, incredulous smile.

"*Basta!*" he said, "threatened men live long. My good Lord of Beauchamp is overcareful for my safety; yet am I not less beholden to him therefor. True it is that these *rascaille* of mine keep careless ward; I would wager that the drawbridge is down even now; matters will never be amended till some knave warder tastes cord or scourge. Here, good archer, are two gold pieces for thy pains; I can see by thy plight that thou hast not spared spur: make cheer here to-night; thou shalt carry back mine answer to Calais betimes to-morrow."

Lanyon drew back with something like aversion.

"I thank your worship," he said sturdily. "I needs must stable and housel here to-night; and a cup of your worship's wine will be right welcome: but we who serve King Edward, under Sir John Hawkwood's pennon, take no guerdon for performance of simple duty, such as mine hath been to-day."

The Lombard bit his lip as he turned toward the dame on his right hand.

"See now, *bella mia*, what stubborn virtue is found in your Islanders. I marvel how, amongst those fogs and frosts, ever was bred a creature so lovable as thy sweet, sinful self."

She laughed, too, as she smote him lightly on the cheek with her jeweled fingers, and, leaning on his shoulder, whispered some words in his ear that chased the gloom from his face instantly.

Half an hour after, having seen his *haquenée* carefully

attended to, Lanyon was sitting at the lower end of the board, doing full justice to such meats and liquors as had never passed his palate till now. Nevertheless, some instinctive distrust and caution withheld him from anything like debauch. When the hour for retiring came, the archer lay down on a pallet in the guard-room among the retainers, few of whom had been so sparing of the wine-cup as himself. Waking with a start toward daybreak, he was aware of sounds from without that had naught to do with dreamland: the tramp of many feet; words of command, spoken low and hurriedly; and a smothered clank of armor. Lanyon sprang to the window, spurning with his foot as he rose the nearest sleeper; looking forth into the cold, gray light, he saw the outer verge lined with men-at arms, and the moat itself—nearly dry as it chanced— filled with crossbowmen. The Kentishman realized the position at once, and accepted it with his wonted placidity.

"By the Mass! a proper gin have I thrust mine head into," he growled; and then turned back into the guard-room, which was now all astir. "Stand not staring and babbling there; but wake your lord, some of ye, and bid him arm, if he would strike a blow for life. Yon crazy doors will stand no siege, I trow; and they are at work there already."

In very truth, the last words were well-nigh drowned in the clattering din of axes, crowbars, and hammers; and long before they had time to don harness, one leaf of the gate was shivered from its hinges, and the courtyard was thronged with spears.

In that sore strait, knowing from the first that resistance was vain, Emeric of Pavia bore himself not unworthily of his soldierly renown: yet he started slightly when, issuing from his chamber in mantle and doublet—sheathed sword in hand—he came face to face with the leader of the assailants. Just overhead, an oil-lamp swung from the key-stone of the arch, beginning to pale already in the dawn-light streaming through the window over against the stairhead.

"My Lord de Chargny," Emeric said, with much outward coolness, "I scarce reckoned on your presence in my poor castle so soon; otherwise would I have striven to receive you in more fitting guise. Now have I no choice but to render myself and these my followers your prisoners, rescue or no rescue; praying only that we be put to fair ransom speedily. Also, would I specially bespeak your courtesy for the fair dame here within my chamber, and for a certain English archer —no servitor of mine—who came hither but newly with message from the Lord Beauchamp."

For some seconds the other answered not, his visage was very pale with the paleness that comes sometimes of great joy, no less than from great sorrow; and in his eyes there was the fierce greed of a miser gloating over the hoard for which he hath delved long in vain. His lips parted twice or thrice before two syllables escaped them.

"Bind him."

The Lombard's white forehead flushed dark red as two esquires, bearing cords, strode out from the throng, and laid hands on him without farther ceremony. He was too proud to demean himself by useless trouble, but his voice was hoarse with anger as he asked—

"Is this fitting treatment of knight by knight? Think ye not ye shall abye it some day?"

De Chargny's harsh, jeering laugh rang out under the vaulted roof.

"Knight by knight, forsooth! *Sang-Dieu!* thou shalt carry thy knighthood to the market-place of St. Omer, and no farther. Dare not thou to plead for others: make thy peace with God, whilst thou hast time; and speak no other word, I warn thee, else will I smite thee on the lips with my gantlet. Have him down, some of you, and see him well secured in saddle. We have naught more to do here; we carry away no prisoners save one; only, the English archer shall abide with us till all is done, for reasons good. And mark me: whoso shall pillage in this castle—were it but a drinking-cup or a *sol parisis*—by the faith of Chargny, he shall die the feldon's death."

When Emeric of Pavia saw that his case was desperate, there was so much of wolf in his evil nature, that he forebore to make moan, but followed his captors sullenly, with one long, lingering look over his shoulder into the chamber he had just left.

Into that same chamber the French captain passed on; and, as he lifted the hangings of the doorway, his rough bearing was exchanged for the courtesy that had won him so many friends in his captivity beyond seas. He bent his plumed head low before the frightened beauty crouching behind the damask curtains of the alcove—more lovely in her disorder than she had been in the pomp of array.

"It irks me much, fair dame," he said, "that I have been forced thus rudely to break your rest. But you have naught worse than fright to fear; neither rapine nor violence shall be wrought here by me or mine. Nay, more; six trusty lances I will leave to conduct you safe to Calais gates: it may be this base *valetaille* will wax insolent and unruly when the reins are on their neck. Some day, perchance, you will thank De Chargny for having rid the world, and you, of as foul faitour as ever wore spurs."

With another grave salute he passed out; leaving the lady something reassured, if not consoled. Doubtless she mourned her paramour for awhile—after the light-minded fashion of lemans; but, ere they saw Calais town, chroniclers aver that a gay French esquire had taught her to dry her tears.

All through the early morning De Chargny and his party marched back, and reached St. Omer ere noon. Two messengers, lightly armed and well mounted, had ridden on far in advance of the main column bearing messages for certain within the town; so that proclamation had been made already, summoning all men that listed—soldiery, citizens or country-folk—to witness an act of *haute justice*, to be wrought presently in the market-place. Lanyon had been told that his detention would be but brief; so he jogged along contentedly enough among the French spearmen in the rear of the column; indeed, having small sympathy with the prisoner, he had a sort of hankering to see how things would end.

When they rode into the market-square, three sides thereof were thronged. Also at the windows there were many spectators; but among them all scarcely one woman was to be seen—a circumstance sufficiently remarkable, considering the curiosity of the sex extends to most ordinary executions. In the center of the fourth side, which had been kept clear, a low scaffold of unhewn planks had been hastily erected: on this stood four men of forbidding appearance, dressed in stained leather doublets—no other than the common hangman of St. Omer and his valets. They had with them none of the usual instruments of their office; only what looked like a common butcher's cleaver, and a coil of leathern thongs. Just here De Chargny reined up his charger; while his men filed off, and ranged themselves on either hand, till only the prisoner and his guards remained in the open space.

Beckoning with his hand for silence, the knight spoke thus:

"Know all men here present, that I, Geoffrey, Seigneur de Chargny, Knight of the Order of St. Denis, have this day, in pursuance of a vow—made on a fragment of the Holy Cross—laid hands on the person of Emeric of Pavia; and purpose here to deal with him after his deserts. Neither by this deed do I hold myself to have broken or enforced the truce, lately contracted betwixt mine own liege lord and the most noble English king. For the said Emeric of Pavia did, by most foul treachery, betray into captivity myself and other barons, knights, and esquires; and likewise cause to be done to death without Calais' gates many—it may be—better men than we. Wherefore, this morning, do I reckon myself to have done public justice, no less than wreaked mine own mortal feud. If I have done wrong, may God and my king assoilzie me; for I take the burden thereof on mine own head and soul."

None answered him a word; and there was a dead silence, while at a sign from their leader his guards cut the thongs which bound the prisoner's ankles; lifted him from the saddle; and set him on the scaffold. On the Lombard's face there was something of the gaunt, wild look of a savage animal nearly hunted down. But he strove to brazen it out still; gazing defiantly round as he stamped his numbed feet, shod in boots of soft Cordovan leather, on which glittered the golden ensigns of knighthood.

Once more through the hush a clear cold voice rang out—

"Emeric of Pavia, one privilege of the order thou hast shamed thou mayest claim still. Wilt thou have priest to shrive thee?"

The other shook his head doggedly, and it seemed as though he would have tried some mocking answer; but his tongue clave to the dry palate, and failed him.

"So be it," De Chargny went on, in the same measured tone. "Then naught hinders the hangman to do his office. Maître Humbert, cleave off his spurs."

A shudder, almost like a convulsion, ran through the prisoner's frame, as the cleaver crashed down close to his heel. And, as the dishonor was complete, he glared round—not defiantly now—to see what was the next torture in store: he had not long to wait.

Out of a narrow street, immediately behind the scaffold, there came a clatter of hoofs; and four huge Normandy stallions—two strong ropes trailing behind each—were led forth, plunging and screaming, as if loathing the work before them.

All the Lombard's hardihood vanished then; his white lips quivered painfully, and one word escaped them in a hissing whisper—

"*Ecartelé!*"

Will Lanyon felt a heavy qualmishness stealing over him; he had reckoned on no such sight as this. And other hearts around St. Omer market-place, besides the stout archer's, waxed faint while the *bourreaux* completed their office as quickly as might be, and bound the prisoner's four limbs securely—each to a rope harness—with the leathern thongs. The Kentishman saw the rearing stallions led out into the middle of the square, bearing in the midst of them what seemed a senseless body: he saw no more; for a deadly sickness made him close his eyes, and grasp his saddle-bow, to save himself from falling. But his ears he could not close. He heard the crack and slash of the whips as they goaded the brute executioners to their gruesome task: then a yell went up—thrice repeated, long drawn, and piercing—such as, for poor humanity's sake, let us hope, has seldom been heard on the hither side of eternal torment: then came silence, broken at last by a great shuddering groan, in which the oppression of five thousand breasts found vent. Opening his eyes once more, Lanyon saw the stones of the square besprinkled with foul red spashes; while in the center, in a broad crimson pool, lay a formless, nameless horror; and, at the four corners, the savage stallions—madder yet with scent of blood—struggled in their halters; each dragging in his harness *something* from contact of which the hardiest recoiled.

While the archer still felt dizzy and faint, a hand

"THE BOURREAUX COMPLETED THEIR OFFICE AS QUICKLY AS MIGHT BE, AND BOUND THE PRISONER'S FOUR LIMBS SECURELY—EACH TO A ROPE HARNESS—WITH THE LEATHERN THONGS."

was laid on his shoulder; and the voice of one of De Chargny's esquires said in his ear—

"Thou art free now, brave Englishman. Make all speed to Calais, and tell to such as list to hear it how my lord deals with double traitors."

Lanyon needed no second bidding. He never drew free breath till the walls of St. Omer were fairly behind him; and he had ridden leagues, before his senses were clear enough to take in commonplace sights and scents and sounds; his bluff, brown face had not recovered its natural color when he stood in presence of the Lord Beauchamp to tell his tale.

The good knight's cheek, too, paled as he listened—crossing himself often—murmuring ejaculations of pity and horror. And in Calais was there never a church or chapel, wherein masses were not sung that night, for the weal of the guilty soul that had gone to its account through passage of such awful agony.

CHAPTER XVIII.

AT BORDEAUX.

For near two years, Ralph Brakespeare went through the weary round of garrison duty with much cheerfulness and alacrity. Yet was he not the less rejoiced, when one day Hawkwood bade him see all prepared for departure on the morrow; inasmuch as he had gotten leave from the Lord Beauchamp to march in command of a reinforcement, destined to join the English armament in Poitou. The route was long; but the esquire would not have it shortened by a single league. Throughout the country, deserted tenements, and fields left fallow, bore token of the fell pestilence, which had spared France no more than the rest of Europe in its progress from east to west—though in Calais, and in other coast towns, through which the keen sea breezes swept freely, it had scarcely been felt. But since the pest had abated of its fury, the pale, panic-stricken survivors had crept back to their daily labor or trade; and all along the road there was no lack of entertainment.

Right pleasant it was, after being cooped up so many months betwixt gray walls—the duresse broken only by rare exercise among bleak *dunes*, or along dreary causeways—to ride on through the fresh summer mornings and breezy afternoons, with constant change of scenery, faces, and objects to vary each day's halt. Crossing the Somme at Abbeville, they were soon clear of the marshy flats of Picardy; and, leaving Arques on their right, wound their way through the green *coteaux* that swell betwixt Rouen and the sea. Albeit a truce prevailed, Hawkwood deemed it prudent to halt in hamlets and small towns than in such cities where the French lay in force; choosing not to risk, with his small company, being embroiled in such chance quarrels as will arise when ancient foes—newly made friends—meet over the wine-cup. So he turned not aside to Rouen; but bearing still coastward, forded the Seine at Caudebec; and so—by Lisieux, Falaise, Pontorson, and Montfort—came safe, toward the end of July, to Aurai, then garrisoned by Sir Thomas Dagworth, the King's Lieutenant in Bretagne.

Here they halted certain days for needful refreshment, both for men and horses; and then set forward again toward Bordeaux, where Ralph of Stafford held command in the room of Lancaster, who had returned to England before Whitsunday. Only by a short week did Hawkwood and his company miss sharing in a great disaster—unless, indeed, their presence might altogether have averted it. For, scarcely had they reached Bordeaux, when news came that the gentle knight, who late entertained them so royally, had been treacherously set upon by Raoul, Lord of Cahors, under the walls of Aurai, and done to death with all his following.

Not long after this, other messengers came; telling how Philip of Valois had found rest at last from troubles and calamity in the shadow of St. Denis's altar;

and how the fiery Duke of Normandy reigned in his stead. Such as were learned in the politics of the day foresaw that the change would not be greatly for the weal of France. The honor of John the Good was as stainless as his courage; but his hand was better fitted to grasp the sword than the scepter or leading-staff: he would imperil an army not less recklessly than he would risk his own person; and was over hot-blooded and inconsiderate, to cope with the wary antagonist that watched him from over the sea. Yet, to all men's wonder, the war smoldered for awhile; only now and then giving tokens of fire lurking beneath the thin crust, like the jets and wreaths of smoke that hover over the Terra di Lavoro.

So, for Brakespeare and his comrades, the old, weary garrison life began again. For even in the skirmishes and chance combats that took place not unfrequently, they were destined to take no share. They heard of that tough passage-of-arms, the memory of which is still kept green in Breton ballads; where—despite Merlin's prophecy—De Beaumanoir and his thirty did at the last prevail over the stark champions who followed Bembro; and where Croquart, the freebooter, setting his back against Ploërmel oak, bore himself so hardily, that to him, above knights and squires of high degree, was assigned that day's palm of valor. They heard, too, how in the country they had so lately left, notable exploits were wrought—how the disaster of the good Lord Beauchamp had been amply avenged by Manny; who brought such plunder into Calais town, that a brave ox fetched but sixteen *sols* in the market-place—and how Henry of Lancaster had pushed his foray farther yet into the French realm; sacking Terouenne, flooding the church with the blood of its townsmen, and carrying fire and sword up to the gates of Arques and St. Omer—and how afterward, by a wench's treachery and an archer's subtlety, Guisnes was taken, and held in despite of the truce. Later yet, they heard how Sir Walter Bentley—left Lieutenant of Bretagne—had gotten great honor by utterly discomfiting Guy de Nesle, King John's marshal, who came forth to provoke him to battle. And, all this while, those who lay at Bordeaux never drew sword in earnest, or lay lance in rest.

Yet this long enforced inaction was, perhaps, better training for Ralph Brakespeare than ceaseless excitement would have been. True, his early luck seemed to have deserted him, and he was fain, so far, to rest on the memory of his first year in arms: before he was six-and-twenty, Ralph had almost learned to laugh at the day-dreams of five years agone. By this time, his character, like his frame, was set; to the vehement ambition and ardor of youth had succeeded the cool, matured resolution of manhood—powerful to will, prompt to execute and patient to endure; he was proof against idle hopes, no less than against groundless fears; and the common chagrins of life took no more hold of his soul, than toil or privation of his body. Yet under all this case-hardness—like a clear water-drop in the depth of crystal—there still abode with him the softness of heart that he inherited from the gentle woman who died in giving him birth. When men, who knew him best, gave Ralph Brakespeare no more credit for such emotion than if he had been an armed effigy, he was just as ready to listen to the cry of a helpless woman, and to avenge her wrongs, as when he rose up in the glee-maiden's defense, under the sign of the " Spur."

With Gian Malatesta he still remained on the same terms of cold, distant civility. As months and years went by, bringing no fitting occasion for the weakening of his enmity, the Italian seemed to have forgotten it altogether. In Bordeaux town—where they most often abode—he found opportunity enough for indulging his tastes; Hawkwood was not over-careful in detecting the misdemeanors of his followers, so long as they interfered not with duty; and on this point Malatesta was faultless. However deep the debauch overnight, the morning always found him alert and clear-headed —ready to carry out any orders whatsoever with his wary hardihood. Directly he was free, he would betake himself straightway to the taverns and stews in which his soul delighted—sowing crowns broadcast among *ribaudes* and roysterers. Play kept his gipsire always full; for at Bordeaux he encountered no such misadventure as had befallen him at Calais.

This chronicle does not aver, that while he tarried on the banks of the Garonne, Ralph Brakespeare bore himself always after the fashion that would have befitted Sir Galahad's esquire, or a Templar holding fast to his vow. When he confessed himself—which at certain seasons he failed not to do—he had, perhaps, as many venial sins to avow as some of his comrades who bore themselves more noisily and jovial; but of broken troth, or ruin of any woman's honor, he could not accuse himself. The blood of Gascony is hotter than its wine; and the dark eyes of more than one fair Bordelaise had looked approvingly—perhaps lovingly—on the stalwart figure and gallant bearing of the English esquire, marveling, half-pityingly, what should make so young a face look so grave. And, more than once, white hands had beckoned stealthily from lattices; or a flower had dropped at his feet as he passed by: for coquetry was not in its infancy even then, and such simple devices prevailed, be sure, north as well as south of the Pyrenees. But pride shrinking from the *amour bourgeois*—for in this class were the temptresses chiefly found—rather than shyness or coldness, kept Ralph's feet safe and clear of the snares. He was not specially cold, or continent, or tender of conscience; but he chose to take his pleasure in places where he troubled no man's peace, and where he could bring on no woman farther dishonor than what she had already taken on herself of free will.

And so, four years passed on; during which the bold Duke of Lancaster, waxing weary, like many another, of the broils of France and Navarre—of petty skirmishes of partisans and mock proposals of peace—traveled eastward to keep his sword bright in war against the Infidel. How in that adventure he miscarried—how through practise of the Duke of Brunswick he fell for awhile into captivity—how, returning, he libeled the Duke's treachery on Cologne cathedral door—how, after interchange of challenge, those two met in the *Pre aux Clercs*, and were made friends by the royal arbiter, without issue of battle—all this is set down in the records of the time. And, every day, things were growing riper for the struggle, final and decisive, betwixt the banners, gules and azure, whose semblances watchmen on Southampton battlements saw bristling in the midnight sky.

But, before the armies were drawn out in array, there happened somewhat which—in nowise affecting the fortunes of nations—had much to do with those of Ralph Brakespeare.

CHAPTER XIX.

HACQUEMONT.

THE truce—or succession of truces—was, as you have heard, very imperfectly observed along all the seaboard from Artois to Bearn. Those in Gascony and Guienne were not less eager than their fellows in the north to infringe it, whensoever and wheresoever they could find fair excuse or chance. The turbulent spirit in those parts was not likely to be checked or allayed by Ralph of Stafford, who commanded then as King Edward's captain-general. That valiant earl, soon after he landed had been himself engaged; encountering the enemy in force under John de Clermont, Marshal of France, and defeating them with shrewd loss; and it was well known that he would be more apt to applaud than reprehend any act of successful daring, though it involved open breach of the peace.

In the early spring of the year of Grace 1355—the last pretense of truce being appointed to expire at the end of the May following—some threescore English got privily under cover of night into the Castle of Nantes, and held it till Guy de Rochefort, governor of the town, brake in by dint of numbers, and slew them to a man. News of this reverse—albeit it was not a grave one, and far removed beyond his own province—caused Stafford to chafe mightily, and to hanker for reprisals.

So, with little delay, he sent forth Sir Walter Breckenridge—a captain of approved valor and experience—at the head of some six-score mounted archers, with the avowed purpose of exploring the country to the northeast of the Garonne, and bringing in supplies; but with secret orders to lose no chance of damaging the adversary, or even of occupying any fortified places that could easily be surprised.

With this company rode forth Sir John Hawkwood and his following. For some three days they advanced steadily into the interior, till they struck the southern banks of the Dordogne, a little to the west of Bergerac, without having seen the flutter of a French pennon, or lighted on any fortalice important enough, either from size or site, to tempt assault. Neither, up to this point, had Breckenridge cared to cumber himself with heavy plunder; choosing to defer the gathering of supplies until his face was turned seaward again. On the fourth day, they halted for some two hours before sunset in a valley not far from Biron; and—the sun not being fully set—sent forth scouts to explore the country round, which, just here, was somewhat hilly and thickly wooded. These returned ere it was fully night, having seen no trace of foe, and no place more considerable than the small straggling town of Biron; this—though it might easily be occupied, might hardly be held. But scarce more than a league from the spot of encampment, they had descried a castle, which Breckenridge guessed at once would be well worth capture.

Position, rather than great size or strength, made Hacquemont valuable. Occupying the entire plateau of a steep eminence, it commanded, not only an extensive view over the valley of the Dordogne and Corvéze, but also the road along which the main traffic of the country passed: for the hills here formed almost a defile. Some of the scouts had crept up under cover of the underwood, almost within bowshot of the walls, and reported that the place seemed very scantily guarded. Moreover, on their way back, they had laid hands on a peasant, from whom, doubtless, fuller information might be drawn. The prisoner was a sullen-looking boor; with the heavy jaw, low brow, and small cunning eyes, that are found near, as well as within the borders of Auvergne. So soon as he recovered from his first fright, he never hesitated betwixt threat of a halter and a bribe of a few silver coins; and told readily enough all that he knew of the castle and its inhabitants. Neither was this treachery unnatural or strange; there was little love in those days betwixt seigneur and villein; nay, the seeds were sown long ago, that a few years later ripened into a black crop of rapine and murder, when, for a brief space, the Jacquerie worked their will.

It appeared that the Baron of Hacquemont had in his youth and manhood won great renown in arms; but, some ten years back, in one of the chance mellays preceding Creçy, had gotten a lance-thrust in the body, and had been so sorely trampled by horse-hoofs, that from that day he never could back destrere or endure weight of harness. So, ever since, he tarried in his castle, peaceably enough, neither molested nor molesting any; keeping there but feeble garrison: every retainer and vassal that could possibly be spared he ever sent forth to do service in the wars; relying, somewhat over-confidently, on the good-will of his neighbors. For as the clown averred with rather an ill grace—the baron was well esteemed and beloved throughout the countryside. Indeed, his repute for piety and courtesy stood so high that, albeit he had been long a widower, certain noble demoiselles of Guienne much affected the society of his two unmarried daughters; looking on Hacquemont as a safe and honorable asylum, even in such troublous times.

Notwithstanding this fair report, Breckenridge felt neither scruple nor remorse in planning the surprise of Hacquemont: only he gave strict charge to all concerned therein to shed no blood needlessly, and to have special care of the safety of the castellan and his family.

While it was yet night, some fifty archers concealed themselves in the brushwood, which in some places grew nearly up to the edge of the castle ditch, and waited their opportunity. Soon after dawn, the drawbridge was lowered, and an empty wain, drawn by two horses and driven by a peasant, came forth. Scarcely had it cleared the archway of the barbican, when from the ambush went up the cry, "St. George Guienne!" and near a score of the fleetest-footed had cast themselves on the drawbridge, before the ancient warder recovered from his panic, or could bestir himself to raise it. Ten minutes after, the flutter of his own banner from the battlements of the keep told Breckenridge, who with the rest of his force was now near at hand, that Hacquemont was won: won, too, without bloodshed; for the scanty garrison rendered themselves without show of resistance, and the castellan, who had not arisen, was made prisoner almost in his couch.

Now ever since, on the night before, the enterprise of the morrow was bruited through the encampment, Ralph Brakespeare had been unwontedly pensive and grave. At first he was affected by a vague bewildermnt, common to all men who encounter some sight or sound that seems strangely familiar to them; though they may not remember where they have seen or heard it before.

Hacquemont.

For a long while Ralph racked his brain, to account to himself for the start and thrill that the first mention of the word sent through his frame: but gradually the lines of a dim memory stood out sharp and clear, till every feature of the picture was vivid, as though it had been limned yester-even.

The weary watch among the sandhills—the flutter of pennon over the alder-clump—the glisten of embroidered surcoat and gleam of gay armor—the merry musical voice ringing out its war-cry—the dizzy crash of the joust—the red westering sun lighting up the perfect face, that even the death-pang could not deform—the last faint whisper of the white lips—all these things came back to him; and once more his heart melted with regret and self-reproach, as it had melted amid the flush of his first triumph, when he looked down on the corpse of his foe.

He remembered how, in those days, he had often caught himself wondering what manner of demoiselle it was who had been honored by De Chastelnaye's love

—whether, after the year of mourning was expired, she had been easily consoled; or if she still lived a maid for her true knight's sake. If so it was, in all likelihood she was abiding at Hacquemont even now. And he—Ralph Brakespeare—who had dealt the first blow to her hope and happiness, was brought here by the chances of war and duty, to trouble and vex her once more. For months and months he had been pining for chance of enterprise. Now that it had come, he loathed it bitterly, and felt great relief at hearing Sir Walter Breckenridge's merciful orders, and at learning that he—himself—would have naught to do with the actual assault.

Thus moodily the esquire rode in his place over the drawbridge into the great courtyard; where, under the arched doorway of the keep, the Baron of Hacquemont awaited his captors—a tall old man, wrapped in a furred gown, and propped on a staff, with thin gray hair, and traces of long illness on his worn features; bearing himself neither timidly nor defiantly, but rather with the quiet confidence of one loth to suspect in others the discourtesy to which he had never abased himself.

Sir Walter Breckenridge was not a whit softer of mood, or more scrupulous, than his brothers-in-arms: yet he felt strangely ashamed of his exploit—almost inclined to excuse it—as he leaped from saddle, and approached the castellan, bowing his head in salute.

"I grieve much, fair lord," he said, "that my duty and mine orders have enforced me thus to trouble your peace, and invade your dwelling. But apprehend not, I pray you, violence or rough usage. We are not base marauders, like Bacon and his fellows, and affect no booty save what is fairly ours by the laws of war. It is needful that I hold this, your castle, for a certain space; yet this shall be done with no great damage to your goods, and with as little constraint on person as may be. Also, shall ye be put to speedy ransom on no hard terms; and thereto I, Walter Breckenridge, pledge my faith."

"I am beholden to you, gentle knight," the castellan answered. "Also in evil fortune do I esteem myself fortunate to have fallen into the hands of so worthy a captain: for, credit me, your renown has reached even these remote parts—so remote, i'faith, that I foolishly held them safe from your forayers. There is little enough to tempt them, God wot: for our country breeds few cattle, and the hands that should have tilled the cornlands are busy far away with spear and crossbow. Nathless, our ransom shall be paid, an' we melt down the last of our silver hanaps. I am the gladder to deal with one of your courtesy and breeding, because there are now abiding with my own children the Demoiselles De Brissac—daughters of the Vicompte Geoffrey, my good friend, and sometime companion-in-arms. They know naught as yet who are their captors; and, I warrant, there is sore flutter in their dovecot yonder."

Following upward the other's glance, Breckenridge saw at a window on the second story of the keep, three girlish faces—differing in type, but all fair specimens of fresh southern beauty—looking down in evident terror on the courtyard, now well-nigh full of armed men. From a narrower casement, rather to the left, another face showed itself alone; a face of rare and royal loveliness even now, though brilliancy of color had faded into ivory whiteness, and the proud dark eyes looked somewhat weary, as though from long watching or weeping. In those eyes there was neither curiosity nor fear; and the lady gazed down on the turmoil beneath, seemingly with no more disquietude than, in other times, she might have watched the tilting, where blunted lances were shivered in her honor. The Englishman could not forbear a smile; but he bent his head once more in lowlier courtesy.

"Hasten, I pray you, to assure those fair and noble demoiselles that no harm is intended them beyond brief duresse in their own chambers. I will take counsel with yonder good knight, who rides with me, and be with you in your presence-chamber above anon."

With these words Breckenridge beckoned to Sir John Hawkwood, who dismounted at once, and the two conferred apart.

Now Ralph Brakespeare, sitting in saddle there, and hearing all that was spoken, had glanced upward with the rest. His eye, after sweeping carelessly over the bright beauty that filled one casement, lighted on the sad pale face framed in the other; and dwelt there as though fascinated. One of the quick instincts that never lie told him that he looked upon her to whom, unwittingly, he had done such mortal harm; the Marguerite, whose name was on Loys de Chastelnaye's lips as he fought, and as he died—told him, moreover, that the girl was worthy of her knight's homage; inasmuch as she had chosen, for his dear sake, to live on alone with her sorrow.

Ralph shrank within himself, as he thought of the horror that would surely break the calm of those solemn eyes, if the lady could guess that she was there set face to face with the man on whose hand was her lover's blood, albeit it was shed in loyal combat: that same excuse never yet healed grief, though it has saved many a feud.

While the esquire mused thus discontentedly, said Breckenridge to Hawkwood—

"Good Sir John, I have ever heard thee reputed cool and wary of wit; also I know that thou art well esteemed by my lord of Stafford: wherefore I would hear your counsel, that I may see if it march with mine own. Lo, thus it stands with us. By happy adventure, and without loss of one life, we have gotten into a fair castle, and one that, meseems, with no great garrison, may easily be held. Yet may I not tarry here: there may be fortalices more vantageous within our swoop; and Earl Ralph, in his present mood, is hard to please. This am I minded to do: leaving here some scanty force, we will push forward yet a dozen leagues to the eastward. Then, if we shall find naught worthier of occupance, we will fall back on Hacquemont, and strengthen its garrison; if otherwise, the spears left here can easily join us as we pass by homeward. More than a score I cannot spare; for I fear no treachery from within, after the old lord hath given parole: furthermore, none, save our men, shall be allowed to keep their arms. Likest my plan, or canst find me better?"

"By the Mass, very hardly," the other answered; "it is both boldly and prudently devised. Doubtless, a score—well chosen—might easily hold the place against tenfold their number, till we of the main body brought them help; for we shall scarce be beyond a long day's ride, and signal from yon keep might be seen from afar."

"Well chosen," the other returned, "truly, there is much in that. Now, Sir John, I were loth to lose your own company, so I pray you to set forward with me; but there are none of my spears to whom I would so readily commit this charge, as those who have of late served under your own immediate training. They number, methinks, something under the score we named. Will it please you to leave them here under command of your esquire yonder? Than him, though he looks somewhat dreamily to-day, I wot we have no starker man-at-arms."

"Your pleasure is mine," the other replied, in his curt, decisive way. "I will give instant orders to that effect."

So the two parted; Breckenridge going straight to the presence-chamber on the first floor of the keep, where the old castellan awaited him.

"Fair lord," the Englishman said, "it is my desire to put no more than needful constraint on yourself or your household, whilst I perform my own duty. I purpose to leave here a certain number of my spears till I pass by again, which I trust will be on the fourth day at farthest. Till then, you shall pledge me your knightly word to countenance no attempt at recoverance from within, and allow none, either by signal or otherwise, to solicit rescue from without: also, your said retainers shall abide unarmed within their lodging;

whilst you, and the noble demoiselles, inhabit your own chambers in the upper part of this same keep. There is no inlet or outlet—so I opine—save through the door at yon stairhead, and of that ye may hold the key; and ye shall have tendance from your handmaidens, and any two of your servitors it may please you to choose. I, on my part, will engage—if, on my return hither, I am minded to hold this castle—to see you convoyed to some near place of safety in French hand, or I will leave you at peace again here. And, whichever befall, if your ransoms are not paid down instantly, I will accept your parole for their discharge. Have I said well?"

A gleam of pleasure lighted up the baron's worn face.

"Right well and mercifully," he answered. "To all that your knighthood has required I will cheerfully pledge myself; and, should any vassal of mine practise treachery, he shall swing on yonder justice-oak so soon as I can deal with mine own again. And, gentle sir, you should not lack my daughters' thanks besides mine own: but the younger is still something bewildered with her fright; and the elder, since she donned mourning for her betrothed, will come into no stranger's company."

So, with many courteous words and the emptying a cup of Gascon wine, the two parted in great amity; and, after man and horse had been moderately refreshed, and orders given for the safe custody of the prisoners, Breckenridge's trumpets sounded the route; and the narrow line of spears wound down the hillside, passing eastward through the defile.

CHAPTER XX.

GIAN MALATESTA'S COUNSEL.

WHILE Hawkwood was disposing all things for the garrisoning of Hacquemont, he was not without doubts and misgivings as to whether it were not wiser to carry Gian Malatesta away, than to leave him there with the rest. He liked the man not a whit better than he did when they marched out of Calais: but since that time the Italian had given no overt cause for complaint; neither had he by look, word, or sign betrayed the faintest enmity to Ralph Brakespeare; so there was no real reason why the two might not safely abide together for so short a space. Also, Sir John knew that the Italian's rare expertness in the use of warlike engines—whereof several of rather antique make were ranged on the battlements—could ill be spared in case of assault. Moreover, it was probable that the somber, jealous nature of the man might take umbrage, if he found himself singled out from his comrades as unfitted to be trusted beyond their commander's sight. Besides all this, Hawkwood had conceived great respect, not only for Brakespeare's thews and sinews, but also for his coolness and nerve; so that he could scarce believe in the esquire's coming to harm in any ordinary peril.

Had the knight wist of the truth, he would have

struck off Malatesta's head with his own hand, rather than have left him at Hacquemont. But, with all his sagacity, he never guessed how, during all those long months of inaction, a foul leaven had been fermenting in his little band, till scarce a savor was left of the old loyal grain. He never guessed how that subtle traitor had lost no chance of embittering irritation into dislike, and weariness into discontent—inflaming, either by taunt or temptation, the evil passions of each in that motley company, whereof scarce half were English-born—till, without any concerted plan, nearly the whole were ripe for mutiny. At first, probably Gian Malatesta began to work without any definite purpose, out of the pure malignity that makes devils impatient of idleness; but for some time past—seeing how the materials molded themselves to his will—he had been looking out for a chance of turning them to account. Never once, throughout all his plotting and scheming, had he lost sight of Brakespeare: despite all his cunning, there was so much of the simple savage in the polished desperado, that he would scarce have cared to build up the edifice of his own fortune, unless its first stone were red-wet with the blood of his enemy. Over such a garrison was Ralph set in charge, on the first occasion of his holding single command.

Without the faintest suspicion of the peril that encompassed him, the esquire was graver and more thoughtful than his wont that morning. The new sense of responsibility might sufficiently account for this; and, as he stood on the eastern battlements watching the hindmost of the column disappear, he repeated Hawkwood's concise orders over and over to himself, till he felt sure of not forgetting one word. Then, with the different keys of the castle at his belt, he visited each lock separately, seeing that all was fast —more especially that of a low building running round one side of the outer bailey, in which the late garrison were confined after their disarming. In this round he was accompanied by Lanyon; who for some time past had been specially attached to his person, much in the capacity of a bâtman of modern days. When the inspection was done, and the guards properly set, it was full time for the midday meal, which was prepared in the large lower chamber of the keep; but to this the esquire felt in no ways inclined to do justice. Sitting down in his place, he ate a few morsels and drank one cup of wine, and then went forth to walk alone on the battlements; never noticing certain dark looks, and sullen glances, leveled at him as he went, chiefly from the upper end of the board.

"Seest thou that?" grumbled Martin Stackpole to his neighbor, Berchtold of Boppart. "His worship can digest no meat eaten in our company. I would the Fiend had the filling of his proud stomach. Perchance, to-morrow we shall hear him taking a lesson on the lute in the bower of those bonny birds, at whom I marked thee casting kites' eyes from thy saddle but now."

The beetle-browed giant slacked not the play of his jaws; but growled out, betwixt two huge mouthfuls, somewhat that might be either assent or curse.

Ralph had certainly intended no slight to his subalterns when he quitted them thus abruptly; but perchance there was more truth in Stackpole's remark than the esquire would have cared to own. The instincts of his birth and breeding—repressed by circumstances and associations—would assert themselves at times, with or without reason. Just now the strident voices, the coarse mirth, and loud blasphemies of the brutal *routiers*, were unutterably distasteful, and the pure, keen air refreshed him more than the wine he had drank. So he paced to and fro, thinking—if the truth must be told—always of Marguerite de Hacquemont. Yet he thought of her, neither with desire of her beauty, nor with the slightest hope of winning her favor; but only with a longing to cast himself at her feet, till he should obtain forgiveness for the great sorrow he had brought upon her—even as he would have craved absolution of a priest for some grave, unshriven sin. It was the very first touch of pure romance in Ralph Brakespeare's life, and the very last that marked it for many a day.

He pursued his solitary walk till the sun was getting low: then he turned into the keep again—hearing but not heeding, voices within the closed doors of the hall—and mounted into the presence-chamber, where he found Lanyon busily engaged in polishing such heavier pieces of armor as the esquire had chosen to lay aside.

After the interchange of a very few words, Ralph sat down in the embrasure of a window looking over the valley of the Dordogne, and fell a-musing once more. His reverie was broken by a voice speaking close to his shoulder.

"A fair prospect, sir esquire," the Lord of Hacquemont said. "I, at least, have never wearied thereof, though I have looked on it nigh threescore years; and Alix, my dame, loved it well, and sat often there till her last sickness waxed sore. That parting was our first real sorrow; and since then, naught has gone aright here. Better had it been for me to have died with younger men at Creçy, than in a chance mellay to have come by such a hurt, as hath turned me into a heavy burden, instead of a prop and defense to mine house. And better had it been for Marguerite, my first-born, to have offered her virginity to God at St. Ursula's altar, than have plighted her faith to the Vicompte de Chastelnaye; albeit my heart was proud enough the day I blessed their betrothal. For knight more perfect never rode out of Limousin; and many notable exploits he wrought before he came to mischance. From a mere youth and ordinary man-at-arms—so his esquire averred—gat he his death-wound; but this have I never wholly credited; no common lance, I warrant it, would have held his own against poor Loys in fair career. But I know not why I trouble you with such matters: rather should I inquire if ye have found sufficient for your needs below? There is no lack of wine in the cellars, and old Réné tells me the larder is indifferently well stored."

Brakespeare had doffed his barret-cap on rising, and stood before the speaker as he would have stood in presence of his king. Only with an effort he constrained himself to answer calmly: for the castellan's last words chimed in unhappily with his own musings.

"I thank your good lordship; there is abundance of all things, and to spare. Rather doth it befit me to ask, if you and those noble demoiselles lack aught that, within the bounds of my duty, may be supplied? Well I trust that your confinement will be brief; and that on the fourth day, at latest, ye will be lightened of our burdensome presence. 'Twill go hard, but Sir Walter Breckenridge will find some fortalice easier to hold than Hacquemont—fair castle though it be."

The castellan smiled gravely.

"We are right well ministered to by Réné, mine ancient esquire, and Gilles, my servitor, who though scarce less infirm than mine own self, are apt enough at such duty. Nay, gentle sir, I must not have you underrate my poor dwelling. There are stronger fortresses, *pardie:* yet, duly victualled and garrisoned, it might withstand a tough siege, even of these new-fangled bombards. 'Tis a quaint old house, too, full of quips and cranks in builders' work. See, now, I will show you one device: it was contrived, doubtless, by some austere ancestor of mine, wishful to check his retainers' mirth if it waxed too wild below."

Speaking thus, the baron pressed the point of his staff on the corner of a large square stone in the center of the presence-chamber, till half its breadth stood up above the floor; revealing an aperture wide enough to admit a broad pair of shoulders.

"Stoop down," the castellan said, lowering his tone. "'Tis somewhat dark now in the hall below, so you will see but dimly. But, if any be talking there, you will hear each whisper, not less distinctly than if you stood by the speaker's shoulder."

More out of courtesy than curiosity, the esquire did as he was bidden. But, before his face had been bent down three seconds, it grew rigid and stern; with a backward gesture of his hand to enforce silence, he began to listen eagerly. This is what he heard:

"Thy counsel savors of the laggard, if not of the craven, Martin Stackpole; nay, pluck not at thy dagger-hilt—I am not so easily frighted as the fat vintner of Bordeaux—but listen. Wherefore should we delay till midnight what may as well be done four hours sooner; and when we can work our pleasure with the strong hand, what cause is there to dally? If thou fearest to trust thy carcase within sword's length of Ralph Brakespeare awake, knowest thou when to find him sleeping on this, his first night of command? And to satisfy thy prudence, shall we sit with our hands folded through the long night-watch, with such plunder and *liesse* near?"

The soft, musical accents contrasted strangely with the voice that broke in, deep and hoarse as the distant bellow of a chafed bull.

"By the beards of the Three Kings, thou wast right, Johann. 'Sweetest bread is quickest baked,' saith our proverb. I am for setting about this gear instantly. *Hagel*, I am waxing meek as a novice for want of a real wild bout. And wine and woman's lips have never so keen a relish, as when men taste them after blood."

"Spoken like Sêr Petronius, of unsaintly memory," Malatesta answered. "Nevertheless, be not over-hasty, my Rhineland Goliath. Bethink thee, that after we have dealt with the esquire, and other one or two English mastiffs, there will be a door—mayhap a strong one—to pass ere we come at the girls and the gold; and oak and iron are not as parchment and glass, even though arms puissant as thine wield lever like a weaver's beam. If those above have time to hang out signal of distress from the keep, and there be daylight for the country-folk to see it, rescue may arise from one quarter or another, and each man may be called to the walls ere dawn. Thou wouldst not have our first free orgie troubled, I trow. Moreover, all our fellows are not so ripe as thee, and me, and honest Martin here; and they will work the best when their veins are fullest: trust me, they shall not lack the spur, if that same can be found in right Gascon wine; after supper, when they have well drunken, I will expound unto them our plan after my poor fashion, and we will to business instantly. Till then, let each go his own way soberly; it is not needful that we three be seen together."

"He speaks well, Berchtold," another voice said. "We had best be guided by him; he hath twice our brains."

So the converse was broken off; and in a few seconds more the hall was empty.

Ralph Brakespeare rose to his feet, with a face perfectly calm, but very set and pale, like that of one who has inhaled some noxious vapor. Taking no note of Lanyon, who approached with open mouth and eyes, he drew the castellan somewhat apart, and told him briefly of the plot hatching below.

Philippe de Hacquemont's courage had ever been unquestioned; and in contempt of peril, while he was able to encounter it, he was surpassed by none of his peers: yet he shook as in an ague fit as he listened.

"My poor girls!" he groaned at last. "Is there no

mercy then in heaven for creatures as pure as its own saints? I vow to Saint Ursula—"

"Your pardon, my lord," Ralph interrupted, plucking him by the sleeve. "We have scant time for counsel, but time enow for prayers. Ye spake anon of the builders' tricks in this castle. Know ye of any whereby man—or better, man and horse—might issue unmarked by any within, till they were fairly beyond the ditch:"

All the martial instincts of the castellan's nature came back at the direct question; he drew himself together like an ancient war-horse at sound of trumpet.

"Of a surety there is such," he said. "In the third stall of the great stable—counting from the right—there is a secret panel, behind which lies a *souterrain*, leading under the castle ditch, and opening at a postern hid in the thickest brushwood, half way down the slope, through which a destrere fully caparisoned may pass. Réné, alone, of all mine household, knows the trick of the spring; and, by God's mercy, he is in attendance here."

"It is, indeed, a blessed chance," Ralph answered, almost reverently. Then he beckoned Lanyon to his side.

"Hark thee hither, Will; and strive to comprehend what thou hearest, for I may expound naught at length. We are in shrewd strait: yon Italian devil hath tampered with our band till—of all I thought true men the morning—I can surely reckon on none save thee. It is their purpose this night to break in here, to plunder, and ravish, and slay. There is a secret issue from the castle; but the noble demoiselles I dare not send forth, even under darkness, lest some loiterer, espying them pass through the courtyard, should give the alarm, and so we and they be set upon at a vantage below. Whilst the door stands yonder they are safe; and, whilst I live, none shall lay hands thereon: the stair is narrow, so that two, mounting abreast, can scarce wield their weapons; and a strong man, fully armed, might hold the platform for a good while against a score. This have I devised. The guards will soon be changed: thou wilt be posted on the north battlements, to which there is access close to the main stable. After seven of the clock, when the rest are set down to supper, René—this good lord's esquire—will come to thee wearing my barret-cap and mantle; he is great of stature, and the masking may pass in the uncertain light: he will unlock the stable, and show thee the outlet. I mind not what beast stands in a certain stall —God send he be strong and speedy; for he may not be changed now without suspicion, nor then without noise, which thou must needs avoid. When thou hast gained the eastward road, ride—I say not as for thy life, but as to save thy soul—till thou come to where Sir John Hawkwood is camped: tell him how we are bestead. The road thou canst not miss; for with such a moon as will be shining then, a boy might track four hundred hoof-prints. Under God's mercy, I have good hope thou wilt bring us aid in time. But if otherwise—"

He crossed himself, lifting his barret-cap from his brow—

"—Then may he assoilzie us all this night, both innocents and sinners. What ails thee, man?" he went on, angrily. "Have thy fool's wits gone wool-gathering, that thou starest on me with such lack-luster eyes?"

The archer's face, indeed, was a picture of sullen bewilderment.

"Fool, indeed," he said, huskily; clutching his brawny throat as though something choked him. "Ah! and I deserve harder names than that, messire, for following faithfully all these years one who sends me forth with a whole skin, while he tarries behind to die. For, naught can save ye but a miracle, I wot: and such are not wrought for landless esquires."

Instead of being touched by his follower's devotion, Ralph's face darkened menacingly.

"I was wrong, then, it seems, in reckoning on thee? It is well. Then Réné shall bear my message, though he seems scarce able for the saddle. But, hearken— when the fray begins, shift for thyself as thou wilt. By the most Holy Rood, thou standest not with me. I had as lieve have traitor at my back as mutineer."

He stopped suddenly, his whole manner changing.

"Nay, nay, I was over-hasty: thine is but a passing humor-fit, and now thou art mine own honest comrade and king's true soldier again. Vex thyself no farther" —the archer had cast himself on his knees, burying his face in the hand that Brakespeare resigned to him for awhile—"but do my bidding heedfully. Should evil befall us here, commend me to Sir John Hawkwood; and tell him that, being in sore perplexity, I acted, according to my poor judgment, as beseemed his honor and mine own; and that well I trust he will never rest till each drop of our blood be avenged. Now stand thou apart: thou goest forth with me anon when I place the guard."

Then Ralph turned to the castellan; who stood by, forgetting his own grievous anxieties, in genuine admiration of the marvelous coolness with which the other met and mastered the situation that had well-nigh paralyzed his own energies.

"Fair lord," he said, "if I have not spoken of bidding your own retainers fight in your defense, it is not that I mistrust their faith or courage. But for the most part they are somewhat aged and war-worn; so, in the front of such as we must mell with to-night, they would be as straw before flame: moreover, weapons and harness could hardly be conveyed to them without giving the alarm; and if half-armed, they must needs be slaughtered like sheep in the shambles. And now it is full time we went about our several tasks; and yours —as well I wot—is far heavier than mine. It beseems not one of my years to give counsel to your wisdom; yet one word I must needs say. For the Holy Virgin's sake, do nothing rashly. All is not lost when I am down; and, when ye least expect it, rescue may be near: there is hope so long as one plank holds fast betwixt you and these ravishers. But, if they be come to the last door, and, looking from the watch-tower ye can discern no sign of help, then, by my mother's honor, sooner would I strike my dagger into the bosom of each noble demoiselle—ay, or cast her with mine own hands from the battlements—than see them fall alive into Gian Malatesta's power."

Each syllable struck on the father's heart like a knell; but his first weakness was past, and he answered steadfastly enough, grasping the esquire's hand in both his own—

"Well hast thou spoken, and wisely. Woe is me, that I can aid thee no more than if I were a bedridden beldame; yet, if I may no longer sway *estoc*, I can still wield *miséricorde*, and it shall do my children the last good office. Would to God, there had been a son born to mine house like unto thee. Wilt thou not tell me the name of him who this night proffers his life more readily for strangers, and enemies to boot, than many would do for their nearest of kin?'"

"Ralph Brakespeare," was the careless answer. "It is of no great repute as yet, and mayhap never will be: but, for such work as we have to do to-night, it may serve as well as a better. And now, my lord, I crave your leave to depart. When I knock thrice on the door at the stairhead, let Réné, I pray you, descend: he shall fasten the last pieces of my heavy armor, ere I send him forth. So, for the present, I bid you farewell: and may the saints send us good deliverance!"

With another cordial hand-pressure, they parted; and Ralph, attended by Lanyon, went forth on his round of duty. Several times during his progress he could not help glancing curiously at certain faces; with a hope of some signs of friendly intelligence, whereby he might have guessed that such an one would fain have warned him of the plot. But none such could he discover; only one man gave him a gruff "good-night:" this was a burly Northumbrian—Miles Swinburne by name—who was posted at the barbican. But Ralph thought within himself that, even if this were not another traitor, he could help but little, and forbore questioning him. Passing through the courtyard on his return—it was now almost dark—he encountered Gian Malatesta.

"I will pray you to take my place at supper to-night," Brakespeare said, "for I am strangely heavy and ill at ease, and have more mind for sleep than meat or drink; also, to go the rounds heedfully an hour before midnight; waking me only if there be cause for alarm. I will to my pallet now, which is laid in the presence-chamber."

All Ralph's rare self-command was needed, to enable him to listen patiently to the Italian's courteous condolence, and smooth assurances that all duty should be exactly performed; but he went his way without betraying himself.

By seven of the clock all who were not on guard were set down to a board plenteously spread, studded, all over with tall *brocs* of wine, that needed only to be plenished from a cask standing hard by. Though almost every man there knew that black deeds were to be wrought that night, never an one ate or drank with appetite less keen, and the mirth soon waxed furious. Hearing this, Brakespeare delayed no longer to give the appointed signal.

The Lord of Hacquemont came down instantly, followed by his squire, the latter bearing lantern, flint, and steel; and silently the two aided Brakespeare to don the last pieces of his armor. In a cautious whisper Réné received his last instructions—he was to tarry at the outer postern till the rescue arrived: then, putting on the disguise aforementioned, the old man stole down the turret stair, and passed into the courtyard unobserved. For several minutes the other two listened; holding their breath till they knew of a certainty that Réné and Lanyon must be safe within the stable, when, in mute thanksgiving, their eyes met.

Then Brakespeare—fully accoutered but for his helmet—knelt reverently before the castellan. In the dim light of the *mortier* they made a very striking group: such pictures have been painted of the Eve of Knighthood, when the neophyte takes leave of his sire before his first vigil in arms.

"Fair lord," the Englishman said, "whether we shall meet again, lieth in God's hand. Lo! here I crave of you your blessing; and, if mine hand hath unwittingly done to death aforetime any dear friend or kinsman of yours, whether we live or die, let there be no enmity betwixt us henceforth forever."

Only Heaven heard the low solemn whisper that passed Philippe de Hacquemont's lips as he bent forward, laying both hands on the other's shoulders; but Ralph felt two big heavy tears, such as are wrung only from the agony of age, drip on his upturned brow. The next instant the castellan had turned abruptly away, as if afraid to trust himself longer, and Ralph was alone in the presence-chamber.

CHAPTER XXI.

AGAINST ODDS.

Bracing his bascinet carefully on, but keeping the vizor up, Brakespeare betook himself to his post of watch. Certain channels were so cunningly pierced in the great stone rose, which formed the center-point of the groined ceiling of the hall, that the minutest feature of the scene below—lighted as it was by several torches—was as easy to distinguish as the faintest sound.

Every man at the long board was fully armed after his own fashion, save that some had laid their head-pieces aside; and the carouse went on, without stint or stay, with a discordant hubbub of talk, broken by bursts of coarse laughter; while each evil face grew eviller to look upon, as it waxed flushed and swollen with drink. The feast was far into its second hour; and Ralph, grown weary of constant espial, only vouchsafed occasional glances below; when Gian Malatesta —sitting in the place of honor betwixt Martin Stackpole and Berchtold, the German—thought the ripe season had come. So, smiting on the table with a flagon to still the uproar, he spoke somewhat as follows:

"Gentle my comrades all; well I deem that to none here present my words will seem strange; for none here but hath cause to quarrel with the fashion in which matters have been ruled of late, and desires to see them amended. Here are four years wasted, wherein we have been forced to live on the bare pittance of our pay; reaping none of those profits and privileges that men of our merit may fairly look for, when carrying on warfare in an alien country. Whether the knight we follow lacks the courage, or the wit, to lead his company aright, matters but little; I am aweary of his service; and so, I wot, are ye all. And is it not enough to endure his discipline, without brooking the insolence of his favorite, who lords it over us worse than his master? Did he not report Martin Stackpole here, for drawing dagger in pure sport on a rascally taverner; and honest Berchtold, for making rough love to a serving-wench, till the knight chid sharply—ay, and threatened with the bastonnade—gallants better born than he or his beggarly esquire? Yet do we deserve all this—yea, that the veriest drudge should laugh us to scorn—if we let slip the chance that Fortune hath given us to-night of making ourselves amends. Besides plate, jewels, and apparel, there is coin enow hoarded in this castle, I will be sworn, to make every man of us rich; for the wine, ye yourselves can speak; and are not the faces that looked forth on us this morning —to say naught of bower-women and handmaidens— fair enough to furnish forth an orgie? When we have wrought our pleasure here, we need but to set forth with our booty, and find safety in a short day's ride; within that distance, as I have certain knowledge, bides stout John Bacon, with a puissant armament. If they have a captain to their mind, what matters it under what king free lances serve? For the hoards I spake of, fear not that we find them: if the baron himself be stubborn, some of his household will prove more manageable; for I have persuasions that would make the dumb to speak. Now, if any of you think that ye owe aught to the brain that hath planned all this gay pastime, grant me, I pray you, the first wooing of the pale girl who stood at the window alone. She is less buxom than her sisters, I trow; nathless, she suits my fancy."

The smooth, round periods tickled their ears, even as some new, delicate flavor might have tickled their palates; they shouted uproarious applause, as they swore, with grisly oaths, that he should have his will; and drank, with hideous jests, to the betrothal. And the listener above felt a hot tingling through the marrow of his bones; while the tough sinews and knotted muscles of his right arm, on which he leaned, swelled out as though they would have burst the mail.

"Ten thousand thanks," the Italian went on, bowing low in mock deference. "I am emboldened by your bounty to ask yet another grace. In dealing with Ralph Brakespeare, aim, I pray you, at disabling him; but spare his life, if it be possible. Lo! here I promise all my share of the coined money to whoso shall deliver him alive into mine hands."

A derisive murmur ran round the table; and Stackpole said, gruffly—

"Hath Sathanas turned saint, that Malatesta preaches mercy?"

The other laughed a little low laugh, as sweet as silver; while he sleeked his glossy mustache with his white fingers—he had drawn off his steel gloves when he sat down.

"Impute not such virtue to a sinner like me, *camarado mio:* I would not have him live; but I would see him die leisurely—after mine own fashion—and not till I have mocked my fill."

The unearthly malignity of the words struck even the drunken ruffians who heard them with a kind of disgust; and there was a pause, while each looked rather blankly on his fellow.

And all the while, right over the bandit's head, there lowered down on him a face, feller and fiercer than his own—the face of the man he doomed.

The silence was broken by Berchtold's hoarse, bellowing tones.

"We might have known thee better, Johann. *Hagel!* an' that be all, we may suit thy fancy even here. If once I get within arm's length of the younker, I will bear him where thou wilt, with no more harm than a rough squeeze. See thou shrink not from thy bargain."

"See thou claim it," Malatesta answered, gibingly. "Puissant is thy hug, my bear of Boppart; but never yet hast thou grappled with so tough a morsel of man's flesh. Now 'tis time we were at work. If I break our revel, my jovial mates, 'tis but that we may fall to later with a heartier good-will. There are two must be dealt with, ere we come to the esquire: Lanyon on the north battlements, and yon other in the barbican. Who will charge himself with these small matters? Let two go on either errand, though one might suffice; for a mace-blow from behind will settle all quickly."

Before any could reply, Ralph had risen to his feet. Not even in that moment of supreme peril had he ever a thought of leaving to his fate, unwarned, the one honest man in that nest of traitors: he only now repented himself of not having trusted him more entirely. He moved swiftly to the window looking toward the barbican, and his stern voice clave the still night air startlingly—

"Swinburne! Miles Swinburne! There is treachery, and I cannot aid thee. Cast thyself into the moat, and flee: 'tis thy last chance for life."

There was uproar among the bandits below, as if an enemy had broken in unawares; and all, catching up their weapons, streamed pellmell into the courtyard. And the trembling girls above clustered closer round the crucifix foot, with smothered screams and moans; and Marguerite de Hacquemont's pale face waxed whiter yet; while her father, after a few muttered words of encouragement, and a whisper to an ancient servitor, went down to his post just within the door. And Ralph Brakespeare, as he pushed the raised flagstone back to its place in the flooring with his heel, locked his vizor deliberately, and mounted the platform of the stair; carrying with him the lighted *mortier*, which he fixed in a nook in the wall. Then, after crossing himself thrice devoutly, he waited patiently for what should ensue; with his great *épée d'armes* drawn, and his mace laid ready to his hand: he would cumber himself with no shield.

For some minutes the turmoil went on below. What had happened in the barbican Ralph could not divine; but, from certain cries of wrath and disappointment, he guessed that Lanyon's escape had been discovered. Soon they all came trooping back again, and feet clattered through the presence-chamber; and the next instant, the narrow stair was thronged with armed men, some of the rearmost bearing torches.

Right in front of the rush was Berchtold of Boppart —his coarse features ablaze with drink and distorted with passion—swaying a massive iron lever, such as was used for bending trebuchets; while a savage grin on his thick lips made the whole expression of his face rather bestial than human. He came on recklessly, with lowered head; intending to drop his crowbar, and grapple. But, the instant he was within fair distance, Ralph's heavy blade came down on the left side of the giant's gorget; griding sheer through plate, and mail, and bone, till it bit deep into the right shoulder; so that the huge corpse fell back almost headless among the startled crowd. Startled—for, though every man there had taken and given good store of hard blows, none had ever looked on so stark a sword-stroke.

During the slight confusion that ensued, and while those in front were freeing themselves of their ghastly cumbrance, Brakespeare's voice was heard. He had no hope of its being listened to; but he knew that every minute was worth a diamond; and was too cool to throw the slightest chance away.

"Hearken," he said, "all ye, whom I thought true and loyal men this morning. Ye may yet 'scape the gallows, an' ye will be guided by me. I know the arch-traitors among ye: one hath paid forfeit already. If ye now retire, and presently deliver bound into mine hands Gian Malatesta and Martin Stackpole, I will engage, on Sir John Hawkwood's behalf, that the rest of ye shall be free to go and seek other service where ye will. Otherwise—"

Over the roar of derision that resounded through the vaulted staircase, could be distinguished the Italian's silvery tones. Yet not he, but another, thrust his way to the front, sword in hand. Then Ralph Brakespeare laughed in his turn, loud and scornfully—

"Ha! honest Martin. Art thou, too, so greedy of thy Judas wages?" And the combat began.

The issue seemed at first very doubtful; Stackpole was strong and subtle of frame, and noted for skill with his weapon; he was clad, too, in harness of proof, and held his own gallantly, despite the disadvantage of ground. But Ralph had reason good for protracting the struggle; and it might have lasted longer, had he not feared straining his muscles by overlong swordplay. At length his arm appeared to sink wearily; deluded by the feint, the other lunged with all his might at the weakest point in his adversary's harness —the upper rim of the throat-piece; a swift motion of Brakespeare's head caused the thrust to glance aside; the next instant a hoarse yell woke up the echoes, and Stackpole fell back, pierced through eye and brain though the bars of his vizor.

For very shame, Gian Malatesta could no longer forbear coming to the front. It was not exactly cowardice that had hitherto kept him in the background; but he ever liked to see others doing his work; moreover, the superstition before alluded to, made him disinclined to pit himself single-handed against the esquire. Now no choice was left him; so, spurning aside the corpse of his comrade, still quivering in the death-pang, he planted himself fairly before his enemy.

"*Corpo di Venere!*" the Italian said, in a slow, suppressed tone. "So we two must play out the play, that yonder bungler began. Thou art at thy old knight-errant's trade; only, flying at higher game than when thou didst buckler the tymbestere. 'Tis my turn now. I play not my life against thine: if, after essaying thee, I prevail not, we will ply arbalest, till thou fallest down there maimed—not slain outright. Die thou shalt not, till—bound hand and foot—thou hast seen how Gian Malatesta can love, and felt how he can hate."

Lest it should seem unnatural that in such a crisis there should be dallying with words, it should be remembered that—if the chronicles of the time speak sooth—men, even in the hottest engagements, found leisure to make orations worthy of being recorded. And furthermore, up to a much later period, the Italians were specially prone to prelude their duels with similar taunts; either intending to envenom their own wrath, or to goad their adversaries into rashness. If, for the very first time since the peril began, Brakespeare's voice shook a little, it surely was not with fear.

"Sêr Malatesta," he said, "for one thing do I render thanks to God: whether I die or live, this night earth must needs be rid of thee. What ailed thy curtal-ax, that it struck not home on Calais causeway? Now, with murder, and ravishment, and cogging of dice, thou hast well-nigh done: for the Devil himself, whom thou

"AND THE NEXT INSTANT THE NARROW STAIR WAS THRONGED WITH ARMED MEN."

servest, will not pluck thee out of Hawkwood's hands. As I hope for Heaven's mercy, so do I believe, within short space, that glib tongue of thine will be raven's food."

Such an involuntary shiver ran through Malatesta's veins, as men are said to feel when others walk over their graves; but he braced himself with an effort; and, muttering a curse on his own folly, attacked Ralph fiercely.

Once again the combat was obstinately protracted; for, if Stackpole were a skilful swordsman, Malatesta was a perfect master of his weapon, and came fresh to its use; while Ralph—though in stature and strength he had decided advantage—was beginning to feel the long strain on his sword-arm. Conscious of this, the esquire determined to risk somewhat to rid himself speedily of his most dangerous foe; so, watching his opportunity, he brought his great *épée d'armes* down, with a swing that must have carried all before it. But the lithe Italian dived down; avoiding the blow so that it swept harmlessly over his shoulder; and the blade, striking full on the stone pillar of the stairway, shivered nearly to the hilt. With a shrill cry of triumph, Malatesta sprang up to press his advantage; but while the cry was still on his lips, the truncheon of steel, hurled with Brakespeare's full force, struck him betwixt the brows; and, losing his footing, he staggered back, stunned and bleeding, into the arms of his followers.

Again the crowd swayed to and fro, discomfited; while the dusky, red glare of the torches cast weird effects of light and shade on the rugged faces working with rage and fear; on the corpses wallowing in their blood; and on the single figure that towered still in its pride of place—erect, unwounded, victorious. Some called for arbalests; others—these of the rearmost— cried shame, on a score being held at bay by one; bidding their fellows in front "Make in," and drag their enemy down by sheer force of numbers. But none cared to trust himself fairly within the sweep of the ponderous mace that Brakespeare brandished, lightly as a riding-wand: moreover, while the Italian was down, the assailants lacked a leader.

After awhile there was a stir in the heart of the throng. Gian Malatesta had recovered his feet, and his senses too; for, evidently in obedience to his order, two men-at-arms advanced abreast, and engaged Brakespeare, thrusting and foining with their long swords; more, it seemed, with purpose of wearying, than of seriously harming him; since neither of them attempted to close. With no great exertion of strength or skill, the esquire parried the double assault; catching the blades on the head or steel handle of his mace, or dashing them aside with a dexterous *moulinet*. But thus his attention was, perforce, entirely engaged; and he never dreamed of fresh danger, till he felt a sharp pang, and a hot gush of blood down the under part of the thigh, where *cuir bouilli* replaced the upper plates of the cuissard.

That felon stroke came from no other than Malatesta. Creeping up, unobserved, behind his fellows, he had leveled a sidelong thrust, with a short, sharp-bladed spear, by which his foe must certainly have been hamstrung, had not a sudden forward movement of Brakespeare's left knee caused the steel to strike some inches above where it was aimed; so that, instead of severing the tendon, it only sank deep into the brawn of the thigh: nevertheless, the hurt was very sore. The Italian knew this as he withdrew the reeking weapon, crying, exultingly, "*Toccato!*"

And Ralph Brakespeare knew it too, as groaning—not in bodily pain, but in bitterness of heart—he leaned heavily against the door at his back. He knew that it could be only a question of moments now, than mere loss of blood would soon render him weaker than the weakest of the frail things he had tried to defend; and that rescue would, after all, come too late. It was not that he shrank from death—*that* he had been ready to meet any day these eight years past—but it may be he thought it hard to die just now, after achieving a feat of arms that must needs have made him famous, had other witnesses been left thereof besides the corpses yonder: keenest regret of all—the good fight had been fought utterly in vain.

From his post within-side the door, Philippe de Hacquemont heard the groan, and guessed that no light cause had drawn it forth. His voice was hollow and full of anguish, as it sounded close to Ralph's ear.

"Ah! woe is me, my son; art thou sped? Then am I too long here; for I have black work to do above. Fare thee well. May God receive our souls, and requite thee in heaven!"

Hastily Ralph made answer; turning his head aside, so that only the castellan should hear.

"Nay, my lord, be not over-hasty. I am sore hurt;

but not so sore but that I can strike another good blow yet; and help may be nearer than we wot of."

He spoke quite calmly; yet, each moment, he was possessed more and more by that somber fury, which made the old Bersekyr never more dangerous than when they had gotten their death-wound; it braced his slackened sinews, coursing hotly through his veins, and driving the sick faintness before it; his fingers gripped the mace handle, as though they would have sunk into the steel; and he gathered himself together for one last plunge into the midst of the assassins, who who still stood aloof, though their work was more than half done. But first he would have one draught of air albeit it was heavy with the smoke of torches and the foul reek of blood: so he cast back his vizor. Passion, even more than exhaustion, had made his face deathly pale; and it was marked, withal, with such a terrible menace, that those who stood nearest shrank back appalled; even as they might have shrunk from one of those armed specters of which ancient legends tell.

At that very instant, when Brakespeare's right foot was planted forward for the spring, there rang out from above a long shriek; such an one as, whether it spring from overwhelming joy or crushing sorrow, can only issue once in a lifetime from any woman's lips; and then, near and clear, a sound familiar to both assailants and assailed, each second waxing nearer and clearer—the war-note of John Hawkwood's trumpet.

There was tumult and uproar on the narrow stair, as the assailants crushed and trampled on each other in eagerness to flee; bearing in the midst of them Gian Malatesta, who struggled furiously to get clear, that he might deal one finishing stroke on his enemy, well-nigh helpless now; for a strong reaction unstrung Ralph's limbs once more, and he sank back half swooning. As the bandits issued into the outer air, a column of armed men streamed out of the stable-door into the moonlight; at the head of whom came a knight, with his vizor up, bearing in his hand a sheathed sword. And a voice, steady and passionless, as though it had commanded some ordinary martial exercise, spoke:

"Hew me down all that carrion: but Gian Malatesta —him with the bright Milan helmet—I charge ye bring to me alive."

It was rather an execution than a combat; for the conscience-stricken mutineers made scarce a semblance of defense: only the Italian fought like a wolf, till he was borne to the ground, and bound securely with a halter. Hawkwood stayed not to watch the performance of his order; but passed straight into the keep, and on through the presence-chamber, picking up a torch that a mutineer had cast away; and so up the steps slippery with blood, till he came to the door athwart which Brakespeare lay in his swoon, as though he would have guarded the threshold to the last. Almost at the same instant it was opened from within by the old castellan. The knight smote his breast with his gantleted hand, till the corslet rang again.

"I have sinned more grievously than I wist of; else, had I been spared the shame of coming thus late."

And stooping, he lifted on his knee the white set face, gazing down on it with real remorse on his own. But Philippe de Hacquemont—who, since he became disabled for arms, had beguiled his leisure by study of chirurgery, till he acquired no mean skill therein—was better able to distinguish betwixt swoon and death.

"Nay, my lord," he said, "things are not come to such a pass. He spake to me right stoutly some few minutes agone. If he have no worse hurt than yon thigh-wound, by God's grace, he shall do well yet. Bind your sword-belt, I pray you, as tightly as you may above the wound whilst I loosen his gorget, and cause him to breathe this essence. See you, now," he went on, after a pause, "the blood is stanching fast, and his lips are no longer so wan. Have him borne so soon as may be, to our chamber above: there he shall be tended as if he were my first-born son."

CHAPTER XXII.

BREATHING-TIME.

LANYON, being on all subjects a man of one idea, was singularly so on the point of duty. Albeit not less anxious than Hawkwood himself, concerning Brakespeare's well or ill-faring, it never occurred to him to look after his master above, while there was work for him to do below. So he cast himself into the mellay with a will, laying about him lustily: he it was, indeed, who actually pinioned Malatesta, and held him down till halters were brought. The Italian gnashed his teeth once, when he saw who it was that thus roughly entreated him; but spake never a word. After awhile Hawkwood came down, and bade Lanyon take three or four with him, who should bear the esquire to the upper chamber of the keep, and cleanse away the traces of combat. Then he beckoned to those who held Malatesta to draw near.

The fastenings of the Italian's helmet had burst in the struggle; and, as he stood bareheaded before his judge, the full moonbeams lighted up the statuesque beauty of his features, already subsiding after the storm of passion into their cynical languor. He knew very well that his doom was sealed: it would have been less idle to look for water in a roadside flint, than for mercy in Hawkwood's face, even before his low bitter tones broke the stillness.

"Gian Malatesta, with what black unshriven sins thy miserable soul hath been laden afore-time, I care not to inquire. One thing I know: of every drop of the blood shed here this night, thou art guilty, in God's sight and mine. Never an one of these"—he glanced at the corpses strewn around, some scarcely still after the death-convulsion—"would have had wit to devise what was easy enow to thy devil's brain. Dullard and wittol am I, to have been hoodwinked by thee thus long. Better had I mixed poison in their every morning draught for those poor knaves, than have trusted thee in their company. But I waste words on thee; thou didst set thy life wittingly on this last hazard, and, having lost, shalt pay speedily. Nevertheless, I may not, as Christian knight, slay soul as well as body. There is a priest, doubtless, within summons; and for shrift, thou shalt have one hour's grace."

The Italian laughed out insolently.

"I thank your saintly worship: of such grace will I none. Even he of Avignon, though they say he holds the keys of heaven and hell, would scarce absolve me if I made confession fair and full. An' monks' tales be true, the Devil will soon have his own; and I care not to vex my master needlessly. I have served him well, and had served him better to-night, if ye had not come to spoil all. Yet what rare sport have I had in my time. *Ohimé!* When I think—"

Over his countenance there stole a pensive expression of half tender regret; such as might become some man of blameless life, recalling the innocence of his childhood or youth.

There was something so ghastly and unnatural in

the covert exultation, that those who stood near—almost strangers to him for the most part—shrank from the hardened blasphemer.

Hawkwood broke in—

"Enough of this: thy blood be upon thine own head. Have him away instantly. Curzon, thou knowest how to deal with him; I gave thee charge concerning this as we rode hither."

"Stay yet an instant," said Malatesta, eagerly, as they were about to lead him off. "It cannot harm ye to answer me one question. Doth Ralph Brakespeare live?"

"Ay, and is likely to live," the knight retorted, with a grim smile. "Otherwise the penance, that thou shall abye presently, had been light compared to that thou shouldst have suffered at mine hands."

Malatesta struck his armed heel on the pavement, till fire flew from the stones.

"I might have guessed it," he muttered. "His star again—his star. On with ye as quickly as ye will. A cadet of Malatesta might well ask for silken cord; but hemp will serve my turn. Hanging, I have heard, is no hard death; at least, so said the half-strangled Zingaro, who cursed us so soon as he could speak, for cutting him down."

Once again the eyes of the two met under the moon.

In the cold cruelty of Hawkwood's glance, there was that which, despite his bravado, real or assumed, made the doomed man shiver.

"Thou knowest many things, good and evil, Gian Malatesta; but, I think, thou knowest not altogether how traitors and suborners die."

Turning without another word, the knight went again into the keep.

If Malatesta's life had been foul and shameful, not less so was his end; worthy indeed of an age barbarous, especially in its punishments. His right hand and tongue, severed while he was yet alive, were nailed against the oak, on which, for many a day after, foul birds of prey held carnival. And so Ralph Brakespeare's ominous words found speedy and terrible fulfilment.

On the third day, Sir Walter Breckenridge came again to Hacquemont with his company, purposing to occupy it with a sufficient force, for he had found no other fortress so much to his mind. But, hearing all that had been attempted there, he was greatly incensed and grieved; and resolved to make such amends as lay in his power—punishment being taken out of his hands —for an outrage, which, if consummated, would have left a blot on his own escutcheon. So, after some friendly conference, Breckenridge consented to withdraw his forces, leaving the castle and everything therein as he had found it; taking the baron's *parole* for ransom of two thousand silver crowns to be paid ere Whitsuntide. Then the English captain set forth on his return to Bordeaux, gathering good store of supplies by the way. He expected little thanks or praise from Ralph of Stafford, who, he knew, had looked for graver results from such an expedition than the harrying of some score or two of homesteads. But the Earl was a chivalrous noble, though a hot partisan; and, having heard the causes of his lieutenant's moderation, averred that all had been well and knightly done.

Sorely discontented was John Hawkwood, as he rode

westward with the rest. He did not repent, truly, of his summary justice. Nevertheless, it left his pennon shorn, for the moment, of immediate following; and his late severity—though none could say it was sterner than discipline demanded—was scarce likely to attract recruits. Also, he was still in no small anxiety concerning his esquire; whom, perforce, he had left at Hacquemont, with Lanyon to attend him. For, soon after Ralph revived from his long swoon, fever ensued; and, for days after Sir John's departure, he hovered betwixt life and death. But the Baron of Hacquemont was no unskilful or careless leech, and his simple remedies were helped by the strong constitution and rare physical energies of the patient. So, one morning, Brakespeare woke from a deep sleep—too weak to stir, but with head cool and senses clear—so clear, that he seemed to guess at once that all had gone well, and for awhile forbore speaking. It was characteristic of the man, and his thorough soldierly instincts, that his first question related to Miles Swinburne. Lanyon answered it in his own plain fashion—

"We found him under the arch of the gate-tower, with his skull crushed like a hazel-nut. It was no light hand bestowed that buffet; and just such an one might have been dealt by the crowbar that we had work to pluck out of big Berchtold's stiff fingers."

"It grieves me that I might not save him," Ralph said; the more so, that in thought I partly did him wrong. I did essay to warn him; but, mayhap, did rather harm than good: he was of the right bulldog breed, that ever runs toward, instead of from, the danger. If I live, I will not fail to see masses sung for his soul. And with yon traitorous scum, how fared it? 'Twere shame if one 'scaped; for they were fairly trapped, I trow."

"Trouble not yourself concerning that, messire," the other answered, chuckling hoarsely. "The most of them had short and sharp shrift. Sir John bade hew all down where they stood, save one; and, I warrant you, we did not the work negligently. That one—your worship guesses who I mean—fared not much better, when his turn came. From the window of this chamber ye can see the topmost branches of the oak, whereon hangs all of Gian Malatesta that gleds and hooded crows see fit to leave; with his tongue and right hand nailed on either side. By St. Giles! 'tis a gruesome sight, and one scarce fit for the eyes of demoiselles to look upon; wherefore the knave met with his deserts just without ken from the castle."

Ralph Brakespeare was stubborn in hatred, as loyal in friendship; and his simple religion enabled him not to mutter one prayer for the weal of his dead enemy.

Here entered the castellan, to relieve the archer on his watch, and to enjoin silence. Indeed, it was not till long after that the patient heard, one by one, all the adventures of that night—how Lanyon's horse had fallen exhausted just within the light of the English campfires; how Hawkwood had leaped to saddle before the tale was half told, and would scarce tarry till twoscore lances were ready to follow; how he had spurred forward through the moonlight, groaning ever and anon, as though in sore pain; and rarely turning his head, though man after man dropped behind, till out of twoscore scarce half drew rein together under Hacquemont mound ; and how Sir John uttered loud and devout thanksgiving when the first clash of arms from within told him it was not yet too late for his trumpet to sound the charge. In Brakespeare's troubled life there had been singularly little of quiet happiness—nothing, certainly, compared to what encompassed him during his slow, steady convalescence. Not the kind old castellan alone, but others in whose behalf he had done his devoir, sought in all ways to do honor to their defender ; white hands were always ready to arrange fresh spring flowers in Ralph's chamber, or to strike on lute or gittern for his pleasure ; and Odille, the Baron's younger daughter—a brilliant brunette of seventeen—would sit by his couch for hours, reading in her low, sweet voice some quaint romaunt or *chronique d'amour*. But more welcome than all this gentle tendance were the visits of one who never sang or touched lute, and who, speaking but little, seldom smiled. Ralph never rested so well as when his pillow had been smoothed by Marguerite de Hacquemont ; and her whispered " Good-night " was a better anodyne than all the songs wherewith the others sought to lull him to sleep. Yet, with all this liking for her society, there mingled not the faintest spark of love : he looked upon the pale girl with no earthly passion, but much as he might have looked on a picture of some beautiful Saint, who won her crown of martyrdom ages agone, in days of Paganrie ; and there ever possessed him that same vague longing to be assoilzied by her of his blood-guiltiness, that he had felt when first he saw her face.

One afternoon, when they chanced to be alone, the

esquire took heart of grace, and faltered out his confession. As Marguerite heard that to the man lying there she owed the barrenness and desolation of her life, she could not repress a shudder and a backward movement of aversion. Brakespeare saw it and covered his face.

" I might have guessed it," he said ; " better had I held my peace. Could I hope to be forgiven ? "

But the true, womanly instinct—purified, not hardened, by long trial—asserted itself as she drew closer to his side than she had ever yet done : leaning over him while she spoke.

" Mine own true knight, before—by Heaven's will, and in fair fight, as I have heard—he went down before your spear, overthrew enemies not a few ; and to never a one of these did he deny mercy, or fair terms of grace. The Holy Virgin forbid, that I show myself harder of heart than he ! Moreover, if my thanks can profit thee, thou hast them by right. Loys de Chastelnaye himself, had he lived, could not have stood forth more gallantly, in fence of the helpless and innocent, than didst thou. May God increase thee in prosperity and honor. Henceforth there is amity between us—by this same token."

Stooping yet lower, she let fall a kiss, cold and light as a snowflake, on his brow.

" Nay, thank me not," she went on, rather more quickly. " I speak only as becomes a Christian maiden. Also, suffer me to depart for a little while : I will to mine oratory ; for never had I sorer need of prayer."

On that subject neither ever opened their lips again ; but Ralph felt lightened of the heavy burden ; and his amendment from that hour was marvelously rapid.

Soon he began to savor that great delight, that none save the sick athlete can thoroughly appreciate—the delight from which perchance the blind Agonistes was not wholly exempt—the delight of returning strength. Ere long, leaning on a crutch, and on Lanyon's brawny shoulder, he contrived to creep into the open air; and a fortnight later, even Philippe of Hacquemont—careful as he was of his patient, and loth to lose him—was fain to confess that the other, with due precautions, might safely take the saddle. He himself had been busy all this while in getting together his ransom; and, when the tale was complete, chose not to delay forwarding it. So, one May morning, there mustered in the courtyard—if not a gallant escort—at least one sufficient to guard the treasure from all petty marauders. And Ralph Brakespeare was fain to bid adieu to Hacquemont.

Odille's bright black eyes were brimful of tears; and the stately Marguerite looked graver than usual, as she hung a slender gold cross and chain round the esquire's neck, praying that it might keep him from sin and harm. But the heaviest heart there was the old castellan's. After Ralph had mounted, the baron held his hand fast betwixt both his own, gazing up into his face with wistful eyes.

"I know not why I am thus foolish," he said, trying to smile; "but hadst thou been born in my house, I were not more loth to let thee go. Yet withal, it glads me to see thee in harness, and once more on the fair road to honor. Only remember this. Shouldst thou grow aweary of warfare, be it soon or late, come back, and make thy home at Hacquemont, if I be alive, I swear by the blessed Saint Ursula thou shalt be thenceforth unto me as my own son."

Ralph clasped his vizor sharply: he was still young enough to be ashamed of showing womanish weakness in woman's presence; so his thanks and farewells were almost lost in his helmet. The next moment his voice rang out sonorous and clear, as he gave the word to march. But they had ridden almost beyond sight of Hacquemont keep, before the air and exercise, for which he had pined so long, braced his spirits to their wonted tone.

They came to Bordeaux in due course, without encountering any adventure, good or evil, by the way. There Ralph received hearty welcome—not from Hawkwood alone, but from other captains also, to whom his prowess had been made known. The Lord of Stafford himself desired to see the strong soldier, who had slain outright two redoubtable swordsmen, and kept near a score of desperate *soudards* at bay. Once again, had he been so minded, the esquire had chance of taking service in the household of a great noble; and once again he courteously put aside all such offers of advancement. Indeed, he was hardly prevailed upon by Breckenridge to accept the twentieth part of the ransom; which, but for him, the Baron of Hacquemont had assuredly never lived to pay. Throughout the English host the exploit was more than a nine days' wonder. When Ralph walked abroad, the camp-followers gathered round him with such a flutter of half-timid curiosity as you may see excited in a modern crowd, when a champion of the prize-ring passes through their midst: even the veteran men-at-arms looked on him with a certain deference; and prophesied to each other that, at no very distant time, Brakespeare's name would be found among a fresh batch of new-made knights.

Ere long the aspect of things was changed in Guienne; for King Edward—seeking to turn to account the endless broils betwixt France and Navarre—sent his son to take command in the south, while he himself once more appeared on the battle-ground of Picardy. So, early in the summer, the Black Prince sailed into the Gironde; and there swarmed to his standard lances and archers, till in October he set forth eastward at the head of a mighty armament. Right though Gascony and the heart of Languedoc he held forward, till his tents were pitched within sight of the Mediterranean, leaving all desolate behind him: for despite the humanity and gentleness so belauded by chroniclers, none made havoc more thoroughly than that famous mirror of chivalry. None were so bold as to cross his path; though the Lords of Armagnac, Bourdon, Foix, and Clermont, with many other famous knights, garrisoned the country—outnumbering the invader with their spears. All these tarried in their entrenchments, and gave no sign while the English banners flaunted over the smoking suburbs of Carcassonne and Narbonne. Before winter closed in, the Prince had brought safe into Bordeaux as many prisoners, and as much plunder, as he chose to cumber himself with.

In the following spring, troubles on the Scots border recalled King Edward to his own realm; but none the less was France harassed by his captains; for Lancaster, landing at Coutantin, joined forces with Duke

Philip of Navarre (King Charles was then in close prison), and the two ceased not to ravage all the Normandy sea-coast.

When news of this came to Bordeaux, the Black Prince would remain idle no longer; but set forth with two thousand lances and six thousand archers on another huge foray through Limousin, La Marche, Auvergne, and Berry; purposing to push forward till he met his cousin Lancaster in Normandy. Working their will on the country, as they had done aforetime, the English marched on without let or hindrance, till Vierzon was stormed, and three famous barons of France had rendered themselves to Edward's mercy, and the walls of Romorantin could hold out no longer against the battering-engines and showers of Greek fire. But no farther dared the invaders advance; for here they had certain news that the misery of his unhappy subjects, the waste of his realm, and the damage of his honor, had at last fairly roused King John, who was even then marching down from Chartres, with an army more than sufficient to encompass and crush his enemy. The Black Prince was too great a captain to press daring to foolhardiness; so he wheeled in his tracks at once, and turned to the southwest, intending to waste Poitou on his return, as he had wasted all the country betwixt the Garonne and Loire.

But this was not so to be. Many times before, and since, have men come to honor unwillingly or unawares; but seldom, surely, hath such good chance befallen soldier, as that which suffered Edward not to pass on his way in peace. King John, in the eagerness of his wrath and the confidence of his power, had made better speed than could have been reckoned on. Day by day, unknown to each other, the distance was lessened betwixt the armies; till, on the seventeenth day of September, Eustace de Ribeaumont and his scouts, riding through the wooded heaths on the banks of Vienne, came suddenly on the English rear-guard.

That same night the Black Prince knew that he was fairly in the toils; and must needs give battle, at such disadvantage of arms as hath seldom been recorded—since the three hundred held Thermopylæ against the hordes of the Persians.

CHAPTER XXIII.

AT BAY.

There are histories—very trite and old—of which the world does not easily grow weary; and the chiefest among such, are those which record how the stronger battalions were forced to humble themselves before the aristarchy of disciplined valor. Wherefore, it may be well worth while to look back, and see what was a-doing around Poitiers on a certain Sabbath morning, five hundred years agone.

More than a league afield, from within ten furlongs of the city gates, stretched the French encampment. Never since Philippe of Valois marched out of Amiens to raise Calais leaguer, had so gallant a host mustered under the Fleur-de-lis; far and wide around the Royal standard—like forest-trees around the tall king-oak—were reared the banners of puissant crown-vassals, and pennons uncounted; and when the forces were set in battle-array that morning, John the Good reviewed twenty thousand lances, and twice that number of meaner degree.

About two miles from the French lines the Black Prince had entrenched himself; taking—as behooved so wise a captain—all possible vantage of ground, which rose thereabouts into a steep acclivity, clothed toward the lower part with brushwood and vineyards, to which there was but one access—a deep narrow lane. In truth, though the quarry was fairly harbored, certain skilful hunters deemed that it might be neither safe nor easy to force him in his lair; and even King John was not so overweening in his confidence as wholly to slight Eustace de Ribeaumont's warning. After careful espial, thus spoke the valiant knight, who won the palm of valor on Calais causeway:

"Sire, we have observed the English; and they may amount to nigh two thousand men-at-arms, four thousand archers, and fifteen hundred footmen; so can they scarce muster more than one battalion. Nevertheless, they have posted themselves strongly and warily. The single road for attack lies through a lane so straight that scarcely can four ride through it abreast; and the hedges on either hand are lined with their archers. At the end of this, amidst vines and thorns, where no horsemen may keep order, are posted their men-at-arms on foot; before these again is drawn up a great body of their archers in shape of a harrow; so that it will be no easy matter to come at them."

King John's brows were overcast. He was none of those who can bear thwarting or disappointment meekly; but he could not choose but hearken, and farther constrained himself to ask counsel from his trusty captain. Thus De Ribeaumont made answer—

"Sire, if ye be ruled by me, ye will attack on foot; sending forward before your vanguard some three hundred choice *gens d'armes*, excellently mounted, who shall break, if it be possible, the body of archers whereof I spake. Then shall your main battalion advance; and coming hand to hand with the English, give the best account of them they may. Such is my poor counsel; and if any man know a shrewder, let him speak it forth in God's name."

The King answered—" Thus shall it be." And then, calling to his marshals, John of Clermont and Arnold D'Andreghen, began after the aforesaid fashion to set the battle in array.

But it was Heaven's will that the unlucky monarch should not be spared a single sorrow in the after-time. Keenest surely of all the torments that beset the ruined gamester, is the remembrance that the heavy stake lay once utterly at his mercy; had he not, in blindness or rashness, cast the chance away.

The trumpets were almost ready to sound, when there rode down from Poitiers in haste a large and motley company; wherein neither pomp of church nor war was lacking; for cross and pillar glittered in the front of many lances. It was the Cardinal Talleyrand de Perigord—that great house bred diplomatists even then—who, with his brother of Capoccio, came to make a last effort at reconciliation. Neither was King John at first averse to listen to such overture. And all that day the peace-makers rode to and fro, striving, as became their office, to avert blood-shedding. The Black Prince must have known himself in sore strait, before he thought of setting his hand to such conditions as these—to surrender all French towns and castles that he held; to give up without ransom all his prisoners; and to make oath that for seven years he would not draw sword against King John. But even to these terms the other would in no wise consent; and the last concession that could be wrung

The Fortunes of a Free Lance.

from him was to the effect, that only on the absolute surrender of the Prince and one hundred of his knights, might the rest pass out free. So the day wore away till eventide, when it was known to either host that they might rest on their arms till dawning.

A marvelous contrast would one have seen, who could have looked down on the several encampments. Round the pavilion of fair red silk, wherein King John lay, were clustered many others scarce less superb; plate and jewels, rich furs, gorgeous panoplies, and golden ornaments were as rife as though the great vassals had mustered for the crowning or the wedding of their king; and the rich wines and meats would have beseemed a court-banquet at the Louvre. The very beasts on which they rode were as full of lustihood as their lords; and more than one pampered destrere sniffed disdainfully at provender that would have been a boon indeed to the lean-flanked English chargers; for in that other entrenchment forage was cruelly short, both for horses and men, and long travel, no less than short rations, had begun to tell wofully. No marvel if the Prince's heart was heavy, as reckoning up that night every lance, spear, and bow under his command, he counted less than ten thousand men.

But in such times of trial natures like his show their brightest side. Taking their pleasure sadly, and too reserved to invite the sympathy of their fellows, in the summer-glow of prosperity they win much esteem, but little love; many adherents, but few friends: like the Alpine plants that thrive best on the verge of eternal snows, they show their softest colors when all the horizon is dark and fraught with storm. So far as we can judge from the rough sketching of his chroniclers, a very singular instance of this temperament was found in Edward of Wales. A soldier to the marrow of his bones, he never breathed freely in the luscious, courtly atmosphere ; and—affecting neither austerity nor seclusion—took scant delight in pageant or pastime: furthermore, it is averred, he was a very pattern of chastity. Fair Joan of Kent, though they were wedded at the last, found, perchance, rather a loyal husband than an ardent wooer. When the light of battle was not shining on his face, we fancy it grave and passionless, as it looks up at us from the Canterbury tomb; touched, too, by that half-melancholy, half-meditative shadow, which—betokening no ill-health—is oftenest found, say physiognomists, in such as shall die young.

But if such an one can count familiar friends, and fewer boon companions, it will be seen, when peril grows urgent, that he has known how to secure the whole trust and love of his soldiery. On the morrow morning, when the last negotiations had failed, and the mediator had departed in discomfiture, there was not one, perchance, of all the ten thousand, but felt his heart wax warm at the hearing of that famous oration —so simple, and earnest, and fitting the time :

"Now, sirs, though we be but a small company, as in regard to the puissance of our enemy, let us not be abashed therefore. For the victory lieth not in multitude of people, but where as God will send it. If it chance that the day shall be ours, we shall be the most honored of all in this world. If we die in our right quarrel, I have the king, my father, and brothers; also, ye have good friends and kinsmen : these shall avenge us, Therefore, I require you, for God's sake, to do your devoirs this day. Also, by his grace and Saint George's, I trust well to bear myself as a good knight."

CHAPTER XXIV.

THE BATTLE.

YET it must not be inferred that in the English camp, even before this, despondency prevailed. A brief discourse, that on the eve of battle ensued in Sir John Hawkwood's tent, may be taken as a fair ensample of the temper of all.

Quoth the knight to the esquire—

"By the Mass, we have small cause to thank yon lither-tongued Cardinal. With all his peace-making, he hath but put off for some few hours what had better been done to-day: right few amongst us will find wherewith to break their fast to-morrow; and it is hard, fighting on an empty stomach. Well, I trust we have seen the last of his smooth face; when there is men's work to do, I like not the meddling of coif or cowl. Now, sith battle must needs ensue, how thinkest thou, my son, it will fare with us?"

"Indifferent ill," Brakespeare answered, carelessly. "An' the French were but puppets, with swords of lath and spears of reed, they could scarce fail to overbear us by mere numbers; for a man's arm must needs tire, even with quintain-play."

"So it would seem," Hawkwood said; "yet I hold not altogether by thine opinion. We shall fight against shrewd odds, 'tis true; nevertheless, against worst thou didst hold thine own at Hacquemont. Wottest thou why? The *rascaille* could not bring their strength to bear, and were constrained to attack, as it were, singly. And thus, in my judgment, it may fall out to-morrow. There is one comfort at the worst for thee and me; if we be taken alive, beyond our harness, horse furniture, and some few silver coins, we have naught to lose; and it may be that some knight of substance will be scarce wealthier than ourselves when they have been put to ransom. Whereas, if against hope we win the victory, there will be other booty for our pains than the spoiling of poor peasants and petty traders; and they will be paid in other fashion than they have been of late. Art not aweary of these petty forays?"

The esquire laughed lightsomely.

"I spake more dolorously than I felt but now. Since your wisdom is thus confident, not for a hundred nobles would I barter my chance to-morrow. We shall have rare sport, whatever befall, and 'tis full time; for that brief bout at Romorantin scarce brushed the rust from our blades. Now if your worship hath no farther commands for me, I will lie me down for awhile; for mine eyes are somewhat heavy."

"Take thy rest, my son," the other answered. "If provant be short, there is less reason thou shouldst stint thyself of slumber."

Ten minutes later Ralph Brakespeare was sleeping as soundly as ever he had done on the eve of merry-making in the olden time.

Soon after sunrise, thus, on either side, the battle was arrayed.

The French were ranged in three battalions, whereof the first was led by the Duke of Orleans, brother of the King; the second by Charles of Normandy, the Dauphin; the third by John himself. The Black Prince maintained much the same order as that in which De Ribeaumont had first espied him; only he kept some of the choicest of his knights mounted in the rear of his archers; and sent the Captal de Buch, with six hundred lances, to skirt the steep mountain rising on the right, with orders to fall on the flank of the enemy when he saw occasion. So the battle began.

In front of Orleans's division advanced the Marshals d'Andreghen and Clermont, with John of Nassau's Germans in support; intending to sweep away the archers lining the hedges and vineyards, and so clear the way for the vanguard. Scarce an English bowstring twanged, till the lane was thronged with enemies. Then, from behind every bush and brier, sprang up a stalwart yeoman; and the cloth-yard shafts hailed down without stint or stay, searching out every joint in the harness, and piercing plate and mail like silk or serge. Soon the defile reeked with slaughter; and over the uproar rose the shrill sounds of brute agony, as the maddened chargers reared and writhed in their pain, trampling the life out of their fallen masters, and spreading disorder to rearward in their struggles to flee. Scarce a tithe of those who had entered forced their way by main strength to the farther opening, and these fared no better than their fellows. For there, achieving his vow, in the forefront of the Prince's battalion, James of Audley made stand; and beyond this the assailants won never a foot of ground; though the contest was very stubborn and hot: for the

French fought as only brave men will fight whose retreat is barred. There Arnold d'Andreghen was stricken down, sorely wounded; and there the question hotly debated but yesterday, whether Clermont or Chandos had the best right to their blazonry, was settled for evermore; for the valiant marshal was down under the horse-hoofs—the gay surcoat dabbled with his life-blood. By this time there was confusion throughout the vanguard; and the infection of disorder began to spread even through the second division of the Dauphin. While these last were still in uncertainty whether to advance or retire, the Captal de Buch came full on their flank with his lances and mounted archers, carrying havoc into their very midst.

In this charge rode Hawkwood and Brakespeare. The esquire's lance was broken at the first onset; but he so bestirred himself with his ponderous mace as to win especial renown where many bore themselves bravely; slaying outright not a few, and taking prisoner Yvon de Montigni a famous knight and powerful baron of Champagne.

The Black Prince soon became aware that the tide of battle had fairly turned; and, divining the right his moment with the instinct of a born strategist, caused his dismounted lances to get speedily to saddle, and bade his own banner advance. While he led forward his division, but before they actually closed, an incident happened worth recording as a singular trait of his character.

Under a bush on his right lay the corpse of a knight, richly attired, round which a group of esquires and archers were gathered. The dead man was none other than Robert of Duras, nephew of that Talleyrand de Perigord, who, but three hours since, had spoken so fairly. Edward was bitterly wroth at what he held to be a visible sign of priestly perfidy; and even at such a moment found leisure to indulge in the grim irony that he inherited from his father.

"Set yon corpse on a shield," he said, "and bear it to Poitiers, as a gift from me to the Lord Cardinal; saying that I salute him by this token."

But Chandos, eager for the onset as in his maiden battle, chafed and murmured aloud; and the Prince himself spurred on more sharply, as though to make up for the delay, till, with a great shock, the main body crossed spears with the division led by the Duke of Athens, High Constable of France. Still the battle waxed hotter and hotter; and still James of Audley held his place as chiefest of the English worthies till, from weariness and loss of blood, he could no longer sit in the saddle, and his esquires drew him by main force out of the mellay; for all the French that had not fled with Normandy and Orleans were fairly engaged; and Warwick and Suffolk could barely hold their own against the battalion commanded by King John in person.

Surely Charles Martel himself, when, centuries before, he met the Saracen on nearly the same ground, though he fought with better fortune, fought not more gallantly. The King and all around him were on foot, and round that one spot swirled the main eddy of the battle; and still John swayed his great battle-ax, never dreaming, as it seemed, of surrendering, though foes grew thicker and friends thinner about him every instant, and though the reddest blood of France was flowing at his feet. For Bourbon, Athens, Chalons, and Beaujeu were down; and Eustace de Ribeaumont cloven to the brain-pan through the chaplet of pearls; and out of Geoffrey de Chargny's cold hand the banner of France had fallen. But the strength, even of despair, must needs have an ending; moreover, the press was so close that it became scarce possible to wield weapon; so John did at last yield. His cousin of Wales, for whom he cried in his distress, was far out of hearing; and Denis de Morbecque, an exiled knight of Artois, had the honor of the surrender. Not long after, Warwick and Cobham came up to disperse the wrangling crowd, and to lead the prisoner, with all due honor, before Edward; who, when he saw the day was fairly won, after discomfiting the Germans, had waited to slake his own thirst and to see to the stanching of James of Audley's wounds.

Thus was achieved this notable victory; wherein the flower of French chivalry was cut down like grass before the scythe, and prisoners were taken outnumbering their captors twofold. It is not hard to fancy what wassail prevailed throughout that night on the plain of Maupertuif; in the pavilion, where the conqueror waited duteously on the vanquished King, consoling him the while with such kind and gracious words as moved some who heard them to weeping; in the tents, where knights and esquires made merry; and under green boughs, where stout yeomen made amends for their three days' fast on rich cates and wines.

Hawkwood himself was moved beyond his wonted staid sobriety. Setting aside his share of booty, he had acquired prisoners enough to make him wealthy with their ransoms beyond his hopes; indeed, in the general panic, chroniclers say, five or six knights or esquires would yield themselves to a common English archer. Yet none of Hawkwood's prisoners matched in importance the knight vanquished by Ralph Brakespeare. The esquire could scarcely refrain from showing surprise, when Yvon de Montigni proffered for his freedom four thousand crowns, to be paid at Bordeaux by Christmas-tide. But he was thrice as joyful, when on the morrow he was bidden to kneel among a score of others, and, at the hands of the Black Prince himself, received the accolade.

Cautiously and slowly, cumbered with the pleasant burden of fresh-gotten wealth, the English host moved southward; and, neither molesting nor molested, passed through Poitou and Saintonge, till they crossed the Garonne, and found jubilant welcome at Bordeaux. Not a few of all ranks obtained furlough there, and crossed the seas for England, there to bestow safely their booty and treasure. Among these, neither Brakespeare nor Hawkwood was numbered; but the first-named sent Lanyon—now regularly attached to his person as body-squire—to bear a message to his father, and gold enough to keep Gillian, his foster-mother, in comfort thenceforth, should she live to five-score.

The meanest archer who fought at Poitiers found himself courted and honored, in some degree, by the quiet people at home; and Lanyon, when he reached Bever, was no worse treated than his fellows. Cicely, the tanner's blue-eyed daughter, a buxom matron now, looked somewhat disdainfully on the stalwart smith, whom she had been till now content to honor; and long afterward, in domestic squabbles, was apt to be severe on the lubbards who were content to spend their strength in forging iron for better men to wield.

Sir Simon Dynevor's dreary face lighted up for an instant, as he broke the seal of his son's missive; but it grew darker and drearier than ever before he had read it through: the letter said no word of return; and he guessed rightly it was meant for an absolutely final farewell.

While Lanyon abode at Bever, he was daily summoned into the knight's presence, and questioned till he had told all, even to the minutest incident, that had befallen his master; and at his departure after no long tarrying—for the esquire was evidently uneasy on English ground—be bore away not only ample guerdon for himself, but a gold chain—an heirloom of the Dynevors—which Sir Simon prayed Ralph Brakespeare to wear for his sake.

CHAPTER XXV.

RALPH AND LANYON WITNESS A TRIAL FOR SORCERY.

ALL that winter at Bordeaux was one long carnival; and French gold flowed like water through the rough hands that had fought so well to win it; but Ralph Brakespeare wasted neither his health nor his substance in such riotous fashion—nay, in some respects, he bore himself more soberly than heretofore. Mere vulgar debauchery seemed to have less temptation for him than ever; and, if Marguerite de Hacquemont's last gift was not a perfect safeguard against sin, it was at least never defiled by touch of *ribaudes*' fingers, or mocked at by drunken *soudards*. Ralph was found in John Hawkwood's company nearly as often as before their positions were changed; and those two acting in concert, with the aid of an established reputation and ample bounty, soon contrived to gather around their pennons no insignificant following of lances. It was, indeed, the nucleus of one of those Free Companies which, ere long, acquired such a terrible reputation throughout central and western Europe. For the better understanding of these matters, it may be worth while to glance at the aspect of the times, and the condition of France.

In the spring of 1357, the Black Prince sailed for England with his state prisoner; having pacified his greedy Gascons with many florins and more fair words, besides committing the province in his absence to four of their great barons. All this while the Dauphin was in Paris; making head, as best he could, against the sore troubles that visited him. He was marvelously patient, politic and persevering for his years, and might even then have, not inaptly, been surnamed "the Wise;" yet it was weary work for such young hands to steer so great a ship through such troublous waters. The three States-General, on their meeting, instead of seeking to stay up the tottering sovereignty, sought to wring concessions from its weakness, clamoring not only for redress of injuries and lightening of burdens, but also for the punishment of alleged misdoers. Neither were the walls of Créve-cœur thick enough to prevent the arch-plotter, who lay in durance there, from fomenting disloyalty. Even before his escape, each measure of sedition might have been traced to Charles of Navarre; and Provost Marcel, his pupil and tool, was not long behind his master either in insolence or ambition. There was a brief cheering gleam, when Raoul de Renneval and the knights of Artois encountered Godefroi de Harcourt near Coutances, and routing him utterly, brought away that valiant rebel's head: then the darkness gathered again. In Paris all was discord and broil, till anarchy came to its climax on the day when the Palais de Justice was stormed by Marcel and his Bluecaps, and the Dauphin's robe was sprinkled with the blood of his marshals. But, though all the horizon looked threatening, there was a tempest just then rising over the rim, compared to which all other troubles were as spring-showers to the hurricane.

The peasantry of France were becoming maddened

with misery. Ten following years had been years of famine; for none cared to cast in seed that should be trampled, ere it grew ripe, by English horse-hoofs, or to press grapes for wine to slake the thirst of Free Companion or forayer; and all this while their lords relaxed not one jot of tyranny, requiring the full tale of bricks, though not a straw-blade was left in the land. Furthermore, with hatred there had of late mingled some germs of contempt: if the villein had no love, he had, perchance, less respect for the baron, who was forward enough to back his bailiff with the strong hand, but rode fast to therear when his king was beset at Poitiers. And so came the Jacquerie.

The deeds enacted in that awful time, from the recital of which the good Canon Froissart shrank, concern us not: it was chiefly in the northern provinces that the pest raged; and its infection spread not far south of the Loire. How the spirit of partisanship for awhile was forgotten—how Flanders and Hainault rode side by side with Picardy and Artois to their vengeance—how Charles the Wise showed himself not more relentless against the murderous ravishers than Charles of Navarre—how Gaston de Foix and the Captal de Buch, returning from the German crusade, couched their lances rgainst a foe fouler than the Moslem, under the walls of Meaux—how, from dawning till the sun was low, the carnage went on, till the lanes round Marne were choked with corpses, and every meadow-nook outside was heaped with dead—how the stillness of utter desolation settled down at length on the nakedness of the land—all these things are matter for a world's history, not for such a chronicle as ours.

After Stephen Marcel paid for fresh treachery with his life, Paris had once more sullenly returned to her allegiance; and the first act of the States-General, meeting there under the presidency of the Dauphin, was to disallow the treaty signed by John in captivity. So once more Picardy, Champagne, Lorraine and Burgundy felt the scourge, while King Edward marched through the unhappy country at the head of a mightier host than had ever yet followed him; till he became weary of wasting; and, half from policy, half from superstition—for, say the annals, his vow to our Lady of Chartres was made in the midst of hail and thunder —he consented at Bretigny to terms of peace.

During the last few months, while a form of truce still endured, it must not be supposed that the restless spirits in the southwest kept themselves peaceably within bounds. Even before the Free Companions drew together in formidable armaments, not a few essayed adventures, for their own profit or pleasure, on a smaller or larger scale.

In the garrison at Bordeaux there had arisen some heart-burning and jealousy; for the Black Prince's lieutenants were too apt to favor their own countrymen, and on slight encouragement Gascons will wax overweening. Among the malcontents, albeit they showed no sign thereof, were Hawkwood and Brakespeare. Though neither murmured nor showed outward discontent, the state of things pleased neither; and one summer day, with scant ceremony or leave-taking—for even then the leaders of companies such as theirs were beginning to act independently—they marched out of Bordeaux; under pretext of checking certain marauders on the French side, who were, in truth, beginning to be troublesome some score of leagues higher up the Garonne.

Whatsoever was their real purpose, it suited not therewith that they should abide in towns or large hamlets; so they rode steadily forward through Carillac, Macaire, and La Raoul till, on the second night, they came to a Benedictine convent, a dependence of the huge monastery in the last-named town, and sought shelter there. To such guests the Prior feared to be otherwise than hospitable; so he received them, with great show of alacrity; and, after some contrivance, room was found for both men and horses within the walls.

From youth upward, as you know, Brakespeare had cherished scant love or reverence for hood or cowl; and in his present quarters he felt strangely ill at ease. Indeed, at the evening meal he bore himself so gloomily—not to say sullenly—that Hawkwood, who seldom concerned himself with others' humor, marveled thereat, and at last was fain to ask the cause. But Ralph replied, curtly, that "Nothing ailed him; only that he had more mind for sleep than for meat or drink;" and so betook himself to his chamber, whither Lanyon, who was to share it, soon followed. They were lodged immediately under Hawkwood, on the ground-floor of a round tower overlooking the private garden of the Prior.

Despite his alleged drowsiness, his couch did not seem to tempt Brakespeare. After being disarmed by his esquire, he advised him to "sleep while he might, for they would march at daybreak:" yet he himself lay not down; and, leaning his arms on the window-sill, looked out moodily into the night. Lanyon was in dreamland almost before his head touched the pallet: but, from long training of bivouac, he slept as lightly as a girl, and sprang up alertly an hour or so later at the touch of a hand upon his shoulder. It was not so dark but that traces of strong emotion were visible on Brakespeare's face.

"Come hither," he said, pointing to the open lattice, "and look out and listen, keeping well in the shadow."

According to his wont, the esquire did as he was bidden without question; and Ralph, too, knelt down in the embrasure.

On one side of the garden, at right angles to the tower, rose a heavy pile of building, in the upper story of which was the Prior's private lodging. There was no sign of life or habitation therein, save a gleam of dusky red light just clearing the level of the soil, evidently slanting upward from some underground chamber. As they listened, there came through the stillness a smothered murmur of voices; and then a sound —too piteously significant to be mistaken—the moan of a woman in extremity of terror or pain. As Lanyon recoiled instinctively, Ralph muttered close to his ear—

"Hearest thou that? *I* heard it before I waked thee. Canst guess what devilry yon shavelings are about to-night? Nay, nor I. But, by St. Giles! I will know ere long. Follow thou me: a child might leap hence into the garden; and we will make shift to climb back, I trow."

Both were lightly clad in jerkin and hosen, and

carried no arms save a dagger. Descending quickly and noiselessly, they crept on till they crouched down by the low window, from which the light streamed: though unglazed, it was guarded by a grating, so close that light and air had some work to pass. Nevertheless, it served Brakespeare's purpose; and this is what he saw:

The chamber was not lofty; but so spacious, that four flambeaux, fixed in iron sockets in the walls, and a huge iron lamp swung in the center, left the furthermost part, beyond a row of supporting pillars, in deep shadow. From the wall opposite the window, ran out a broad stone ledge, like a dais. On this, in rude armchairs, the center one of which was somewhat higher than the others, and had some pretensions to ornament, sat three Benedictine monks. Two of these were strangers to Brakespeare; but in the chief he recognized the Prior. At a table immediately in front of these, set not far below the dais, a man dressed in the long robe and square coif affected by lawyers, was reading out, in a quick monotonous voice, some documents that he had recently been copying; on some the ink was scarcely dry. A trial of some sort was evidently proceeding; and the accused could be no other than the woman crouching low, in shame or terror, betwixt her guards. Her face was bowed in her hands; but, even in that ungraceful posture, the rare grace of her lithe figure, and the perfect contour of every limb, could not be dissembled. When she suddenly looked up, uncovering her face, Ralph was fairly startled by its loveliness— utterly unlike, if not excelling, anything he had seen in all his wanderings. The complexion was by nature dazzlingly fair, though the peach-blossom of the soft cheek was blanched now; but, in all other respects, there was an oriental stamp on her beauty. The long, languishing eyes, the whites of which were strongly tinged with blue, shaded by wealth of trailing lashes— the smooth, fine hair, that flashed back the torchlight like polished jet—the full, delicate mouth, and crimson lips, so apt to mold themselves into a mutinous smile —spoke plainly enough of redder and richer blood than flows in the veins of Japhet's descendants. There was as much of petulance as of contrition or appeal in the gesture, as she wrung her slender white hands, gazing eagerly in the faces of her judges. In two of those faces there was nothing remarkable.

The Prior was a portly, pompous churchman, rather benevolent-looking than otherwise; though, by virtue of his office, he bore himself austerely; and the round, rubicund visage on his left betokened no worse vices than indulgence and love of luxury. But the countenance of the right-hand monk was one of those not pleasant to remember, and therefore not easily forgotten. Sallow and atrabilious, its pallor none would impute to fast or vigil, even if the heavy animal jaw, and cruel, sensual mouth, had not told that, if ever such an one achieved saintliness, it would be at the cost of many hard battles with the lusts of the flesh. In his eyes there was no calm, judicial severity, but rather such a fierce eagerness as springs from unslaked desire, or bitter hate; also, it might be noted that when the prisoner's appealing glances roved all around, they never dwelt, even for an instant, on this man's face.

The whole scene seemed to Brakespeare a ghastly

mockery. He could scarce bring himself to believe that the three solemn judges, and their busy legal assessor, and the four armed guards—to say nothing of the other figures grouped in the dim background— were all required to deal with a frail girl, no more fit for rough handling than a May-fly. He looked on, and listened, like one in a dream. There was a brief pause, after the man of law had finished reading; then the Prior spoke, clearing his throat importantly—

"Thou, whom men call La Mauricaulde—some time novice in the nunnery of Mount Carmel, but having escaped thence at prompting of Sathanas, if not by his actual aid—thou knowest well wherefore thou art now set on trial; and hast heard what these have witnessed against thee. Such testimony it avails not to deny; neither may thy life be in anywise excused, whereby, not scandal alone, but great damage hath been wrought. For do we not know how—having once drunken of the cup of thy witcheries—divers of all stations have set at naught, not only their fair repute, but all duties of religion; so that finally, being wasted away in mind and body, no less than in substance, they have died miserably, rather like miscreants than chrissom men? Also, by trustworthy witness it hath been averred that thou hast been seen in full practise of thy accursed enchantments. Hath not Guillaume Chapellier, sexton of La Marmoude, made oath, that he watched thee in the graveyard at such work as these lips of mine shall not be defiled by rehearsing? And did not Antoine Tournon, returning home by night, see thee pass overhead through the air, borne on some devilish creature, the likeness of which he could not set forth for his extreme fear? Now, therefore, I adjure thee, in the name of the most Holy Trinity, to make full confession —if the familiar spirit by the which, as I well believe, thou art possessed, will suffer thee to speak. So, though thy life be forfeit, may some pain be spared to thy sinful body, and peradventure some profit may accrue to thy more sinful soul."

The girl—she was scarce yet in the prime of womanhood—rose up upon her feet, smoothing her hair from her brow with her soft, white fingers—the action was simply mechanical, its lithe dexterity suggesting long use of the mirror. Her voice trembled, so that at first it was scarcely audible; but gradually it slid into such melody as Ralph had never listened to; and a marked foreign accent only added to its charm:

"Ah, reverend father, be patient—if not merciful. There are none to witness on my behalf; and, could I find words, fear hath left me no strength to plead. Freely will I confess that for years past, since under the robe of a priest now dead, and under cover of the night, I had escaped from the good Carmelites, I have led life of *courtisane*. Also, may I not deny that for my poor sake substance hath been wasted, and some blood shed. Yet not seldom did I refuse gifts thrust upon me, rather than impoverish my lovers; and when any of such came to hurt, or fell into sore sickness, none bemoaned them more than I. Sore hath been my shame and sin: yet—if ye will hear the truth—sore have been my temptations. The blood of our race flows never tamely or orderly, either in love or malice; and, though of malice against any I am free, I have ever been too apt to love. Rightly have men called me **La Mauri-**

caulde; for of Moresco parents was I born, and from them was I taken by the Baron of Rocheguyon and his dame, since defunct; who, thinking to do a deed of charity, would have me baptized, being then ten years old, and nurtured me till I entered on my novitiate. Now, for all these sins of mine am I willing to do such penance as your reverend wisdom shall adjudge; and of all the wealth that hath accrued to me will I make free gift to your Order; craving only leave to be let go forth on my way barefoot, so that none dwelling hereabouts shall look on my face again."

"Nay," said the Prior, sternly, yet not so harshly as he had spoken before, 'tis too late now for such proffers. Thy goods, no less than thy life, are already forfeit. Nor is this full confession: thou hast said naught of the arts and enchantments by which thou hast wrought; nor of the Familiar by which, as we believe, thou art possessed."

She shrugged her round, white shoulders, in a sort of pettish despair; and her delicate mouth began to pout.

"Alas! I have used no worse witcheries than men find elsewhere in bright eyes, and red lips, and white hands. Neither have I been possessed by any other devil than he who tempts all frail womankind. Maître Guillaume Chapellier must have had an evil dream: not for a carcanet of rubies would I set foot in a graveyard after sundown. When Antoine Tournon, the fisherman, brought me his ware, his eyes were often heavy with wine; he must have drained many a *broc*, that night he saw me fly across Garonne. I have never been mounted on aught lighter of foot than Blanchefleur, my fair palfrey, who will never feed from my hand again. Surely your wisdom will not listen to such idle tales. If ye press me to death never so hardly, I can confess no more. Father Ignace knows—"

Here, for the first time, the girl looked full at the Benedictine sitting on the right. The monk's cheek reddened, not in a single healthy flush, but in irregular patches; and his eyes too waxed bloodshot.

"Why callest thou on me?" he said, hoarsely. "I know naught more than others of thine accursed sorceries. Speak out: and let us hear what falsity the Succubus within thee will utter through thy lips."

His savage glance made the girl cower like the lash of a whip. She was too frightened to use her vantage, if any she possessed.

"I meant nothing," she murmured; "only I—I thought—I hoped—"

And her voice died away in quick, convulsive sobbing, while her head drooped on her hands again. The Prior, turning his head, looked somewhat doubtfully at either of his assistants—like a man who, having determined on a disagreeable duty, would not be sorry to have it gainsaid.

"Since the accused, or, rather, the demon clothed in her flesh, is obdurate," he said, "we have no choice but to apply the uttermost question."

Both gave assent, but in a different fashion—the one, with reluctance more evident even than that of his superior—the other, with absolute eagerness. The Prior beckoned with his hand; and out of the shadow behind the pillars four men, dressed in close black jerkins, that left the arms and legs bare, came forward;

two of whom took each a flambeau from the wall, while the others laid hands on the prisoner's shoulder. At the first touch the girl shivered, as though in an ague-fit; but let them lead her away without resistance. The three judges, too, arose and followed; and the eyes of those without followed too.

In the dark recess there was fixed an engine, the use of which Brakespeare knew at once, though it was the first time he had looked upon a rack. The torches made the place so light, that he lost none of the preliminaries of the torture. He saw the *questionnaires* tear off the girl's garments roughly, till she stood almost as Phryne before the Areophagites; he saw the face of the Benedictine, called Ignace, swollen with passion, as his eyes gloated on the nude beauty, with an eagerness that could not be mistaken now; he saw the needless violence with which the victim was prostrated and bound. Ralph closed his eyes here; and a cold sweat, breaking out on his brow, rained down his face. Then there came the creaking of pulleys—then a terrible shriek—then another, smothered, as though it came through a gag—then utter silence. And the Prior's voice, so hoarse and changed that none would have known it, said—

"Devil or no devil, I can endure no more of this. Set her loose: see you not she has fainted? And clothe her decently again, in Christ's name."

When Ralph looked once more, the three monks had resumed their seats, and were conferring in an undertone. At last the Prior spoke aloud to the scribe—

"Jehan, write that we, the sworn judges here

present—to wit, Aldobrand, Prior of the Order of St. Benedict at La Meilleraye; Ignatius, Sub-prior; and Paul, Almoner of that same house—have heard the testimony urged against the woman of loose life called La Mauricaulde, dwelling for six years past at the *manoir* of Vergerac, suspected on good ground of dealing with the Evil One, or of actual possession by a familiar spirit. Furthermore, that, having failed in bringing to full confession the said accused, we did, in our presence, cause to be applied the extreme torture of the question, and that the accused swooned thereunder without having given intelligible word or sign. Wherefore we, the said justiciaries—not deeming that our powers extend even unto death—have judged it better to proceed no farther; but to send the said prisoner, under a safe escort, to Agen, there to be dealt with as it shall seem fit to our Lord the Bishop, High Justiciary of this province. Whereto we set our several hands and seals."

While this was being completed, low moans were heard in the recess, and one of the *questionnaires* came forward.

"The prisoner hath revived, Monseigneur. How is it your pleasure she shall be dealt with?"

"See her well guarded to her cell," the Prior answered, "and let Brother Cyril, the mediciner, attend her there. She must needs find strength for travel ere noon to-morrow. It were better that thou, Brother Ignace, should see to this; and, perforce, thou must ride with the escort to Agen. As for me, I will to my chamber; for I feel so strangely ill at ease, that, lacking fresh air and a cup of wine, I fear to swoon."

Ralph Brakespeare had seen and heard enough. He did not wait to watch the half-fainting figure carried away by the jailers; but strode back swiftly through the garden till he came under the window of his chamber. There, not trusting himself to speak, he motioned to Lanyon to stoop; and, setting his foot on the esquire's broad shoulders, swung himself through the lattice: then he let down his sword-belt, and with it drew up Lanyon after him. When they were both within, said Ralph in a whisper—

"Tarry thou here, and watch or sleep if thou wilt. I go to speak with Sir John Hawkwood."

CHAPTER XXVI.

RALPH PAYS A MIDNIGHT VISIT TO HAWKWOOD.

The sights and sounds that wrought so potently on Brakespeare and his esquire had, it seemed, in no wise affected those who rested above; for all was perfectly still there, till Ralph laid his hand on the latch. But before he raised it, Hawkwood's quick imperious tones were heard from within.

"Curzon! Peter Curzon! up with thee, and see who tries the door."

When Ralph entered, the knight sat upright on his couch, with his sheathed sword across his knee: he guessed at once that a visit at such an hour was not for naught, and bade his esquire withdraw, and keep watch without. There was no lack of light in the chamber; for a mortier burned there, besides the one that Ralph carried; and Hawkwood scanned his comrade's face intently, till the door was closed on them.

"What ails thee, man? Art sickening of fever or ague? I had thought thee proof against such fits."

While Brakespeare told very briefly and simply what he had seen and heard, the other's countenance changed from anxiety to indifference; and he even smiled slightly as he made answer—

"Certes, 'tis barbarous cruelty; for the girl, I doubt not, is no worse than many another *bonne gouge*. Yet

I see not how it can be hindered; nor, in plain truth, how it concerns thee or me."

Brakespeare bit his under lip sharply, for the other's coolness chafed rather than calmed his heated blood.

"Under your pleasure," he said, "it concerns me thus far. Knowing the road that they must travel, it will be easy to catch them in ambushment. 'Tis not unlikely that the girl may be taken out of their hands, at cost of a few dry blows; monks and their following are cattle quickly cowed; but, whether or nay, the holy men shall not play out their sport without speaking three words with me."

Hawkwood bent his brows in evident perplexity and vexation. Thoroughly independent by nature, and hardened by training, he thought no more of danger when it was worth his while to incur it, than of the daily bread he ate; but of gratuitous risk he had a virtuous horror. Yet he had not lived so long in Ralph Brakespeare's company, without discovering that the other was ill to turn from his purpose—whether good or evil—when it was once set. They were on equal terms too, now; and, despite his vantage of years and experience, he could only counsel, not command.

"Under my pleasure—that hath little to do with it, I trow," he said, in some bitterness. "Thou knowest not what a hornet's nest thou art bringing about thine ears; nor what venom lies in priestly stings—and all to save a *ribaude's* slender wrists from straining. Nevertheless, I may not cross thy fancy: thou art sober enough as a rule, God wot; neither can I forget, it was much such a quarrel that brought us first together. How many spears wilt thou need, to help thee in this mad freak?"

"Eight will well suffice, besides my body-esquire," Ralph answered. "If they travel with stronger escort than is like, we can make light work of such *rascaille*, taken unawares, at odds of three to one. I doubt not, but we shall overtake thee ere thou comest to the night's halt, without having blunted a sword blade. None the less do I thank thee heartily, for not having withstood me in this matter."

Hawkwood was too politic to mar a concession once made by after-sullenness. So he answered quite cheerfully—

"Enough said. Only I trust thou dost not purpose to carry with thee the wench, after thou hast rescued her. 'Twould be evil ensample for our *soudards*, who are ever fond of such baggage."

Ralph laughed, in spite of himself. "Fear me not: rescue once wrought, we go our several ways. The bird is well able to shift for herself, I dare swear, despite her gay plumage. When her wings are free, she will not be lightly limed again."

"That is well," Hawkwood answered; "now, betake thee to thy couch again, and sleep or wake as thou wilt. But I see not wherefore I should lose my rest, because thou art moon-stricken. Our trumpets will sound at dawn, and we will order this matter as we ride."

So they parted; and Brakespeare, after confiding his plan to Lanyon, to the other's huge contentment, cast himself on his pallet. But day broke, without either having accomplished more than a brief feverish doze.

CHAPTER XXVII.

SACRILEGE.

IF the time seemed long to certain of the Free Companions till they were fairly in saddle, the monks were not less eager to be rid of their guests; and the Prior himself deigned to come forth to speed their departure, though the hour was before Prime. Hawkwood took his leave with due acknowledgment; but Brakespeare kept aloof, feigning to busy himself with inspection of accoutrements, and such matters. He could not bring himself to interchange even the forms of courtesy with any one who had countenanced last night's loathsome work; albeit, the object of his special aversion—the Sub-prior—was not in presence.

So the lances filed out two abreast, and moved eastward along the right bank of the Garonne. The road never diverged far from the river, though it followed not all its windings; and led through an undulating country, evidently naturally fertile, though at that remote period there was far less of tilth than woodland. They might have ridden some three leagues or so, when they reached a spot so exactly suited for ambush, that, after interchange of glances, both the leaders drew bridle. There was forest-ground both to front and rear; and the summer foliage of the hazels and hornbeams fringing the glade was so thick that no eyes, unless specially watchful, would be likely to detect the glimmer of armor ten fathoms from the road; while the branches of the undergrowth were not so strongly tangled but that a barded destrere might easily burst through.

Up to this point, none save Lanyon and Hawkwood guessed at Brakespeare's purpose. But, so soon as they had halted, that knight moved back to the center of the column, so that all might hear, and spake thus—

"I would have you all to wit, that the work I am now setting about is of mine own choosing, and such as Sir John Hawkwood, my brother-in-arms—though he willeth not to hinder it—doth in no wise countenance or approve. Also, I needs must aver, that from the same there is to be reaped no great profit or honor. Briefly, it is mine intent to lie in ambushment here till there shall pass a company from the *moustier*, where we lay last night, conveying to Agen a woman, falsely, I believe, accused of sorcery; who hath been already grievously tormented, and will there be barbarously done to death. It is no light matter, some will think, to balk churchmen of their will. But the burden, whether of sin or shame, I take on mine own shoulders. Those who bide with me shall risk no more than a brief brush with the escort; scarce enough, perchance, to stay the stomachs of such as are gluttons of hard blows. Beyond myself, and this, my esquire, eight spears will suffice; but I enforce none to such duty, neither shall any serve me for naught. Each and every one who stands this day at my back, shall receive beyond his usual wage ten silver crowns; which, should harm befall me, Sir John Hawkwood will see discharged. Let such as mine offer pleases, make answer."

There arose a clamor of many voices, scarce kept within bounds by habits of discipline. There were but few in that godless company who would not have broken sanctuary for less guerdon than was now proffered; furthermore, such a passage of arms was the very pastime for which they had been wearying; and, above all, Sir Ralph Brakespeare was a special favorite. So, nearly every man there volunteered his service; such as kept silence being either older or wiser than their fellows, or more immediately attached to Hawkwood's own person. Quickly—and seemingly at hap-hazard, so as to offend none, yet with real regard to the character of each—Brakespeare made his choice; and after a few more words exchanged between the leaders, the main body moved forward, while the ambush proceeded to ensconce themselves. They left the road some rods farther on, so that, when they were posted, the brushwood in their front, for some distance beyond either flank, was undisturbed.

The time dragged on wearily as is its wont when eyes and ears are on the strain. But, a little before noon, sound of voices and tramp of hoofs came nearer and nearer, till the foremost riders were fairly within the glade. Ralph had certainly undervalued both their numbers and their quality. The wealthy Benedictines of La Raoul could afford to pay their retainers handsomely. If the weapons and harness of the escort were scarce bright enough to please a critical eye, there were among them some solid veterans, able to hold their own with ordinary troopers. First came some dozen mounted spearmen, and about the same number of arbalestriers on foot; then two Benedictine monks; some little distance in the rear, so as to be just out of their ear-shot, rode Ignace, the Sub-prior—his bridle-rein fastened by a cord to that of the mule on which sat a veiled woman, whose wrists were bound; and six more armed horsemen brought up the rear.

Step by step, so cautiously that the brushwood rustled no more than might have been accounted for by the summer breeze, Ralph had pushed his charger forward, till he got unobserved within a lance's length of the road. As those two passed, he could hear the prisoner's plaintive voice answering, what seemed to have been a threat from her guardian—

"Ah, holy father! Be not so merciless. Much would I do to win your favor, yet I cannot do all. The love, even of such as I, is not to be enforced, especially by such rough wooing as yours."

There was, perchance, the slightest shade of mocking coquetry in the last syllables. At any rate, so the Benedictine interpreted them; for he purpled with passion as he gripped her wrist, so violently as to wring from her a moan of pain.

"Darest thou yet again to deride me? Hast not learned—"

Before the menace was complete, the signal rang out through the hazels—

"Brakespeare! Brakespeare!"

And Ralph's terrible mace had stricken from the saddle one of the rearmost horsemen; and, with Lanyon at his shoulder, he had engaged the others hand to hand, leaving his followers to deal with the main body of the escort.

Taken at sore disadvantage—for there was scarce time for spearman to couch lance, or archer to bend arbalest—the Benedictine soldiers stood for awhile stoutly to their arms. But though they fought doggedly, they fought not with the thorough good-will of their adversaries. Moreover, the Free Companions, specially those on the English side, had already laid the foundation of their evil renown, and their tender mercies were known to be cruel. So, first one, then another, dropped his point, till there rose a general cry for quarter, and the struggle in front and center was quickly over. At the first onset the monks huddled together like frightened sheep; but the Sub-prior soon bethought himself that no harm could befall his own sacred person, and was thus cool enough to watch the issue narrowly. When he saw that this was no longer doubtful, something strangely like a blasphemy sped through his clenched teeth; and he drew closer to the prisoner, sliding his right hand into the breast of his robe.

"Spawn of Sathanas!" the Benedictine said. "Thinkest thou thou shalt 'scape, to make mock at Ignace once more among thy paramours?"

Then from under the dark robe came a bright flash; and, with one smothered shriek, the girl sank sideways to the ground, with a dagger buried to the hilt in her right side.

Now all this while sharp work was going on to the rearward; for, though Ralph and his esquire soon disposed each of another opponent, there still were left three to deal with; and, with one of these Brakespeare found no child's play. In the very heat of the conflict, his ear caught the death-cry; and, glancing over his shoulder, he barely missed seeing the murder done. A groan of wrath burst from the Free Companion, as his mace descended full on his adversary's head, crushing bascinet and brain-pan together; then, wheeling his charger in a demivolte, and letting his weapon swing by its wrist-chain, he swept the Sub-prior clean from the saddle with a buffet. That act of sacrilege would assuredly have arrested the conflict, had it not been already ended; for the two who still made stand against Lanyon instantly cast down their arms, unwilling to farther provoke one who could so entreat God's anointed minister.

The other monks were well-nigh distraught with terror; and sat wringing their hands, and gazing appealingly in the faces of the group of prisoners and captors mingled pell-mell, that gathered round the spot —near the senseless body of the Sub-prior—where Ralph sat, his vizor up, with La Mauricaulde's head on his knees. That she was dying fast was plain; for the ripe pomegranate lips were blue already, and the blossom of her cheek was faded; but her eyes, as the silky lashes were lifted slowly, retained their wonderful witchery; and her voice was not less caressing than her gesture, as she stroked Ralph's hand, with her soft white fingers.

"*Ah! beau seigneur*, was it chance that brought you to poor Zulma's rescue? For never, to my knowledge, did we meet before. You have been kinder and braver than all who swore they loved me. Dearly would I have liked to pay you in mine own fashion; but 'tis too late. I know not whither I go, only I have good hope 'twill be among mine own kind, where priests have no dominion. Tell Father Ignace, when he wakes, that I liked his stab better than his embrace, after all. I pray you grace me with one kiss on my cheek: 'tis not cold yet, and it hath been called soft, ere now. I am proud that the last lips I taste—and I have tasted many—should be noble as yours, *mon gentil chevalier.*"

All his manhood sorely shaken, he stooped to bestow the caress; the girl sighed twice or thrice wearily; then there came a shiver, rather than a struggle, and the knight laid the fair, frail corpse very gently on the forest grass.

By this time the Sub-prior's senses had returned; and the first blank bewilderment of his face was succeeded by the distortion of mingled rage and fear. Yet less of the first than of the last was there expressed. The priestly garb was a safe conduct, seldom, if ever, violated; the Benedictine could scarce believe the rude buffet to have been other than an unlucky accident; so his tone was scarce less arrogant than if he had been dealing with an offender in his own chapter-house.

"Whose hand was laid on me but now? If 'twas by misadventure, only by sharp penance can it be purified; if otherwise, better had it been stricken with the palsy. Let me hear the truth, lest on the innocent as well as the guilty should fall the Church's anathema."

The dullest-witted of the lookers-on guessed that a

storm of passion on Ralph Brakespeare's face would have been less dangerous than its black resolve, as he, too, arose and stood betwixt the murdered girl and her slayer.

" 'Twas I dealt thee that buffet. Canst guess why I smote thee with gantlet instead of mace? 'Twas because I would not thou shouldst die in honest soldier-fashion, when there were hempen cords to the fore. If there be virtue in thine office, call on heaven to work a present miracle: for naught else shall save thee from a dog's death."

The Benedictine recoiled, speechless with terror; but his brethren smote upon their breasts with loud outcry; and in the murmur of surprise and disapproval that ran through the circle, joined the voice of more than one Free Companion. Brakespeare turned sharply toward the malcontents—

"I will not argue this matter. If any man be minded to take the monk's part, let him step forth, and I— waiving the privileges of command—will meet him blade to blade. If I be worsted, deal with yonder shaveling as ye will. Perchance, ye may overbear me and mine with odds; but not otherwise shall the hound 'scape halter."

A significant silence ensued. The speaker was, as aforesaid, both liked and admired by his followers; besides this, a terrible prestige still hung round his name, and none cared singly to feel the weight of the arm that kept the stair at Hacquemont. Ralph smiled, somewhat scornfully.

"Meseems me, the monk will lack champions. Stand thou forth, Diedrich Schwartz; thou art more of heathen than of Christian, I have heard; let us see now whether thy talk over thy wine-cup be drunkard's vaunt, or whether thou wilt earn double wage by doing, for once in thy life, a righteous deed. Wilt thou fill the hangman's office? If it mislike thee, and none other can be found, I will set mine own hand to the rope."

The man whom he addressed—a huge red-bearded Bohemian—came forward, eagerly.

"I thank your worship," he growled; "the task is entirely to my humor. When black cattle wax vicious, 'tis full time they were haltered. Let me deal with him; I warrant you, I cure him of goring."

The preparations for execution were soon made; but, while Lanyon and another were binding the Benedictine's arms, he broke suddenly from their hold, and groveled in the grass at Ralph's knees, screaming for mercy, and crying that the other could not mean thus to punish a priest, for having laid hands on one possessed with a devil.

Ralph spurned the unhappy wretch with his mailed foot, as he glanced at the corpse lying near.

"'Possessed with a devil?' Marry, thou wilt have better acquaintance with devils soon, though thou wilt scarce meet them in such fair guise."

Then they dragged the Benedictine away, to where the Bohemian waited under a stout oak limb. But the hoarse voice ceased not to shriek out a ghastly medley of prayers and curses, till the halter choked it. When all was over, Brakespeare approached the other two Benedictines, who crouched by their mules, with their faces buried in their robes.

"We make not prisoners and take no ransom of such as ye and your following," he said. "Ye are free to return to your *moustiers* when ye will; and, if ye care to save yon carrion from the crows, ye may send and fetch it home after sundown: only, let none presume to pass this way again before."

Soldiers and monks were but too glad to escape so easily from such sacrilegious company; and, within brief space, the glade was clear to all but the Free Companions.

Before they set forward, Ralph bade Lanyon and another lift the girl's corpse and carry it deep into the woodland, far out of sight of the road. There in the light soil, with their swords for mattocks, they soon dug a rude grave-pit, deep enough to be safe from ravages of bird or beast; and there, under canopy of greenery, rest La Mauricaulde's bones—not less quietly, perchance, than many who sleep under cathedral aisles.

Very silent and thoughtful were the Free Companions, as they rode on through the forest-land; and their leader spoke to none till they rejoined the main body under Hawkwood, at the village where they halted for the night. Sir John's brow grew overcast when he heard what had been done, and he cared not to disguise his displeasure. Indeed, betwixt the two knights there rose a coolness, not soon abated, and which never thoroughly wore away.

CHAPTER XXVIII.

LES TARDS-VENUS.

Though Ralph Brakespeare never so long as he lived repented having taken God's vengeance into his own hands, it follows not that he was insensible to the consequences of the act. It had been better for him, so far as his credit was concerned, to have sacked and burned a dozen castles than to have set at naught the sanctity of that one cowl. He soon found out that in the eyes of many, neither fanatical nor over-righteous, he was held guilty of the sin for which there is no forgiveness, and, therefore, marked with a heavier brand than others whose lives were stained by all imaginable cruelty and rapine. He could scarce chafe or complain now, if knights of blameless repute—whose hands were clear off aught worse than honorable bloosheding—should shrink from his fellowship in peace, and choose that even on a stricken field some space should divide their pennons. At certain times he felt a gloomy satisfaction in the thought, that each day widened the gulf dividing him from the class in which place must needs have been found for him, had he not been cheated of his birthright; but at others, a dreary sense of isolation oppressed him—the more so, as Hawkwood's manner continued reserved and cold.

The knight was not, in reality, especially shocked by

Ralph's summary justice; but he was shrewd enough to be aware that there was peril in the close companionship of one who lay under the Church's ban and probably thought that he would one day or another have scandals enough of his own to answer for without having art or part in overt sacrilege. Nevertheless, he took care to avoid anything like a rupture; and as it suited neither of their purposes to return to Bordeaux, the two held on amicably together; having established themselves for the nonce at the castle called La Perrache —a detached fortress on the left bank of the Lotte, to the north of Aiguillon, which was too scantily garrisoned to offer even a show of resistance.

If Brakespeare had fallen into the disfavor of his brother-in-arms, it was far otherwise with the greater part of those who followed their several pennons. Those desperate Ishmaelites regarded with admiring awe the man who had trampled under his heel the superstitions from which they themselves were not wholly exempt; and felt a sort of pride in being associated with the terror attaching to his name; for they rejoiced rather than otherwise in evil repute, so long as it made them more formidable to their foes; even as the Schwarz-Reiters in later times were wont to blacken their persons, horses and harness, before going into battle. Had any expedition been on foot, promising much profit at the cost of much peril, when their forces must needs be divided, not a few would have deserted Hawkwood to take their chance under the other pennon.

Soon after the events lately recorded ensued the peace of Bretigni. Thenceforward the disorders, especially in the southern and eastern provinces of the French realm, became more and more outrageous. Nor is this wonder, when it is considered what numbers of mercenaries, used for ten years past to the license of free quarters in a half-conquered country, were now disbanded to find service, or support themselves as best they might; with scanty means too, for their booty or wage was wasted as soon as won. Some, indeed, absolutely refused to surrender to the French deputies the fortresses which they held; asserting they were soldiers of Navarre, not of King Edward, whose orders they now chose to set at naught. Neither did these at first lack excuse from the conduct of many of the other party, since the Barons of Languedoc—headed by De la Marche, D'Armagnac, Comminges, and Chatillon—were more than loth to transfer their allegiance; while Poitou, La Rochellois, and Saintonge clung no less obstinately to their ancient fealty. So that it was more than a year before the remonstrances of John the Good—enforced by his cousin, James of Bourbon, in person—took effect, or that Chandos was able to establish himself in peace at Niort, as lieutenant-general of all the fair domains ceded to England at Bretigni.

The scattered malcontents soon drew together, either cleaving to their old commanders, or choosing new leaders, till they waxed so strong and bold, that they feared not to storm the fair town of Joinville on the Marne, wherein half the riches of Champagne were stored. There the *Tards-Venus*, as they called themselves mockingly, abode for a while; proving that if they came late, they came in bitter earnest; for all the fertile region, hitherto innocent of ravage, they made desolate, up to the gates of Langres. When little was left worth the harrying, the Free Companions rode southward through Burgundy; despoiling after their pleasure (for none dared make head against them) all the neighborhood of Besançon, Dijon and Beaune; and putting Guerche to pillage and sack. By the middle of Lent, Seguin de Bastefol, Guy de Pin, the Bastard of Breteuil, and their fellows, grew satiate of vulgar sport, and resolved to fly at higher game. So they pushed forward down the banks of the Sâone, with the avowed purpose of reaching Avignon, and enforcing the Church to contribute liberally to their necessities; and over wine-cup or dice-box already began to count up the ransoms to be wrung from Pope or Cardinal. But thus far they did not penetrate without hindrance. Tidings of these things reached John the Good in Paris, to his sore grief and anger: so, without delay, the king sent letters to his cousin of Bourbon—then tarrying at Montpellier—bidding him march presently with a sufficient force to the chastisement of the freebooters. Nothing loth, that famous captain gathered from Auvergne, Limousin, Provence and Dauphiny, a goodly armament, and marched from Agen northward, till, some few leagues from Lyons, he came to where the Free Companions lay.

A very Babel of tongues might have been heard on the hill of Brignais; for English, Germans, Brabanters, Flemings, Hainaulters and Gascons mingled there; and their harness was motley as their tongues. But the spirit of nationality was well supplied by the spirit of partisanship, and there was no disunion in the strange encampment; nor was discipline less rigid than if all had been bred on the same soil, and had fought from boyhood under the same standard. The freebooters, like the buccaneers of later date, observed times and seasons in their devilry, bearing themselves ever most soberly on the eve of battle. Among those who had cast in their lot of late with the *Tards-Venus*, were Hawkwood and Brakespeare. La Perrache was no safe abiding-place for them since Jacques of Bourbon had mustered his armament; and there was no choice but to unite themselves with the main body speedily, for such as wished not to be cut off in detail.

Ralph was no longer an impulsive aspirant, but a tough, hardened adventurer, with whom dreams of chivalric glory were as things of the past; yet some instincts of gentle birth and breeding, after the rough usage and evil communication of a dozen years, were still vivid enough to make him feel uneasy in his present company. And on that April morning—looking forth, while they waited for Bourbon's onset—the knight felt that he would have given much to have found himself among the assailants rather than the assailed. Something of this he hinted to his brother-in-arms, but met with scant sympathy or encouragement there.

" 'Tis somewhat late in the day to be overnice," Hawkwood said, bitterly. " If any scruples beset thee, choke them, I pray thee, even as thou didst throttle the monk. Bestir thyself with that mace of thine doughtily to-day. By the Mass, thou never hadst better reason. Seest thou yon banner in the van of their first battalion? It bears the blazon of Arnaut de Cervole, called the Arch-Priest. There is little of the priest about him, save in his title, they say; nevertheless, I were loth to see thee alive at his mercy. But for that matter, every man here will fight like a penned rat; and our plans were right warily laid yester-night: if I err not, some of those gay pennons will be smirched ere all is done."

Of a truth, the Free Companions, in preparing for battle, had displayed no mean strategy. They had great vantage of ground in their favor, being entrenched on the plateau of a hill—not high, but exceeding steep —the which could only be ascended slantwise. Moreover, by their method of encampment they had so cunningly dissembled their real force, that the French scouts reported their enemy to muster but some five thousand, instead of thrice as many, which was their actual strength.

It was in vain that Arnaut de Cervole, and other captains of approved wisdom, discredited these tidings; relying rather on the sure intelligence they had before obtained. Jacques de Bourbon was not to be gainsaid; and many knights, smarting under the disgrace and damage endured already from the freebooters, backed him in his rash resolve. So the trumpet sounded the assault—the valiant Arch-Priest leading the vanguard.

Now in the Free Companions there were many imperfectly harnessed and rudely weaponed, who could have made a poor stand against the charge of men-at arms. These were ranged all along the hillside, with huge piles of flints and other missiles ready to their hands, and plied them with effect scarcely less deadly than that of the English bows at Poitiers. Here, as heretofore, the unwieldy column armed *cap-à-pie* spent its strength in furious efforts to come to close quarters with enemies safe from their agility and vantage-ground; all the while the stones kept hailing down, beating in bascinets and breastplates, maiming where they did not slay; Jacques de Bourbon, bringing up the second battalion in support, did but make confusion worse confounded instead of giving succor.

When the turmoil was at its densest, and the assailants were thoroughly in disorder, the main body of the Free Companies, perfectly horsed and armed, and in admirable order, advanced by a secret road round the hill, and fell upon the flank of the French with shortened lances. The issue of the day was not long doubtful after that. Though Cervole, Beaujeu, Châlons, Forêtz and Vienne bore themselves right worthily, they could make no head against the freebooters; who, as Froissart hath it, " fought so hardily that it was marvel." One hundred knights and barons rendered themselves prisoners there; and scarcely did a remnant of the goodly armament that had marched through Lyons a few days since make their way thither, with Jacques de Bourbon and his son; each of whom carried back his death-wound.

Brakespeare's scruples and discontent troubled him not a whit while blows were changed—indeed, his prowess that day was acknowledged and admired by many usually grudging of praise—but he had little heart to join in the mad revels and uncouth rejoicings with which the victory was celebrated; neither did the doings of the next few weeks reconcile him more to his fellows in command.

There was wild work all through the country of

Forêtz while the marauding band roamed hither and thither unchecked, sparing only the fortresses; and these rather because they cared not to waste time in siege than because they feared to attack. At the last the country became so absolutely desolate that it could find provender for man and horses no longer; so the Free Companions were fain to separate. The larger division marched southward still, till Guy de Pin, with the advanced guard, stormed Pont du St. Esprit. There the freebooters from all parts drew together; so that Pope Innocent, in his palace at Avignon, but seven leagues off, trembled exceedingly, and caused to be proclaimed a solemn croisade against these enemies of God and man; promising remission a *pœnâ et culpâ* to all such as should stand betwixt Holy Church and danger. Not many, in truth, were tempted to follow where promises were rife, but pay was lacking; yet enough to enable the Cardinal of Ostea to make some front during the early summer, and to hold the marauders in check, till an abler soldier and a better diplomatist came across the Alps, and the Marquis of Montferrat took the matter in his own hand. He so wrought with the Free Companies that, stipulating for present largesse of sixty thousand florins, and— strangest condition of all—plenary absolution from the Pope, they consented to follow this renowned captain to the wars in Lombardy; and so the realm of France found some breathing-space from torment.

When Guy de Pin and the others marched southward, some three thousand men-at-arms tarried with Seguin de Bastefol, who lost no time in occupying the strong town of Anse, on the Sâone, which he held long after, in despite of King or Pope; sucking in, like some monstrous cuttle-fish, the very life-blood of the fertile country round. Here, too, Hawkwood and Brakespeare had their headquarters; acknowledging Seguin de Bastefol as their nominal leader, yet going forth and returning at their own pleasure, and acting in most respects as independent captains.

CHAPTER XXIX.

ON FORAY.

THE country for leagues round Anse soon grew more impoverished and drained, till it could barely victual the powerful garrison lying there; so that the freebooters were forced to go farther afield, till often several days' march would separate them from the town. Brakespeare especially affected these distant expeditions, for to the old restless impatience of inaction was added dislike of present associations and circumstances. He always felt as if a weight were lifted from his lungs, when he was fairly out of sight of the banks of the Sâone. In some respects Ralph was not more delicate of dealing than his fellows. No scruples withheld him from robbing with the strong hand whatsoever pleased him, or from enriching himself and his followers at the cost of those whom—despite the mock peace of Bretigni—he still chose to esteem enemies. But he would allow no needless violence, much less anything of brutal license; his followers soon got to know that while on active service they must take their pleasure after his fashion, not their own; and sharp examples had taught them to beware of one who never spoke twice without striking, and striking to fell purpose. Nevertheless, Ralph kept his place in the favor, if not in the love, of his adherents;

if they growled sometimes in their beards, they would allow none other to speak disparagingly of him in their hearing; and if they had no tales of debauch to tell on their return, none in the garrison had so much coin to spare for revel or *ribaude* as those who rode under the *two splintered lances, crossed, on a sable field*.

On a certain morning, late in the autumn of 1361, Brakespeare crossed the Sâone into Burgundy, intending to visit a region into which neither he nor any of his comrades had yet penetrated—that stretching northward from the Haute-Rhone toward the border of Savoy. Distance, difficulty of access, and reputed poverty, had been the causes of this immunity. Of the two former, Ralph had learned to think lightly of late, and of the last he chose now to judge for himself. The first day's march led through country already thoroughly explored and exhausted; neither on the second did anything notable occur. The only dwellings above the degree of a peasant's hovel that they passed, were a few poverty-sticken manoirs and gaunt, lonely towers where no plunder was likely to pay the peril of assault; and those who hunt for profit care not to meddle with a wolf's lair. By noon on the third day they had come down on the river, and were fain to keep the road, such as it was, that followed its windings. The rocky, woody country all around, that succeeded flat sandy plains, was ill-traveling for barded chargers. They were nearly abreast of the rapids, now called the *Saut du Rhone*, when the scouts—who, after Brakespeare's unvarying wont, had been sent in advance—came back with tidings that some short distance in the front they had descried a great and fair castle. Brakespeare halted his party instantly, and rode forward himself to reconnoiter, accompanied only by Lanyon.

The last two years had changed the esquire more than his master. He deemed it his duty to adapt his demeanor in some fashion to their altered fortunes; and had so far succeeded, that the stolid simplicity of his countenance was now replaced by a sort of saturnine gravity, which suited well his slow brevity of speech. Moreover, his bearing had long ceased to be clownish or awkward; and, whether on foot or in saddle, he looked from head to heel a tried, sturdy soldier.

After some three or four furlongs of steep ascent, the woodland ended abruptly, and some hundred yards or so a level clearing extended beyond, which had to be crossed before arriving at the barbican. Under cover of the trees, the knight made long and careful survey before he spoke.

"A brave outside, by Saint Giles! If the withinside answers thereto, it will be well worth the winning. What thinkest thou? Ha?"

Unless directly questioned, Lanyon never dreamed of giving his opinion, and even now there passed his lips only one word—

"If—"

Ralph shook himself somewhat impatiently. "A plague on thy raven's beak! Is it so long since it was wetted that thou must needs croak? We will prove what thine 'Ifs' are worth ere night. Bring up my spears forthwith. There is a shrewd storm gathering in the west. If yon walls find us naught better, they shall find us roof-bield, and save harness from rusting."

The castle owed little of its strength to art. Around two sides of the cliff, whose plateau it nearly covered, ran a ravine escarped by nature, and so deep that one, standing on the brink, looked down on the topmost branches of the pines that found roothold among the rocks beneath. The walls, in most places, rose sheer from the farther verge, so that nothing without wings could have passed along; and the only access to the gate was across the narrowest part of the gorge, where a platform of masonry jutted forth on either side, joined in the midst by a *pont-levis* that could be raised or lowered at pleasure. It seemed as if those who fortified the place had deemed it so nearly impregnable as to care little for ordinary outwork; for the barbican was built rather for show than for defense—being, in truth, little more than an arch surmounted by battlements. But the ponderous gate-tower beyond was a small fortress in itself; and there the garrison was evidently intended to make its first serious stand. As soon as his party came up, Brakespeare dismounted all save such as were needed to take charge of the horses; and, causing the cumbrous lances to be piled, gave his brief orders for the assault, in case the castle should not be rendered peaceably.

Then very warily they crept forward on foot; yet not so warily but that they were described from a loophole, or *tourelle;* for on the battlement no watchman showed himself. Three or four quick notes of alarm were sounded on a bugle within, and as the leader of the Free Companions—deeming farther precaution useless—set foot on the level clearing, the drawbridge rose with provoking slowness, till it hung in air midway betwixt the two platforms, leaving a chasm some three fathoms across.

Brakespeare seemed no more disconcerted than if such an accident had entered into his plan of attack. Seeing that the place could not now be carried by surprise, he advanced his company, in regular order and no undue haste, across the open space; and, passing through the gates of the barbican, stood forth alone on the platform, and bade his trumpet sound a parley. After a brief delay, an elderly knight in full armor, save for the vizor, appeared behind the battlements of the gate-tower, and demanded, in set phrase, to be informed wherefore trespass was made on the lands of La Roche Dagon, and a challenge sounded at its gates; farther, under what standard the intruders served.

"I am here for mine own pleasure," Brakespeare answered; "and I follow none other standard than King Edward's when it is flying. But, for the nonce, I hold with the Free Company lying at Anse, under Sir Seguin de Bastefol's command. It is my purpose to lodge within your walls to-night, and it may be for some space after. Now, therefore, say quickly whether ye be minded to give me free admittance, or if I must make entry after mine own fashion."

The Frenchman's countenance fell at the mention of the Free Companies; but it grew dark and angry at Ralph's last words, though he constrained himself to speak with some formality.

"Sir knight—for I perceive that your spurs are golden, though your manners scarce answer your degree—I may not reply to your demand without conference with the high and puissant dame whom I serve; for the Countess Bertha orders all things here, since it pleased Heaven to afflict our good Lord of La Roche Dagon with palsy."

So, with a stiff obeisance, the Frenchman withdrew, but returned instantly to say that the Countess chose to make answer in person. Lances and arbalests began to bristle all along the battlements of the gate-tower; in strange contrast to these was the apparition that soon filled one of the center crenelles.

A beautiful woman, though her beauty was of an uncommon type. The outline of the haughty aquiline features might have been softer, and the curve of the crimson, sensual lips less decided; the small head, too, would have seemed overloaded by the masses of red-gold hair that grew far down on the broad low brow if the slender neck had not carried it so imperially. Only the upper part of her figure was visible, yet somehow Ralph guessed it to be tall and shapely. She leaned forward over the battlements—not eagerly or anxiously, but with a sort of indolent grace—as though she had been looking down on a spectacle prepared for her amusement. Brakespeare, standing bareheaded beneath her, was near enough to the glitter of her great tawny eyes, and her voice was wondrously sweet and clear, even now, when its tones were mocking.

"So, *beau chevalier*, you purpose, my seneschal tells me, to honor our poor dwelling with your company, whether it likes us or not. It grieves me to seem niggard or churlish; nevertheless, I counsel you to prick forward, ere darkness and rain overtake you, to some other shelter. Unless ye have martlet's wings, and can lodge in their nests, ye will find no shelter to-night at La Roche Dagon."

Brakespeare's cheek reddened under the deep tan of sun and weather. But he made answer with grave courtesy—

"I feared that such would be your answer, noble lady. Yet I would your own lips had not spoken it. I care not to bandy challenges with dames. I knew not your castle had so fair a commander; nevertheless, I may not, without shame, be turned back. I pray you withdraw, and bid your followers within do their *devoir*, whilst I and mine will essay what simple men may do without aid of miracle."

Her slender hand waved a gay defiance, and the next instant—instead of the proud beautiful face—the grim visage of an arbalestrier peered out, and Ralph stepped back from the platform into the shadow of the barbican arch.

"Who hath charge of the grappling-iron—Gilbert Fleming? That is well. See there is no fray in the rope, and that it be fast to the ring. Thou hast, too, the short curtal-ax I bade thee have sharpened at Anse? Lanyon, do thou make haste and rid me of jambarde and brassart. I needs must have my limbs free for this gear." As he spoke, the knight unbuckled his sword-belt and cast down his gantlet. From mere force of habitual obedience, the squire knelt down and busied himself with stud and buckle; but he looked up imploringly in his master's face.

"I beseech your worship, be not overrash. Consider that here is no case of fall into ditch or moat, whence ye might 'scape with bruise or drenching: bones would be like cracked eggshells, once they touched the rocks at the bottom yonder. In God's name suffer me to try this adventure. I am the lighter of the twain, and will scarce be missed, God wot, if aught miscarry."

Ralph's palm fell roughly, but not unkindly, on his follower's shoulder.

"Of what pratest thou, blockhead? Lighter than I —with all that mass of brawn? And how would those stiff bow-legs of thine twine round the rope? By what right lead I these spears, if I care not to be foremost in peril? No more words; but see the rope be fast, so that it yield not with my weight; and lay hands on me, so I roll not sidelong when the drawbridge comes down. Gilbert Fleming, thou art quick of eye and steady of hand; do thou cast the hook."

Grumbling and muttering in his beard, Lanyon completed his task; but the others murmured applause, as their leader followed out on to the platform the trooper who carried the grappling-rope. At the first throw the iron held fast round one of the lowering chains. Six or seven of the Free Companions kept the rope tight with all their weight and strength; and before the garrison were aware of his intent, Brakespeare had swung himself up, hand over hand, and was crouched at the top of the steep sloping planks, with his left arm twined round the supporting posts of the handrail. His face was turned toward the barbican, so that his back was toward the danger—the sorest trial of nerve, all soldiers say—below him the ghastly, naked rocks, twenty fathoms down, peered out through the rank herbage and roots of pines; yet he plied his ax as coolly and skilfully as if he had been felling an oak, till the staple flew from the woodwork, and one of the supporting chains dangled loose. Then he crept cautiously to the other side of the *pont-levis*, and, twining his arm yet more firmly, began the same work there. But long ere this the garrison had recovered from their amazement, and more than one quarrel had glanced off Ralph's bascinet and breastplate; an arbalestrier, wiser than his fellows, was just taking aim at one of the assailant's unprotected limbs, when a voice issued from the bartizan at the angle of the gate-tower—

"Hold! let none shoot another bolt without my command."

It was the Countess Bertha who spoke; she had chosen to retreat no farther than where she could watch all that passed in safety.

Over the rattle of iron and the splintering of beams, the clear, imperious tones smote on Ralph Brakespeare's ear, and a thrill of proud pleasure tingled through his veins. He felt, for the moment, less like a freebooter setting his life on a desperate hazard for the chance of booty, than a knight displaying his prowess under the eyes of the queen of the tournament, whose glove was to be the victor's guerdon. The corded muscles of his fore arm tightened, as he threw double strength into three more blows that finished his work. Then the *pont-levis* came crashing down, with a shock that made the solid masonry of its supports to tremble. It was well for Ralph that he had given warning beforehand, so that strong and nimble hands were ready there; for the shock was so stunning that his grasp loosened, and he was rolling sideways toward the chasm, when Lanyon and Fleming caught his shoulders, and drew him back under the barbican.

In a few seconds the effect of the fall passed off; the esquire had begun to buckle on his master's armor with much more alacrity than he had shown in doffing it; and the Free Companions were crowding forward emulously for the assault, whose result no man doubted now. They had dealt with such matters too often not to know how little chance oak and iron stood against ax and lever, wielded as they knew how to wield them. But as they tarried till their leader was fully armed, a white kerchief fluttered from the loophole of the bartizan; and the next moment the beautiful *châtelaine* looked from the same center crenelle; Ralph came forth in time to hear her first words.

"I cry you mercy, *beau chevalier*. Had I known what a Paladin stood before our gates, I had never dreamed of barring them, and had thought our poor roof honored by his tarrying here. I think there lives never another, betwixt Rhone and Garonne, who would have dared such feat as hath just dazzled mine eyes. You are right welcome to La Roche Dagon, though 'tis somewhat late to say so. Enter, I pray you, and deal with us as you list; remembering only that we have rendered ourselves without blood-shedding, and that our garrison is mainly made up of pages and tiring-maids, commanded by a weak woman in the place of a palsied old man."

There was something of mockery still in her tone; but only enough to be pleasantly provocative—no trace of the cold disdain that had marked her first speech. Once more Brakespeare's heart leaped up under his corslet, as he bowed low in acknowledgment. But when, before setting foot on the drawbridge, he faced round on his followers, his speech was curt and stern as asual.

"Mark me now, sirs. I have not periled my life here for naught. I know not how long it may suit me to hold this castle; but I purpose not to yield it again without sufficient ransom, in which ye all will have due share. Howbeit I give ye fair warning that I will have no brawl or license here, much less rough usage of women or weaklings. I quarrel not with an honest carouse; but if ye break bounds, look to it. He who offends in such wise shall have shorter time to repent himself than had Jean Cabestal, near Trevoux. Ye have not forgotten how it fared with him. Now, let half of your number fall back and bring up the destreres, and the rest follow me orderly."

Even while he was speaking, the great gates beyond the drawbridge swung slowly open, and the Free Companions filed into the base-court two abreast.

CHAPTER XXX.

BEWITCHED.

SIR RALPH BRAKESPEARE stood in the base-court—leaning on his great *epée d'armes*, which he had girt on again—while his men formed into two ranks much like a modern company taking open order. He was puzzled by a certain embarrassment and uncertainty as to what step was next to be taken. He did not care to force himself into the presence of the *châtelaine* in the rough guise of a victorious enemy, yet he felt keenly the absurdity of reversing their real positions. He was not bewitched enough as yet, to forget that with romantic chivalry a Free Companion had naught to do. So he pondered, till his reverie was broken by the voice of the ancient seneschal, praying him to visit the Countess in her presence-chamber.

Bertha de la Roche Dagon was sitting in a chair of state, carved with armorial bearings, at the upper end of the presence-chamber; behind her several of her household—both male and female—were ranged in a half-circle. All of these were more or less richly attired; but one was distinguished from the rest, not only by the gorgeousness of the dress, but by the singular perfection of form and feature—a tall, slim page, who stood close to his mistress's shoulder, with a flush of anger on his clear olive cheeks, and angry fire in his big black eyes. He was gnawing his lips, too, like one

The Fortunes of a Free Lance.

who has been sharply chidden, and would fain answer if he dared. As the Englishman entered, the lady rose and advanced to meet him. Even in those few steps the wondrous grace of her gait was visible; though, till she moved, none would have believed that a figure so tall and stately could sway itself so lissomely. The close tunic of dark blue velvet, bordered with gold, over the silken skirt of a paler shade, did justice to her superb bust and to her waist—girlish still—though the lady was in the prime of womanhood.

"I pray you believe, sir knight," she said, "that I design not to cozen you of your rights. Soft words pass not for coin, I know; and in fair gold pieces shall our ransom be paid, if ye will be patient with us. Entreat us ever so roughly—we can do no more. We are prisoners rendered to your mercy; yet I think we shall find no churlish jailer. Suffer me for this one night to do the honors of my poor dwelling, as though it were still mine own. You shall not fare the worse for sitting as guest where you might lord it as master."

The strong soldier whom she addressed colored like a bashful boy as he muttered some broken sentences of assurance, to the effect that no violence need be feared from his band, and that all in the castle, even to the lowest, should be gently and honorably dealt with. Furthermore, he prayed the Countess to order the household, for the present, in all things as heretofore. Then, under pretext of looking to the bestowal of his men and their horses, he withdrew, carrying with him some whispered words of thanks, and followed by a glance and smile which conveyed something more than the thistledown promises of coquetry.

When the door was fairly closed, the Countess Bertha turned toward her household—

"All goes fairly thus far," she said. "See that nothing be lacking to keep these English strangers in good humor; and above all, that our supper be rightly set forth. And, Mathilde, see they make ready the white robe bordered with seed-pearl. I would be brave to-night. Now leave me, all. Stay—Réné, do thou wait. I have a special errand for thee."

For some moments after they were alone, the Countess gazed at her page with a kind of indolent curiosity and disdain.

"Art thou mad?" she said, at last, "to give rein to thy malapert humor in others' presence? Also, I fain would know what made thy *Seigniorie* so sullen. How long would the gates have stood, when the drawbridge was down? Wouldst thou have made all here incur the hazard of sack and pillage; and should I bandy words of defiance with this knight, when smooth words are as easy to speak?"

The page stamped his foot petulantly. In truth, his manner was rather that of a jealous lover than of a spoiled domestic.

"As easy to speak—I doubt not that. Also, it was easy enough to bid them forbear shooting, when, in another second, Gilles Montigny would have sent a bolt through the freebooter's thigh. The bridge was not down then, I wot."

She smiled—rather, it seemed, at her own thoughts than at his speech.

"'Tis better as it is. I had scarce forgiven myself, if so proper a knight had been maimed under mine eyes. *Pardi*, I mind not when I looked upon his fellow."

Réné d'Andelot's heart grew sick within him, as he saw her face soften into a languid tenderness; while her eyelids drooped, and the scarlet lips parted, like those of one wrapped in a pleasant dream. He knew how to interpret those signs only too well.

"Let him look to himself," he said, hoarsely. "If he but look on thee overboldly to-night, I will see if his skin be dagger-proof. Let them hang me from the battlements an hour after. I care not."

Her eyes opened, wide and scornful.

"Thou foolish malapert. Thinkest thou I cannot guard my own honor; or that if I chose to take new paramour, thou shouldst hinder me? Know, that if I have graced thee above thy merit, thou art none the less my sworn servitor. Howbeit, I were loth to see thee harmed. Be not so rash as to measure thyself against him; he would crush thee, like a gadfly in his gantlet. Now, away with thee. I have weightier matters on hand than the appeasing of thy peevish humors."

The page threw back his handsome head. At first it seemed as if the mere pride of manhood asserted itself against the cruel cynicism; but he either lacked the nerve, or feared to trust himself to speak. After one long, appealing look, under which the lady's face neither quailed nor softened, he turned and left the room hurriedly.

The Free Companions, when outward bound, were not wont to be burdened with much baggage. Nevertheless, they carried always some few sumpter beasts in their train, and Sir Ralph Brakespeare was not so ill-provided but that he was able to exchange the coarse jerkin and hose usually worn under harness for more suitable garments before he again appeared in the *châtelaine's* presence.

While this was a-doing, said the knight to the esquire—

"How likest thou our lodging, Will? and what thinkest thou of the dame who rendered herself so graciously?"

"The lodging is fair enough after a fashion," the other answered, doggedly; "yet, under your worship's pleasure, I should not care to abide long here. Certes, the dame is fair enough after a fashion too; yet—"

Ralph turned sharp round on his follower.

"Thy trick of grumbling is past the healing, else should I be wroth with thee. Thou hast haunted taverns, and followed *ribaudes*, till thou art unfit to judge of aught more delicate. Where, I prithee, hast thou ever looked on beauty that could compare with the Countess Bertha's?"

"'Tis somewhat hard, messire," Lanyon muttered, "that your worship first requires my opinion, and then should quarrel with it. 'Tis a rare face, I own, and I know not that I have seen it matched in flesh of blood; but ye must needs remember that picture hanging in the Abbey church of Haultvaux—brought from Italy, I have heard—wherein the temptation of the blessed Saint Anthony is set forth. Marry, over the holy man's shoulder there hangs a thing that—even to the color of the hair cr eyes—might stand for the portrait of this brave dame."

"Tush!" Brakespeare broke in, in undisguised anger now; "I was fool to question thee. Keep thy murmurs of ill-omen to thyself, I charge thee; and spread not discontent in our band. Be not too liberal of the wine-cup to-night. I would not that any of our men overstepped decent bounds; and I think thy brains are wool-gathering already. I bade Gilbert Fleming have the drawbridge repaired. That gear must be all in order ere 'tis fully nightfall. See to it presently. Likewise have the keys in safe keeping. I have no farther need of thee here."

The sturdy soldier shook his ears like a great hound that has been sharply chidden or chastised.

"I am no breeder of mutinies," he answered, "and no drunkard or brawler. Had I guessed your knighthood would have chafed thereat, I had kept my unsavory comparison betwixt my teeth; or, for the matter of that, I would have likened the lady to one of heaven's angels. I will about that smith's work now. It will be supper-time soon, and the storm will scarce hold off another hour."

If the castle of La Roche Dagon had harbored honored and welcome guests, the tables could scarce have been more richly or carefully set forth than they were for that evening meal. The Countess Bertha was either too proud, or too politic, to make pretense of poverty which might scarce have been believed. The eyes of many a freebooter glistened greedily, as they roved over massive tankards, salvers and ewers of rich plate scattered over the board with seeming carelessness—almost hiding the napery of the cross-table on the dais at which the *châtelaine* sat, with a vacant chair on either side. Close behind her stood two female attendants, and Réné d'Andelot, the page. Only six covers in all were laid at that table; three of these were designed for the knight who had held parley at the battlements, and two others of like degree—also somewhat advanced in years—whose pennons were ranged under the banner of La Roche Dagon.

Brakespeare came in somewhat late. Albeit he had full trust in Lanyon, he chose to go the rounds himself, and see that the guards—all of his own men—were duly set. The Countess Bertha's glances had wandered more than once impatiently toward the door by which he needs must enter; and, as the English knight advanced up the body of the hall, they rested on him—first critically, then approvingly. In very truth, it would have been hard to light on a finer ensample of mature manhood than Ralph presented at this time. His plain, close-fitting dress displayed—perhaps to more advantage than gorgeous or quaintly-fashioned apparel would have done—his deep square chest and long sinewy limbs: he bore himself erect and lightsomely, like one trained by unceasing exercise; and his step was quick and springy—like that of one used to the weight of harness, and rejoicing in unwonted freedom—as, in obedience to the *châtelaine's* gesture, he approached and seated himself in the chair on her left hand.

She saw his glance turn inquiringly to the still vacant chair on her right, and answered it.

"It hath been so, these two years; yea, ever since the good lord, my husband, was stricken with the palsy. For we cease not to hope that he will one day be enabled to sit in his old place and rule his own household again; though 'tis weary work waiting on him, and he seems past mediciner's skill."

A little sigh rounded off the speech; but there was no sign of rooted sorrow on the lady's face. Perchance time had worn off the keen edge of her domestic troubles, or she had found distraction, if not consolation— for nothing could be gayer than her humor thenceforward. It was wonderful to see with what tact she smoothed away the difficulties of her position; contriving to reconcile the courtesy of the hostess with the humility of the captive. All the while the by-play of eloquent glances, and of lithe white hands, so graceful in their restlessness, went on, till Ralph's blood waxed hotter than could be accounted for by the rich wine which he drank not sparingly; and he could scarce forbear a start and a shiver, when her sleeve—by chance, so it seemed—brushed his; and Réné d'Andelot's handsome face waxed wan and gray, and prematurely aged, in its look of pain.

There was deep carouse in the body of the hall; but the Free Companions—partly from fear of their leader partly in deference to the presence in which they sat— indulged in no rude license or loudness of talk, and pledged the Burgundians of La Roche Dagon as cordially as if they had fed and feasted side by side for years.

Supper was nearly over, when Lanyon—who had been absent for some short space—returned. His beard was dank, his garments splashed with rain, and his whole bearing seemed more bluff and uncouth than usual, as, advancing to the dais with rather scant ceremony, he laid a huge bunch of keys on the table before his leader. The knight bit his lip, frowning.

"I beseech you, pardon my follower's rudeness, noble lady. 'Tis a clumsy knave, though an honest. When I bade him have the keys in charge, I wist not that he would clash them down here thus unmannerly—as if this, your castle, were a prison, and I your chief jailer!"

The Countess laid her little hand on his wrist, very lightly—yet not so lightly but that it set his strong pulses bounding—and bent over till her heavy red-gold braids brushed his check.

"And if it were so?" she murmured. "I have heard of prisons so pleasant, and jailers so gentle, that the captive cared not to go forth when the gates were unbarred. Perchance I may pine hereafter; but 'tis long since I have felt so light of heart as I do this night. Ah! if you knew how dull and dreary La Roche Dagon has been, this many a day—"

For several seconds Ralph was silent. When he answered, it was in the same undertone, and thenceforward the converse of the twain became more confidential. This was noted by others besides Réné d'Andelot; Mathilde and Jeanne exchanged smiles and meaning glances; and freebooter nudged Burgundian in the body of the hall, muttering rude jests and coarse surmises; but of these signs of intelligence neither the knight nor the lady took heed; nor, had the Countess Bertha been aware thereof, would they have troubled her a whit. When the game was fairly afoot, that daring huntress of Man would press it through the heart of a crowd, no less than through a solitude, and shrank no more from the display of her caprice than did Cleopatra or Faustina, when—in presence of a thousand courtly sycophants—they leaned on a fresh favorite's breast. She could not even spare a glance for the unhappy boy whose caresses were scarcely cold on her cheek; though his face might have moved a devil's pity, as he stood there, behind her shoulder, driving his nails into his palms, as if he would abate agony of mind by the body's pain.

It was more the habit of courtly training, than because she cared for excuse or disguise, that caused her to say aloud as she rose to withdraw—

"I leave you to the wine-cup now, *beau chevalier*. If you weary thereof, and care to listen to the lute, Jeanne here strikes it right deftly, and Mathilde's voice is sweeter at least than the brawling of the wind without. You will be right welcome in my bower-chamber."

As Ralph rose and drew back to give the lady passage, their hands met. If the contact was accidental, not so was the pressure of the slender fingers that tingled through his arms to the shoulder-blade.

Legends speak of magical palaces and gardens, where the actual presence of the enchanter was needed to make the jewels sparkle and the flowers bloom, and where—this wanting—everything became again scentless, colorless, tasteless. Of just such a dreary change the Free Companion was sensible, as the door closed behind dame and demoiselles. A dull gray mist seemed to fall suddenly over the banqueting-hall, and he was sorely tempted to rise and follow instantly. But a vague shame and sense of ridicule withheld him; so he enforced himself to remain and carry on some formal talk with the Burgundian knights—who, on their part, were little disposed to be either convivial or communicative. They were not only discontented at the rendering of the castle without a blow, but very anxious concerning their own ransom; for they knew enough of their wilful Countess to be sure that, in making terms for herself, she would not be overcareful of the interests of her retainers.

Ralph farther appeased his conscience by going round the guards with Lanyon when he rose from supper. The storm had come on in earnest, and a thick mantle was hardly proof against the fierce, driving rain; so that the esquire could not wonder that the rounds were hurriedly made. Neither did he marvel, though he was very ill pleased, when he was told that his services would be needed no more that night. He gazed after his master, as the other strode away with the haste of one who cares not to be questioned, and crossing himself devoutly, exclaimed—

"Now may Heaven stand this night betwixt him and harm! Unless there be special grace to help, he will scarce come out of it like good Saint Anthony."

CHAPTER XXXI.

A RERE-SUPPER.

THE bower-chamber at La Roche Dagon was both large and lofty, yet there was nothing there of ponderous grandeur. The walls, to half their heights, were covered with soft arras hangings of bright colors, skilfully blended; and the rich furniture was designed rather for ease and idlesse than for pomp and parade. Indeed, about the whole apartment there was an air of Saracenic luxury; and this was increased by the subdued light of waxen tapers, and by the perfumed vapors ascending in light-blue cloudlets from the two quaintly-carved silver thuribles. The chamber was sufficiently lighted in the daytime by a single window —not of stiff lancet shape, but with broad casements between the mullions, and with flowing tracery above of arch and quatrefoil—looking over the deepest part of the ravine.

On a couch, so broad and low that it might almost be called an *estrade*, the *châtelaine* reclined. The background of amaranth velvet enhanced the effect of a brilliant complexion and dazzlingly white skin, and brought out in strong relief the curves of a superb figure. And on hand and arm there was flash and shimmer of gems, as she swung gently to and fro a delicate gold-handled fan of flamingo feathers. Ralph Brakespeare did not mar the effect of the fair picture, sitting on a cushion close to the lady's feet, his elbow resting on the *estrade*. His dress, as has been said before, became him right well, though it was perfectly plain; the only ornament he wore was the chain, Sir Simon Dynevor's gift. A thin thread of gold that supported Marguerite de Hacquemont's cross was scarce visible round his neck, and the cross itself was hidden in his doublet. Within the last few hours Ralph had marvelously changed. The lines of his visage, usually hard and stern, had softened, and in his outward guise he no more resembled the rough *chevaucheur* who summoned La Roche Dagon to surrender than does the Emir, issuing curled and perfumed from his bath, the dusty wayfarer across the desert.

The lute-playing and singing were done; and though the *demoiselles d'honneur* still remained in presence, they were withdrawn discreetly out of earshot. Near a table in another corner, whereon conserves and wines of divers sorts were placed, Réné d'Andelot leaned against the wall, his head bent low on his breast, and seemingly taking no heed of anything that was passing; but in his face there was a black look, half cunning, half vicious, more dangerous than its late suppressed fury. And all the while the storm raged on outside, and from the gorge beneath there came up a sound, like the roaring of a great sea, from the tormented pines. The converse betwixt those two on the *estrade* had for some time past been low and often broken; indeed, it may well be that either spoke often at random, without fully realizing the import of the words. At length the lady roused herself impatiently, as if she would fain have shaken off some overpowering influence.

"I know not if it is the tempest loading the air," she said, "but I feel strangely athirst, and my lips are parched. Réné, give me to drink of yon sherbet; and this fair knight shall pledge me in a beaker of Cyprus wine."

With an unsteady hand the youth performed his mistress's bidding—or, rather, half thereof—for the salver, which he presented kneeling, bore only one cup.

The Countess looked sharply at her page, as she took it.

"Didst thou not hear me aright, when I said Sir Ralph Brakespeare would pledge me? Wherefore hast thou not poured for him also?"

Réné d'Andelot rose hastily and answered—looking not at his mistress, but full at the Free Companion—

"Very noble dame, as you said rightly to-night, I am your sworn servitor, in matters small or great, for life or for death; but to this Englishman owe I neither service nor homage. Let him pour for himself, an he list. He shall die of drought ere I aid him to slake his thirst."

Never, since he went near to beard his own father in his own hall, had Ralph Brakespeare endured insolence of word, look, or gesture from any man; and of late he had been so accustomed to see others bow themselves to his will, that for an instant or two he felt more surprised than angry. But he checked his rising choler—remembering from whom the provocation came. The ridicule of a serious quarrel with that slender stripling struck him at once, and he even tried to avert the storm gathering on the *châtelaine's* brow.

"Nay, chafe not, gentlest lady, nor hold yourself accountable for your menial's discourtesy. If I war not with women, I brawl not with boys. Perchance yon springald will learn better manners ere we part company; but 'tis not in your presence I would give the lesson. The Cyprus wine will not lose its savor, or I pledge you with less good-will, if I be mine own cup-bearer."

The wrath of the beautiful tyrant was not so easily appeased. It was strange to see how the melting hazel eyes roused themselves from languor and froze into cruelty, as they were riveted on their victim.

"I am partly to blame," she said, "for not having before chastised thy malapert humors. But this shall be speedily amended, and by sharp schooling. Begone now; and presume not to appear again in my presence, till thou hast learned to comport thyself as beseems thy station. And ye, too, Jeanne and Mathilde, may retire. I would confer with this knight touching ransom, and other grave matters, alone. Ye may wait my coming in my tiring-chamber."

The last words were spoken carelessly; yet with a kind of defiance. It was evident, that anger had only made her more recklessly bent on the accomplishing of her wayward will. Once again Réné d'Andelot seemed tempted to open revolt, and once again his nerve failed him; but as he bowed his head in mock humility and withdrew, there came over his face the

[IN A VERY FEW SECONDS, BRAKESPEARE HAD WRENCHED HIMSELF LOOSE, AND ONE LONG SWING OF HIS BRAWNY ARMS LAUNCHED THE UNHAPPY PAGE SHEER INTO THE AIR, LIKE A STONE FROM A PETRARY.]

same set, vicious look that had possessed it awhile ago.

So, for the first time, those two were alone together. It could scarcely be of ransom, or such solemn matters, that they were speaking in those low murmurs—broken by gaps of silence more and more prolonged. Their heads drew so perilously close together, that the red-gold tresses almost touched the crisp brown curls; and the lady's round white arm leaned against, if it did not actually press, the puissant shoulder of her companion. The turmoil in Brakespeare's blood waxed hotter and hotter. He had never in all his life before been proved by stronger temptation than may be found in light and facile amours : furthermore, he had almost forgotten the sound of a high-born woman's voice; and such an one would have carried dangerous music even had it spoken commonplaces; his senses had not been so blunted by rough camp-life as to be unable to appreciate keenly the appliances of luxury around him; he cared not to resist the delicious languor stealing over him, and half closed his eyes, as though the vaporous incense drowsed them. When he opened them again, they met other eyes glancing downward, with a challenge that the veriest novice could scarce have misunderstood, or the sternest saint resisted, even had his draught been pressed from nenuphar instead of purple Cyprus grapes. Nearer and lower the lovely witch-face bowed itself, till fragrant breath was warm on his cheek; nearer and nearer yet—till moist crimson lips were laid on his own, and clung there thirstingly.

The caress was scarce begun, when from the farther

side of the chamber there came a rustle, as of arras violently torn aside, and, though Brakespeare sprang to his feet with the dexterity of one familiar with sudden danger, he was only just in time. With one bound Réné d'Andelot cleared the space between the secret door by which he had found entrance and the *estrade*, and struck full at the Free Companion's broad breast with a long poignard; but, swift as was the onset, Ralph yet had time to ward the blow, and caught the thin keen blade in his left forearm, which it pierced from side to side. The next second, without the semblance of a wrestle, the page was down under his enemy's knee.

Brakespeare's countenance could be stern and menacing enough at times; but seldom, even in heat of battle, had it expressed actual ferocity; and surely had it been so possessed by such a murderous devil as now, when, pressing his knee firmer on the writhing figure beneath him, and setting his teeth—more in wrath than in pain—he drew the dagger slowly out of the wound. Not much blood followed; for it was chiefly a cordage of muscles that the steel had penetrated; and the limb, for the moment at least, was not disabled; for the page was caught up like an infant in the other's mighty grasp, and as the Free Companion strode toward the oriel-window, he muttered aloud—

"Thou gay hornet, we will be troubled no more with thy stinging, and thou shalt have thy lesson for once and aye."

And all this while Bertha de la Roche Dagon bore herself thus: she frowned slightly at the first rustle of the arras—partly, perhaps, chafing at the untimely intrusion; partly vexed at her own imprudence in having forgotten to draw the bolt of the masked door —but she never shrieked or trembled, or shrank during the brief struggle—only her lips parted eagerly, and the pupils of her great hazel eyes dilated, like those of some beautiful tigress, who, from under the shadow of a date-palm, watches the yellow sand flying up round the death-duel that is to decide which of the two tawny rivals shall be her mate. Neither did she disturb the indolent grace of her attitude—much less interfere by word or gesture—though she guessed at Brakespeare's fell purpose before he tore open the casement with his left hand.

And Réné d'Andelot guessed at his doom. He had looked forth from that window often enough to have measured the depth of the hideous chasm. He could remember, too, what a shapeless, battered corpse was lifted from the boulders, when Charlot was seized with a dizzy fit, and fell where the gorge was shallower than here. As he lay pressed back against the window-ledge, his face was lashed by the driving rain; and, glancing sidelong, he caught glimpses of the black billows of tossing pine-boughs, tossed hither and thither by the raving wind. No marvel that he struggled with a strength and obstinacy surprising in one so delicate of frame—striving to strangle his enemy— twining his slender fingers round his adversary's throat, and twisting them in his doublet-collar when his grasp was loosened. Even the spasms of despair could not struggle long against such awful odds of weight and strength. In a few seconds Brakespeare had wrenched himself loose; and one long swing of his brawny arms launched the unhappy page sheer into the air, like a stone from a petrary.

Up to this instant, Réné d'Andelot had fought as mute as a wild cat; but now there went up through the darkness a single long shriek—rising high above the howling of the wind, the booming of the pines, and the roar of the mountain stream, swollen to a torrent now—startling the freebooters, still deep in carouse, though they were little apt to disquiet themselves at sound of distress or pain. And then the voice of the storm broke out more savagely than ever, like that of a wild beast rejoicing over a dainty morsel just cast into its den.

Even Ralph Brakespeare's blood—heated by divers evil passions—was chilled and checked as he listened; but it rose again quickly to fever heat as he closed the casement, and turned inward again toward the *estrade*, where Bertha de la Roche Dagon lay.

She did not attempt to upbraid him, or affect regret for the deed just wrought; but rather seemed anxious to make herself accessory thereto; for her tongue neither spared endearments, nor her eyes promises, as she bound his arm with her own waist-scarf. Then the intercepted caress was renewed, and followed by many another; and then—on those two fell the rosy cloud, the uttermost skirts whereof are dark with sin. Soon the green wound began to tingle; but the knight felt it no more than did Lancelot the smart of his gashed hand, after the grating was once wrenched away that barred him from Queen Guenever's bower.

Then, and for many a day after, his better angel gave place to Belial. Yet Ralph did experience one brief pang of remorse and shame, when he marked the fragment of a thin gold chain hanging to his doublet collar, and wist that Marguerite de Hacquemont's cross was either lost in the black ravine, or locked in the stiffened fingers of the murdered man.

CHAPTER XXXII.

BEGUILED.

MORNING broke—still and cloudless, as though the night had been innocent of storm or crime. Of the last, at least, no proofs remained, for the torrent had done its work thoroughly; and Réné d'Andelot's corpse, after making sport for eddy and rapid, found rest at last in a black pool ten fathoms deep in the Rhone. Yet none in the castle doubted that the page had come by foul play, nor by whose hand he had been done to death; and not a few—who, while he lived, had hated the spoiled favorite—thought of him half regretfully now. There were swollen eyelids among the women of the household; and Mathilde's cheeks all that day were deathly white. It was long before her voice was in tune for *rondelai*. Some even among the rough freebooters shrugged their shoulders, and looked askance at their leader, when, two hours before noon, he appeared in the midst of them.

The most heedless of the *routiers* could not fail to detect a marked change in Sir Ralph Brakespeare. His manner, usually so steady and cool, was now hurried; his eyes were unnaturally bright, and his cheek flushed as though with fever; the very tone of his voice seemed altered. He scarcely spoke with any but Lanyon, and with him very briefly; saying that he had determined to tarry at La Roche Dagon till the ransom of the castle, and of the three Burgundian knights, should be paid; but that these last were at liberty to depart on their parole, to collect the money on their own fiefs, and that with them should go forth all the able soldiery of the garrison; so that, even with less careful ward than the Free Companions were like to keep, there should be no danger of rescue from within. The habits of discipline and submission were too deeply rooted in Lanyon to allow him to question: but his face was very gloomy as he listened, and he was scarce out of the knight's presence when his discontent broke forth.

"A murrain on her witch-face! I guessed how it would be. The glamour is fairly over him, and St. Anthony himself could scarce help us now. The ransom should needs be heavy. Thrice its tale would not pay for the spoiling of the best lance in all the Free Companies."

From that day an utterly new life began for Ralph Brakespeare. His world henceforth was bounded by the demesnes of La Roche Dagon; and his thoughts seemed to travel no farther than his feet. He would scarcely absent himself from the Countess Bertha's presence, even for the time necessary to perform the light duties of inspection and parade; when they went a hawking, he was ever close at her bridle-rein; and of an evening, along the castle walls, their shadows moved side by side.

Only on the formal visits that she paid to her husband's sick chamber was Bertha alone; for her lover would never cross its threshold. And on bright, warm days, when Count Hugues's chair was carried forth on the battlements, if Ralph chanced to come near the spot where the poor paralytic sat blinking in the sun, he would turn hastily away: besotted and bewitched as he was, he was still sufficiently his old self to shrink from looking on the stricken face and blanched hair of the man whose helplessness he had dishonored. He never confessed these scruples to his mistress; for he cared not to provoke the light, mocking laugh that rose to her lips too readily.

There is no such thorough bondage as that of these strong, masculine natures, when it is once complete: there are no half-measures in their folly or self-abandonment. When the Danite—shorn and blind—toiled in the stifling prison-house of Gaza, he was not a verier thrall than on that summer night, in the Valley of Sorec, when the breeze lifted his shaggy locks laid on Delilah's lap. Men, tenfold better and wiser than the Free Lance, have acted in the spirit of Philip Van Arteveld:

> " Now be they armies, cities, peoples, priests,
>   That quarrel with my love—wise men or fools,
>   True friend or foemen—they but waste the wrath,
>   Their wit, their words, their counsel. Here I stand
>   Upon the firm foundation of my faith,
>   To yon fair outcast plighted; and the storm,
>   That Princes from their palaces shakes down—
>   Though it should vex and rend me—should not strain
>   The seeming silken texture of that tie."

The Burgundian knights returned, bringing the due tale of their ransom—that of the castle and its inmates had been ready this long time—yet Sir Ralph Brakespeare gave no signs of departure, whereat his men wondered at first, and then murmured. It would have been irksome to them to be cooped up within walls, even with more distractions to idleness than could be found at La Roche Dagon. True it was, that each had received more than his full share of the ransom money, and that the greediest could scarce quarrel with the amount. But the gold that they could not spend burned in their pouches; and, though they were gorged here with dainty food and drink, they came to think there was more savor in the flesh-spots of Anse, and in the wine that they once cursed as over-new. There, at least, they could carouse after their own fashion, unfettered by the lightest rules of decorum; while here, their leader seemed determined to monopolize license.

So they grumbled and growled, till one day the discontent came to a head; and Gilbert Fleming was put forth to expound it—a sturdy veteran, not given to wild debauch or reckless improvidence, wherefore he stood high in his captain's favor, who trusted him next to his own body-squire. The *routier* delivered himself of his mission warily; for Brakespeare's temper had grown more uneven of late, and none cared to provoke it. On the present occasion, however, the knight listened patiently; pondering awhile, before, he made answer in his own grave, calm way—

"There is truth and reason in what thou sayest, good comrade. Neither may I deny that, in such times, 'tis waste of approved *gens d'armes*, to keep them at garrison of a fortress whence no foray is made. I purpose not to ride forth hence yet awhile:

nevertheless, all such as care not to tarry here with me, have my free leave to betake themselves to Anse again. I doubt not, still bides there Sir John Hawkwood—a better captain than I—who will receive you gladly. When I return thither—if ye be so minded—ye can ride under my pennon again; and, forasmuch as ye all have borne yourselves discreetly during your sojourn here, I will add to your full pay certain largesse; and will wish you heartily 'Good-speed.'"

Gilbert Fleming could have looked for no better answer: yet his countenance fell when he told it to his fellows; and he seemed inclined to quarrel with the alacrity some of them displayed in closing with their leader's offer. That same day, before noon, the Free Lances were mustered in the courtyard of La Roche Dagon. Then it was found that only some ten or twelve, and these by no means the choicest of the band, chose to remain there, and share Brakespeare's fortunes to the end—a miserably insufficient garrison for the place. To this effect Gilbert Fleming expressed himself. Sir Ralph Brakespeare smiled coldly.

"Trouble not thyself concerning that. It may be that others will soon draw to me when they know that my pennon is pitched here; and if it be otherwise, the place is right easy to defend, and hard to assail. While the drawbridge is up there is no danger of surprise; and should any try the trick of the rope and grappling-iron, the mangonel we fixed for that special purpose will sweep them off like flies. We are amply victualed, too, and yon well never can fail. In these two bags is the largesse whereof I spake; see ye divide it fairly at your first halt—each man taking his share without wrangle. And now, Gilbert Fleming, lead forth thy party without farther parley. Ye are late on the road already, if ye would sleep at Vertpré. Fare ye will, my merry men all; and fair chance befall you till we foregather again!"

No answer came; and the Free Companions looked at each other somewhat shamefacedly, as, without another word, the knight turned on his heel and mounted the staircase leading to the presence-chamber above. But the awkward pause did not last long; and, if any had scruples as leaving his leader in the lurch, they soon vanished in speculations as to the probable amount of largesse, and reckonings as to how many carouses it would furnish at Anse. None guessed at the heaviness of heart that—despite his indifference, real or assumed—oppressed Ralph Brakespeare, as, some minutes later, he leaned from a window, whence a last twinkle of spear-heads was visible in the skirts of the woodland. He was absolutely proof against fear, and had no thought of personal peril; yet he could not shake off a vague sense of desolation, and consciousness of folly. So a voyager, who, left by his own choice alone on the shore of some marvelously lovely tropical isle, watches the white sails of his comrades' vessel blending with the purple horizon; and knows that, when they return, they will, perchance, find naught to bring away but a heap of bones.

The knight's reverie was broken by a sound, betwixt a grunt and a groan, close behind him; and, turning sharply, he confronted Lanyon, before the other had time to clear his countenance of its gloom.

"I can guess wherefore thou art here," said Ralph, slowly and bitterly. "To complain, doubtless. Thou has done so aforetime, with less reason. By Saint Giles! I marvel thou wentest not forth with the rest. This place misliked thee from the first, and matters will scarce be mended now."

The esquire had shifted uneasily at first under his master's glance, like one detected in some breach of good manners. But he stood his ground stoutly enough now.

"It pleases your worship to be merry. I am dull at conceiving a jest; and this seems to me a sorry one. But my memory is better than my wit; and I mind well the words ye spake when we two stood together in Bever court. 'Honest Will, I pray thou mayest never repent having cast in thy lot with mine.' Have I grown dishonest, then, to have such words cast in my teeth? I repent naught but not having kept to myself my likes and dislikes: so will I offend no more. I came but to ask if your worship had any command concerning the ordering of the garrison left here?"

Ralph's face softened, more naturally than it had done since the fatal fever-fit possessed him.

"Go to: thou art even too honest for the company thou art keeping. I prithee forgive my taunt, and forget it: I am strangely distempered of late, and speak at random sometimes. For good or evil hap, we two must needs cleave together; I never thought otherwise. I will come to thee anon below, and look myself to the ordering of these matters."

When the Countess heard from her lover's lips all that had been done that forenoon, her arched brows were bent—thoughtfully, to say the least of it; and, though she was afterward more lavish than usual of her caresses, Ralph was tormented by a disagreeable impression that she felt no overwhelming pleasure or gratitude for the sacrifice made for her sake.

If the truth must be told—the spoiled beauty was already beginning to weary and repent of her fancy. Every thorough coquette prizes a conquest less from the moment that it is perfectly assured and complete—especially if there be no rival to dispute it. And Bertha de la Roche Dagon was cruel in her luxury and caprice beyond her fellows; with her, the Circean cup lacked savor without a spice of treachery.

Her paramour was too single-hearted in guilt, and too honest in dishonor, to suit her long. She had never been bound by anything ruder than rose-chains: no wonder that steel rivets galled her dainty wrists. Indeed, those two had few real sympathies in common. Ralph Brakespeare was not of the stuff of which minions are made; he had earned his mistress with a crime, and he would have risked a dozen lives besides his own to carry out one of her whims; but he could not turn himself into a troubadour; and the delicate *finesses* without which—on palates like Bertha's—dalliance must soon pall, were as strange to him as tapestry-work would have been to his fingers, hardened by grip of sword-hilt and mace. He was not jealous—for the very simple reason that there was no living creature in the castle whom he could suspect—but he was, perchance, in many ways too exacting. Besides, this, if he was enslaved, he declined to wear the badge of bondage openly; his manner was often too imperious for the taste of the lovely despot who had domineered over mankind from her girlhood; and she soon found that he was no puppet to be played with and cast aside or taken up again.

Altogether, the *châtelaine* began to realize that she had made a grave mistake, and to cast about for means of amending it. But these did not suggest themselves easily. She had ever been too haughty, or too careless, to choose a confidant; and she was not one of those who glean counsel in the highway. So she pondered and fretted inwardly—doubling the devotion of her manner toward her lover all the while, till at last she fell back on what is often the first—always the last—resource of woman in her extremity, and sent for her confessor.

Some two leagues distant was a Cistercian monastery, founded about a century later than the great Abbaye de Cisteaux. The said House had been wont, from its establishment, to minister to the spiritual necessities of La Roche Dagon, and a certain Father Jerome had discharged this particular duty for many years. It was an onerous office, certainly, if not a responsible one, especially since the Countess Bertha came to reign there. Sir Ralph Brakespeare, as you know, liked not cowl and scapular; but for very shame he could not have objected to the visit paid, outwardly, no less to the lord than to the lady of the castle; and it was in the ante-chamber of her husband's apartment that the Countess chose to lighten her soul of its burden. There, at least, she was safe from the only interruption she dreaded.

Father Jerome had listened so often to that incorrigible penitent's confessions, that the mention of any ordinary sin would not have stirred the apathy of his placid face, and he would have mumbled absolution as a matter of form. But on the present occasion his visage was ominously grim.

"My daughter," he said, "without special license of my Superior, I may not complete thy shrift. The sin of adultery is—as I have warned thee aforetime—sufficiently heinous; but the guilt is tenfold when it is shared by one lying under ban of Holy Church. Knowest thou not that yonder godless kinght is guilty of the blood of an anointed priest—no other than the Sub-prior of the Benedictine House at La Meilleraye—whom he hanged by the neck like a felon, while, in discharge of his duty, the holy man was convoying to Agen a convicted sorceress?"

Now the lady was perfectly familiar with the whole tale. Before the Free Lances had been three days at La Roche Dagon, some of them had vaunted this deed of their leader as rather redounding to his credit, and it soon filtered through the entire household. But the devoutest matron could not have looked more virtuously horrified than did the Countess Bertha now. She played the part of amazement and remorse so admirably as almost to impose on the auditor. Ere long, Father Jerome judged it best to relent; and, on certain conditions, no longer to withhold absolution. Then, in all amity, the two began to confer together, till they had laid the frame-work of their plan.

CHAPTER XXXIII.

HEAVENLY INSTRUMENTS.

Few fortresses built before the beginning of the fourteenth century were unprovided with means of exit and access besides the main entrance by the barbican and *pont-levis*. The castle of La Roche Dagon to the south and west was made nearly impregnable by the deep scarped ravine. On the other two, the walls—pierced only by narrow loopholes and arrow-slits—were high and massive enough to set at naught all the rude artillery in use before gunpowder came into vogue. Pickax and battering-ram would have made no more impression there than on the living rock; while the nature of the ground forbade attack by *chattefeux* or *belfroi*. But on this other side existed a secret passage, very similar to the one above described at Hacquemont: only that here the tunnel—issuing from one of the dungeons—extended much farther, and debouched about midway on the hill—which trended downward steeply, though not abruptly—by an iron trap-door, level with the surface, and so concealed under boulders and briers as to defy detection. Indeed, unless these had been cleared away from without, it could not have been lifted from within. The passage had not been used for many years, and few in the household were aware of its existence;

neither was this among the secrets that Bertha had thought fit to confide to her lover. The keys of the several doors it traversed were not kept with the others; but always lay in the *châtelaine's* private coffer.

On the fourth day after his first visit the confessor returned; and once again Sir Ralph Brakespeare saw him arrive with some surprise and displeasure. He was getting used to all manner of caprices and whims; but this sudden access of devotion puzzled him exceedingly. Looking deliciously demure and innocent, Bertha coaxed her frowning lover.

"Thou wouldst not have me all a heathen, *mon gentil ami?* When the good father came last I was confessed but not shriven—wottest thou why? He judged me to have sinned of late so heinously, that, without conferring with the Abbot, he dared not absolve me. And whose fault is it, that I have so erred? Wilt thou grudge this one half hour to my soul's peace? Or is it because there is none on earth thou canst be jealous of, that thou art grown jealous of Heaven?"

As a matter of course the lady carried her point. Her religious exercises were somewhat long; for the second hour found her still closeted with her confessor. By this time everything was settled: yet evidently there had been some debate; for the Countess Bertha's face, though neither sorrowful nor displeased, was unwontedly pensive.

"I would I had a more express promise, reverend father. If all tales are true, the mercies of Holy Church are sometimes cruel; and, though I would fain be rid of yon Englishman, I were loth to give him up to the doomsman, much more the torturer. I should not sleep for many a night, if I thought he came by foul usage—and I love not ugly dreams."

She gave the prettiest shiver of her round white shoulders, as she looked up pleadingly; but the monk showed no signs of relenting, and answered almost rudely—

"Thou hast heard our terms, my daughter. On no others will our House risk its vassals in thine aid—to say naught of the *preux chevalier*, Guiscard de Champrecour, who leads them. Choose thou, once and for all; either to live on in open shame with this accursed Freebooter, or to render up him and his esquire—who abetted in that foul sacrilege—without farther question. I have paltered with thee overlong on this matter."

She sighed once; but before the sigh was fairly ended she smiled.

"Be it as thou wilt, and let no more words be wasted. Ay—and does Guiscard de Champrecour lead your soldiers? I saw him win a tilting prize at Lyons. A marvelous fair knight, albeit something overbold with his glances."

The monk had hard work to look grave—it was so easy to read what was passing in his penitent's mind. He guessed at once that with that sigh the old love was buried, and with the smile a new one was born.

"Then, before midnight, our forces shall be without the postern," he said, rising, "counting on finding bars and bolts undone. The page Aymery, who serves in poor Réné d'Andelot's room, may be trusted so far; and none can watch him, since the secret stair of issue descends from yon chamber, where my lord the Count lies. As for thee, my daughter, thou hast naught to do but to use this liquor, deftly, at the right season. 'Tis utterly tasteless and harmless to life: yet there was never yet human brain that could think, or muscles stir, for twelve hours after it hath been swallowed. Take it, with my benison."

He held out a tiny vial of thick dark glass, which the lady carefully concealed in the bodice of her robe; and then somewhat abruptly they parted: the man's black fanaticism and the woman's selfish sensuality were not sufficient to prevent them from feeling uneasy in each other's presence till the treachery was complete.

That night Brakespeare supped alone, as had been his wont for some time past, with the *châtelaine* in her bower-chamber. From the first moment of their meeting, Bertha had never been more dangerously seductive; and Ralph yielded to her fascinations the more easily, because he had reproached himself since for his churlishness in the matter of the confessor that morning; indeed, he would have expressed his penitence, if his lips had not been stopped in a pleasant fashion. Generally, the lady needed some pressing before she would accompany herself on her lute; but now she took it up unasked, and sung more than one *virelai* in a voice wondrously sweet, though not especially well tutored or strong. So, as the night wore on, the witch kept weaving charm after charm, till her victim was more helpless under the spell than when he first reclined at her dainty feet. Suddenly the countess, who had been glancing twice or thrice impatiently toward the oriel-window, begged her lover to draw the curtain closer athwart the casement; saying that the moonbeams streaming in vexed her, she knew not why. The instant Ralph's back was turned she drew the vial from her bosom, and, unstopping it with swift dexterity, emptied it into the cup that stood nearly full at her elbow. When Brakespeare returned to her side, she had raised the goblet to her lips and seemed to drink; but never a drop passed them.

"You weary of my wine, if not of me, *mon doux ami*," she whispered; "'tis an hour since you pledged me. Do me right now in this beaker, whose savor I have proved already."

Her hand never shook as she held it out; and she looked right into his eyes while he drank.

For one brief instant the minutest feature of the scene stood out before Ralph's vision with supernatural clearness, like objects lighted up by a brief flash of lightning, and abode in his memory as if they had been seared there. To his dying day, he never forgot the quaint arabesques in the pattern of the arras, nor the chasing of the silver hanap he had just drained, nor the amaranth velvet of the *chatelaine's* tunic. He could even remember how the slightest flush on one of her delicate cheeks showed that his last caress had been something too rude. Then there came a hot surge and whirl in his brain—then a heavy stupor, slackening sinew and muscle, so that he scarce had strength to stagger back and sink down on the *estrade*, groping blindly for his poignard hilt. And then came a horror of great darkness.

Bertha de la Roche Dagon's face was full at first of

Brakespeare ; Or,

CHAPTER XXXIV.

IN THE SHADOW OF DEATH.

ERTHA !"

e voice was faint, and hollow, and bewildered—
the voice of one who, having been buried by
p in a trance, wakes within the sepulcher.
en there was a clank of fetters, and through the
ess another voice spoke.
ow, St. Giles be praised that he lives yet !—
h I know not wherefore I should rejoice thereat.
ord Sir Ralph, I fear me it fares ill with you.
er may I aid you ; for I lie here like a log in these
d gyves."
t is Will Lanyon, surely," Brakespeare said in a
r tone. "In God's name, what is this place, and
ame we here ?"
eshrew me if can altogether expound it," the
e replied. "My brains are swimming yet with
roke that felled me ; and, furthermore, we were
ht here in a close litter ; but I take it, though I
not rightly how time hath gone, we are but some
agues from La Roche Dagon—a malison on every
therein. I wot well that we are in priests' hands,
hough mine eyes were bandaged when the litter
ed, I have heard since no clank of spur—only
atter of sandaled feet. Neither know I how the

"SHE STOOPED AND KISSED HIM TWICE OR THRICE."

mocking triumph, as she bent
to assure herself that he wa
But it softened for an instant
him twice or thrice, passiona

"'Tis pity. Ah me! 'tis p
Then she sprang up, stamp
at her own weakness; and v
bower-chamber, locking it be

An hour later, Lanyon sti
his door open stealthily; but,
feet or grasp a weapon, a par
his head, and left him sensele

By midnight the massacre
Companions were taken w
though they died hard and d
serious resistance. Before da
been flung into the ravine, and
had taken from the countess
and reward.

castle was surprised. The French rats crept up a sewer, perchance; but they did their work cleanly.

Not one of our company is left alive save us twain; ere they led me out, they counted the corpses."

Once more the fetters rattled, and there was a sound of a brief convulsive struggle, as if the knight had striven furiously to rise. Then Ralph's voice, hollower than it had sounded at first, was heard.

"And the Countess Bertha—hast thou naught to tell concerning her? She was with me surely when I fell down in this trance. If they have harmed a hair of her head—"

Lanyon's laugh broke in, hard and jarring.

"Be not uneasy thereanent! Yon winsome lady stands in no peril that is not of her own seeking. Mine eyes were not so heavy but that I saw her smile as she looked down from the presence-chamber into the courtyard, just after the last of our men had been dealt with. A proper knight, too, stood by her side; and, if I err not, her hand rested right lovingly on his shoulder. I dare be sworn, she could tell the secret of the trance in which your worship hath lain so long."

The next minute the honest esquire could have bitten his tongue out for the words it had spoken,; for there came through the darkness a sound, more terrible to hear than wail, or shriek, or groan—the sob that breaks from a strong man's breast when some awful agony is tearing at his heart-strings.

While Lanyon was devising some rude form of consolation, a key rattled in the wards of the lock, and four Cistercian monks appeared, two of whom carried torches. Of the pair who entered last, one was the friar Jerome. Ths other's features were almost buried in his cowl; but his robe and scapular were of finer texture; and the beads of the rosary swinging at his girdle were richly wrought in gold, such as were only worn by high Church dignitaries. The torchbearers held their flambeaux over the stone bench to which Brakespeare was fettered by a broad iron chain doubled round his waist, with heavy manacles on wrists and ankles, so that their superiors might contemplate the prisoners at their leisure. For several minutes the two monks feasted their eyes greedily in silence. Then the Abbot—for such he was—drew near with slow, cautious steps, like a hunter peering into a pitfall in which some terrible wild beast is trapped.

"So," the Cistercian said in a low, bitter voice, "Heaven hath delivered thee into our hands at last. Thou owest the Church a heavy debt; thinkest thou to pass forth hence, till thou hast paid the uttermost farthing?"

The Free Lance's face was deathly white, and the late agony had left it pinched and drawn; but his bold brown eyes never blenched, and his lip curled instead of trembling.

"Heaven works with rare instruments, it seems— a false harlot, a juggling monk, and drugged wine! Nevertheless, sith it is as thou sayest, and the debt must be paid, I marvel ye have not set about writing quittance already. In such matters you holy men are not wont to be long-suffering."

The Abbot drew back a pace or two hastily, crossing himself.

"Peace, thou blasphemer! Make not thine accompt

with God heavier than it now stands. Thou knowest not what or whom thou defiest. In cases like thine, 'tis mercy to cause the soul to pass to judgment through sharp bodily penance, if so may be purchased some remission of eternal torment. Thy hardihood will be more than human, if it outlast the proofs of our *questionnaires.*"

Before the ghastly threat Sir Ralph Brakespeare's visage fell not a whit; yet there was something like compassion in his glance as he turned toward the corner where, fettered not less heavily than himself, lay Lanyon, the esquire.

" We who wear spurs change defiances with our peers, not with women or monks," he said, " and boasts, even in a free man's mouth, are idle. I am no hardier than my fellows, that I wot of; yet under trial I trust to bear myself not dastardly. When flesh may endure no longer, why—ye may laugh your fill. I have scant skill at pleading, and naught wherewith to bribe; nathless I would ye would consider, that 'twere hard justice to deal with yon poor follower of mine as ye deal with me. On the day when the deed which ye call sacrilege was wrought, I said, 'The burden, whether of sin or shame, I take upon mine own shoulders.' So say I now. What he did—'twas little enough, God wot—he did under mine orders. If his life be forfeit, let him die like a Chrisom man, though a sinful one; not piecemeal, like a scotched snake."

Lanyon could not stir a limb, but he lifted his head impatiently.

" Nay, nay, Messire Ralph. Shame me not before this reverend company. If my sinews be not so tough as thine, they will stand some straining ere they crack. They call him churl in Kentishland, who drinks his full at the feast, and tries to escape the reckoning. I was right ready to take art and part in yon deed; and I am ready now to abye it. Let these holy men deal with us according to our deserts; surely their wisdom cannot err."

His very eagerness betrayed him into a form of address more familiar than he had used toward his master for many years—perhaps since they had been boys together—and there was anxiety in his eyes, as if he had been soliciting some great boon.

The Cistercian Abbot threw back his cowl—revealing features cast in a fine patrician mold, though marred by the stamp of supercilious austerity—and gazed steadily at the speaker, moved into something like admiration by the sturdy simplicity of self-sacrifice.

"Thou art honest, at least," he said, "and it shall not fare the worse with thee therefore. Also thou hast well said, that it is not for such as ye to prescribe the fashion or measure of your punishment. Only be sure, when it is noised abroad, it shall serve as a warning to malefactors, and an ensample that, when Holy Church setteth her hand to the work, she doeth it not negligently. Now we have respite for one hour, during the which the reverend father here shall receive your confession; so that at the fitting moment ye may be absolved—for we may not slay the soul with the body. Brother Jerome, I leave thee to thine office. Do thou advise us when it is ended."

Drawing his robe closer around him, lest it should be defiled by touch of the excommunicate, the Abbot swept out of the dungeon, followed by the two monks, each of whom, before departing, fixed his torch in a socket projecting from the wall.

Though the Free Lance had grown more than negligent in religious duties, he was by no means an infidel; nor—despite his late open rupture with the Church—was he inclined to spurn her aid in the last extremity. Nevertheless, he felt an unconquerable aversion to be shrived by the priest who, he felt sure, had been the accomplice in, if not the concoctor of, the plot against his life and liberty. And, even could this have been overcome, it were the veriest mockery to profess himself at peace with the world and all God's creatures while the memory of Bertha de la Roche Dagon's treachery lay like molten iron on his heart. If his fingers, even at that moment, could have closed round her delicate neck, they would scarce, perchance, have pressed it more rudely than they had often done in caress: yet Ralph felt as if another hour on the rack, and another century of purgatory, would have been a cheap price to pay for having the false witch fairly at his mercy. He could not, for a moment, decide whether to reject or accept the services of the friar, who stood there telling his beads, showing no sign of interest on his heavy, apathetic face.

At length the knight motioned with his hand, as though to intimate that he wished Lanyon's confession to precede his own. So the Cistercian kneeled down by the farther stone bench, and bending down his ear, prepared to listen.

But the esquire seemed in no hurry to begin. For the last few moments his eyes had been closed and his brows bent, like those of a man striving to collect his thoughts. And it was with a quaint half-smile that he spoke at last.

"I cry your reverence mercy. But, an' ye fear not to come so near mine unholy carcass, I would crave of you one slight service—to thrust your hand into my breast, and pluck forth what ye will find hanging there next the skin."

Half reluctant, Father Jerome did as he was desired. When the doublet and shirt were undone, there was found a broad piece of flattened gold, strung to a chain of steel-wire links rudely twisted; which by long pressure had worn a sort of furrow in the hairy chest and brawny throat.

"What meaneth this token?" exclaimed the monk, suspiciously. "How can it concern me, or advantage thee, at such a time? I command thee, confess if these signs have aught to do with Black Art or Cabala. Unhappy wretch! Learn that, under this roof, the Prince of Darkness hath no power."

The smile grew broader on Lanyon's lip.

"If Black Art hath aught to do therewith, a holy man must answer it—no other than Abbot Hildebrand of Haultvaux; whom my master and I encountered on the road the morning we set forth from home. The signs ye see he carved with his own hand; and with these very words he bespoke me when he bestowed it. Marry! 'tis no marvel I remember them; for I conned them over to myself nigh an hundred times in that day's journey, and ever since they have come as pat to my mind as an *Ave*. 'Tis a rare chance that your reverences' *routiers* found it not: they thought it scarce worth while to search narrowly the person of a poor esquire. '*Thou comest of the right bulldog breed*'— my lord Abbot was pleased to say—'*and will never be far from thy master's heel, in weather fair or foul; so that, if he lie in sore peril, thou thyself wilt be in as evil case. If ye be come to such a pass that there is no hope of help from man, and ye have brief time to make your peace with God, show that gold coin to the priest that shall shrive thee, and adjure him, by his vow of charity, to carry it straight to his Superior, or the churchman highest in authority that shall chance to be near. If the token be discerned by one who hath the power of life or death, or whose intercession may avail, I dare aver that ye shall both go forth for that once scot-free—ay, though there be holy blood upon your hands, or the guilt of sacrilege upon your souls.*' Surely now, if ever, is the time to put this to proof. So thus do I discharge me of Abbot Hildebrand's message. If it carry no weight here, it's no fault of mine. Good father, the gold piece is in your hand: deal with it as seemeth best to your wisdom."

After this—surely the longest speech that his tongue ever framed—the esquire settled himself on his bench again as composedly as if it had been his pallet, and waited the result with much more outward indifference than his master; for, during the last few moments, the knight's face had grown eager and wondering. Father Jerome rose to his feet in much vexation and perplexity. He had given himself, and gained from others, much credit for having entrapped such important captives; and was inclined to chafe at the faintest chance of their escape from condign punishment; yet he stood too much in awe of his haughty and irascible Superior to venture to suppress the token on his own responsibility. After pondering awhile, and muttering a few words that were lost in his cowl, he plucked a flambeau from the wall, and left the dungeon, clanging the door behind him.

When the prisoners were fairly alone, said Ralph—

"By St. Giles! I am as easy to beguile as a dottrel; but I thought at least I was safe with thee. Father Hildebrand knew thee better than I, when he chose thee to carry his embassage. I had as soon thought of finding a troth-piece round thy bull's neck, as yon token. Peradventure, 'twill not help us, yet none the less I own that the Abbot meant kindly, and that thou art the very pearl of secret-keepers."

Had the light been less dim, the esquire's cheeks might have been seen to flush. In certain things he was simple as the day he started from Bever, and his master's praise was as pleasant to his ears as ever.

"Mock me not, messire," he said. "I have done no more than any carrier-pigeon, rightly trained. Moreover, we know not if it will profit it, as yet."

"We shall know right soon," the other answered; and then there was silence again.

Meanwhile Father Jerome was closeted with his Superior. The Abbot was no less puzzled and perplexed than the monk had been, when the token was laid before him; but in different wise. For it was clear that he was able to decipher the engraving thereon, and only doubted how to act.

"We are placed in a shrewd strait," he said, twisting the gold piece nervously in his fingers. "By this token, Hildebrand of Haultvaux expressly requires that the bearer hereof, and the gentilhomme whom he serves, shall be assoilzied and set free for once, be they gnilty of any crime whatsoever. 'Tis a strange request, but Hildebrand never speaks nor acts like other men; and his demands may be not lightly gainsayed. None hath wrought more diligently for the advancement of our Order than he; and, standing high in King Edward's favor, he hath never misused it. He is keen to discern, and slow to forget, when his will is crossed, and hath sure intelligence of all that passes here; and his cousin, the Cardinal of Ostia, would surely espouse his kinsman's quarrel. 'Twere rash policy to incur his Eminence's displeasure just now, for since Pope Innocent's health hath begun to fail, his name is in many mouths at Avignon. Moreover, I have reflected—though this alone, I profess, should not have withheld me—that we are not so far from Anse but that, if news came thither of our *haute justice*, Seguin de Bastefol may ride out hither, and avenge it. *Benedicite!* On scantier pretext these godless knaves have wasted holy places with fire and sword. Nay, it boots not to gloom over it, Brother Jerome. I am vexed, not less than thou art; yet am I minded to meddle no farther with God's vengeance, but on certain conditions to let these malefactors go free. I will take good heed that Hildebrand be informed of this our courtesy, and I doubt not that one day it shall be amply repaid. So, do thou attend me to the dungeon once more; and bid Jacquot, our jailer, follow with his tools. If they needs must go forth, we will be quit of their accursed presence speedily."

Neither Brakespeare nor Lanyon thought the aspect of things more encouraging, when the Cistercians entered the dungeon once more, followed by a man bearing a basket filled with uncouth iron instruments. The uppermost thought in both their minds was, that the Abbot, provoked by their stubbornness, had shortened the time of respite, and that the forbidding attendant was none other than the torturer. Neither had the Superior's brow relaxed aught of its severity, as he bespoke the chief prisoner.

" If ye have not altogether forgotten how to pray, ye will bend your stubborn knees before Heaven in thanksgiving for little less than a miracle. Your lives are safe. It hath pleased my brother of Haultvaux—for what reason I cannot guess, since never in less worthy cause hath saintly voice been upraised—to plead so specially in your behalf that I may not slight his intercession. So space for repentance is given you. There is good reason that your lives be amended, for ye are even now as men raised from the dead. Yet, on these conditions only shall ye pass out free. Ye shall swear on the most Holy Sacrament, hereafter to molest neither the castle of Roche Dagon, nor any now dwelling therein; and not only to exact no reprisals for this night's work from any—gentle or simple, clerk or lay—but to reveal what hath befallen thee to none. And furthermore, in after-time, that ye will cut off your own hands at the wrists sooner than lay them on, or touch irreverently, an anointed priest. Perchance ye will set your vow at naught. In such a case, your blood be on your own heads. From that instant ye are laden with mine anathema, from which none living, save our Holy Father himself, can discharge you. Are ye ready to make oath?"

It will scarce be credited that the Free Companion should have hesitated before he answered; nevertheless it was so. That same inveterate stubbornness of character which, from boyhood upward, had been his bane, asserted itself even under the shadow of death, and chafed under the light condition by which his release was fettered. But there was some reason even in his self-will. He soon began to reflect that it might be very long before his power equaled his will, if he were to go forth bent on revenge—a revenge that, after all, could only light on such as manhood is bound to spare. Besides, the outer world had never looked so pleasant to him as now. There surely was much work to be done, and, perchance, fair sport to be found therein, even if monks were wily and paramours untrue. Also, if he had been entrapped by one shaveling, he owed his life to the kindly forethought of another, whom he had entreated but roughly when they parted. Weighing all these things, he was fain to confess that he had found mercy beyond his deserts. So, on his own and his follower's behalf, he proffered to take the prescribed oath; and even added some formal acknowledgment. The Abbot whispered in Father Jerome's ear, who departed hastily, and then beckoned to the jailer to strike off the prisoners' fetters. Before this was fully accomplished the friar returned, followed by two monks, one of whom carried the golden pyx, the other a canvas sack. When the double oath had been duly administered, the Abbot undid the strings of the bag and shook out its contents on the floor—a gip-sire and a chain.

"These were taken from your several persons last night," he said. "All that appertaineth to you is restored, saving horses, arms and harness—with the which it were sin to furnish you. The soldiery of the Church are no miscreant plunderers, and our House hath no need of your gold; even for charitable use, our hands shall not be defiled therewith. May it help you to better ends than ye have compasssed heretofore. And now—go in peace; peradventure this sharp lesson may yet profit you. Brother Clement, bring here bread and water, lest they wax faint by the way; and then have them forth privately by the south postern."

So, with slow, dignified steps, the Abbot moved away; but on the threshold he turned, and glanced back into the cell. It may be he had feigned more vexation than he felt when he found himself constrained to remit the sentence—at any rate, his last look was not unkindly. There was noble blood in the Cistercian's veins, and cloister training had not wholly quenched the martial instincts born with him. In spite of himself, he had been impressed from the first by the bearing of both the prisoners, and knew not whether to admire most the cool resolution of the knight or the blunt simplicity of the esquire: the last wave of his hand might well have been mistaken for a benison.

Jerome, the friar, was less magnanimous; his visage was strangely dark and malign for a man of peace, as he followed his Superior out.

When the victuals were brought, Ralph drank eagerly

of the water; but his throat was still too parched to swallow a morsel of the coarse rye bread. Lanyon's appetite seemed in no wise impaired; and his jaws made play with the frugal fare, lustily as ever they had done with the spiced meats of La Roche Dagon.

Ten minutes later, the two stood free under the night, and were striding swiftly away—their faces turned toward the west. The monk who unlocked the postern had pointed out to them the track, whence there was no danger of straying for such as could take their bearings from the stars. Ere long the open air and brisk exercise began to tell; and—mind and body shaking off the languor of the drug—the old, elastic strength glowed throughout Brakespeare's frame. Nevertheless, he continued moody and thoughtful, and did not seem disposed to break the long silence. They had been walking something over an hour, when, on a crest of rising ground near a wood, the knight stopped abruptly. Following the direction of the other's gaze, Lanyon guessed easily at the reason of the halt. Battlements and towers stood up black against the dusky horizon, broken here and there by broad streaks and thin lines of light.

Sir Ralph Brakespeare shivered from head to heel where he stood; and his bare fingers pressed his follower's shoulder like an iron gantlet.

"Canst thou guess who sups with the Countess Bertha to-night?" he whispered hoarsely. "And thinkest thou, if we craved it humbly at the gate, we might be fed with their broken victuals? Or, perchance, the noble lady might fling us alms from her bower window? Wouldst have no stomach for such dole? Nay, nay—pride suits not with beggars, and we are naught else now."

There was puzzlement, akin to alarm, on the esquire's countenance. During all the years that they had traveled, over rough roads and smooth, through sunshine and storm, together, he had never heard his master so wild of speech.

"The potion works still in your worship's brain," he said, "or ye would not talk so distemperedly. Did ye not swear, scarce an hour agone, to meddle no more with La Roche Dagon? How doth it concern us to know on whom the witch-lady now practises glamour? Marry, I wot my gipsire is heavier than when we two left Bever behind us; and that fair gold chain is worth more than the bezants ye carried in yours. If we were hopeful then, wherefore should we be hopeless now? We have grown wiser in the world's ways at least, and better masters of our weapons. It will be hard if we carve not out another fortune; we have enow to purvey us with horse and harness; and see if some stout hearts troop not to your pennon, when once it flutters again."

The knight's passion-fit had already passed off; but he shook his head gloomily as, after another long look at the towers of La Roche Dagon, he turned to resume his journey.

"Thou are right, in a fashion, Will; yet not wholly so. We are not so slack of sinew, or scant of breath, but that we can breast another hill; but it will be wearier work winning up, and the prospect will be scarce as fair as from that we have climbed. Furthermore, I avouch to thee, that the blood of those poor knaves, slain yonder, lies heavy on my heart. If they had died in fair fight against great odds, it had been well. But it irks me to think of their being butchered like beeves."

"Your worship's conscience is too tender," the esquire answered, in perfect good faith. "It was but a chance of war, like another. I have no mind for rack, or pincers, or such devilries, I own; but so the pain be brief, I see not why a *routier* should stand upon the fashion of his death."

The simple philosophy did not quite convince Brakespeare; but he cared not to argue the question then; and so silence ensued, broken only by brief consultation where the road divided or seemed doubtful, till after sunrise, when nearly half the distance dividing them from Anse was accomplished. At a small hamlet they refreshed themselves with food and rough country wine; and then set forward, Lanyon—as he had done on the first day they marched forth together—carrying the provant. After another scant meal they rested somewhat longer; so that the twilight was closing in fast as they came down on the ferry of the Loire over against Anse: they stood within the gates of the town soon after the sounding of curfew.

CHAPTER XXXV.

EASTWARD HO.

In most lives, be they ever so peaceful or blameless, there are certain moments that may never be recalled in after years without a hot flush and tingling like shame, even though they are linked with no memory of guilt or dishonor. At such times, men, neither romantic nor over-sensitive, have wished in all sincerity that their tongues had been dumb forever, rather than utter the tale that must needs be told. Nerves, strong enough in the midst of deadly peril, have grown womanly weak ere now under such a trial. Well and nobly spoke the old provost to the messenger from Flodden Field:

> Thou hast not shamed to face us,
> Nor to speak thy ghastly tale;
> Standing—thou, a knight, a captain—
> Here alive within thy mail.
> Now, as my God shall judge me,
> I hold it braver done,
> Than hadst thou tarried in thy place,
> And died above my son.

When Ralph Brakespeare set his back against the door in Hacquemont keep, and made ready to hold the stair against odds of a score to one, he felt no such sinking of the heart as now when he entered the

chamber where Seguin de Bastefol and other chiefs of
Free Lances sat at supper, and was fain to confess all
that had befallen him. There was little fellow-feeling
or comradeship among these marauders, recruited, as
they were, from divers countries; but many there
would liever have provoked the captain of a fair
clump of spears than the man who, quite unarmed,
and with never a blade at his back, sat in the midst of
them—with a face too resolute to be penitent, yet too
sad for defiance—to tell, so far as his oath of secrecy
allowed, the story of his own folly and its punishment. So, when it was ended, there were neither
gibes, nor taunts, nor jests, nor laughter; but only
sullen murmurs of disapproval, easier to bear.

Yet one man singled himself out from his fellows,
and ranged himself at once on Brakespeare's side.

John Hawkwood was a wily adventurer, thoroughly
unscrupulous, and relentless at times, as his afterhistory proves; but he was free from the meanness of
the petty plunderer; and it was foreign to his natnre
to press hardly on a comrade in adversity, or even
to exult unseasonably in the fulfilment of his own
prophecies.

" 'Tis an evil mischance," he said, cheerily, as he
made room for Ralph next to himself; "yet not so
evil but it may be amended. There is the furnishing
of more than one lance in that fair gold chain, that by
some miracle still hangs round thy neck, to say naught
of thy balas ruby. Didst thou blind the *soudards'*
eyes with *gramarie*, so that they saw it not glitter ?
Each man here is free to choose his own captain, and
I know naught of our trade if thou long lackest fol-

lowing. Moreover, I will aid thee according to my power; and I will confer with thee on these things ere we sleep. Pledge me now heartily: thou art no winebibber, I know; but a cup or two beyond thy stint will do no harm to-night. Trouble wears more than travel, and thou hast had enow of both, God wot."

The geniality of the speaker influenced not only the man he addressed but others in presence there. Thenceforth, Brakespeare's misadventure was an object rather of rough sympathy than blame or scorn. He himself was the more moved by Hawkwood's manner, because, of late, had been marked toward him by a certain coldness and reserve. That even the two spake long and earnestly together; and, before they parted, much of their future plans was nearly matured.

Hawkwood's proffers of assistance to his comrade, though liberal enough, were not unconditional. He did not attempt to reduce the other to a mere subaltern with no independent power; but made it clearly understood that the command of their united followers was to be vested in himself, and that no expedition should be undertaken without his especial sanction. At the same time Brakespeare was left free to part company whensoever he pleased—first repaying the sums now advanced; in pledge whereof, the gold chain, at Ralph's express desire, was placed in Hawkwood's hands. This, at least, was better than parting outright with the heirloom; the ruby he still retained on his finger. All this may seem exceeding unromantic, and something unchivalrous; but both were hard, practical men, and they liked each other none the worse because the matter was arranged in an honest, businesslike fashion. When all was definitely settled, the elder knight began to unfold his design.

"I have pondered much of late," he said, "having in truth little else to do, and thus much is clear to me—that it is not for our advantage to tarry longer here. This realm of France hath been so vexed and ravaged from border to border, that there is little left therein worth the harrying. Even this corner of Burgundy, that had 'scaped till the *Tards Venus* came down, is so naked now that it can scarce purvey us with forage; mine ears are weary with the plaint of those wretched peasants; and to look on their frightened famished faces is worse than listening to their moan. I care not greatly, as thou knowest, for meddling with priests, and we have seized and put to ransom all such fortresses as might safely be assailed; so that, in this wise, we needs must hold our hands—unless we would set ourselves at open war with one or both the kings; for Edward cannot, for very shame, sit still whilst the peace of Bretigny s trampled on. Art thou of my mind so far?"

"Yea so," Ralph assented. "We have grazed all down bare within sweep of our tether, and 'tis best to seek fresh pasturage. I care not how soon, or how far afield we stray."

"That is well," Hawkwood said; "hearken then to me. Thou hast heard, belike—for those here have never ceased to grumble that they marched not south with Guyot du Pin and the Bastard of Breteuil—of the early doings at Pont St. Esprit, and how our fellows wasted all up to Avignon gate, till Innocent waxed sick with fright, and the cardinals hid themselves in hole and corner like hunted mice. But, mayhap, thou hast not heard—sith 'tis but late and in thine absence —how all these things were concluded. For, at the last, John, Margrave of Montserrat, on behalf of the Pope, proffered sixty thousand golden crowns, and plenary absolution to boot, for the Free Lances to leave the Church in peace, and follow his own banner into Lombardy, where he wages war with the Milanese. Witless and wilful would our comrades have been had they haggled over such terms; so, two months agone, they marched thitherward, light of conscience, and heavy of purse; and ere this, I wot, they have done wight service, with profit to themselves, no less than to their captain. Now I am minded—when we two have gathered sufficient following—to follow in their track. I have spoken lately with certain who know the country well; and, unless I err greatly, there will be, for years to come, work enow therein—ay! and large wage to boot—for such as fight for their own hand. Wilt thou ride on that road with me? 'Tis but turning bridle again when thou art aweary of my company."

"Ay, and willingly," the other made answer; "an' ye fear not infection of ill-luck. Misfortune, so some think, carries a taint like the plague."

"Tush!" Hawkwood said, pleasantly; "I have never leisure for superstitious fancies, and leave such to old wives or astrologers. Blame rather ill-management than ill-luck, when matters go awry. If a knight will air his valor in defense of *ribaude*, and make martyr of felon priest, and let high-born paramour set foot on his neck—those that came back from La Roche

Dagon told rare tales!—he must needs look to come by scathe or scorn. But thou hast been sharply schooled against such vanities; and, if I see thee falling again into temptation, thou shalt not lack due warning of thine elder—not thy better—in arms."

In more cordiality than had subsisted between them for some time past, the two parted for the night. On the very next morning Sir Ralph Brakespeare began to furnish himself anew; and his name was reckoned once more among the captains and leaders in Anse.

Little, indeed, is known accurately concerning the military economy of those famous Companies; for no annalist ever rose among themselves, and even Jehan de Froissart's zeal would scarce have tempted him within sight of their camp-fires. Nevertheless, something we may infer. Division of booty in certain proportion was substituted for regular pay; and the Freebooters came and went as it pleased them, enlisting for no definite time of service. Yet that there were difference of rank fixed and maintained, is clear. The lowest grade were the *coutilliers*, or spearmen, lightly harnessed and imperfectly armed, who performed the duties of grooms or pages to the full lances; above these last were certain squadron leaders, answering to the knights-bachelors and bannerets in the feudal army; while the movements of the main body were directed by one or more chiefs, answering to our generals of brigade.

Hawkwood was not over-confident, in asserting that spears would soon gather round his comrade's pennon. If Brakespeare had been somewhat stern in discipline, and imperious—apt rather to repel than invite familiarity; he was known to be free-handed, even to lavishness; and when there was danger in the front he only asked to be followed. In speaking of the misadventure at La Roche Dagon, the *routiers* did not forget how the castle was won: weighing the exploit of the *pont-levis* against the night surprise and the drugged drink, the scale turned rather in Ralph's favor. Any man might be excused for being taken unawares by secret passages, or woman's wile; if their captain had paid dearly for his own love-fit, perchance he might be less severe hereafter in judging others who broke bounds; and they liked him none the worse since he had shown that he was not temptation-proof. Little sympathy, and less regret, was expressed for those who came by their deaths when the place was retaken; those reckless *soudards* were more inclined to pity a comrade for losing his money at the dice than for losing his life in battle or brawl.

Sir Ralph Brakespeare was much in the position of a favorite captain, who having just lost a vessel—rather by the visitation of God than through his own ignorance or cowardice—when he begins to fit out again, finds less difficulty in manning his ship than many merchants who have plodded on through their profession, steering clear both of brilliant success and grave disasters.

It soon became noised abroad that Hawkwood and Brakespeare proposed to sever themselves from the Companies lying at Anse, and set forth for Lombardy. Rumors—vague, but tempting—of the success of those who had already marched thither, had come back across the Alps; so that, when the knights finally mustered their followers, no fewer than fourscore lances, and nigh two hundred spearmen and *coutilliers*, were ranged under their command. Seguin de Bastefol was sorely inclined to take umbrage at so large a defection; but independent action was the very root and essence of Free Companies; and he knew that neither of those two was likely to be dissuaded nor gainsayed. Moreover, he himself had begun to find the country round Anse too strait for him, and to think of moving westward toward his native Gascony. This, indeed, he did not long afterward, turning by the way to storm Brieux, ravaging and devastating Auvergne from Clermont to Ussoire. So Seguin de Bastefol swallowed the necessity with a tolerably good grace; and when he bade his comrades "Go and prosper in the devil's name!" this, according to his peculiar ideas, was rather a benison than a ban.

The events and preparations just related extended over the space of several months; and the spring of 1362 was far advanced when the adventurers rode forth from Anse. They bore to the southeast, by Grenoble and Briançon, and crossed the Alps under Mont Genevre, by the pass through which, more than a century later, Charles VIII. descended, bringing with him a mighty armament and heavy train of artillery. It was a long march and a toilsome; for the road was rough to travel, even in summer, and was more than fetlock deep in snow on the higher grounds: yet they had not lost horse or man when they came down on the Piedmontese plains near Susa. Thenceforward the journey was easy, and they moved steadily on—meeting with no let or hindrance—by way of Asti and Alexandria, till they fixed themselves for the present on the south bank of the Po; waiting to see how the tide of events would turn.

By this time John of Montserrat, warring with the Lords of Milan, had made such good use of the spears he hired at Pont St. Esprit, that Barnabo and Galeas Visconti were fain to sue for peace. When this was once concluded, the Margrave—a prince no less politic than bold—began to cast about how he might best deliver himself of a burden both cumbersome and costly; for it was needful not only to provide the Freebooters with food and pay, but also with constant work. Once in idleness, they waxed dangerous; and, like the familiars of necromancy, were apt to turn and rend their masters. From this perplexity he was relieved by the offer of the Pisan deputies to take off his hands such of the Free Lances as he could spare; and so the White Company—then chiefly, though not entirely composed of English—passed into the pay of the Republic. To this Company Hawkwood and Brakespeare joined themselves; and were received as those are like to be who bring with them no mean reputation, and a following answering thereto.

It was not long before the elder knight began to gather into his own hand the reins of authority, hitherto somewhat slackly held by the two or three esteemed chiefs of the White Company. Only one of those—Simon Burnley by name—could lay claim to any real military skill; and he was such a thorough debauchee that it was hard to reckon when his senses would be fit to use. So the eyes of all men began to turn to the quiet, staid commander—slow of speech, but whose cool brain and steady nerves were ever ready to profit by advantage, or battle with calamity.

Ralph Brakespeare watched his comrade's rise not alone without envy but without emulation; though he was neither gloomy nor despondent, the shadow of his last misadventure passed not away from him when others forgot it. He seemed loth to take upon himself any responsibility of command; in field or on parade his voice was clear and sonorous as ever; but in counsel-chamber it was never heard. Hawkwood at first made efforts, not a few, to draw the other out of the background, as if unwilling to engross the chances of advancement; but after awhile he desisted, and left Brakespeare to follow his own devices, while he addressed himself steadfastly to the task of building up his own fortunes.

Under the careful training of that skilful strategist, the materials of the Free Companies—already molded into shape by fifteen years of incessant warfare—was developed to a military perfection forgotten in Europe since the Roman Legionaries ceased to be. On the harness and equipment, no less than on the training of his veterans, Hawkwood bestowed thought and care. It was easy to conceive how poor a front raw peasant-levies and citizen-soldiery must have shown when set face to face with such troops as Villani describes:

"These English were all lusty young men, most of them born and brought up in the long wars between the French and English; warm, eager, and practised in slaughter and rapine, for which they are always ready to draw their swords, with very little care for their personal safety; but in matters of discipline very obedient to their commanders. However, in their camps and cantonments, through disorderly and overbearing boldness, they lay scattered about in great irregularity, and with so little caution that a bold, resolute body of men might, in that state, easily give them a shameful defeat. The armor of almost all were cuirasses, their breasts covered with a steel coat of mail, gantlets, and armor on the thighs and legs, daggers and broadswords; all of them had long tilting lances, which, after dismounting from their horses, they were very dexterous in handling. Every man had one or two pages, and some of them more, according to their ability to maintain them. On taking off their armor, it was the business of their pages to keep them bright and clean; so that when they came to action their arms shone like looking-glass, and thus gave them a more terrifying appearance. Others among them were archers; their bows long, and made of yew. They were very expert in using them, and did great service in action. Their manner of fighting in the field was almost always on foot. The horses were given in charge to the pages. The body they formed was very compact and almost round; each lance was held by two men in the same manner as a spear is handled in hunting the wild boar; and thus close embodied, with their lances pointed low, and with slow steps they marched up to the enemy with terrible outcry, and very difficult it was to break or disunite them."

Nevertheless, fortune was tardy in rewarding the great *Condottiere's* pains. The winter expedition through the Val de Nievole, though an admirable test of hardihood and endurance, could scarcely be classed above a predatory expedition, from which was reaped no permanent advantage; and when, in the summer of 1364, he first appears as the leader of the Pisan forces in a regular engagement, he led them not to victory but to a rude reverse. True it is, that at Barga those of the White Company encountered not municipal troops alone, but many of their ancient comrades—both German and English—who had been lured from their own ranks by fair proffer of florins. It was wolf set against wolf, and deadly rending ensued; yet was the defeat not doubtful, and Malatesta, who commanded the Florentine host—cousin to him whose doings and death have been recorded in this chronicle—pressed his advantage right up to the gates of Pisa. Never, since he first drew sword, did Sir Ralph Brakespeare show more desperate valor than in covering that retreat, wherein he gat two sore wounds, besides being crushed under his dead charger. Hardly did Lanyon and others who struck into the rescue bear the knight alive into the town.

So once more Ralph's iron constitution had a sharp trial; and the stark muscles and sinews slackened, till they could no longer lift the weary arm. There were no white hands to smooth his pillow, and no soft voice to sing him to sleep, as at Hacquemont. Nevertheless the knight found a careful nurse and a cheery withal, in a certain matron, buxom though well stricken in years—wife of the clothier in whose house he had lodged ever since he first joined the White Company. The *condottiere*, even so early in their service, were apt to entreat somewhat roughly the good citizens, on whose pay they throve till they waxed wanton; so that murmurs not a few, and some shrill complaints, had already been heard in Pisa. But Sir Ralph Brakespeare's name was in itself a safeguard; the boldest ruffler presumed not to brawl under the eaves of the house where he dwelt, much less molest its inmates; and he himself treated his hosts not with moderation only but with courtesy. In his sickness he had his reward.

If Dame Giacinta had watched by the sick-bed of her own son—she had never borne a living child, yet the matronly instincts were not less strong in her ample breast—she could not have been more earnest in her tending. Garrulous by nature, she could govern her tongue at need and, not till it was safe for her patient to listen did she try her best to amuse him. She had a pleasant voice too, and the *lingua toscana* was musical then as now; and Ralph would lay for hours listening to her prattle, seldom exerting himself to speak, but answering her now and then with a smile; with which encouragement the dame was more than content. Lanyon, too, was always within call; for little duty was going on, since the late defeat caused the Pisan garrison to keep within the gates. On the whole, the knight's convalescence advanced comfortably enough.

One day early Dame Giacinta came into the sick chamber, dressed in deep mourning, with a countenance unusually downcast and demure; praying for leave to absent herself some two hours, which she purposed to spend at her devotions in the cathedral church hard by. When she returned the cloud had cleared somewhat from her countenance; though still pensive, she lapsed rapidly into her wonted talkative mood, and was very ready to answer Ralph's questions as to the causes of her heaviness. This was the tale she had to tell; to which the Free Companion listened till the summer day waned into twilight.

CHAPTER XXXVI.

DAME GIACINTA'S TALE.*

"You must know, most noble *cavaliere*"—Dame Giacinta began—"that I was not city bred, but born some four leagues hence, on the lands of the Vidoni, which stretch along Lake Bientina; in the service of which family I abode till the castle and fief changed masters; then I came hither to abide with mine uncle, in whose house Matteo, my good man, found me and wedded me—despite my thirty years. The Florentines slew my father before I knew his face; and in that same battle Messer Geronimo Vidoni was wounded mortally. His widow, Donna Agatha, was very kind to my mother, and would have her always near her own person, albeit she was too weakly to be of great use as bowerwoman; and when, five years later, I was left an orphan, caused me to be educated—it may be somewhat above my station; whilst she lived I never lost her favor, though she was too wise to spoil me. Her son, too, was pleased to show me no small favor. Messer Marco was but a youth when he became head of his house; but

* Some may remember to have seen the main incidents of this chapter more graphically set forth in a few verses that appeared three years ago in "Temple Bar," signed by Robert Buchanan. I have tried to make the plagiarism palpable by adhering even to manner; but it is better to make it still plainer by this confession.

both in bearing and spirit he was older than his years. Such as knew him well liked him well, for he was true, and brave, and generous to the heart's core; but he was no general favorite with men or women, being rough and curt of speech and something imperious of manner; neither did he affect the company of neighbors. Even in hunting or hawking he mostly took his pleasure alone, and seldom cared to show himself in the tilt-yard —holding all other courtly pastimes in utter scorn. The Lady Agatha used sometimes to lament this to me, and to wish that Messer Marco could be prevailed on to wed. A gentle, fitting helpmate—she thought—might do much toward causing him to take such a place among his equals as beseemed the chief of the Vidoni. So she cast her eyes round about heedfully, till they lit on a damsel of good birth and breeding—daughter to one of the Spinetti—who had just returned home from the Carmelite convent, where she had been nurtured by the special care of the Abbess.

"Doubtless the Lady Maddalena was rarely beautiful: but, had I been a man, I would as lieve have wived with one of the fair saints that Sêr Giotto limned so deftly. Her cheeks might have been as snowflakes, for all the love or anger ever brought out thereon; her eyes might have been wrought in sapphire; and her very smile—she smiled but seldom, save the mark!— was frozen too. I do not think, at first, Messer Marco was much drawn toward the maiden; but in most things he let his mother have her way, and perchance was somewhat weary of hearing from her lips 'that if he cared not for wedlock, it still was his bounden duty in such troublous times to provide his house with an heir;'

so he gave assent a little sullenly, making condition that he should be troubled with no formal wooing. Indeed he scarce saw the bride half a score of times before he brought her home.

"The change that came over Messer Marco within a year was near akin to witchcraft. I was appointed the Lady Maddalena's own tiring-woman, so, I saw it all. Before they had been married two months he loved her with all his soul and strength; but she never seemed to notice his passion—much less to return it. It angered me past patience to watch his full brown face waxing thin and drawn, and his eyes hollower and brighter, while morning or evening brought no change in her small, white, demure face. It would have been better if she had shown fear or loathing of him than that deathly coldness; but she would only draw herself slowly away if he came too near, or murmur, if he wrung her hand too hard, 'I pray you be not so rough, you crush my fingers'—looking all the while like a virgin martyr. I cannot guess if the Lady Agatha found out that she had made a mistake. She was not the woman to confess such things to any living creature; if it was so, she had not long space to repent herself; for the marsh fever carried her off suddenly in the eighth month after the wedding. She passed away at last very happily and calmly, blessing both her children, and praying that God, in his own time, would be pleased to remove from them the curse of barrenness.

"My good mistress would scarce have been happy, even in heaven, if she could have seen how things went on after she died. Messer Marco grew weary of wooing his white statue—moreover he fancied she mourned his mother less than was becoming. His temper grew fierce at times, and his tongue would utter wild words when it slipped its bridle. From being sober as an anchorite, he betook himself to deep drinking—though I never saw him utterly besotted with wine. All the while his wife never stirred one of her baby fingers to beckon him back from the road he was treading—but looked on, placid and meek—smiling perchance, now and then, a little scornfully—just as if she had been watching, from a safe distance, the gambols of a big boarhound. I began to hate her—I know not why— and I think she perceived this: though her words were always sweet and meek, her voice seemed to grow harder while speaking to me at times.

"When we first heard of our bride, there was much talk of her piety; and she took marvelous good care to keep up her credit for the same at Castel Vidoni. *Benedicité!* the good old chaplain who had shrived the Vidoni and their household for a score of years might not serve our new mistress's turn. She prayed from the first to be allowed to keep her own confessor—a brother of the Franciscan monastery at Gallano—who had waited on her in her father's house ever since she left the Carmelite convent. Poor Donna Agatha, I remember, thought the request very reasonable, and worthy of such a paragon as she had chosen; and Messer Marco objected to nothing then; nor indeed up to the very last did he interfere with his wife's religious exercises.

"I am but a chattering beldame now, and then I was not a jot quicker of wit or of sight than other tiring-women; yet I profess that I disliked and distrusted

Fra Rèmo's sallow face from the first instant I set eyes on it. He might look as cool and saintly as he would, and droop the lids over his greedy black eyes, and press his lips together to keep down bitter words; but he could not keep the round red spots from coming out on his cheek-bone, nor his fingers from quivering under his robe. The first time I marked those signs was one evening, when wild weather constrained him to tarry at the castle, for the floods were out. Donna Agatha was ill at ease, so the monk sat at supper with my master and mistress alone—'twas the merest form; he touched naught but bread and fair water. It was my duty to stand behind the Lady Maddalena's chair, to fetch aught she might require from her chamber. Messer Marco had not yet fallen into the evil habits whereof I spake; but the night was sultry, and he had been less sparing of the flask than usual: his mood seemed somewhat jocund, and once—speaking to his wife—he put forth his hand and pinched her ear betwixt his fingers.

"My goodman was ever too easily moved to jealousy —the saints wot, with little cause—but he never would have chafed at seeing such a caress bestowed on me by my cousin. It was marvel to see the Lady Maddalena shrink away as though her husband's touch profaned her; yet I watched her not so narrowly as I did the priest. It was a light scandal, after all, to make the blood flush so in his cheek, and set his fingers twitching in his sleeve. I understood none of these things then; but the time came when I understood them all. As I said, matters went from bad to worse after Donna Agatha's death, and came at last to this—

that the Lady Maddalena would no longer share her husband's chamber, alleging that she feared his violent humors, especially when heated by wine. Perchance, Messer Marco was ashamed to contradict her; anyhow, he let her have her own way, sullenly. Thenceforward, she lived almost like a recluse; never going abroad save when, at stated times, she went in her litter to confession or other religious exercise in the Church of San Francisco at Gallano; Fra Rèmo came very rarely to Castel Vidoni, fearing, it was thought, insult if not injury; for our lord had looked askance at him more than once lately, vouchsafing no greeting beyond a growl in his beard.

"In our household there was one Guiseppe Bandello, whose father and grandsire had been falconers before him to the Vidoni—a faithful servant enough and exceeding expert in his calling, but cross-grained in temper, and disliked by all save Messer Marco, who trusted him entirely. For some time Guiseppe's countenance had been gloomier than usual, and he went about muttering to himself as though some load on his mind troubled him; but none of us cared to ask what ailed him. One day he and Messer Marco went out, as was their wont, hawking alone together. I chanced to be crossing the great hall when they returned, and I saw from my lord's face that something had perturbed him strangely, so that I could not forbear questioning him; but he only laughed out loud—though all the while his lips twisted and writhed as though in pain—and bade me send him in wine speedily, for his mouth was parched with drought; saying that nothing worse had happened than that his fair falcon

Bianca had spiked herself on a heron's beak, so that the twain lay dead together by the side of the marish. As I was leaving the hall, he called me back sharply, and asked whether my lady did not purpose on the morrow to visit the church at Gallano. I answered him yea; for she had charged me to see that her litter was ready early, though she would have none of my company. He nodded his head without speaking—draining two or three beakers of wine, but tasting no food—called for a fresh horse, and rode forth alone; though it was past the hour of the Angelus, and the skies were overcast.

"Nigh ten days ago, Fra Rèmo had set forth for Rome on some special mission; he was much trusted and esteemed by his Order, and it was thought would ere long rise high therein. Her confessor had been absent more than once before, and then the Lady Maddalena was wont to be shriven always by a certain Fra Anselmo—an aged monk, of great repute for sanctity. On such occasions I had noticed that my lady's devout exercises were gotten over much quicker than when Fra Rèmo guided them. All that night and the next morning passed without any signs of Messer Marco. My lady never troubled herself concerning his movements, and asked no questions now as to whither he was gone, or for how long: but she went to Gallano as she had purposed, and had been home again some two hours when my lord returned.

"I was looking from the window into the courtyard when he rode in, and I hasted down to ask what ailed him. I thought for sure he was sickening of the same fever that carried off his mother. His lips looked black and parched, and his eyes burned like lamps in the midst of his wan face; and, instead of sitting in saddle tall and square, he seemed all bent and shrunken together; and his chin was down on his breast, as if he were too weak to lift it. His voice, too, when he spoke, was quite weak and piping, though it got stronger afterward. He said there was naught amiss with him, save perchance some slight chill from the night dews, and that he would be well again when he had eaten and drunken. He bade me tell them hasten with supper, and pray the Lady Maddalena not to fail to bear him company thereat, as it was the feast day of San Marco, his patron: for on occasion of fast or vigil my mistress kept her own chamber. Right few words were spoken at supper; but Messer Marco's manner was so different from what it had been of late—so very quiet and gentle —that my lady's pale blue eyes opened wide in surprise more than once. He seemed to have forgotten his hunger and thirst though, for he scarce eat anything, and drank only a cup or so till supper was over; then he prayed my lady to pledge him before she rose from the table, from a certain flagon which had stood before him untouched.

"'Tis Monte-pulciano, near a century old—a very rare wine,' said he, 'so rare, that only once, Maddalena *mia*, have you tasted it. My father had but six flasks thereof; he drained one the day I was born; another you deigned to taste when you crossed this threshold as bride; and 'tis my fancy—I know not why—to empty another to-night. I pray you balk it not. If you will drink to naught else, drink to my better life and manners—both, I shame to say, need amending.'

"My lady bowed her head very coldly, as she took the cup in both her little hands; yet she seemed to like the flavor of the liquor, for her draught was longer than I had ever seen it. Generally she would only sip like a bird. All the while Messer Marco's eyes were fixed on her so eagerly that he himself forgot to drink.

"'Heaven prosper your good intent,' she said, in her meek, quiet way, as she set the cup down; and so passed out of the hall, as light as a shadow.

"It was my lady's fancy to bide mostly alone in her inner chamber, whence opened her oratory; so I sate with my broidery-work in the outer room, within hearing of her silver bell. I might have been there an hour or so, and had fallen a-musing over my work, when the door opened, and my mistress stood there, beckoning. I saw at once she was in mortal sickness or pain; for she was deathly white, and kept gasping and moaning, with her two hands clasped hard across her breast. I carried her back to her bed, and then shrieked for help as loud as I was able. When the other bower-women came I ran down myself to the hall —to tell my lord what had happened. He did not seem to heed me, but sat there like a man in a dream, and when I plucked him by the sleeve, and cried to him 'for Christ's sake to come quickly,' he only shook me off, and said in a hoarse, hollow voice—

"'Bid her sleep; all will be well, when she sleeps.'

"I dared not stay, lest my help should be needed upstairs, so I hastened back thither, but I was too late to be of use; and later still was the leech, though he dwelt hard by, and was summoned by a servitor on the first alarm. My lady never spoke one word that could be understood, but only shivered and moaned. And the moans and the shudders grew weaker and weaker, till she lay at last—still and cold—like a crushed white lily.

"I had small liking for my mistress, as I have owned; but I felt as sorry then as if I had loved her; and I was weeping and making moan amongst the other women gathered round the bed, when Messer Marco's voice from the doorway made me start and turn.

"'Wherefore this outcry?' he asked. 'Fear ye not to wake her? for she must needs be sleeping.'

"Then Sêr Geronimo, the leech, came out of the shadow—trembling; for wild tales had gone abroad of late concerning Messer Marco's temper.

"'Alas! my lord,' he said, 'be not deceived; slumbers such as these can only be broken by the judgment-trumpet. The noble Lady Maddalena's spirit has passed away but now, from some sudden seizure, as I think, of the heart.'

"Messer Marco looked at him—in the same dreamy way as he had looked at me in the hall but now.

"'Ay, and is it so?' he said. 'Then hath earth lost a fair saint, and heaven gained a fair-faced angel. Now I know what I have to do.' And so went out.

"A dreadful suspicion shot across my mind, making me cold and faint; but I had known my master even from boyhood, when there was a kind heart's core under the rough rind, and I could not leave him alone just then. So I followed him out, and caught him by the mantle and prayed him—as well as I could, for my chattering teeth—to let me do somewhat to help him in his sorrow. He drew himself out of my grasp—so quickly that I thought he was angered, saying—

"'Nay, touch me not, good Giacinta; I have no ailment thou canst heal. Trust me; I am best alone. But call me hither my page Pietro. He must carry a message forthwith.'

"I stood without and listened while my master bespoke the page.

"'Ride down at speed to the Franciscan convent at Gallano; and, after commending me to the Prior, bid him see that neither mass nor trental, nor any due office be omitted for the rest of thy lady's soul. She hath deserved well of their Order, and the first word of her decease should set all the bells a-tolling. And specially pray Fra Rèmo to come up hither instantly. I heard yesternight that he would be home earlier than he had reckoned on, and by this time he may well be returned. As he shrived thy lady living, so let him assoilzie her dead. None other, with my good leave, shall usurp his ministry.'

"So Pietro departed. Messer Marco locked himself in his own chamber; while the women, as in duty bound, laid out decently the lovely white corpse. It might have been some two hours before Fra Rèmo arrived. My master had heard of his coming ere I did; but I saw their meeting in that same room where I had been sitting, as I told you. Beyond this again, there was a third apartment, used only as an antechamber. Fra Rèmo's countenance was very much changed; there was a kind of blank horror thereon, hard to describe, and purple circles under his eyes, as if marked with a brush; brace his lips as he would, he could not keep them from twitching; nevertheless, in fair set terms, he began to condole with my master—suggesting the duty of resignation and so forth ; and furthermore, that the change (albeit so sudden) must needs have been for the benefit of the departed lady. Messer Marco cut him short at once.

"'Trouble not yourself, reverend father, concerning a graceless sinner, when a saint lies within there, waiting your last offices. Nathless, though I bear my burdens after mine own fashion, I may not spurn your consolations : when your ministry is fully performed, you will find me ready to receive them here.'

"Then Messer Marco bade all go forth, save Pietro the page. Into his ear he whispered some words that I could not catch; but I questioned the boy when he came out and learned that he had been bidden to fetch from below two goblets, and the jeweled flagon holding the famous Monte-pulciano. I knew not why, but the chill fluttering at my heart increased every instant, and there was a faint sickly savor in my nostrils like the savor of death. So I crouched down behind the curtains in the third or antechamber, while Pietro passed through after leaving the wine ; and, when I heard the door locked from within, I crept forward and laid mine eye to the keyhole—through which it was easy both to see and hear. Messer Marco sat with his elbows resting on the table and his face buried in his hands. He never stirred till the door of the inner room opened softly, and Fra Rèmo came forth. The monk looked still more ill at ease than he had done half an hour agone. He kept wetting his parched lips with his tongue ; and I could see his eyes turn, first in surprise, then in eagerness, toward the great golden flagon. Certes, Messer Marco saw this as well as I, for he smiled in a strange fashion as he beckoned the other to draw near.

"'Reverend father,' he said, 'you are continent in diet and drink, as in all things else, I know; nevertheless, your vow forbids you not to touch wine for mere health's sake. Albeit we are neither of us in mood for feasting, a draught of this rare liquor may serve as a cordial now, to keep our hearts from fainting in their heaviness. Do me right, I pray you, in this one goblet.'

"So Messer Marco took up the flagon; and with a steady hand poured out the precious liquor, that sparkled in the lamplight though it gurgled out slowly like oil. The monk drank with such fierce eagerness that I doubt if a fly could have slaked its thirst from his empty goblet; but Messer Marco's was scarcely tasted when he set it down; he half concealed the cup with the broad sleeve of his mantlet, so that for awhile Fra Rèmo noticed this not.

"'Now shall we be better able to speak of my loss,' Vidoni said. 'A cruel one, is it not, reverend father? And so cruelly sudden too! I fear me, I never prized aright my sainted Maddalena, while she tarried with me. Ah! she was too good for earth, and too gentle for one rude and unmannerly as I; yet, peradventure —I speak this humbly and under correction—it might have been better if she had thought her husband's soul worth caring for when her own was safe; and if she had beckoned him sometimes to follow along the narrow path whereof you priests discourse, instead of letting him hurry down the broad road after his own devices.'

"'Nay, nay, fair son,' the monk answered, huskily. 'Wrong not so the dead, I beseech you. That devout lady was no less anxious, I well believe, for your eternal weal than for her own; and you were ever named in her prayers.'

"My master's laugh was like the bark of an angered hound.

"'Then she had her own method of showing her carefulness, even as she had her own method of discharging wifely duty. You were her confessor, Fra Rèmo; wherefore you have not to learn that, for these years past, I have won from her neither favor nor mark of tenderness—more than sister might bestow on brother. Ay! even of such she waxed more niggard day by day. Yet I strove for her love harder than many men strive for heaven; and, even when my mood seemed roughest, unless my brain were distraught by drink, I watched for some sign of softening or glance of pity, as one perishing of famine waits for the food that will never come. I deemed it mine own fault, for having mated myself with one far above my level; and tried to think it not strange that angels should keep their wings from soiling. I well-nigh laughed at first, when, two days agone, Giuseppe, my falconer, came to me with a strange tale. 'Tis a shrewd knave, though, a sullen, and hath eyes like one of his own hawks— eyes, Fra Rèmo, that from the top of a high pine-tree can pierce even into a lady's bower. Ha! why look you so aghast? Can it be that your favorite penitent kept back somewhat at her last confession? Take another cup of Monte-pulciano. 'Twill stop the fluttering of your pulse, mayhap. "Her last confession," said I? No, no. Her *last* you heard not; I will tell you why.'

"My heart stopped beating, as, looking through the keyhole, I saw the friar's face turn from sallow to ashen-gray, till its color might have matched his robe.

"'What think you of my scheme?' Messer Marco went on. 'The maddest freak surely that ever crossed a drunkard's brain, yet rare sport came of it. I knew that my pious dame purposed to attend at your Church of San Francisco this morning—there, in your reverence's absence, to confess herself to Fra Anselmo. So I rode down, and lay in Gallano yesternight, and caused a fashioner with whom I have dealt to provide me with a Franciscan habit. Also, very early in the morning I caused a forged message to be conveyed to the said Fra Anselmo, bidding him set off instantly, to attend the deathbed of that wealthy and devout widow Catania Pratellesi. The holy man, unwitting of the more honorable penitent then on her road, went forth with speed. It repented me to beguile his age and infirmity; but there was no other way; and so only could I compass mine end. In my Franciscan's robe and cowl I lurked in shady corners of the church—peering out from the porch now and then—till my Maddalena's litter drew up at the gate. Then I slid stealthily into a certain confessional, and drew the bolt. So my wife came; and, finding the door shut, guessed that none other than Fra Anselmo could be within. And thus it came about that I heard—Fra Rèmo, can you guess what I heard? Aha! There's blood enough in your cheeks now, even without a second draught of Monte-pulciano.'

"In truth, a dark red flush had surged over the monk's face and brow, up to the tonsure. I thought the falling sickness was upon him as he stood up—rocking on his hands that rested on the table—with awful fear and rage in his staring eyes. Messer Marco rose up too, and with his strong arm thrust the priest back rudely into his chair.

"'Sit down!' he went on, low through his teeth. 'Sit down—or, by Christ's body! you shall feel my dagger-point. I have not yet said *all* my say. I heard, that—instead of a pure maiden I brought home a harlot in thought—ay, and soon after, a harlot in deed. I learnt that oftentimes, when she shrunk from my lawful caress, as though it were taint, her lips were reeking from kisses, and the prints of lustful fingers were fresh on her neck. I learnt, too, *who* it was that trained her to dishonor, taught her to carry her shame haughtily, and how to hoodwink her cuckold. I let her finish, and mumbled out something that passed for absolution—I doubt if it helps her much now—so she departed, lightened in spirit, and ready to sin again. I called her by no hard names when we met; only I prayed earnestly that she would sup with me. She did so to-night and she drank of that same liquor which so tickled your palate. An hour later she lay within there; waiting—as she had done a score of times before, Fra Rèmo—waiting for you—cold as you found her. Ha! have I touched you more nearly now? And do you feel aught working in your veins—save Monte-pulciano a century old? *Per Dio!* You have rare luck: never an one in Sacred College hath tasted better liquor than that which brings you death—you a simple priest. Now, whether ye like it or not, you shall drain one more cup to the days that are gone, and your pleasant paramour. Ye will not? Nay then'—leaping up, he caught the monk by the throat.

"I could find no voice to scream; but I beat on the door till my hands bled, and made shift to call on my master by his name. If he heard, he heeded not; for he never turned his head nor shifted his knee or his hand after once he got the friar down. I could not take my eye from the keyhole, though the iron seemed to burn it. I could not faint either, or shut mine ears against the hard breathing, and the horrible choking gurgle, and the hoarse rattle that ended all. When at last Messer Marco rose, shaking himself, there lay on the floor, beyond, a ghastly tumbled gray heap; from which stretched out two sandaled feet, still quivering. After a pause, my master walked toward the door. The power to move came back to me then, in the very extremity of my fear; for I thought that he was angered at my watching, and was coming forth to slay me likewise. So I staggered to one of the windows—I know not how—and strove to hide myself under the curtains. Whilst I was cowering there, Messer Marco's voice sounded close to my ear, speaking low and gently, as I had never heard it speak since the night his mother died.

"'Ah! my poor Giacinta, thou hast seen, then, and knowest all. I have a lie ready for the rest of mine household to account for yonder carrion, but I palter not so with thee. Thou mayest betray me if thou wilt —I think thou wilt not. Fear not that any, save one, shall come to blame for what hath been done here; if needs be, I will avouch my own handiwork. Go and call Pietro now: for I must to Pisa to-night—there to take counsel with my trusty cousin, who shall advise me whether it be best for me to bide or flee."

"Betray him! He might well be safe against that. I straightened myself and strove hard to be calm, whilst my master's call rang through the corridor! and, shortly after, I heard him charge the page to see his sorrel saddled instantly, and to send once again for the leech—who had already left the castle—for that Fra Rèmo had fallen down in a fit. Then he returned and passed into the innermost chamber, closing the door behind him. Besides this, there was between us the chamber in which the other corpse lay: nevertheless, I could hear quite plainly, my Lord Marco sobbing as though his heart were broken—as in very truth it was—and I could hear him calling the dead woman by all manner of fond manes, such as he had never used since the old days when he did not think the winning of her love was utterly hopeless. Then, by Heaven's grace, I too fell a weeping—for I think, without those tears, my brain would have turned with grief and horror. At last the steps of Sêr Geronimo the leech, and others, were heard in the corridor without, and they knocked for admittance. Then my master came forth and crossed the second chamber, without glancing aside at the friar's corpse. Indeed, I think he would have gone out without noticing me; but I felt, I cannot tell why, that I should look upon his face no more; so I stopped him, and knelt down before them all, and pressed my lips upon his hand—though it was blackened with guilt now, it had stroked my head kindly when I was a little child—and prayed that God would help and forgive him. I doubt if he understood my words; but he tried to smile as he stooped his haggard face down close to mine, and just touched my forehead with his lips. Then—speaking to none else, and staring always straight before him—he went out; and two minutes later I heard the rattle of his horse's hoofs in the courtyard beneath.

"I dared not go with the rest into the second chamber; but they told me afterward that Sér Geronimo shook his head as he knelt by Fra Rèmo's corpse, and that others besides him noticed purple marks on the throat that could scarce be accounted for by the fit of the falling sickness. But it was the business of none there to be over-curious; and the Franciscans, when they heard the news, and came to fetch their dead away, raised no question: perchance Fra Anselmo had warned his brethren to avoid unprofitable scandal. Unprofitable, of a truth, it would have been: before dawn, the sorrel wandered back with splashes of blood on saddle and housing; and those who went forth to search found Marco Vidoni stone-dead in a pine-wood, not a league from his own gate. Riding through the dark at furious speed, his skull had been dashed against a trunk leaning somewhat athwart the road, and he could not have lived a second after the shock.

"Bernando Vidoni, the cousin of whom my poor master spake, soon came from Pisa, and saw the double funeral celebrated with due pomp and solemnity. He was a good man and a kindly, and would have driven none of the old household forth. But few of us had the heart to take service under a new master; and I went with the rest to this city, where some of my kindred abode; and before I had tarried very long with these my good Matteo found me out and wooed and wedded me. We have been very happy since, in our humdrum fashion; but always when this day comes round, I rise with a heart as heavy as lead, and it is never lightened till I have recited many *Aves*, and spent some space in prayer. And, should bread be harder to win than it hath ever been with us, I will still find coins enow to provide a mass in behalf of all who passed to their compt that night unannealed, and a special one to boot for poor Messer Marco's soul."

CHAPTER XXXVII.

BEFORE Sir Ralph Brakespeare was fit to sit in saddle his term of service was ended. The honest burghers were greatly discouraged by the defeat at Cascina; and, looking at their empty treasury, they dared no longer maintain those terrible mercenaries who were apt to wax disorderly on less pretext than arrears of pay. So it was resolved to let them depart, as soon as the city could clear scores with the White Company. From their financial difficulty the council was relieved by Giovanni Agnello—a man of ambition larger than his fortune—who proffered a loan of 30,000 crowns, on condition he should be at once invested with the Doge's mantle. The money came from much deeper coffers than those of Agnello; for it was found by Barnabo Visconti, of whom the other was but the tool and hireling. The *condottieri* cared not a jot whence their wage came, if the tale was full, and the metal rang true: so on the present occasion they took it—grumbling, as a matter of course—and went their way, to turn their Ishmaelitish hands against every one who might be safely laid under tribute, now that peace was concluded betwixt Florence and Pisa.

Thenceforward began for Ralph Brakespeare a life more evil and unknightly than any he had yet led. If the freebooters that Hawkwood commanded were not as merciless in rapine as those who followed Werner—

self-styled "The Enemy of God"—yet their exactions and outrages were sufficient to wring a cry from all the country betwixt Arno and Lake Trasimene; till at last the Siennese, goaded beyond endurance, turned to bay. It was even such a battle as when the shepherd lad went forth with sling and stone to fight with the harnessed champion of Gath; and once again the right triumphed over the unright, and against odds of strength and skill: Hawkwood—if not utterly routed—was forced to give ground, and retire for awhile into the neighboring territory. But there again he found his path beset with thorns—and sharp ones to boot—no other than the German lances who had lately taken hire with Perugia. These, with the civic militia at their back, soon took the field; and the White Company met with a second reverse—heavier than that which had befallen them before Sienna.

It was now that Hawkwood's great strategic talent came really into play. No mere chief of *condottieri* could have kept the bands of discipline and mutual interest unstrained, that held together six thousand marauders, more dangerous under defeat than after victory, and prone to mutiny at the least check on their license. It was a hard and anxious time, not only for the famous captain himself, but for his subalterns in command. Those three years counted for ten in aging Ralph Brakespeare; before they were ended there were deeper lines in his face, and more silver streaks in his brown beard, than were warranted by twoscore summers. He was not so much discouraged by ill-luck—indeed, at times he thought that he and his comrades scarcely merited better—but he was heartily sick of the life he led; and would have turned his back upon Italy long before, had he not held it shame to leave in time of sore strait an ancient brother-in-arms, who had stood by himself in adversity; for all debts, save this one, were cancelled long ago, and Brakespeare was free to go whither he would. Those two were excellent friends now, and there was small danger of their being divided by difference of opinion; for Hawkwood took no man into his council, and preferred bearing the whole burden of ill success on his own shoulder to sharing his authority, even in name. Patiently and warily—exacting from the country through which he moved, or where he tarried, only such contributions as were sufficient amply to maintain his spears—he bided his time, till he felt himself strong enough once more to adventure himself on a stricken field. The tide of fortune had turned thenceforward. Up to the day when all Florence came to see him laid in a sumptuous tomb, once only could any have boasted that they had seen John Hawkwood's back.

In the spring of 1367 he marched into the territory of Sienna; and again—not despairing, but flushed with the memory of their last success—the citizens came forth to meet him. This time heaven helped not the weaker battalions. The first onset of the *condottieri* bore down all before it, and the overthrow of the Siennese was so complete that the pursuit and slaughter were carried to the foot of the hill that the city crowns. While the terror of his victory was still fresh, Hawkwood marched forward on Perugia. The German lances were no longer to the fore, and the bridge of San Gianni saw the defeat of Conchiano bloodily avenged. For the next two years Hawkwood's company lived at free quarters in the territory of Sienna and Perugia—none daring to molest them, or to withhold what they pleased to require. Then they took service again under a new master.

Barnabo Visconti, casting about his keen eyes in search of the proper instrument to carry out his large and crafty designs, found none so likely as the English captain. It was, indeed, the custom of that politic prince to pension the chiefs of the adventurers—even when he did not require their active service—so as to insure, at least, that their arms were not turned against himself. Having now taken Hawkwood into full pay, he sent him to raise the siege of Minciato, now invested by the Florentines, from whom the town had revolted. It soon appeared that Visconti had neither chosen unwisely nor wasted his wages. Hawkwood stood aloof, provoking the enemy and eluding battle, till they waxed wroth and rash, so that they were fain to engage on any terms; and, being drawn into an ambush, were routed with great slaughter and shame. Thus the siege of San Minciato was raised; and, that the town afterward fell into the hands of the Florentines was no fault of Hawkwood's, but of treachery within the walls. Nevertheless, in this service the English captain abode not long. Barnabo's promises were better than his pay, and the insults of young Ambrosio Visconti were hard to brook. So, in the following year, he listened readily enough to the proffers of Cardinal Biturcense, Pope Gregory's legate, and ranged himself under the Holy Gonfalon against his late master.

Here two paths—which for over twenty years had

run side by side—divided forever and aye. The very morning that Hawkwood announced to his spears that they served the Pope now, instead of Visconti, Brakespeare craved speech with him alone.

"I blame not what thou hast done," Ralph said. "Thy brain is wiser than mine, and thy conscience, I dare swear, every whit as tender. Nevertheless, thou goest this day farther than I care to follow. I have run up no score with Mother Church that I wot of, since we cried quits down there in Bourgogne; but I will not take her pay, nor blunt sword in her cause. So I am come to say farewell ere I ride back again, and see what is a-doing beyond Alps. Good luck go with thee, whether thou fightest for Pope, or Prince, or Kaiser; and may men deal with thee even as thou hast dealt with me "

Hawkwood was bitterly vexed, and something angered; but he was too wise to try persuasion when the other's purpose was set, and too proud, perchance, to use entreaty; so, with kind and courteous adieus, and a gift of a rich jewel, he let his ancient comrade depart. Ere night those two had gripped hands for the last time; and before dawn Sir Ralph Brakespeare rode westward out of Bologna, with Lanyon and five others in his train.

The aspect of things in France during the last eight years had greatly changed. Some names of note were borne no longer on the muster-roll of either army, and others had arisen destined to be yet more famous. Henry of Lancaster's sword, that had never yet had time to gather rust, hung idle now over his tomb in Leicester chancel. King John, a prisoner again by his own free-will, had eaten away his generous heart in Savoy Palace; and prelates and peers, who had set him at naught while living, flocked to do honor to his bones when they were laid near those of his father, under St. Denis's altar. Charles the Wise was each day proving himself more worthy of his title and inheritance; better advisers, too, and more fortunate if not more valorous soldiers, were around him than those who had served his father. The war-cry, "St. Yves Guesclin," had been heard often and loudly since it rang out in the streets of Mantes; and nobles who awhile ago would not have glanced aside as the poor Breton knight passed by, veiled bonnet now in presence of the Contable, first of Castile, then of France.

Sharp work had been going on beyond the Pyrenees, wherein almost all the worthies of King Edward's wars took part. It is well known how Pedro the Cruel— having taxed the patience of all men to the uttermost, till the Church laid him under her anathema, and not a Spaniard would draw sword in his defense when Henry of Transtamare ousted him from his throne— by the help of Edward of Wales, was set up once thereon, and permitted to do a little more of the devil's work. Surely in an evil hour the Black Prince opened his ears to the whine of the crippled leopard, and shut them against the advice of the wise counselors and valiant knights who besought him to hold his hand. Thenceforward his own life began to darken so drearily that some scarce remembered the glories of its dawning and its noon. Fair fortune in the field abode with him to the last; scarcely at Creçy or Poictiers was achieved a victory more complete than at Niajarra; and the hand that clove right to the center of the Breton battalion, and received Bertrand du Guesclin's sword, could scarce be said to have lost its strength or cunning. But the Black Prince soon grew sick of the caprice and cruelty and falsehood of the tyrant whom he was not ashamed to champion, and wended back his way discontentedly across the Pyrenees. Perchance he was not greatly grieved when, awhile after, the news came that Henry the Bastard reigned over Castile unquestioned, having avenged the blood of Blanche of Bourbon at the cost of fratricide. Edward's frank and generous nature was so hardened and embittered now that neither conscience, nor the pangs of the dire malady he brought with him from Spain, warned him to forbear oppression. The vassals of Aquitaine had suffered sorely before the last burden of the *fouage* tax caused them to wax restive and carry their complaints before Charles the Wise. If the pretexts on which the English King first took up arms were light and flimsy, those of the second armament were more shadowy still; and a subtler casuist than Simon Tibbald might have been puzzled to gloss over stern facts, so as to make his sovereign appear in this matter void of offense.

He of Toulouse, and the other preachers who thundered forth anathemas and promises from all French pulpits, had easier text to work upon. They spared not to improve the occasion; claiming as a mere right the help of Heaven, whose hand, they said, was already laid heavily on their most terrible enemy. The seed fell on fertile grounds. The memories of Creçy and Poictiers were faded now and dim. Few of the credulous and eager ears that listened now had heard the whistle of cloth-yard shafts; or, if they had heard, it had been as the patter of a summer shower, instead of the rush of storm-rain. Men had confidence, too, in their new ruler, knowing him to be not only bold but cool and capable, and generous without being prodigal; whether mercenaries were to be hired, or munitions provided, he would have value for every coin in his full treasury; and Charles had been for years past husbanding his crown revenues.

In truth, this second war began with evil omen and auspice to the Red Cross. In the very first year thereof a sore gap, that never could be filled, was made in the roll of English worthies. In a mere skirmish on the bridge of Lussac, the spear of a Breton squire sped straighter to its mark than the best lances of France had done on fifty stricken fields. An hour later John Chandos lay a-dying; and the moan made in Mortemer was prolonged throughout Guienne and Aquitaine, and taken up in England from the Welsh Marches to the Scottish Border; and many voices echoed the words of the Black Prince when the news were brought to Bordeaux:

"God help us, then! We have lost all on the hither side of the seas!"

A pompous epitaph would ill have served the strong, simple champion; over his tomb only these words were written:

> Je, Jehan Chandault, des Angloise capitaine,
> Fort chevalier, de Poictou seneschal
> Apres avoir fait guerre tres lointaine
> Au rois Francois, tant a pied qu'a cheval,

> Et pris Bertrand de Guesclin en un val,
> Les Poitevins pres Lussac, me diffirent,
> A Mortemer, mon corps enterrer firent,
> En un cerceuil eleve tout de neuf,
> L'au mil trois cens avec soirante-neuf.

Sorrow and bodily anguish only made the Black Prince more hard and bitter. The first year of the war was marked by a deed that would have brought dishonor on a holier cause. There was sharp provocation. Edward had ever held the Bishop of Limoges in great trust and honor, and bestowed on him great favor: when the town revolted it was but natural that he should be sorely angered. He swore his great oath —saith Jehan Froissart—which he never had yet broken—"by his father's soul"—that he would set hand to no other enterprise till he had made priest and burgher pay for their treachery; and, mustering at Cognac his vassals from Poitou, Saintonge, and Gascony, together with the Free Lances from Hainault, compassed the city in close leaguer.

There were bold spirits within the walls; and Villemur, Beaufort, and De la Roche did their devoirs as knights and captains with hearty good will; but neither skill nor courage availed against the steady advance of the English miners, who, for one long month, pushed forward their sap, till they came to tell the Prince that he had but to give the word, and the way should be made plain over ditch and rampart into the heart of the town. All night long the props smoldered in the mines; just after dawn a great flake of the wall crushed down outward, and the English trumpets sounded assault. Right in front of the stormers, when gate and barrier were down, a litter was borne: thereon was laid one who never would mount war-horse more; who, with death in his own face, and eyes heavy with pain, gloated over the carnage, and checked it not till three thousand innocents had atoned for the treason of their master. This was the man who, when the sun was setting over the field of Poictiers, ere he would sup, served his royal captive on bended knee; and spake such gentle and generous words that some were moved to tears who held such weakness in scorn. The old chivalry flashed forth for an instant, once, before all was done, when the litter drew near the spot where John de Villemur and Hugh de la Roche had set their backs to the wall, and with fourscore more held their ground against thrice that number, led on by Lancaster, Cambridge and Pembroke. To those valiant men-at-arms the Black Prince listened, when at last they proffered to surrender, and gave them fair quarter; though the shrieks of women and children, ringing in his ears since daybreak, had found them deaf as an adder's. Then leaving a heap of ghastly ruins behind him, in place of a goodly city, Edward marched back on Bordeaux. There he escaped not long God's visitation; for he lost suddenly his eldest son, and the fatal dropsy grew upon him till he was fain to listen to the advice of his leeches, and to sail from Aquitaine for the last time.

A striking picture, albeit a somber, might have been made of that last assembly in the audience-hall of Bordeaux; when all the Gascon and Poitevin barons paid their last act of fealty, and bade their suzerain farewell, kissing him on the mouth. We need not follow the

Black Prince on the dreary homeward voyage; graver historians, indeed, have found nothing worthy of record concerning his latter days.

Before the spring of 1371 all these things had been performed; and men were still speaking with knit brows and bated breath of the sack of Limoges, as Sir Ralph Brakespeare rode down the westward slopes of Mont Genevre.

CHAPTER XXXVIII.

Though Charles the Wise in the last seven years had wrought infinite good to his realm, both within and without its borders, there were certain evils that his patient tact could not abate, much less root out utterly. In the more distant provinces—not to speak of the debatable ground over which the Lilies of France and the Red Cross of England floated by turns—not a little of oppression and misrule still prevailed ; and the voice of the poor and needy in their distress, though it went up shrill and often, waxed faint before it reached the throne.

Heaviest among the burdens of the land, now as heretofore, were the terrible Free Companies. There was brief respite from the plague of the canker-worms while the wars were raging in Spain, for large bodies of the Freebooters fought there under the Black Prince's banner, and Bertrand du Guesclin exacted from his mercenaries the full value of their hire, setting them ever in front of the battle. So thousands of those marauders left their bones to whiten beyond the Pyrenees; yet thousands found their way back, by twos, and threes, and scores, and began to draw together in bands; greedy, and reckless, and merciless as ever. Among those who sat down before the doomed city of Limoges were found Perducas d'Albret, Lanuis, the Bastards of L'Esperre and Breteuil, and many other names of evil omen and repute. And be sure they bore their full part in the Devil's carnival that ensued when the siege was over, and the sack begun. As Sir Ralph Brakespeare rode westward from the Lower Alps, through Dauphigne, Viverais and Auvergne, he passed along a track whence few could have emerged without paying toll in purse or person: for divers of the castles perched on the platforms of basalt cliffs and limestone hills were garrisoned now by captains of Free Companies. But albeit those wolves would have battened on one of their fellows, crippled or helpless, not less ravenously than on strange flesh, they lost not their cunning instinct when most an hungered. From their posts of espial, looking down on mountain pass or forest gorge, their scouts saw the little company of seven wending warily along. They scented gold in the valise strapped on Lanyon's croupe, and licked their chaps as they snarled to each other that the gray was too tough and too strong to mell with. Neither did they guess that the stalwart figure towering on his mighty destrere a span above the tallest of his following, might once have been familiar to the eyes of some of them; and so Ralph Brakespeare passed through the midst of his ancient comrades, unwelcomed and unharmed.

On a certain afternoon in April their journey was well-nigh done, for the peaks of the hill-range trending eastward of Mount Cantal loomed now in their rear misty-blue, and the Dordogne flowed on their left through a broadening valley. Lanyon had that tenacious memory for external objects not uncommon with men of slow reasoning power and stolid temperament.

At a certain spot he checked his horse, and let the others pass him, while he peered curiously around till his face began to lighten with a pleased look of recognition, like that of one who, after long absence, finds himself again on familiar ground. Glancing backward over his shoulder often, as was his constant habit when on the march, Sir Ralph Brakespeare saw his follower's halt, and marveled a little thereat.

"What is it, Will?" he said, reining back a little, so that there might be no need to raise his voice. "See'st thou sign of ambush in the oak copse yonder? Mayhap thine eyes are sharper than mine; yet I thought but now 'twas hardly cover enough for a scanty clump of spears."

"Nay, my lord," the other replied. He had fallen into this form of address toward his master from hearing others use it so frequently; but the courtly air of Italy had in nowise softened his manner, and his voice was gruffer than ever. "Nay, I suspect no ambushment. 'Twould be hard measure an' we were trapped so near our harboring, but this place brings back old times apace—ay, and the sharpest course that ever I ran in saddle. A long bowshot in front, where the track turned sharply, the poor beast under me came headlong down, and across that broken ground I ran, stumbling from breathlessness at every step till I broke in among their camp-fires. Under the lee of yon oak wood, Sir John Hawkwood's pennon was pitched. By Saint Giles! I see the good knight's face now, waxing white and grim as I stammered out my news. Marry, my joints have grown stiffer since then; I doubt if I could match now either the ride or the run."

A quaint expression, something akin to melancholy, softened the speaker's rugged face, and a wistful look came into Ralph Brakespeare's eyes, though he answered cheerily—

"What wouldst thou have, grumbler? Thinkest thou that time will stand still for thee and me? Fifteen long years—years not of idleness either—have slipped by since then, and they must needs have set their mark on us both; yet we have stomach and strength left for a hard day's work, I trow. Nathless, we have earned some space of rest and refreshment. We shall find both at Hacquemont, and a brave welcome to boot, unless all are dead who said 'God-speed' when we set forth. Let us put forward; our cattle are fresh now, and I would fain housel ere dark, lest our coming startle the good folk there or put them overmuch to coil."

So the little troop passed on, making good speed wheresoever the ground allowed it. An hour after sundown they passed up the narrow roadway leading to the barbican gate of Hacquemont; and Lanyon, by his master's orders, woke up the echoes without—and perchance the warder within—by a long shrill bugle-call.

Out of a loophole over the portcullis there peered forth in the twilight an old, sour, withered face, and a cracked voice asked, half querulously, half timorously, "Who waited without, and what was their pleasure?"

"I would fain know if the Lord Philippe of Hacquemont yet lives; or, if he be dead, who holds this castle in his place?"

The ancient warder did not recognize the deep, stern tones that indeed were scarce so staid as their wont, yet he felt it was no open enemy or traitorous marauder that spoke, so he answered almost cheerfully—

"Yes, messire, our good baron yet lives; albeit his strength seemeth to diminish daily, and 'tis long since he hath left his chamber. Once more I pray you of your courtesy to declare to me your names, that I may deliver them to my lord forthwith, if he be waking. He must needs have been startled by your bugle blast."

"Say, then, that Ralph Brakespeare waits to pay to the Lord of Hacquemont his humble duty, and craves, for the sake of old acquaintance, one night's shelter at least for his following."

There was a rattle of iron as if ponderous keys had fallen, and a cry of astonishment from above.

"Holy St. Ursula! Will my lord ever forgive me when he knows whom I have kept waiting at his gate? A malison on these dim eyes and dull ears, that looked on and listened to the savior of us all like a stranger! Lo, I come instantly. None other save your own voice should announce your comiug."

As the horseman filed in under the barbican arch, other servitors had gathered in the courtyard, bearing torches; and these marveled greatly to see crusty old André—so chary of courtesy to man, woman or child—cast himself on his knees, embracing the mailed foot of the foremost rider more devoutly than he had ever saluted relic or crucifix. But first one, then another of the more ancient retainers recognized the face and figure of the stranger; and throughout the group there ran loud murmurs of wonder and welcome, as they knew that once more there stood within the walls of Hacquemont the champion whose name had never been long off the household's lips since the night of the battle on the stairs.

While Brakespeare unhelmed himself after dismounting, he bade a page standing by go before him to announce his coming, for he feared the effect of sudden surprise on the sick castellan. Two other servants, bearing torches, marshaled the knight with all reverence into the keep, and through the presence-chamber. Near the top of the upper stair he turned and looked back. All that had happened in those long years became for an instant a vague, distant memory, and every incident of that one night stood out clear and sharp, like the feature of a landscape when a hill-mist lifts suddenly. It seemed but yestereven that he stood waiting the onslaught with the *mortier* burning in that niche on the right; he heard again the trample of iron-shod feet in the presence-chamber below; he saw again the crowd of visages deformed by greed, and cruelty, and lust, surging up the stair; he saw the whirl of the crowbar swayed by the German giant; plainer than all, the dark, beautiful face, and the evil, lustrous eyes on which carrion-birds had battened long ago. He saw all this with his hand touching a notch in the pillar, where his sword, as it shivered, cleft away a cantle of stone, and his pulse leaped up— as it had never done since, in any one of the battles and forays in which he had borne a forward part—as he muttered, half aloud—

"*Pardie!* 'twas a royal fray."

There was very little of vanity in that strong, simple nature; not more than twice or thrice in a career rife with adventure and feats of arms had Ralph Brakespeare indulged in the luxury of self-praise. He almost laughed in scorn of his own weakness as he turned again to follow his torch-bearers, who had already half mounted the third stair; but his face was grave enough as he stood at the curtained doorway of the chamber whence issued broad gleams of light and the low murmur of voices—a chamber that he remembered right well, for he had lain long therein, when the chances for him were even of life and death.

Such a group as this Ralph Brakespeare looked upon, as, leaving the attendants without, he passed inward alone.

In a huge fauteuil, facing the door, and drawn close to the hearth whereon logs were burning, sat the Baron of Hacquemont. The dark green chair-hangings sweeping to the floor on either side, threw out in relief his hair and beard of intense dead white. His wan, weary face was pinched and drawn with pain, and his pale fleshless hands were working nervously as they rested on his furred robe. Over the back of the chair, holding an essence-vial, leaned a dark, handsome lady, wearing widow's weeds: a little withdrawn in the background were two other figures; one, a tall man on the hither side of middle age, with features delicately chiseled, but wearing rather a sad and pensive expression; the other the page that had been sent forward to announce Brakespeare.

Treading heedfully, so as to deaden the rattle of his harness, and speaking never a word, the knight moved forward, and knelt at the castellan's feet—even as he had knelt on that night when those two interchanged farewell in the presence-chamber. Very slowly, with an effort painful to witness, Philippe de Hacquemont lifted one trembling hand till it rested on the other's bowed head. His voice, scarcely raised above a whisper, first broke the silence.

"I render thanks to our gentle Lord Jesus, and I vow a chalice to blessed St. Ursula, my son, for this our meeting. Thou comest late—yet not too late—for we have not grown weary of waiting. Lift up thy face, I pray thee, that I may look upon it again. Changed —ah me!—sorely, sorely changed. Time hath dealt more roughly with thee than with me. What hast thou, at thy years, to do with gray hairs and a furrowed brow?"

Ralph strove to answer lightly, but his voice was hoarse and husky.

"Ay, my good lord; flesh and blood wear faster than Milan steel, even if it have no chance to rust. Such as I have no cause to grumble, so long as we can carry harness and couch lance. I would I had found yourself in better case. I had hoped to have lighted on you where you love to sit—in the oriel you wot of."

The baron shook his head, and there flitted across his lip the semblance of his old melancholy smile.

"Nay, nay, my son; such hope was overweening. From this chamber I never shall stir till they bear me out to the chapel below, chanting the *Miserere*. Others, too, have changed, it seems, besides me and thee. Thou hast forgotten one old friend at least; not one glance hast thou vouchsafed to Odille, who waits thy greeting."

Rising hastily to his feet, Brakespeare stood face to face with the dark lady in widow's weeds. Fifteen years had matured sparkling loveliness into stately beauty, and the features were to him as the features of a stranger: but he knew the frank, kind, bright eyes instantly again. Her voice, as she welcomed him, had not lost its ring, and the hand she held forth to meet Ralph's lips was soft as ever.

"I, too, return thanks for your coming, Sir Knight —ah, we heard long ago, how and where you won your golden spurs. I think 'twill put new life into my father's veins, he hath not spoken or looked so like himself these months past. You are never long out of his thoughts, but chiefly at this season—you wot why —he wearies for your presence, or, at the least, to learn how you are faring. Never a pilgrim, or minstrel, or wayfarer, coming from afar, housels here, but is questioned concerning Sir Ralph Brakespeare; and not a few have spoken of your doings: though since you crossed the Alps, tidings reached us more rarely."

A dark red flush rose on the knight's brow. Though oftentimes, during the wild *condottieri* life, he had felt sharp twinges of shame, he had never loathed it so bitterly as now—standing, perhaps, for the first time these many years, in the presence of a pure gentlewoman, born of a race whose escutcheon was clear from any stain of felonrie.

"Perchance 'tis best so, noble lady," he answered curtly; "no good report, even if they magnified not the evil, could have been spoken concerning me of late. We who followed Hawkwood can claim no better credit than earning our hire honestly. I am heartsick of such warfare where none knoweth under what banner he will fight on the morrow; and I have done therewith for ever and aye. I crave your pardon if I touch a green wound rudely, but it irks me to look on you first in widow's weeds."

"I have worn them these four years," she said, bowing her head on her breast—"since, in a skirmish before Villefranche, my dear lord and husband, Amaury de Champrécourt, was slain. It pleased God our marriage should be childless, so I came straightway hither to be my father's nurse. Out of my sorrow came this much of good, for my presence hath been sorely needed here since our poor Marguerite died."

Ralph had expected this. From the first moment that he rose up and looked on Odille standing alone behind the baron's chair, he felt sure that one place was vacant in that family, and another filled in the household of heaven. He knew that the pale, patient mourner's days of waiting were ended, and that the great brown eyes, once dim with tears, had brightened once again with the light that should never be quenched, so they rested on the face of Loys de Chastelnaye; nevertheless, he drew back, blenching a little, like one stricken by a sharp disappointment. It was almost a mockery to express sorrow upon such a change, yet some such words would his lips have tried to frame had not Odille spoken first, as if she read his thoughts.

"You need not be grieved," she said; "none of us were wicked enough to begrudge her her rest She spoke of you on the day she died, and bade me deliver to you her kind farewell if ever we met again." Glancing downward here, she broke off suddenly, "Sainte Marie! I might have guessed it. This great joy hath overtaxed my father's strength."

Of a truth, the baron's eyelids were fast closed, and though his face could scarce wax whiter, a fixed deathly look, possessed it now.

"Nay, you need not fear," Odille went on in a whisper, as she bathed her father's forehead with the essence; "'tis but one of the fainting fits that are common with him of late. Yet 'twill be best that you leave us alone for awhile. I will descend when he settles to slumber; he mostly drowses after such swoons. Messire Gualtier here will take heed to the bestowal of your retinue; for yourself, you wot well that all within these walls is at your disposing, not less than when you held us in gage."

The tall, grave man before mentioned came forward out of the background, and bent low before the knight, who followed him from the chamber without speaking again. An hour later Ralph sat alone at supper, with strangely little appetite for one who had ridden so far and fast; and even Gualtier de Marsan ministered to him, sparing no jot of the observance due from squire to knight, and answering all questions with ready courtesy. Nevertheless, if Brakespeare had been less busy with his own thoughts, or had chanced to glance suddenly over his shoulder, he might have been puzzled by the look—half of inquiry, half of disquietude—that ever and anon broke through the calm of other dreamy eyes.

Later in the evening the Lady of Champrécourt descended, and from her Ralph learned that Gualtier de Marsan was near of kin to her deceased husband, and had been his body esquire.

"My dear Amaury loved him as his own right hand."

Odille said; "and it was Gualtier who—himself sorely wounded—save my lord's body from plunderers' hands at Villefranche; since then he hath abode with us here. I had not the heart to bid him go forth, poor as he is, and without kinsmen to care for him now. Furthermore, he is very gentle and skilful in his tendance of my father, who likes him well."

Another than her listener would perchance have noticed a consciousness in the lady's manner, like that of one who perforce makes excuse, and the treacherous blush over her cheeks. But Ralph's eyes, that could catch a glimmer of a spear-head half a league away, saw naught of this, and he changed the subject, so soon as he could do so courteously, for others that touched him more nearly.

Those two sat late in discourse, but Odille's "fair good-night" was the merest form of words. It was long since the Free Companion had rested on so soft a couch, or in such a richly-furnished chamber; but sleep, that had seldom been coy in guard-room or bivouac, stood obstinately aloof; and he rose soon after dawn, more feverish and weary than he had often been in the old times after ten hours on outpost.

There was nothing strange in this. Most seafarers say that their first night on shore is sure to be broken. They miss the sway of the surge, the hiss of the cloven water, the creak of the cordage, the tramp of feet overhead, albeit all those sounds had become an abomination to them of late. It is only after the second or third day that they begin to enjoy the land comforts they have pined for. There are few keener pleasures in this life than the slow natural reaction leading to complete repose.

Just so it fared with Ralph Brakespeare. As day followed day, he settled more and more into his place in the household, till at last Hacquemont seemed to him more like to home than Bever had ever been in his boyhood. The time never hung heavy on his hand. In the morning he would direct the martial exercises of the archers and men-at-arms—the garrison was more numerous and efficient than it had been formerly; after the nooning, he would ride forth with Odille and two or three attendants a-hawking along the valley of the Corréze, where there was no lack of quarry; for the Baron had recovered strength marvelously, and they feared not to leave him for some space alone. All his evenings were spent in that upper chamber, where Philippe de Hacquemont listened with a keenness like that of childhood to such stories of wild adventure as the Free Lance was not ashamed to tell; while Odille sat over her broidery-work, glancing up ever and anon with a low exclamation of fear, or pity, or wonder, and the prettiest shiver of her round white shoulders; and Gualtier de Marsan stood in the background, a look of disquietude, that could scarce be termed discontent, darkening more and more on his sad, handsome face. It was a thoroughly domestic household throughout. Lanyon's rugged visage softened into a sort of stolid beatitude, under the benign influence of the place. His voice could not soften itself; but it was never heard to grumble; his manner toward his juniors and inferiors was almost paternal, after a gruff fashion; and he even struck up a friendship, to the wonder of all, with cross-grained old Gilles, the warder. The *routiers* who had come with Ralph Brakespeare from beyond the Alps—though not one of them, since early boyhood, had probably dwelt three nights in amity under a reputable roof—were discreet enough to rule themselves according to the spirit of the time. They had not forgotten how prompt and pitiless their leader had shown himself in punishment of excesses, for which there was some shadow of excuse, if they were not fools enough to fancy that the edge of his sword had blunted, or his arm grown slow to smite, because neither had been lifted of late in any but mimic broil.

All through that summer, too, there was a lull in the war-storm, that for so many years past had been blowing—with change of quarters, it is true, but almost without slack, athwart the realm of France—or, at least, it broke forth only in brief fitful gusts at certain points of the southern frontier. Barons and knights not a few, both in Poitou and Limousin, had fallen away from their English fealty; but the Red Cross still held its own throughout Aquitaine, and John of Lancaster, holding court in Bordeaux, had leisure to think of consoling his widowhood and sating his ambition by marriage with Constance of Castile—a fair, gentle princess, if the chroniclers may be believed. Yet it was an ill-advised match after all. Wise men shook their heads as they asked what luck could come with Pedro the Cruel's daughter. So, indeed, it befell —not for the first or the last time a Spanish alliance brought with it a curse—but none the less merrily the espousal feast was held in Bordeaux, and none the less gallantly did knight and ladies ride in from all the borders of Guienne, bringing wedding gifts and all good wishes; and in the autumn John of Lancaster sailed away for England with his new-made bride, never heeding—if he knew it—that Henry of Transtamare, the Spanish King, had in his wrath and fear sent embassage to Charles the Wise, offering to make common cause against England to the uttermost of his power; for there wanted not many in his realm who still held Henry the Bastard as an usurper, and would have listened readily enough to John of Lancaster, had the Duke been bold enough to claim the crown of Castile in right of his wife. It is not hard to guess what manner of answer the ambassador carried back to Leon. Even had not that strong voice of Bertrand du Guesclin been close to his ear with counsel and encouragement, Charles would scarce have hesitated to close readily with the proffered alliance against Edward. And so another black cloud rose on the horizon that already looked dark enough for England.

So throughout the autumn and winter Sir Ralph Brakespeare's followers tarried in peace at Hacquemont, neither molested nor molesting ; for the castle was far enough from any frontier to be out of the track of regular organized inroads, and with such an addition to its garrison it was far too tough an enterprise for the strongest of the scattered Free Companies to meddle with.

It fell on a certain day in the early spring of 1372 that the knight and the castellan sat together alone; for Odille, under a safe escort led by Gualtier de Marsan, had gone to visit her aunt, Abbess of the Convent of St. Ursula, some three leagues distant. The Baron of Hacquemont had sat silent for awhile, with eyes half closed, evidently musing. At length he spoke, gazing intently in his companion's face, with a very anxious look on his own.

"My son, had it not been sin to question God's will, I should have marveled a year agone why it pleased him to keep this weak taper of mine flickering on while so many brave torches were quenched utterly. I marvel not now. Doubtless there was a purpose in this, as in all other things good or evil, which befall us. Canst thou guess? Nay, I wot well thou canst not, what hath been on my mind; waking always, ay, and sleeping sometimes—these many days and nights past? Let me now say forth my say. Albeit my strength is wonderfully sustained, it is not always I am able for long discourse, so, though my speech may seem strange—yea, even if it mislike thee—hinder me not, I pray thee, till I have told thee all my mind."

Then slowly and painfully, halting often, rather from lack of breath than lack of words, Philippe de Hacquemont set forth the project which he had brooded over till it seemed mature. But a very few words will expound it sufficiently for our purpose. The wish nearest and dearest to the Baron's heart was that Ralph Brakespeare should wed Odille, and be to him thenceforth in very deed as his own son, inheriting Hacquemont, and all its fair appanage.

"If there should be no male heir of my adoption," the Baron said, "the fief must needs lapse to the Crown. True, out of all my revenues, which of late have far more than sufficed our needs, I have laid by money sufficient for Odille's maintenance, should she live threescore years. The money is at usage in safe hands, and even if she came empty-handed, there would ever be refuge open to her in St. Ursula's House yonder; but she is over-young and fair to wear out her days in mourning, and her nursing task here must needs soon be done. I should go to Alix, my dame and Marguerite, my daughter, with a right quiet spirit, if I knew in these troublous times I left her a guardianship like thine. Where betwixt the Alps and the Pyrenees could we look for starker arm or braver heart?"

The Free Companion's face, especially of late years, was not lightly betrayed into an expression of any violent emotion whatsoever; yet there passed across it now, legibly enough, wonderment at first, then a great gratitude, then the darkness of a greater doubt. He cleared his throat once or twice, and shifted uneasily where he sat like one puzzled how best to frame a reply. When he did speak, his thanks were frank and hearty enough to satisfy a more exacting listener than the kind old castellan, yet he did not for an instant feign to believe that the path before them lay open and clear.

"Like should match with like," he ended with one of his rare smiles. "The Lady Odille deserves younger and gentler bridegroom than I. Nay, my lord, I guess what you would say, but we who ride with our lives in our hands count not our age by years. A bird liker her plumage would be more fitting mate; such for example as Messire Gualtier de Marsan."

Few had ever seen on Philippe de Hacquemont's benign brow so dark a frown as settled on it then.

"I looked for sober answer from thee, not mockery or gibe," he said. "Hath the House of Hacquemont become so poor and lowly that the last of its daughters should mate with one who hath barely won silver spurs? who hath gained no *los* save in tilt-yard? 'Tis a kindly youth enough, with a rare knack at *virelai* or viol, and faithful doubtless, after his fashion. Yet sooner than see Odille's hand laid in his, troth-plight, I would see her safe behind the convent's grate. If I thought he had presumed—"

And the weak tired eyes flashed out as they had not done for many a day. But Ralph Brakespeare broke in, his voice grave even to sternness—

"You make me repent my frank speaking, my lord," he said. "Such baseness never was in me as to impute to the Sieur de Marsan or your daughter any thought unbeseeming their several conditions. I dare avouch the one as pure as snow, the other true as steel. I spake of the gallant only as an ensample of what your heir should be in outward seeming."

Even before old age and long sickness had tamed him, Philippe de Hacquemont never could nourish resentment or suspicion long. His brow cleared swiftly; and then those two fell into long earnest discourse, bringing about a result with which both seemed content. It seemed that Ralph Brakespeare had a strange hankering to set foot in England once more before severing himself from it forever. So it was settled that he and his body squire should ride to Bordeaux the following week, and take ship thence, returning to Hacquemont after a very brief sojourn beyond the seas; that during this absence the castellan should broach the project they had then been discussing to his daughter, using—so it was solemnly agreed—no undue influence to sway her decision, and that the knight, on his coming again, should accept her answer.

CHAPTER XXXIX.

No let or hindrance befell Brakespeare and his squire on their journey to Bordeaux. While in garrison there long ago, Ralph had had acquaintance with divers merchants and burghers of the better class. With one of these he bestowed three horses and harness, for he was minded to land in England in the guise of a peaceful traveler, bearing no outward signs of his profession or estate beyond estoc and dagger and golden spurs. The communication between Bordeaux and Southampton, if not so rapid, was nearly as constant then as nowadays. The breeze blew steady and strong from the southeast, and the galliott on which they embarked was a moderately swift sailer, and staggered along under press of sail at fair speed—even through the rollers of the Biscayan Bay. So on the fifth morning they were slipping along under the lee of the Wight, and anchored safely in port before noon. The knight had left the chiefest part of his worldly wealth at Hacquemont, but the leathern belts, which both he and his followers wore under their doublets, were well stuffed with bezants and golden crowns. So, with little delay or difficulty, they provided themselves in Southampton town with two stout *haquenées* and a pack-horse to carry their mails, and a three days' ride brought them to Southwark without distressing their cattle.

Fully a quarter of a century had passed away since those two rode last through Kentish Street, yet not a feature of the place seemed changed. The heavy gables and hanging eaves of the houses on either side looked not a whit more weather-beaten; the window-panes of horn or glass not a whit duskier with dust or grime. The same hideous shapes of beggary, sickness, and decrepitude beset the travelers—croaking or screeching for alms; the same ill-favored faces of cut-purse or bravo peered out at the tavern doorways; and there, on the right, abode—a trifle more faint and blurred, perchance, but still plain for the passer-by to read—the legend

JOHN BRAKESPEARE, ARMORER.

Out of the low-browed hoard, as before, broad red gleams shot athwart the roadway; and, as before, there rang out from within, in a certain rude rhythm, the chime of hammered steel. Ralph felt half disappointed when, as he drew bridle, there came forward—not the burly figure he had first seen there, but another man; younger, taller, and slighter, yet, withal, bearing so strong a stamp of family resemblance that the knight framed his first question accordingly.

"Good youth, I would fain inquire concerning your father, who sometime traded here. It is five-and-twenty years since he and I foregathered, and our acquaintance was but brief; yet I would fain hear that he lives and thrives."

After a quick downward glance at the rider's spurs, the artisan doffed his bonnet.

"I thank your knightly worship," he said, in a round,

mellow voice, very like the one that Ralph remembered
—" my father yet lives, in marvelous good health, considering his years. He hath long been highly reputed among our burgesses, and is greatly trusted in our Ward : in good sooth the matters of Common Council need at times wise and wary handling. Nevertheless, not seldom he cometh among us here in the forge for brief exercise or pastime ; and if he sees any of our 'prentices slack, he will still doff furred gown and show them how to wield forehammer. Hath your worship any commands for my father ? He is now within, and above stair."

" Under your favor," the knight replied, " I will presently visit him." So flinging his bridle to Lanyon, he dismounted.

" May I know who thus honors our poor house ? " the young armorer asked, as he went first up the dark, creaking stair.

" Thou shalt know anon," Ralph replied, sinking his voice, " though the honor is not worth the naming. But I would fain see if my likeness hath wholly passed from thy father's memory. Let me, I pray thee, enter first."

John Brakespeare was sitting alone, poring over some parchments by the light of an oil-lamp, for twilight was fast closing in. His crisp short hair and strong beard were both more white than gray; but there was little change in the hale, ruddy cheeks; the moist, merry eyes, and the ready, pleasant smile. His frame had waxed somewhat heavy and corpulent; but —draped in the full, dark robe—it was not devoid of a certain portly dignity. He rose slowly to his feet, peering under his hand, into the half-darkness at the farther end of the low-browed chamber. Before the burgess could speak, Ralph strode forward and stood within the circle of the lamplight.

"God save you, Master Brakespeare," he said. "Have you never a greeting for an old friend?"

Long and anxiously the other gazed in the speaker's face before he made answer.

"I—I crave your worship's pardon," he said hesitatingly; "the accent of your voice seemeth not altogether strange to mine ears; yet I mind not that mine eyes have ever before rested on your face."

Ralph laughed half sadly, half in mirth at the other's evident bewilderment.

"Ay, is it so? Now I, for my part, have been jostled to and fro through many lands, and have seen and heard some strange things; yet heard I never of a stranger bargain than was struck in yon street below, five-and-twenty years agone, when a wayfaring youth asked thee for no less a boon than the loan of thy good name, and thou wert rash enough to trust him therewith. Wilt thou not pledge me now in one poor cup of wine in requital for the stoup we two drained together that night, under the sign of the 'Spur?'"

The old armorer's eyes opened wide and bright in amazement, with the light of joyful recognition from them, as he stooped forward holding forth two brown, brawny hands which the next instant were gripped heartily in Sir Ralph's.

"Wittol that I was! These weary parchments must needs have dazed my sight. Surely, surely, noble sir, I remember all as though it were yestereven, the poor glee-maiden's dance—God sain her, and others who died in the Great Plague!—and the stark wrestling bout wherein the foreign ruffler's curls gat a soiling, and your service-taking under Sir John Hawkwood, and all our pleasant discourse together. We have had word of you since, trust me, we have had word of you. We had a brave carouse—had we not, Dickon, my son? —the day when the news came hitherward that our noble Prince had himself graced you with the accolade on Poictiers field. Ay, and aftert hat Harry Gauntlett (his father lives hard by) brought home from Bordeaux such a strange tale that even I who had seen your sinews proven could scarce believe, albeit he had it, so he swore, from eye-witnesses: how in some French castle you held a stair-head with your single blade, slaying outright two famous swordsmen, and keeping the Italian we wot of and a score more at bay till help came, and the devil gat his own. And how, thereby, a noble family was saved from murder and worse. Afterward we heard that you had ridden beyond Alps with Sir John Hawkwood's spears, and since then— naught."

The same cloud that had come over Brakespeare's countenance when Odille de Champrecourt spoke of his recent past, crossed it again, though slighter in shade.

"Thou hast heard enough, good friend," he answered, curtly; "and all the best news. Of what hath been done in these last years I care not greatly to speak. Nevertheless, at supper to-night, if it pleases thee to play the host, thou shalt listen till thou art aweary. If, when thou hast heard all, thou judgest that I have brought thy name to no discredit, it is well."

The armorer had fallen back a pace or two, and there was something of deference, if not of constraint, in his manner, as if he half repented the freedom of his first greeting.

"I looked for no less an honor," he said; "truly it grieves me that I may not crave your knighthood to tarry wholly under my roof; but since Dickon here is wived, we have never a guest-chamber. I wot your worship travels not alone. Well, I trust your body-squire at least will taste of our cheer to-night. My son will take good heed he lacks nothing."

"Thou art scarce like to remember him who holds my bridle below," Brakespeare replied. "These dozen years past he carries my pennon."

But John Brakespeare, it seemed, had not forgotten the Kentishman, and bustling down to the doorway more nimbly than might have been looked for from his weight in years, bestowed on the esquire a welcome more familiar, if not heartier, than that with which he had received the knight.

Long and pleasant talk ensued that night both above and below stair, but as it turned all on matters which have already been set forth in this chronicle, it need not be recorded; and there was no stint of good wine either. Though Sir Ralph Brakespeare rarely, if ever, broke the temperate habits of his early youth, his follower was less abstemious; and when, on the stroke of midnight, the squire followed his master toward their hostel, the solemnity of his gait, and the increased stolidity of manner, showed that strong liquor had wrought its uttermost on his seasoned brain. It was after some trouble and loud knocking that they gained admittance—for the "Spur," as of old, was an inn of fair repute, and harbored few lodgers but such as kept decent hours. While they waited under the dark porch Ralph had leisure to recall how he had last lingered there, and the current of his thoughts may be guessed from the words that hove from him half aloud, with something like a sigh.

"Dead—in the past year, too. 'Twas too dainty a morsel for the plague pit."

Once before dawn he started from sleep, fancying that a low voice whispered in his ear, "So may all the saints have you in their keeping." Not without a twinge of reproach he remembered that through all these years, save when Marguerite de Hacquemont's kiss was laid on his brow, no lips had touched him so pure as the poor glee-maiden's. Early on the morrow the knight and his squire were in saddle, and Ralph had pledged his host in a stirrup-cup—a stranger, though, for he who ruled sometime at the "Spur," slept this many a day in St. Olave's churchyard—and made such good speed along the Kentish highway that they laid that night at Tunbridge. You may guess whither they were bound.

On the morning Ralph Fitzwarenne was cut adrift from his home, once and for all he averred in the stubbornness of his heart that his father should never again—save at his own express desire—look on his face whether in life or death. 'Twas one of those rash vows that, perchance, are better broken than kept; but there was no fear or no hope that it should ever be broken now. Thus much the Free Companion had learned the night before in conversation with the armorer. True, that desire for his return had never been expressly spoken, yet from the tidings Lanyon brought back Ralph could guess at somewhat of the longing that had filled Simon Dynevor's desolate heart. After that the dispensation of God left him wifeless and childless. That was a sour, saturnine face of his father's; yet once, at least, he had seen it soften toward him. And now as there rose against the sky-line the wooded ridge that bounded the demesnes of Bever, Brakespeare was oppressed, for the first time since he crossed it last, with a vague misgiving that it had been better if he had not come back so late.

A Dynevor was still lord of Bever; for it chanced that one of that house—not near of kin to the last possessor—had done good service in the French and Scots wars, and King Edward, rather than disturb an ancient name, waived the Crown's right to the lapsed fief.

So those two rode on moodily and silently, till at a certain point where the road ran through a wooded hollow Brakespeare drew rein and spoke, glancing over his shoulder at his squire—

"Dost thou remember?"

"Ay, right well, my lord," Lanyon made answer in his slow, sturdy way. "Just here the good Abbot Hildebrand bestowed on me the blessing that your worship would have none of, and a broad gold piece to boot. God rest his soul, say I, for that same bezant did enfranchise us both when we stood in sore need of ransom."

Ralph bent his brow. "Sayest thou 'God rest his

soul' at venture, or hast thou heard aught lately concerning that same priest?"

"No later than yesternight at Tunbridge," the squire made answer. "He died scarce a year since, it seems. They were speaking of his grand funeral, and of the dole made for him through all the countryside. He was hugely missed—not alone for his large charities, but because of late he ever withstood the King and his councilors with great boldness, when it was question of farther grinding down the Commons."

Ralph turned his horse's head away with an impatient thrust of the spur. The lapse of five-and-twenty years, and the memory that he owed his life to the dead man's intercession, had not taught him so far to forget the wrong wrought while he was yet unborn, as to say "Amen" to the benison on Abbot Hildebrand's soul. But within a furlong the knight checked his *haquenée* to a foot-pace again, as if he were loth to hurry past the old familiar places. Yon oak to the left still towered above the woodland, tall and bare as when he brought down with the crossbow he could scarce lift to his shoulder the raven perched on the topmost withered limb. On that knoll on the verge of the forest-ground he first blooded Fay, the sleuthbrache, at deer. How proud he was of her when he saw her stoop her back muzzle to the tainted ground, and never lift it from the trail till the sprang at the throat of the great hart—not so sorely wounded but that he could stand bravely at bay. In that meadow he rode his first gallop on Philip Kemy's charger, and he remembered how, on that tilt-ground, nearer yet to the castle wall, he had felt his veins tingling, when a saddle was first emptied by his lance. He had sent away steeds enow riderless since then, God wot, and perchance might do the same for many more, but that hot, proud flush he never would feel again.

The sun was setting as they rode into the little hamlet of Bever, and drew up before the modest roadside hostel, that seldom, if ever, had housed guest above yeoman's degree: but the Free Companion was not apt to quarrel with his lodging or his fare, and refreshed himself quite contentedly with what they were pleased to set before him. Nor was the squire a whit more dainty. When supper was ended Ralph inquired after one Gillian, sometime wife of one of Sir Simon Dynevor's foresters.

"Her goodman is long dead," the ale-wife answered, "and Dame Gillian is well-nigh doting; but she dwells in her old cottage, and is as well cared for as if she were franklin's widow, forsooth! Her foster-child—Ralph Fitzwarenne, we used to call him—hath won an earldom, they say, beyond the seas, and sent her long ago more gold crowns than she will live to spend."

So Ralph strode away alone through the twilight, leaving Lanyon to dispose of his time as seemed to him good. There were bright gleams of firelight shot through the window of Dame Gillian's cottage, though the evening was warm, and there was the sound of a fresh young voice chanting one of the low monotonous ballads with which nurses are wont to sooth children to sleep. When the knight knocked softly the chanting ceased, and in a second or two the latch was lifted from within, the door half opened cautiously, and a voice, half mirthful, half pettish, spoke from behind it.

"How now, Dickon? What fooling is this? Thou art a full hour too soon. Thou mayst not enter, nor may I stir forth, for the grandame hath scarce begun to doze."

"It is not Dickon," Brakespeare answered, smiling, despite his heaviness of mood; "neither is my visit to thee, fair maiden; but rather to the reverend person who, it seems, sleeps not yet."

The girl started back with a suppressed cry, and nearly thrust-to the door. But somehow the deep, stern voice reassured rather than alarmed her; so she peered forth again, this time revealing a pretty blond head, and a merry, mischievous face, lit up by arch blue eyes.

"Save you, gentle stranger," she said, "for I guess you gentle unknown, even as you guessed me fair unseen. What is your errand to my grandame? I fear me you will scarce get speech with her to-night. She wanders much of late, even in talk with her gossips and me, and is especially crossed-grained at her wakings."

"Nevertheless, under your leave, I will make essay," the knight replied, as he bowed his head and doffed his barret-cap on entering—for the doorway was not built for visitors of his stature. The girl gave a shy upward glance as she made way for him to pass—a certain awe tempering her admiration of the stranger's tall, martial figure and stately bearing.

"Suffer me to arouse her," she whispered; "'twill be best so." But the caution was needless; for just then the figure in the armed-chair by the hearth stirred, and a cracked, piping voice cried querulously—

"How now, Janet? What new freak is this, thou

arrant gill-flirt? When thou art not gadding abroad, thou art ever contriving mischief at home. Can I not close mine eyes but thou must be chattering with one of thy losel sweethearts? Thy father shall take order with thee when he cometh home."

"Hush, hush, grannam!" the girl said, hastily. "Shame not thyself and me with such words; 'tis no sweetheart of mine, but a gallant gentleman come to visit thee. Stay; I will get more light."

And as she stooped over the blaze, candle in hand, the rose on her cheek flushed to peony. The old woman stirred in her chair more uneasily than before, with the quick, suspicious terror of dotage.

"What have I to do wi' gentlefolk?" she grumbled. "Janet—Janet, I say—come nearer to me. This visit bodes us no good; let him tell his errand quickly or begone."

The girl set the candle on the mantel-spike, and glanced up once again at Brakespeare, rather, it seemed, in apology than in inquiry.

"Nay, dame," the knight answered very gently; "I mean no harm, God wot, to thee or thine. I thought 'twould please thee to hear tidings of one thou hast not seen these many, many years; I mean Ralph Fitz-warenne."

The crone began to mumble under her breath; at left she muttered aloud—

"Warenne? ay, ay, I mind the name, for sure—a brave house. I served them as long as any were left to serve; but old Sir Ralph—he who was slain along with my goodman up away in the North—was the last of the race, for his shrewish sister counts for naught.

My poor lady, Maude—ay, ay, I remember, she had died ere that in child-bed; and Ralph Fitzwarenne—he was her son—for sure I remember him well enough, and with good cause; 'twas ever a stubborn child, and waxed harder to rule as he grew older. He would scarce come to good, I fear me. He died long ago beyond the seas."

"Be not wroth, noble sir," the girl broke in, timidly; for Ralph's brow was bent like one in anger or pain. "She wanders sadly, as I told you; specially when speaking of old times."

"Nay," he answered; "I am not like to be wroth; for she nursed me, and I have rested my head on her knee many and many a time when there was no other to whom I might make moan. Mother Gillian, hast thou not a kiss to spare for thy foster-son—not one kind word for Ralph Fitzwarenne?"

He knelt by the armed-chair as he spoke, and his deep, strong voice shook like a woman's, while he gazed up pleadingly into the withered old face that, for awhile, gave no answering sign. At last the dame's eyes lighted up with a startled gleam, as, leaning forward, the beldame thrust the speaker back with all the strength of her lean, shaking hand.

"Thou!—thou Ralph Fitzwarenne?" she cried. "Nay, nay, the dead come not back in such gallant guise. He died—died long ago."

"How knowest thou that?" Ralph asked, drooping his head despondingly. This was the only roof in England where he had hoped to meet with real welcome. Such a welcome as it was!

"I heard it for sure," she said, shivering and chatter

ing her teeth; "or I dreamed it. Ay, ay, I dreamed it thrice, and morning dreams come ever true."

He rose to his feet with a long, weary sigh, and turned Janet, who stood gazing on with wide blue eyes and red lips parted—much as a Provençale peasant-wench might have gazed on Roland the Paladin.

"Canst thou not persuade her?"

The girl roused herself with a start, and leaning over her grandame began to soothe and scold her alternately, like a fractious child.

"Are not ashamed," she said at last, "thus to entreat the noble gentleman on whose bounty thou hast lived so long?"

The crone raised herself up, and once more her eyes gleamed, but this time with the light of avarice.

"Ay, ay, 'twas a brave largesse, and a timely," she muttered, "but 'tis well-nigh spent. Had yon tall stranger been Master Ralph, or had he brought sure tidings concerning him, he would scarce have come empty-handed."

The girl's cheek flushed brighter than ever with honest shame, and she wrung her hands—very small and white they were for a forester's daughter—despairingly.

"Nay, vex not thyself, my child," the knight said softly, "'tis not her fault, poor soul. I had liever have found thy grandame in her grave than thus sorely changed. So kindly and cheery she used to be; but God's will be done. Here, dame, I will cumber thee with my presence no longer. If thou wilt not believe in the presence of Ralph Fitzwarenne in flesh and blood, mayhap thou wilt believe his is not fairy gold."

He laid a heavy purse softly in her lap, sickening at heart. In very truth, the crone was a spectacle at once ghastly and grotesque, as she fumbled at the purse-strings with shaking fingers, and then dabbled them in the coin—mumbling the while, and wagging her withered jaws, as a toothless wolf might do over a dainty morsel. The girl followed Brakespeare as he crossed the threshold.

"You will not deem us all ungrateful, noble sir? I would my father were at home to thank you better than I; but he is away to the town after certain matters pertaining to his forest-craft. He will pay his duty to your worship betimes in the morning, and "—she glanced up again with that half-coquettish shyness—"you will not think me so light of conduct as her chiding would import. I am betrothed to Dickon since Martinmas, and he is to my father as a son already."

The knight bent his lofty head till his lips touched the smooth, upturned brow. Dick Staveley, jealous and choleric as he was, need never have begrudged his sweetheart that salute; yet it dwelt long in Janet's memory. Its grave, kindly courtesy—so different from anything to which she had been accustomed—made her shrink a little that evening from the boisterous caresses which had hitherto satisfied her entirely.

"I had guessed as much," he said. "What is left in yon purse after they have buried thy grandam shall go toward thy dowry. Fare thee well, pretty child, thou canst have so few sins of thine own to answer, thou mayst sometimes spare an orison for poor Ralph Brakespeare."

The girl stood watching the stately figure till it was wholly lost in shadow, and then sighing a little, she wist not why, turned back into the cottage to find her grandame still mumbling and chuckling over the gold.

The knight returned not straight to his hostel, but walked a furlong or two farther on, to a spot of rising ground, bare of trees, whence there was fair view of the castle. By this time the moon had risen, bringing out in sharp relief turret and battlement and bartizan. Lights were shining through many of the narrow window-slits, and sound of voices, with sometimes bursts of laughter, came across the castle-ditch through the still, warm night. And the moon rose higher and higher, and the stars came out one by one till their tale was full; and still Ralph stood with lips tightly compressed, and hands resting crossed on his sword-hilt. When at length he had gazed his fill he turned sharply on his heel, and looking neither to the right nor to the left, nor glancing once over his shoulder, retraced his steps toward the inn, where he found Lanyon awaiting in their common chamber. Had the squire been talkative and inquisitive, instead of marvelously stolid and taciturn, something in the knight's face would have forbidden question. So, with scarcely a word exchanged, those two lay down on their pallets, and took their rest—or unrest—till the dawning.

Rumors of the visitors' names and quality had oozed out somehow through Bever hamlet; so when the knight came forth to mount the *haquenée* which the squire held ready, he found besides Dame Gillian's son a small knot of idlers at the hostel door. After brief converse with the ranger, the knight put foot in stirrup;

even as he did so, he looked rather wistfully around the circle, to see if no old acquaintance had found his way thither. Among the bystanders there were several old enough to have remembered Ralph Fitzwarenne, but not a single face expressed aught beyond indifferent curiosity, and one or two loured with a vague disappointment; for reports of fabulous wealth and reckless liberality had spread through the village, and some who stood there had half expected that gold pieces would be scattered broadcast to be gathered by whoso chose to stoop for them.

And so Ralph Brakespeare turned his back, for the very last time, on the place of his nurture, if not of his nativity; and only one voice—his foster-brother's—wished him "God-speed."

They had ridden a league or more before the knight broke silence.

"And how didst thou disport thyself betwixt supper and bed-time, Will? An' thou hadst not better luck than I, we might have spared our journey hitherward."

"I scarce know what your worship calls good luck," the other answered, even more gruffly than his wont. "Sometimes 'tis better luck to miss folk than to find them. Our old mill still clacks merrily as ever, but strangers gather the grist thereof. My father drained his large posset ten years agone. He drank deeper, they say, after the Black Pest carried off my step-dame —whether for joy or sorrow, God knoweth; and the rest of my kindred have wandered away, none can tell me whither. So I bethought me I would go up to the forge, and drink a cup of honest John Burnley's ale, and ask after the health of Cicely, his wife—mine ancient sweetheart. She was gracious enough, and he seemed ever glad of my company, when I was here last on your worship's errand."

"Didst thou see them?" the knight inquired, marking that the other paused as if there were no more to tell.

"I heard them," Lanyon answered, with a grim laugh, "and that sufficed me. By Saint Giles! my step-dame's tongue never jangled faster or shriller than did Cicely's yestereven. Yea—once I heard so shrewd a clatter that I guess she proved whether John Burnley's costard or her distaff were the toughest. I care not to thrust myself in where dry blows and hard words are agoing; so I even withdrew myself warily to whence I came, and called for a pottle at mine own cost for the good of our inn. 'Twas but poor muddy liquor, but the ale-wife suffered me to drink it in peace."

The knight looked hard at his follower, doubting—and not for the first time either—whether, under that heavy, stolid exterior, there lay not a better philosophy than any he himself could boast of.

"Good sooth, I envy thee," he said—not in irony or bitterness. "Here have I been disquieting myself because Gillian, my foster-mother, knew me not again, having fallen into dotage; and I waxed wroth with the poor folk yonder, for that their welcome was naught. What are we that man, or woman either, who have their own daily task to do, and their own kith and kin to care for—should carry us in their memories for half a life-time. What! Babble they that the love of our native country never dies? *Basta!* Minstrels' fables all. A man's true country is wheresoever a man's lot is cast, and where such as care for him dwell—be they never so few. An' I hunger to cross the seas again, write me down driveler."

"Our welcome at Hacquemont was not cold," the squire said simply. "I wot there is watching and waiting for us even now; and I would we were within hail of my gruff gossip, Gilles."

Brakespeare smiled, as if his thoughts had been turned to a pleasanter current. Then they rode onward cheerily enough, and the next afternoon found them once more housed at the "Spur."

CHAPTER XL.

A BRIEF halt in London was absolutely needful, for their cattle had traveled far and fast of late, and neither the knight nor the squire—even without their harness—were a light load for horseflesh. So, on the following day Sir Ralph Brakespeare strode forth about noon alone. He crossed London Bridge, and passing through the Chepe, issued forth by Ludgate into the open fields, and so held onward (past the Savoy) through the hamlet of Charing, till he came to Westminster—a town, even at that period, of no mean importance; for besides only mere courtiers and ecclesiastics, not a few knights and nobles had their lodging in the neighborhood of the Palace and the Abbey.

Furthermore, as trade ever follows custom, clothiers, armorers and goldsmiths—to say nothing of butchers, bakers and vintners—had built for themselves booths, dwellings and warehouses all about, so that in Westminster streets were to be found, more irregular, perchance, in their architecture, but scarcely less busy than some in the heart of the City.

Brakespeare was passing one of these, the lodging evidently of some personage of importance—when his eye was attracted by the rare beauty of a charger whose bridle was held by two dismounted squires, and by the blazonry on the *cointise* that seemed familiar to him. In the rear was mustered a troop of some score retainers, gallantly mounted and richly armed. Almost immediately he for whom they waited came forth—a goodly knight, and of a marvelous presence still, albeit both beard and hair were white as hoar frost, and he moved under his gorgeous plate armor with firm elastic step. As with a soothing word or two the old noble laid his hand on the withers of the fretting destrere, his glance encountered Brakespeare's. For a second or two each gazed on the other in the vague fashion of one who racks his memory to give the name to a resemblance. Recognition dawned on Ralph first; and, as he made a hasty step forward, he bared his head—not alone with the reverence due to superior age, but partly from the force of old habit—for the last time those two met there had been betwixt them the difference that must always exist betwixt a leader of armies and a nameless subaltern.

"Sir Walter Breckenridge, if I mistake not," he said, in his clear, bold voice. "My good lord, I scarce need inquire after your health. You carry more lightly than the rest of us the score of years that have slipped by since last I looked upon your face. Belike you have forgotten Sir John Hawkwood and Ralph Brakespeare, his esquire."

The old knight's countenance lighted up cordially as he reached out his gantleted hand across the saddle-tree.

"By God's body! I have forgotten neither," he answered. "No, nor how that same squire saved mine honor, and the ransom of Hacquemont to boot, against such odds as seldom have been heard of, save in *Jong-*

leurs' tales. Though 'twas mine evil hap to miss Poictiers, I heard how worthily you there won golden spurs; and we live not so far to the West but that we have heard how, of late, beyond Alps, the Free Lances have borne all before them; and who hath led their companies. Only it grieves me that so much *los* was not won under the Red Cross, rather than under the banner of Prince or Pope. Surely thou wilt not pass my lodging without draining one hanap therein to our ancient accointance. Though I am boune to visit our lord the King at Windsor, my business is not so pressing but that, for so fair a purpose, I can spare a poor half-hour."

So the two went together into the presence-chamber —hung with costly arras, and otherwise richly decorated, after the fashion of the time—and Sir Ralph did his host right, in a mighty beaker. The gallants of those days drank as they fought—right royally—and carried off, easily enough, a morning draught that would have set the steadiest of modern brains a-working.

After brief interchange of question and answer, quoth Sir Walter Breckenridge—

"Thou mindest what I said anon—how it grieved me to think so stark a blade had been wielded so long in the service of an alien. Now, might not this be yet amended? A word in thine ear. My lord the King never stood in more need than now of tried soldiers. Not I alone, but many others, opine that since sore sickness forced Prince Edward to quit Aquitaine, our foothold therein is scarce so firm as heretofore. I have had much talk with Sir Guiscard d'Angla, the Poitevin envoy, since he hath tarried here—a wise and valiant captain, I warrant him, not given to evil foreboding—and he hath plainly averred that matters out yonder need wary handling. Now the Lord John of Pembroke, who goeth forth thither as the King's lieutenant—though he hath a right good courage and right goodwill, hath scarce the brain for such a task; yet—an' he will hearken to counsel—I fear not but that all will go well with us yet. Glad man were I, if I could persuade thee to cast in thy lot with us. He sails presently from Southampton for La Rochelle. Albeit, thine own following be meager just now, the Free Lances will gather to the sound of thy name like hounds to the horn."

The other bit his lip, as he answered with some bitterness—

"'Tis an apt comparison, *pardie!* Surely they are but hounds at the best, and but ravening ones to boot; and I—though you are pleased to overrate my poor repute—am but the huntsman, unversed in the laws of noble venerie. I marvel that your lordship should choose to seek sport in such company!"

"Nay, nay," Breckenridge broke in; "I will not hear thee so miscall thyself. Blacker tales have been told of Knolles than ever were laid to thine account: yet Chandos himself, while he lived, thought it not shame to couch lance in his company, and few stand higher in the King's favor than he. 'Twas but lately John Menstreworth abyed dearly the maligning him. Didst thou not see yon grim head grinning down from the bridge-house tower? Our liege is no niggard of his bounty to such as serve him faithfully. Three years agone he would have paid my poor deserts with the barony of Welland, and a fair fief to boot; but I have more than sufficeth my needs, and none to inherit such honors; also, I love the old name, so, with all gratitude, I said him nay. Come, wilt thou not be ruled by me? Thou art not minded, I trust, to take part against us."

"Nay, verily," Ralph replied. "I have no such thought; though 'tis long since I took King Edward's wages, were I arrayed against the Red Cross, I should seem unto myself but a renegade. Nevertheless, I am under promise to return to a certain place in France —marry, 'tis no secret, your lordship knows the place, 'tis no other than Hacquemont—before binding myself by any engagement whatsoever. 'Tis a quiet nook, beyond the sound of French or English trumpets; and I see not why I should not tarry there for awhile, neither molesting nor molested, taking part with neither side. I have earned some respite, I trow, for —save when I have been ailing of wounds—the harness has scarce been off my shoulders these twenty years."

The elder knight shook his head rather sorrowfully.

" 'Tis a pleasant dream," he said, "and the saints forbid I should grudge thee thy rest so fairly earned; yet, 'tis a dream scarce like to come true. To sit with folded hands in such times as these is not for the like of thee and me. Sometime back, the good Bishop of Rochester preached at Westminster on the blessing of peace, and so forth. His discourse pleased none of us that listened, my lord the King least of all, judging from his frown; yet the text hath rung in mine ears ever since, 'All they that take the sword, shall perish with the sword.'"

Ralph barely repressed a start. That same thought had been in his mind many and many a time, but it had never before been put in words.

"Your words have truth and reason, my lord," he said; "and, trust me, I will ponder thereon heedfully. I will bring you mine answer to Bordeaux, or to such other place as you may please to appoint, within one month after I set foot in France, and I purpose to set forth thither straightway. Will this suffice you?"

"It must, perforce, sith better may not be," quoth Breckenridge, rising; "but 'twill scarce delay thy journey to take passage in my ship from Southampton, and suffer me to see you safe on shore. Since Duke John of Lancaster's marriage and the contract of the younger Infanta to his brother of Cambridge, the Spaniard hath waxed venomous, and his corsairs are abroad in those seas, so that the passage is scarce safe for merchantmen without convoy. How sayest thou? This grace, at least, thou wilt scarce deny me?"

Ralph had no choice but to accept gratefully; and so, with more courteous words on either side, they parted, having made compact to meet at Southampton that day se'ennight.

No farther incident marked the remainder of Brakespeare's stay in Southwark. After taking kindly leave of the armorer, and bestowing on his family such gifts as he could prevail on them to accept, the knight once more took the road, and arrived safe at Southampton the day before the appointed time.

For a full fortnight beyond the time appointed for their sailing, the transports lay idle off the town, for the cumbrous vessels of that time never ventured forth from harbor when the breezes were contrary. During that weary waiting Ralph had ample leisure to pass in review the chiefs of the expedition under whose convoy he was to sail. The more so, as, for reasons not hard to understand, he would be as yet presented to none of these, but tarried under the same roof with Sir Walter Breckenridge, without revealing his own name or quality. The Free Companion, like most other successful adventurers, had no mean skill in physiognomy, and the judgment that he formed of men at first sight was rarely far from truth.

John of Pembroke was older, and perchance wiser, than when he was trapped at Puirenon, and was fain to humble himself by crying on Chandos for succor; yet that quick, impulsive manner, and those bright, unsteady eyes, betokened one better fitted to lead a desperate assault or headlong charge than to rule the destinies of a province, or control the movements of a mighty armament. Neither did the force then actually sent forth seem proportionate to the object it was destined to achieve. Sir Guiscard d'Angle had assured King Edward that there was no lack of lances in Poitou and Guienne ready to be hired, and that gold was more needed there than steel. So the treasure-ship was laden with nobles and florins enow to maintain for a full year's space three thousand fighting men; but there embarked with the Earl, besides his own household, scarce a score of knights, each with his immediate retainers. Truly, among them were numbered names of no mean renown—those of Beaufort, Curzon, Grimstone, Morton, Whitaker, and Breckenridge, were right well known on either side of the narrow seas

At length the wind veered round to the no..nwest, and getting aboard with what speed they might, the English sailed out of Southampton with good hope and courage, praying only that the breeze might hold till they reached Rochelle; for few, if any, of them dreamed of their landing being disputed. This confidence was somewhat abated when, after a prosperous voyage, they sighted the southern point of the Poitevin coast—for there the lookouts in the mast-turrets descried a dark line of shipping anchored in the sheltering lee of the Isle of Ré, barring entrance to the harbor. The vessel that carried Breckenridge and Brakespeare sailed better than the most part of her fellows, and held her place throughout in the vaward division of the little squadron, so that those were among the first to be aware of the presence of an enemy.

Quoth the elder knight to the younger—

"I have done thee a right good turn, it seems, in persuading thee to take passage with me. Lo! now thou wilt have to take thy chance of landing with the rest of us, and thy full share of hard blows also, belike —whether thon wilt or no."

"Trouble not yourself, my good lord," the other made answer, cheerily. "For your kind intent I am none the less beholden to you. Nevertheless, I am as well pleased that it is not against France alone we shall fight presently—if fight we must. Yon gaudy pennon of Gules and Or that I saw floundering in the last gleam of sunshine is not blazoned with the Lilies I trow : rather should it be borne by the Spaniards of whom ye spake—albeit those are no corsairs, but mighty warships."

"Those hawk's eyne of thine are keen, then, as ever," Breckenridge replied. "Never an one of our watchmen hath told us so much ; yet I doubt not. Even such as thou sayest is the banner of Castile. Now I will below and arm me ; but how to furnish thee forth I know not. There is no lack of harness aboard, but none, I trow, like to fit one of thy size and stature."

"Fear not for me," Brakespeare said. "My mails are not heavy, yet they hold that shall serve my turn to-day."

Nevertheless, when the Free Companion came on deck again, there was no outward change in his attire, save that he wore a plain bascinet. His squire, too, was accoutered with a light headpiece and a stout leathern gipon.

"Are thou distraught ? " Breckenridge asked discontentedly, as he too came on deck, armed in plate from head to heel, " or bearest thou some charm, to make quarrels and javelins glint off from clothier's ware like hailstones ? "

By way of answer the other opened the breast of his doublet, revealing beneath a mail-shirt, woven in steel links, exceeding fine, that glittered like silver broidery —one of those masterpieces of the hammerman's art, rare even in Milan armories.

"I have proved it," he said, with a quiet smile. "Ludovico Sforza wore this under his vest on the day when I met him by the way, and, guessing him unarmed, thought to spear him as I would have speared a marsh-hog—for blacker traitor and fouler murderer never drew breath. I smote him full on the breast, and the shock was so rude that his neck brake, and he lay dead where he fell. I thought 'twas sorcery that my lance had not gone thorow; but when we stripped him, though there was a sore bruise above the midriff, the skin was barely grazed."

The old knight nodded his head as if well pleased. Of a truth the time was short for discourse, for the Spaniard's line was now so close that the great ramparts and towers of their warships, full of spearmen and arbalestriers, were plainly discerned. They had weighed anchor when the English first came into sight, and having gotten the windward, were now bearing down full sail.

So the battle began. That it should have been vainly contested against such unequal odds redounds not less to the honor of the Red Cross than any victory achieved since Poictiers. For, not only was the Spaniard far superior in numbers, but his vessels, compared to the English, were as caravels to cock-boats; and, furthermore, besides crossbows and cannon they carried divers warlike engines flinging great bars of iron, huge stones, and leaded beams—the full shock of which no ordinary hull might withstand. Nevertheless, those who fought under John of Pembroke bare themselves with such valor and skilful seamanship that—at the cost of many sorely wounded, and not a few slain outright by the enemy's artillery—they held their own, even to the going down of the sun, with actual loss of only two provision barges with all aboard. For, saith Froissart, " They handled their spears, which were well steeled, so briskly, and gave such terrible strokes, that none dared to come anear, unless he was well armed and sheltered."

Slowly, as night fell, the two fleets drew apart, and cast anchor, waiting—the one side with eager confidence, the other with stubborn, if hopeless, courage —for what the morrow should bring forth.

Now the engagement took place not so far from the shore but that it could be plainly discerned from the ramparts of Rochelle. Sir John Harpenden—a valiant and trusty captain, who then was seneschal of the town —spared neither threats nor entreaties to induce the citizens to embark in the vessels and barges lying in the port to the aid of their fellows, who were manifestly overborne ; but the Rochellois, with French sympathies at their hearts, in nowise listened—excusing themselves with some show of reason; alleging that they had their own gates to guard, and that —lacking practise on the sea—they were ill-fitted to cope thereon with the Spaniard ; but that they were ready with their service should battle ensue on shore. When the seneschal saw that he wasted breath, and was not like to prevail, he bethought himself how best he could act for the clearing of his own honor. So on the turn of the tide John Harpenden, and three other Poitevin knights who also were minded at all risks to keep faith with their suzerain—embarked in four open barges, and carried to Pembroke and Guiscard d'Angle the heavy message that they must trust no longer to aid or countenance from La Rochelle, but only to the strength of their own arms, and to the mercy of God.

CHAPTER XLI.

When the sun had fairly risen on the morning of the eve of St. John Baptist, and the tide was at the full, the Spaniards weighed anchor to the sound of trumpet and drum, and having once more taken the wind of the English, bore down in full battle-array, intending fairly to surround the smaller squadron. Forty great ships of war and thirteen galleys made up their line; and among their captains—besides Ambrosio de Boccanera, their Admiral—were Hernando de Leon, Roderigo de Rosas, and many other Castilian worthies. And so the combat was renewed with bitterer ferocity than before, for the Spaniards recognized not without shame, how few and ill-provided were those who had held them so long at bay; and the English fought like born bulldogs as they were —knowing that hope of retreat or succor there was none—and bent on biting to the last. Neither did Guiscard d'Angle and his Poitevins bear themselves a whit less gallantly. Whatever his defects as a general, none questioned that John of Pembroke bore himself that day as a valiant knight, or that he was ably seconded by each and every one who sailed from Southampton in his company. Yet the end could not be doubtful. Besides the fearful artillery and terrible engines before mentioned, another devilish contrivance was, for the first time in civilized warfare, brought into play, and the weaker side had not only to elude the shock of huge prows beetling over their own decks, and the crash of lead and iron, but also the contact of fire-ships. Mortal thews and sinews, however tough, must wear out at last; and the handiwork of shipwrights, if ever so cunning, cannot hold out forever. So 'tis no marvel if, as the day wore on, the cry of " St. George Guienne " waxed fainter, and the luck of Castile began to prevail.

In such a condition as this Brakespeare and Breckenridge found themselves about an hour before noon. Awhile agone, with great toil and danger, they had shaken off one of those fire-ships; yet their sails had been all ablaze, and hung now in blackened rags from the yards, so that the craft could no longer be handled, and weltered right along in the water. Nevertheless, before they were quite disabled, they had hurtled through the enemy's line, and now lay on the outer verge of the fight, nearest to the shore. There was a brief lull in the storm that had been harassing them ever since daybreak; a very brief one though, for not three cables' length off a huge Spanish galley was working round, like an armed man taking space to run his course, and all knew she only waited to get to windward to bear down and finish the work already half done.

With a long breath, like a gasp, Sir Walter Breckenridge lifted his vizor and looked on his companion, whose face was already bare. On either visage there was a certain seriousness, but that of the elder knight was the gloomier of the twain.

" These accursed Spaniards wear not pointless

stings." He glanced rather ruefully round the deck, slippery with blood and cumbered with wounded—the corpses had been cast overboard without ruth or scruple. "Eftsoons must we make choice betwixt surrendering to ransom or drowning where we stand; for our seams are strained even to bursting, and they tell me of a shrewd leak in the hold. 'Tis the part of a wise man, surely, to choose prison for a brief while, rather than the deep sea forever and aye; but as we wax old we wax stubborn, and for myself I doubt. What thinkest thou? Thou hast good right to speak, for never an one of King Edward's lieges hath wrought for him more doughtily than thou hast done since yesternoon."

"It is my trade," the other answered coolly. "A day's work more or less matters little in a year's tale. The pleasant passage at your lordship's cost, is, so far, scarce overpaid. But my lips are parched with drought, I fain would slake them, I own; I warrant Lanyon here, if ye will grant him leave, would ferret out a flask of the rare liquor we drank last night at supper. There is time enow for a parting cup yet, whilst yon lumbering caravel hangs in the wind."

He spoke quite simply and naturally, not in reckless bravado, or in the ghastly merriment of despair; but rather like a man who hath stood too often on the very brink of the Dark River to blench when he needs must set foot therein. The heart of the veteran soldier waxed warm with genuine admiration, and he smiled outright as he signed to Lanyon to obey. In a few seconds the squire returned bearing a goodly flagon and a silver tankard, which last he filled to the brim with a steady, practised hand. Brakespeare drained it to the last drop, and Breckenridge, when it was filled again, did him reason in like manner. They pledged each other—these two—with as hearty good-will as if they had quenched their thirst after a tourney to the sound of flutes and clarions; yet they had no better music then than the groans of the wounded round their feet, and the gurgle—each minute more and more ominously loud—of the water pouring through the rift in the hold.

Then said the Free Companion—

"My lord Sir Walter, ye well can guard your own honor without counsel of mine, and well I wot that when ye speak the word 'surrender,' ye will have done all that beseems a Christian knight—and more. But for myself, I am not minded to see the withinside of a Spanish prison; moreover, I have a tryst to keep within brief space, the which, if I live, I will not fail. That I will stand by thee to the last, it needs not to aver; but when there is naught left here for me to do I purpose to shift for myself by swimming. My squire here is a born water-dog; we have swam for our sport, ere this, a longer space than lies betwixt us and the shore. The tide, too, is at the slack, and there is floating wreck enow about, whereon to rest if our arms shall tire."

The old knight smiled again—this time very sadly.

"'Tis a brave design," he said, "and, if it be within compass of man's strength or hardihood, I doubt not thou wilt achieve it. Thou must carry thine answer concerning the matters we spake of to Bordeaux to other than me, for I know of a surety that this day Walter Breckenridge dealeth his last sword-stroke.

Still I trust that thy mind will be swayed aright, and that thou mayest yet do King Edward bright service. And so God keep and prosper thee."

Even while their hands were locked together, each glanced over his shoulder to windward. Not half a bow-shot off the great Spanish warship bore down under press of sail, her decks crowded with spearmen, and her towers bristling with crossbows. In the forward turret stood a knight wearing a gorgeous surcoat over bright plate armor, who ever and anon turned his head, motioning to the steersman with his drawn sword. This was none other than Ponce de Leon, brother to Hernando, the Vice-Admiral, and one of the famousest knights in Castile. The huge black stem forged nearer, as though purposing to strike the English craft amidships, and sink it with the mere shock; but at the last moment the galley's helm was jammed hard down, so that her sails shivered in the wind, and she ranged up to her enemy broadside on. As the bulwarks touched, the Spaniard cast out his grapples, and then ensued a mellay, fierce and obstinate—albeit the English fought not alone against vantage of numbers, but of ground also—for as the gunwales touched, the deck and bulwarks were much higher than those of the transport.

Eager and fearless as in his first fray, old Walter Breckenridge cast himself into the teeth of the Spanish boarders, and, repelling their first onslaught, gained footing himself on the enemy's deck and crossed blades with Ponce de Leon. So gallantly, indeed, did the doughty veteran bestir himself, that Ralph, though he had work enough on his own hands, could not refrain

THE FREE COMPANION DRAGGED HIS VICTIM ACROSS THE DECK, THROUGH THE SKIRTS OF
THE THRONG, AND PLUNGED OVER THE WEATHER BULWARK.

from glancing sometimes over his shoulder to watch the sword-play on his left. Suddenly a cry—half of wrath, half of warning—broke from the Free Companion's lips, but it came too late. Walter Breckenridge, fully engaged with the foe in his front, wist not of the blow leveled sidelong at him, till the mace descended where the neck joins the spine. 'Twas a felon stroke, but so starkly delivered that the brave old knight dropped dead in his tracks with scarce a quiver in his lower limbs—like an ox felled in the shambles. Ponce de Leon turned, in hot anger, to see who had dared to interfere with his handiwork; but he had no chance to chide the offender. Ralph Brakespeare marked who dealt the blow—a tall, dark-visaged hidalgo—and swore under his breast a bitter oath that he would have that man's life, at whatsoever peril of his own. But he chose a surer way than combat after the rules of warfare; wherein, by stress of numbers, he might have been balked of his vengeance, and lose liberty to boot.

Flinging down his *estoc*, so that both hands were free, he drove headlong through the press, and in another second those two were knit in grapple. The Spaniard's mace was useless; but plucking his poignard from his sheath he smote his assailant with it on the breast, fair and full. The Toledan blade shivered like glass on the Milan mail-shirt, and before any were aware of his intent, the Free Companion had dragged his victim, choking and struggling—in a grasp against which the gorget was poor fence—across the deck, through the skirts of the throng, and plunged over the weather-bulwark, keeping the fetter-lock of his fingers fast. With a splash that might have been heard over all the battle din, the two bodies struck the water together, but only one rose to the surface—the other the deep sea kept for her own, to have and to hold until the day when, perforce, she must render up her dead.

Lanyon, as you know, was standing within ear-shot when his master first spoke of swimming; and incontinently, without farther orders, he began to make ready in this wise:

There was still a goodly quantity of liquor left in the flask that he carried back to the cabin; so, putting it to his lips, he drained it to the very dregs, muttering to himself some gruff apology about keeping out the cold. Then he cast loose his cumbrous leather gipon, and doffed his bascinet, so that he stood bareheaded in tight-fitting jerkin and hose. Then he took out of an iron-bound coffer a broad leathern belt, and thrust into this, when he had buckled it round his waist, a light dudgeon-dagger. Thus accoutred, he emerged on deck, just at the moment when the Spaniard cast out his grappling-ladders. The esquire had evidently no purpose of taking part in the mellay. He was a very glutton of hard blows at proper times and seasons; but he was none of those hair-brained desperadoes who fight for fighting sake, and would as soon have thought of thrusting himself into a feast whereto he was not bidden as into a fray where he had no concern. So he climbed up a little way into the lee rigging, where, for the nonce, he was out of danger, save from stray missiles, and followed keenly and coolly every movement of his master's, intending to guide his own thereby. Seeing Brakespeare disappear with his prey in his grip over the bulwark of the Spanish galley, Lanyon drew a long slow breath, after the fashion of practised divers, and, without more ado, leaped head-foremost into the water.

So it befell that, when the Free Companion came up panting after the long plunge, the first sound in his ears was a familiar voice close by.

"Hither away, my lord. Hither away."

And as he dashed the brine out of his eyes, he saw rising on the crest of the swell the shaggy head and bull-neck of his old retainer.

So many and diverse were the phases of peril those two had faced together, that both master and man took such matters now with incredible equanimity.

"Ha, ha! thou art here, then?" was all the knight said. Then with one hand he unclasped his bascinet, and, tossing it away, turned himself about, and led the way shoreward. They might have advanced some half a furlong when a great cry from behind made both swimmers look back.

Mere weight of numbers had forced the English back to the deck of their own vessel, and there the fray was waged savagely as ever; for the stout squires and sturdy yeomen fought on the more doggedly, because, since their leader was down, there was none cared to take upon himself to cry "Surrender;" and the Spaniards, enraged by such obstinacy, were little minded to show quarter. So they hurtled to and fro, never heeding the gurgle of the water rushing into the hold under their feet, or the gunwale's sinking till it touched the water's edge. All at once came a heel to leeward, the green, foam-flecked surge swept in amidships up to the waists of the combatants, and turning herself clear of the grapples, the English craft foundered bodily, carrying with her the dead, the wounded, and the living, who were scarce in better case: for, of those who went down alive, all harnessed, into the ghastly whirlpool, not one in ten saw light again. Among the drowned were Ponce de Leon, and more than three other renowned Castilian captains besides; so when awhile later the Spaniards stripped Breckenridge of his armor, and flung his corpse over with the rest, a gallant company waited for him down there, twenty fathoms deep, though never an one of the sleepers when he came among them turned on his pillow.

"God rest their souls," quoth the knight, through his set teeth.

"Amen," said the squire.

And with that brief funeral oration each set his face again shoreward, and swam on silently. For awhile they made good steady way; the tide, which was at its slack, neither aiding nor impeding their progress. But they were still some distance from the nearest rocky promontory opposite the Isle de Ré, when Ralph Brakespeare began to draw his strokes more and mote slowly, and his strength was plainly well-nigh spent.

"A plague on this mail-shirt," he said, hoarsely, as Lanyon ranged up alongside. "On land it weighed no more than if it had been woven of silk; but it is a shrewd weight to carry through water, and cramps my arms to boot. I shall sleep with old Walter Breckenridge to-night after all, so shift for thyself, honest

Will. If thou dost win safe back to Hacquemont, tell them that I tried hard to keep tryst."

For the first time in all his life the sturdy Kentishman's heart fluttered like a girl's; yet he constrained himself to speak cheerily—

"Nay, nay, my lord, 'tis not yet come to such a pass as to think of farewells. For the matter of that, whether ye sink or swim, I am minded to keep your company. Take breath for a brief space, resting your hands on my shoulders—so. Fear not to trust yourself; I profess I feel not your weight."

For a minute or two there was silence, broken only by the knight's deep laboring breath, during which Lanyon's small keen eyes roved anxiously round over the smooth sea.

"What is that?" he cried out at last, leaping breast-high from the water. "By the Mass! if I mistake not, we are saved! Yon wave breaking in a smooth sea must needs break on a rock awash, and 'twill be hard if we find not standing-ground thereon till the cramps pass off."

Some twoscore strokes brought them to the spot, and the squire's hopes proved to be well founded. It was one of the small sunken islets common along that dangerous coast, that at ebb-tide are nearly bare. The water on it now scarcely more than covered it, and there was so little swell that the swimmers had no difficulty in keeping hand and foothold. When the strain on his sinews was once slackened, Ralph Brakespeare breathed freely again, and his numbed limbs grew lissom and strong once more in the bright sunshine. Before the water on the rock grew waist-deep, he was sufficiently refreshed to trust again to the mercy of the deep; so, swimming slowly in on the back of the young flood-tide, without farther danger or mishap they set foot on the reefs at last, and scrambled safely to shore. While he took needful rest, sitting on the brown sands, Ralph looked anxiously seaward, and to his practised eyes and ears it was plain that the battle was done. The roar and rattle of the Spanish artillery had ceased altogether, and the shout that came across the water was as the shout of triumph, not of combat; the throng of ships was beginning to disentangle itself into something like regular lines, while every pennon that could be discerned bore the arms of Castile. At length the knight arose, shaking himself impatiently—

"A sorry sight," he muttered, "a sorry sight. Though if stout Walter Breckenridge were alive and free, I know not why I should greatly care. Come on, and let us hear what they are saying in Rochelle; albeit, if we find no old acquaintance there, we are like to fare foully, both in food and lodging. The beggarly citizens are scarce like to give us either for charity."

"We need not be beholden to them for such matters," the squire made answer, with the gruff chuckle which always betokened approval of himself or others. "'Twas not for naught I girt myself with this belt before starting. It felt parlous heavy when your worship looked so wan, and I was fumbling with the buckle when mine eye lighted on yon blessed rock. Marry, 'tis as well I slipped it not."

As he smote on the leather with his brawny hand, there came from within a pleasant jangle of gold.

Craving favor at strangers' hands was so repugnant to Ralph Brakespeare's nature that he felt scarcely less grateful to Lanyon for his providence than if he had saved his life twice over ; yet he only said—

" I thank thee."

He strode onward without lifting his head from his breast, and with this acknowledgment the squire was more than content.

The event of the long battle was known ere this in Rochelle, and the townsmen in their hearts were not a little pleased thereat; yet they thought it best to refrain from public rejoicing, not knowing how soon they might have to give account for their slackness in rendering aid when it was so bitterly needed. And they did wisely ; for on the following day—being the feast of St. John—six hundred Gascon and English spears, headed by the Captal de Buch, Percy Freville, and Devereux, marched into the town. Much incensed and grieved were these famous captains when they found they had come too late; and were fain, that same afternoon, to look on from the walls while the Spaniards weighed anchor to beat of drum and flourish of trumpet—the pennons at the mast-heads, blazoned with the arms of Castile and Arragon, trailing to the sea—and steered for the coast of Galicia, if with not much booty aboard, with prisoners worth goodly ransom.

CHAPTER XLII.

AMONG the lances who rode into La Rochelle behind the Captal de Buch, Sir Ralph Brakespeare encountered several old acquaintances, but few ancient comrades; for in those days men were not so eager as heretofore to take service under the Red Cross, and the most famous captains of the English party were fain not to be over nice in the choice of their recruits, so long as these last could do a day's work worthy their large hire. He himself was tempted by more than one fair proffer to join at once the squadron that rode northward from La Rochelle into Brittany, after leaving in the castle garrison sufficient to overawe the lukewarm and rebellious burghers; but having resisted the persuasions of Sir Walter Breckenridge, for whom he had a real esteem and liking, the Free Companion was little likely to listen to those of comparative strangers. So, after three days' tarriance in the town, the knight and squire turned their faces southward, and made their way to Bordeaux as speedily as two sorry *haquenées* could carry them. There they found both horses and harness in full as good case as they had left them, and good cheer to boot, in the house of the merchant who had these in charge. The worthy Bordelais held himself, in truth, highly honored by receiving under his roof so renowned a soldier, and was sore grieved that his guest could in nowise be prevailed upon to abide there over one night. Ralph Brakespeare had been sensible for some time past of a strange hankering to find himself once more with his friends at Hacquemont, and, as the distance lessened between them, this grew stronger. He slept brokenly, though it was long since his head had rested on so soft a pillow, and was afoot at an hour that even his host—himself no sluggard— thought untimeous. He hurried over the leave-takings too, as fast as courtesy permitted, and vaulted on his destrere as springily as when he first backed the roan —whose bones were dust these many years—under the sign of the " Spur "; shaking himself as he lighted on the war-saddle till corselet and cuissard rattled again.

In very deed, Ralph was gladder to don harness that morning than ever he had been to doff it. His sober civilian's attire had grown hateful to him of late, and had all along seemed to him, as it were, a disguise. Even the Milan shirt that, since the morning of the sea-fight, he had continued to wear under his doublet, was but a sorry substitute for the familiar armor, under which his shoulders seemed to move more naturally than under silk or serge. Somewhat of this same feeling stirred in Lanyon's more stolid temperament. Long rest and bounteous provender, too, had made their cattle full of lustihood; so more jocundly than they had ridden of late, the two traced back their road along the banks of the Dordogne; the knight turning his head ever and anon to pass a pleasant word to his squire, who kept his distance to the rear as regularly as if they had been on the line of march. Nothing of moment befell them, either on the road or at the two hostelries in which they were fain to abide; and the third evening had barely closed in when a faint red gleam on the left—a little lower than the lowest of the rising stars—told them they were within ken of the watch-tower at Hacquemont.

Quoth the knight, as he drew bridle and halted, while the squire, without waiting farther sign, ranged up alongside—

"How thinkest thou, Will? Shall we find all well up yonder? 'Tis a shrewd chance, but that something hath miscarried. The good baron, as thou knowest, was but weakling when we set forth, and, unless by God's special grace, was scarce likely to mend. Yet —I wot not why—I am too light of heart greatly to fear."

" 'Twould ill become me to be wiser than your worship," the other answered, with his hoarse chuckle. "I would warrant them all as thriving as when we parted—unless, perchance, my gossip Gilles, through very weariness of drinking alone, hath been too liberal with the wine-pot for his health. He and I grumbled on well enough together, and none other cared for the company of the cross-grained old knave."

The knight nodded his head, like one well pleased at finding an echo to his own feelings, and, giving his destrere the spur, rode sharply up the steep, winding ascent before them. So once again they drew bridle on the plateau before the barbican of Hacquemont; and once again, obeying his lord's sign, the squire sounded a long shrill blast on his bugle, dwelling in peculiar fashion on the last notes. After brief delay the faint light streaming through a window-slit above was darkened by a man's head and shoulders, and a voice like the grating of a hand-saw croaked out into the night air—

"Mine eyes are no better than a newt's, by starlight; yet surely they are but two. The marauding *rascaille* are full of schemes and counterfeits, yet would I swear that no other living man than my *compere* Guillaume wound that blast."

"And for once thou wouldst swear truth, my gossip Gilles," the squire made answer from without; "though I have heard thee swear as stoutly to tales that none of us could swallow. Be deliverly with thy keys, I pray thee; our cattle are somewhat heated with travel, and the night air waxes chill."

"At thy japes again, so soon?" the other grumbled. "*Pardie*, it is well thou returnest not alone. There hath been waiting and watching within for the coming of the knight thou servest. My good lord Sir Ralph, you are heartily welcome."

Within a few minutes, the Free Companion, using less ceremony than aforetime, had made his way to the apartment above which served Philippe de Hacquemont both as bed and presence-chamber. It struck him at once how wonderfully unchanged was everything since he passed under that same doorway a full year agone. There was the same wan, white-haired figure reclining—perhaps a little more listlessly—in the great arm-chair hung with green; the same stately lady bending anxiously over her father's shoulder; the same dark, handsome face looking wistfully out of the dusky background; and for the welcome, that surely was not changed, or if so, was even warmer than heretofore.

Those hawk's eyes of Ralph Brakespeare's, as hath been heard already, were strangely dull at discerning certain signs and tokens that others less keen of sight would have read easily enow. He never noted the bright color sink in Odille's cheek, nor how her cold hand trembled as he lifted it to his lips; nor how, during that salute, though it savored of naught warmer than such courtesy as is usual between knight and dame, De Marsan's eyes flashed through the dusk while his fingers were twined and twisted like those of one who has hard work to keep some mad impulse down. Yet Gualtier had so far recovered his self-command when his turn for greeting came as to bear himself in all respects as befitted his station. However cordial might be the kindness betwixt them, in those days there was little familiar intercourse betwixt knight and esquire.

That evening was scarce long enough for the telling of all that had befallen the travelers since they rode out of Hacquemont. It was good to see how the poor old Baron's eyes sparkled, and his bowed, broken figure straightened itself, as he heard of the great sea-battle. Before the story was half ended, the color had come back to the Lady of Champrécourt's cheek, and she listened scarce less eagerly than her father; and Gualtier de Marsan drew nearer in involuntary eagerness and attention, biting his lip, though, savagely while the narrator spoke, with simplicity that formed part and parcel of his nature, of what would have furnished most men with a theme to their old age Once, when the tale was nearly done, the Baron's glance turned toward his daughter, and he muttered half aloud—

"Mark that! Markest thou that, Odille?"

And the Lady of Champrécourt's dark eyelashes went down, and the color died out of her cheek this time not to return again so soon. This befell when Ralph told how—when the deadly numbness grew on him as he swam—he had committed to Lanyon the message for Hacquemont concerning the tryst he had bound himself to keep there.

That night nothing was said beyond the questions and replies that needs must pass, when friends have been long parted, betwixt those that have gone forth and those who have tarried behind; and somewhat before the usual hour each and all betook themselves to their chambers, to rest or wake as seemed to them good: but early on the morrow the Baron sent for Brakespeare to his chamber, and without long preamble, broke into the subject nearest his heart.

"The saints have listened to my prayers and my words to boot," he said, "in so far that I have lived to see thee return once again, my son; yet well I know that the respite is but short, and groweth shorter, not daily, but hourly. Sin and shame it were if I dallied longer when no hindrance that I wot of, but thou shouldst presently become my son in very deed, no less than in name. I have spoken to Odille, and I dare aver thou wilt find naught hinders."

The Free Companion arose from his seat, and strode twice or thrice through the chamber before he made answer in a voice much less steady than common—

"My good lord, you cannot doubt my gratitude, for the Lady of Champrécourt's hand were a royal gift for a man of thrice my merit and degree. Yet, under your favor, I crave you to remember that 'twas agreed betwixt us that her own free-will should in nowise unduly be swayed. She loves you from the very bottom of her pure heart, I know, and to do your pleasure it may be would imperil her life's happiness, or aught short of her soul's welfare; wherefore I fain would hear now of your own lips if this part of our pact hath been kept to the letter."

The castellan frowned as he made answer—vexed, perchance, rather at his own thoughts and misgivings than at the other's frank speaking.

"Thou art something overnice, my son; nevertheless, to quiet thy scruples, I do solemnly affirm that I have in no wise used, much less strained, fatherly authority in this matter. If thou willest Odille's hand 'twill be given, I do verily believe, with a good and free-will. Her liking and esteem for thee date not from yesterday; time and sorrow have somewhat tamed her, and, perchance, she will be more chary of her blushes and her smiles than if this had been her first wooing; but if she saith 'yea,' there will come to thee a wife as leal and tender as heart of man could desire."

Since his childhood Philippe de Hacquemont had never wittingly lied to any living creature, and it is most certain he believed himself to be speaking simple truth now. He forgot—perhaps he had schooled himself to forget—the piteous pleading glances, eager handclasps, heavy sighs, and many other mute eloquencies, more persuasive than such rude instruments of parental tyranny as threats, upbraiding, curses, or even bolts and bars. But such as it was, the answer fully satisfied Ralph, and that same day, before noon, in his own frank, straightforward fashion, he required an answer to his suit from the Lady of Champrécourt.

Sitting white and still as a statue, with a dull, mechanical smile flickering about her lips, Odille listened to her suitor's brief pleading, and made answer instantly, as if afraid to trust herself at all—

"Good friend, I will not palter with you. I had never thought again to doff my widow's weeds, but if your thought is as my father's—that my hand will make you happier—it is freely yours. That poor gift will scarce pay the debt you laid on Hacquemont when you saved all the household from a cruel death, and us women from dishonor crueller far. There is little left in me of the Odille who used to chant to you *virelais* long ago, but if I can minister greatly to your pleasure, I am ready henceforth to share your pains and sorrows, and to bear myself in all things as befits a humble, true, and loyal wife; so may Our Lady aid me and the blessed Saint Ursula."

Over Ralph's grateful joy, over Philippe de Hacquemont's triumph, it is needless to tarry. The news took none in the castle very much by surprise, unless it was Gilles, the ancient warder, who—since about thirty winters agone he lost a spouse, more bitter and crossgrained than himself—had come to consider marrying and giving in marriage as a thing contrary to nature, and rather repugnant to the will of God.

In those troublous times all pomps and ceremonies were much curtailed, and it was a very quiet wedding; nevertheless it was needful that certain preparations should be made and guests bidden, for the castellan was not mindful that the contract should be slurred over, or done in secret, as if it were one he was ashamed of. Furthermore, from the neighboring town of Bergerac was summoned a scrivener learned in the law, by whom dowers, deeds and parchments were engrossed, setting forth that Philippe, Baron of Hacquemont, being then well stricken in years, and devoid of male issue, did thereby solemnly adopt as his heir and successor Sir Ralph Brakespeare, licensed henceforth to bear the name and arms of Hacquemont. All this was duly witnessed, signed and sealed.

On one of these errands Gualtier de Marsan had ridden far and fast ; and, as he returned, got drenched in a rain-storm. That same night he was seized with shivering fits, and on the morrow was in fierce fever ; which, on the morning fixed for the wedding, had fairly mastered his brain. The esquire was a great favorite at Hacquemont, with the household, and the Free Companion himself was right sorry for his state, and had more than once visited the sick-chamber. But at each of these visits the raving seemed to break forth with fresh violence, and at last the leech forbade entrance to any save himself and the nurse. For many reasons the marriage could not be put off ; indeed it would have been useless to propose to the old castellan any such delay.

So Ralph Brakespeare and the Lady of Champrécourt knit hands and plighted troth before the chapel altar— under evil auspices, in truth, with darkening shadows all around. Emotion and excitement had told heavily of late on the Baron of Hacquemont, and it was plain to all that with a few more turns of the hour-glass his life's sand must run out. And as the scanty bridal-train passed from the chapel through the court, there rang out from a window far above a terrible cry, followed by a burst of maniac laughter—sending a thrill through the stoutest heart there, and causing the bride to shiver like an aspen. Those sounds came from the sick-chamber where Gualtier de Marsan lay, tossing like a rudderless barque very near the fork of the Dark River—whereof one length winds slowly back through the pleasant meadow-lands of Life, while the other hurries on, swift and straight, into the deep Dead Sea.

CHAPTER XLIII.

PHILLIPPE DE HACQUEMONT had gauged very justly the measure of mercy meted out in answer to his prayers. He did survive to see his favorite project fulfilled, but barely more. It seemed as though he had braced himself for this one object, partly by an effort of the will, and when it was accomplished was not eager to prolong the struggle. He would sit for hours without speaking, and not caring much, as it seemed, to be spoken to; quite happy in his own thoughts, and in watching the new-married pair, sitting—also rather silent—together. Then again he would brighten up for awhile into something like his old self. On one of these last occasions he desired to confer with Ralph alone, and thus bespoke him—

"My fair son, I have, as thou knowest, done all that lies within my power to confirm thee in thine heirship here; and—forasmuch as there liveth no male, near of my kin—it importeth no one man that I wot of to oust thee from thine heritage. Nevertheless, that thou wilt enjoy it unto the end peacefully, without hindrance or peril, I may not hope. Whilst the present troubles of our realm endure, few—whether they be great or small—have leisure to concern themselves with their neighbors' affairs; and it may be long before news is brought to Paris that this worn-out carcass of mine is laid in the grave: but when Charles the Wise shall know how things stand here, thinkest thou our politic King will sit with folded hands, whilst the fair fief of Hacquemont is held by one who oweth him not fealty, and who will send never a spear to the muster even should the Oriflamme be raised. Moreover in these times I hold it not possible for a trained soldier to lie supine, taking his ease at home, and siding neither with England nor France. True it is that certain fortresses are even now held with a strong hand by certain who take service on either side as it suits their humor, bearing allegiance to none. I would not have thee ranged among these mistrustful thieves, and well I trust thou hast forsworn their company forever and aye. When I proffered thee Odille, and chose thee for mine heir, I took no promise from thee concerning this matter, neither do I seek to bind thee now. Nevertheless I freely aver that hadst thou been in open arms against my lord our King, I could not in honor or conscience have set mine hand to either contract; but thou camest from beyond Alps—a Free Lance in very truth—owing fealty to none. Neither would it be more strange to see thee, being English born, do thy devoir under the Lilies, than to hear of all the knights and barons of Gascony and Poitou, who cry, 'St. George Guienne!' Once more I require of thee no promise, but I charge thee, when I am gone, weigh all these things heedfully, putting no violence on thyself, and then to decide as seemeth best for thine own honor, and for the safety of the dear child I leave in thy guard."

Ralph's brows were bent as he listened, and his answer came but slowly.

"My lord and father, your speech is wise and generous as ever. Trust me, not now for the first time do I ponder these things and ever find myself in the same strait; yet I scarce know why it should be thus with me. I have never home-tie beyond the seas, and here I had many such, even before the last seven days made them sevenfold stronger. For ten years I have been fighting yonder for hireling's pay, scarce knowing—and to speak sooth, scarce caring—if the banner under which I lay down at night should be ranged against me on the morrow. Such scruples are as much misplaced in my heart as would be the Cross of St. Louis on my breast; yet I cannot away with them altogether. May be I shall wax wiser and better able to discern the right path after biding here for awhile. Be sure of this, I will constrain myself much, rather than in any wise imperil the welfare of my dear lady, your daughter."

"Thou sayest well, and I am content," the castellan replied. Then, after taking breath, he went on more earnestly than before. "Mark me now. Unless I grossly err, over things in these parts there will shortly come a great change. Since his fleet was swept away under thine eyes before Rochelle, there hath been shrewd ebb in King Edward's power. Poitou he ever ruled rather by fear than love, and the malcontents there have waxed outspoken and bold; in Guienne too, his lieutenants have rather weakened than strengthened his hands. Thou knowest what tidings have come to Bergerac of late. The Constable's staff in Du Guesclin's grasp is no gilded bauble; Moncontour, St. Sévere, Soubise, and many other strong places have gone down before him. The valiant Captal de Buch is prisoner, neither will our King be overspeedy in putting him to ransom. Even now, if common report be true, the chiefest of the Poitevins, who still hold the Red Cross, are closely penned in Thouars, and unless succor come from England are under covenant to surrender by an appointed day. *Pardie*, if matters go on thus, such as dwell in France and deny fealty to her suzerain will stand like lonely trees—a ready mark both for the blast and leveling."

" There is reason in all this," the other answered, gravely. " That the battle hath gone hard against Edward of late, I may not deny. Yet, having heard much concerning him, and seen somewhat of that king in early days, and heard more from those who have been near his person—for instance, stout Walter Breckenridge, whom God assoilzie!—I guess that he will not lightly relinquish that which it hath cost so much time and gold and blood to attain. Men wax not less stubborn as they wax older, till they begin to dote ; and had you, my lord, looked on his face as I did, day by day during Calais leaguer, you would, I think, share my faith that he will essay one great emprise at the least, ere he listen to any such terms of treaty as France would deign to propose. Yon armament under Penebroke which so heavily miscarried was, I know, meant only as the forerunner of a mightier one. The cry for help from Thouars must needs bring things to an issue ; King Edward cannot be deaf thereto for very shame. I dare aver, ere this there is chafe and stir at Windsor, and that the *arrière-ban* hath gone forth already, from the Scottish Border southward, throughout the length and breadth of the land. I am minded to bide here quiet for awhile, marking warily the changes of the times—Hacquemont, as I have heard you say, hath ever lain somewhat remote from the war turmoil. 'Twill be easy to send forth scouts ever and anon who shall bring us word if it rolls our way. Thus far do I subscribe to your opinion, my good lord: if King Edward should lose foothold in Guienne, or keep it only on the seaboard, 'twere sheer madness to keep his pennon flying over a few scattered castles—for the Constable to sack piecemeal at his leisure. I mind well the words that were ever in John Hawkwood's mouth, when somewhat had to be done at which he guessed we might have qualms—we were not nice of stomach, God wot—'Necessity hath no law,' quoth he. He picked up the proverb from a priest, yet 'tis truth, perchance, for all that; and I will strive to comfort myself therewith—as better men have done, I trow—at a fitting season; the saints guide my judgment to guess when it hath come."

"Amen," the old castellan answered, as he leaned back, closing his eyes, with a long sigh. "We will speak farther of these matters, but not now; I am too weary. Fetch Odille to me, I pray thee. Now that my time is so short, I begrudge her being long out of my presence. I bade her go to inquire concerning the health of Messire Gualtier; 'tis a gentle youth and a kindly—yea, also, I have done him some wrong in my thoughts of late. I am well pleased to hear that he is mending fast."

Truly said Philippe de Hacquemont that his time was short; it was shorter even than he counted on, and on worldly matters he spoke again never a word. Early on the morrow they found him quite dead, "Lying as he had smiled." The change had come so quietly that the page who slept in the chamber never guessed that aught had gone amiss, till he drew the curtain and let the light stream in on the set, white face.

Though for months past Odile must have looked upon her father's death as a question of days, and could hardly—for his own sake—have wished his life prolonged, it was only natural she should regret him deeply; but time passed on till the fullest period of filial mourning was expired, and still the lady seemed unable to shake off the sorrow that seldom allowed a smile to flicker on her lips, and kept her eyes often heavy with tears. In her husband's presence she did, indeed, force herself to be cheerful; but even to him—unsuspicious and easily satisfied as he was—the effort was sometimes apparent. Yet Ralph never murmured, even to himself, and was indeed perfectly happy in his honest way. Action and some sort of exercise in the open air had become part and parcel of his nature. He was Seigneur of Hacquemont till any chose to dispute his title, and the succession brought business enough and to spare on his hands, for the fief—though not overwealthy—was broad, and counted many scattered vassals, with all of whom Ralph chose to make acquaintance face to face. The tried soldier always loves to know on what material he may count in case of need. Since the warfare had grown desultory, the country was not so sorely drained of its youth and manhood, and among the peasantry there were not a few rough-hewn stocks that might easily be trimmed into soldierly shape. The choicest of these—allured, partly by large pay, partly by their seigneur's great renown in arms—were easily persuaded to enter his immediate service. Once in the castle, the training of such went on rapidly ; so its garrison soon became more formidable than that of many fortresses thrice as important. Hawk and hound, too, Brakespeare followed keenly as ever, though he was fain to follow them alone ; for since her father's death the Lady Odille had never been strong enough to go far afield. One way or another, he usually found himself in saddle in early morning, and was rarely home much before sundown. He was perfectly content if his wife showed any interest—to do her justice, she generally did—in the sport or business of the day ; and in the seventh heaven if she could be persuaded, after supper, to take up her lute and sing to him some ditty—were it ever so sad.

Sometimes, but rarely, Gualtier de Marsan would take his turn at the viol. Sickness had left heavy traces on the esquire, and his strength seemed to return very slowly. It was with difficulty he forced himself to take needful food and drink, and he was equal to no exercise ; so 'tis no marvel if his cheeks still continued hollow and wan, and if the dark circles under his wistfull eyes passed not away. Though he and the Lady Odille were thrown perforce much into each other's company, they spoke but seldom—so far as any knew—and then concerning the most trivial matters. They would sit for hours in the presence-chamber—Odille in the great oriel, Gaultier in the recess of a distant window, gazing out wearily, with listless eyes that marked not a feature of the landscape betwixt them and the distant hills.

The household was made up of ancient retainers and others, born in the family service; simple, God-fearing folk the most part, part of whose creed it was to honor their master, and to speak no evil of dignities. Even the spearmen, who had come from beyond Alps—at first from policy, or awe of Brakespeare's anger, afterward from habit—had fallen into the same quiet, humdrum ways, and even in their drink carried themselves decently—snoring over their liquor if they chanced to take a cup too much, instead of wrangling or rowing over it as heretofore. The battered, weather-beaten *soudards* had begun to value aright the comforts of chimney-corner and roof-bield, and had lost all taste for the perilous excitement of foray or bivouac. They waxed lusty, too, on much sleep and large provender; though Ralph was but in jest when he called them sometimes " fat, lazy knaves," there was more truth in the words than he wist of. All things considered, it was scarce likely that any of Hacquemont would trouble themselves to spy upon their *châtelaine*, much less to cavil at her ways. Nevertheless, one man there watched the aspect of matters with growing discontent.

Under Lanyon's rough, blunt exterior there were hidden—as may have been seen in the course of this chronicle—certain sparks of intelligence and shrewd common sense. Moreover, his wits were quickened by the incitement that all others there lacked: he loved from the very bottom of his heart the master he had followed so long through foul and fair weather, and he cared for no other created thing. Day by day his humor grew more somber and taciturn—shunning the companionship of his gossip the warder, and repelling all social advances from others. The *routiers* grumbled to each other that their comrade had waxed proud of stomach in his old age, and prone to stand on his dignity as body-squire to the Lord of Hacquemont. Nothing could be farther from the truth; Lanyon thought just as humbly of his own merits, and was just as little likely to exact more respect from others than is due from man to man, as he was on the morning he followed Ralph out of Sir Simon Dynevor's presence; but he was weighed down by suspicions he could not away with—by a secret that was none of his own seeking, of which he could not unburden himself. Thoroughly dauntless by nature, and hardened by incessant training, the esquire would have faced almost any peril to which mortal flesh is liable without the quickening of a pulse or the quivering of a nerve. From one thing he would have shrunk as a girl might shrink from the first sight of bloodshed. That thing was—the hinting to Sir Ralph Brakespeare a doubt of his wife's purity. So he kept silence, growling under his breath, grinding his teeth, and snarling on occasion like a chafed wolf, and there was the wolfish glare in his small keen eyes as they lighted on De Marsan, toward whom his manner was at times blunt, even to rudeness. These signs of his dislike could scarce always have escaped the object thereof; but if Gualtier noticed, he did not seem to heed them. When the other's bearing was unusually churlish, the younger esquire would open his great sad eyes a little, with a look of languid wonder, and let the lids droop again as he fell back into his reverie. Graver matters, clearly, were busying his thoughts than an old *routier's* fits of evil temper.

All this while Philippe de Hacquemont's prophecies seemed drawing nearer and nearer to their fulfilment.

When the message came to Windsor from the faithful Poitevins beleaguered in Thouars, after one long fit of despondency, King Edward rose up in ire, and swore a great oath that long before the day appointed —failing his rescue—for the town's surrender, he would succor them with such an armament as never yet had set foot on the shores of France. Thus far Ralph Brakespeare, too, had been right in his auguries. The *arrière-ban* went through every nook and corner of England, from the Tweed to the Tamar, and drew together four thousand lances and twenty thousand archers, for whom four hundred transports waited in Southampton Water. Scarce one of the names then famous in our realm for valor, wisdom, power, or pure lineage, was absent from that muster-roll. The Black Prince roused himself from the apathy of long sickness, and—having first set his house in order, and disposed all things for his son's succession—dragged himself on shipboard, though his shrunken limbs were scarce fit to bear harness, and the great armament set forth.

But the stars, in their courses, fought against King Edward. For nine weary weeks the fleet did battle with wind and waves, weltering to and fro—sometimes within sight of Breton cliffs, sometimes driven far back again to the westward, but never fairly weathering Ouissant Isle, much less nearing Rochelle, the port for which they were bound. At the last provision began to fail, and King Edward was fain to put about, and steer again for his own land; crying out—so the chroniclers say—in the bitterness of his discomfiture,

"Never was king who had drawn sword so seldom, and yet proved so stubborn a foe, as Charles of France."

So those in Thouars were left to their fate, which was soon decided in this wise:

About the time of the sailing of the English fleet, Thomas Felton, seneschal of Bordeaux, and Archibald de Grailly, uncle of the Captal de Buch, had mustered some three hundred lances who marched northward to Niort, and found there encamped many—both of Gascony and Bretagne, and the united forces made up a formidable army. From these captains word was sent to Thouars, that of King Edward's presence in person there now seemed faint hope; but that they, at any rate, were willing to strike in and aid to the uttermost of their power. Then ensued in Thouars sharp debate —albeit it was debate of one against many—for stout John de Partenay stood well-nigh alone in his sentence, " that whether their suzerain came to the rescue or no, it still behooved them to fight it out to the last." The others alleged with much show of reason that by the terms of their covenant, failing succor from England by some one of the royal blood, they were bounden to render the town, and once more to pledge fealty to France. The voice of the many prevailed. On the eve of Michaelmas Day, those who watched from the towers saw the flaunt of many pennons, but among them the standard of England was not found. They were the ensigns of a great host—led by the Dukes of Berry, Bourbon, Burgundy, and Du Guesclin—coming to claim fulfilment of their contract. On the next day, the Lilies floated again over nearly the last stronghold of England in Poitou.

Thenceforward the tide of warfare seems never to have turned. The great Constable roved hither and thither, with a thousand lances at his back, reducing one after another all such towns and castles as still maintained a show of fealty to the Red Cross. John of Montfort himself—faithful in either fortune to the ally who had loaded him with benefits—was forced to flee from his duchy of Brittany to seek refuge beyond seas; and soon it came to pass, that Charles the Wise could fairly call his own all the territory lying betwixt Seine and Garonne.

Now of all these things Ralph, Seigneur of Hacquemont, was duly informed by scouts or otherwise. He lay too far inland to be within reach of summons when Grailly and Felton mustered their lances at Bordeaux, so that he had not been forced as yet to declare himself for either side; but he wist right well that the question could not be staved off much longer. Indeed, it was seldom absent from his mind now. His inclination still set the other way, yet he was cool and wary enough to recognize that open rebellion might soon become absolute madness—nay, that delay even might be dangerous.

While he thus halted betwixt two opinions, the autumn came round in which Thouars fell.

CHAPTER XLIV.

On a certain October morning the Lord of Hacquemont's horses waited without the barbican. Most indeed, in the castle, thought their lord had already ridden forth; but Ralph had suddenly bethought him of some repairs needed in divers parts of the walls and battlements, and as he was to ride near where the masons dwelt he determined to visit these before getting to saddle. Looking at the state of his defenses, and remembering how soon they might be needed, brought his thoughts naturally into the channel in which they had run often of late. He soon fell a-musing earnestly, and scarce knowing what he did, entered one of the small jutting tourelles, and sat down there. The weather was close and sultry, and the half-drowse into which deep reveries so often merge was stealing over him when he was roused by the sound of voices drawing nearer and nearer till they came close. It was manifest the speakers had halted, and were leaning over the battlements within a pace or two of Ralph's shoulder. The entrance to the tourelle was so narrow that none—unless standing exactly in front—would guess at the presence of any withinside.

Never once since the night when he looked on at the Convent of La Mellieraye, had the Free Companion played the eavesdropper. His first impulse now was to rise and discover himself instantly, but the words that smote his ear chained him where he sat, motionless and helpless as one over whose sleeping head a Hand of Glory has been waved. They were uttered in the soft, rich tones of Gualtier de Marsan.

"Nay, dear and gentle lady, make not, for very pity's sake, my task harder than I have set it to myself. Well ye wot that if ye forbid me to depart I needs must tarry here whatsoever the agony I shall abye. If it please you to drain my heart's blood slowly, I begrudge not, God knoweth, a drop thereof, nevertheless once again I say have mercy, and bid me go forth."

There was a sound as of a smothered sob, and then another voice spoke. The listener within knew it very well. It had sung him to sleep many years ago, when the fever of his sore wound made him restless. It had spoken the words of troth-plight, without faltering, before the chapel altar yonder; but it had never sounded so strangely sweet as now.

"It is you who are cruel, Gualtier, not I. Life here is dreary—sometimes almost too heavy to bear—but how thinkest thou will it fare with me when I am alone—quite alone? Ah me! I trust the masses said for his soul have assoilzied my dead father for having tempted me to mortal sin, and given hand without heart: my penance, at least, still endures, and will endure so long as my husband and I shall live. Wife's duty I have ever rendered; but wife's love I never can; and he is so good, and brave, and generous; so true and so sure of my truth, I grow half wild sometimes with remorse and shame. I shall madden quite, if I be left alone with my thoughts. *Mon doux ami*, tell me, at least, what hath prompted this sudden resolve of yours?"

The round music had died out of De Marsan's tones; they now sounded hard and hoarse, as those of a man wrestling with sharp bodily pain.

"It is because my heart waxeth weaker, so my body waxeth stronger. 'Tis but lately, since the fever left me, that my pulse hath begun to beat; and now I may not endure to look on things that erstwhile I saw like one in a dream. Ah! gracious lady, you and the holy saints know that never till this day hath word or salute passed betwixt us, but such as may become our several stations—nay, such as my lord, your husband, himself might approve and, in my very conscience, I believe that I have spoken no more than is needful now; but when the blood boils, the brain whirls, neither may I answer for what might ensue. If no worse befall, I might undergo your displeasure, and be fain to depart in bitterness. Thus far under sharp trial I have held fast to my duty and mine honor; ere I lose such cold comfort, it is best I go forth. My kinsman of Montauban waits me ever now; there will be sharp work a-doing ere long in Guienne, and even if death come not quickly, there is no medicine for the wrung heart like the shivering of lances."

"Death?" Odille said very wearily. "Death cometh not at our times and seasons. Better perchance had it been for us all, hadst thou never risen from that sick-bed yonder; but, Gualtier, I hinder thee no more. We will part as thou sayest, whilst neither conscience carries aught that need shame us at confession. If God will that we suffer long, he will perchance give strength to endure. We will speak of these things anon. Help me to my chamber now. I am so faint that I fear to swoon."

Slowly, without a glance withinside, the two passed the entry of the turret, and Ralph was left alone.

Alone—yea alone for evermore now—more lonely than when awhile back he found the heritage of his father in the hands of a stranger, and no welcome in the eyes of the woman who nursed him. Alone— without hope that the curse of loneliness would be lifted this side the grave, for the wife to whom he had given his large, honest love, if she had not proved unworthy of the trust, felt it, at the best, an irksome burden to be borne in patience till Heaven, in its mercy, should see fit to lighten her thereof. Only then did he realize what had been the happiness of these months past; the deep, quiet, happiness—no more resembling the fierce fever-fit that had possessed him at La Roche Dagon than does the red gleam piercing through the rift of storm-clouds a bright, calm, summer's day. There was no taint, at least, on Odille's honor or his own; and she had called him "good, generous, and true." There was some comfort in that; nevertheless, the strong soldier shivered from head to heel as he rose, blinking dizzily as he passed out into the light like one lately smitten with sunstroke.

It so chanced that Ralph encountered none of his household on his way to the barbican, without which Lanyon waited for him with their horse. One glance at his lord's countenance turned the esquire more sick with fear than when, far out in the deep sea, he heard that the other's strength was failing; but he asked never a question either then or thereafter.

Ralph flung himself into the saddle without a word, and rode furiously down the steep descent, and half a league farther into the wood before he drew rein. Then he fell into a walk and wandered on a by-road—seemingly without aim or purpose and not knowing that he was followed, for when wheeling about suddenly, as from some fresh impulse, he came face to face with Lanyon, he started in a sort of surprise.

"Art thou there?" he said. "Mayhap thou canst tell me on what business we came forth, for it hath slipped my brain."

It was a second or two before the esquire could get rid of the choking lump in his throat.

"Nay, I wot not," he said gruffly, "unless it had something to do with the repairing of the defenses up yonder."

At the word there came over Ralph of Hacquemont's ghastly face a light something akin to the old light of battle.

"Defenses," he muttered. "By God's body! it was even so. They may be proved ere long. Do thou ride down, and bid the knave masons get to work betimes to-morrow; as for me I will hie back straight to the castle. I am strangely ill at ease to-day, but the chapellan is leech enow to cure me with blood-letting."

So turning bridle, the knight rode off at speed, leaving Lanyon utterly aghast.

"His eyes are open then—whether for the better or for the worse, God knoweth. I would avouch our lady free from sin; yet mayhap that will not save yonder springald's white neck from the twisting." Thus muttering, the esquire went his way to do his lord's bidding.

On that day, one of those rare conjunctions of time and circumstances mere chance could hardly bring about befell at Hacquemont. As Ralph turned the last corner of the ascent, he caught the glimmer of steel through the trees, and found the plateau under the barbican occupied by a clump of spears, sitting in saddle before the raised drawbridge. The leader of the party rode out and with all reverence delivered a sealed parchment.

"I will pray your seigneurie—for I guess that I speak to none other than the Lord of Hacquemont—to peruse this at your leisure, and then to give me mine answer, which I am bidden to bear back at speed to my good lord, Sir Olivier de Clisson, the High Constable."

From mere force of habit, Ralph's self-command returned when need was urgent. His manner was quite calm and courteous as he prayed the French knight to enter and refresh himself and his following, while the letter was a-reading.

"I must trust to my chapellan to interpret it," he said, with a half-smile; "I am so poor a scholar."

But the other declined, with many thanks, saying that he was straitly charged to bear back the answer without breaking bread at Hacquemont, or even quitting saddle.

The missive was very brief. It required Ralph, self-styled Lord of Hacquemont, to present himself forthwith at Poictiers, with sufficient following, ready to serve under Bertrand de Guesclin's banner wheresoever he should direct. It farther set forth that, in case of such submission, and considering Sir Ralph Brakespeare's high renown in arms, King Charles would be pleased to accept his homage, and confirm him in his fief and honors; but failing this, he was bidden to make ready to defend himself *à l'outrance*—expecting no better terms than are dealt to obstinate traitors.

Ralph took the parchment from the chapellan, when the other had finished reading, and, holding it in his hand, paced to and fro through the presence-chamber, as was his wont when deep in thought. The first stunning effect of the blow that had stricken him that morning had passed away, and he was now able to weigh matters without passion, if not without bitterness.

Lo, the time had come whereof he and Philippe de Hacquemont had spoken together. What had he promised then, when both had agreed that to hold a solitary castle for King Edward would be no better than madness? This was the season at which he had prayed the saints to guide his judgment aright; he had promised too, at whatsoever constraint to himself, to provide for Odille's welfare. Why should not that promise be kept to the letter, even if wise saws and proverbs of expediency were cast to the winds? Would it not be indeed for her good, if she were set free once more—free to bestow her love where she would, without sin or shame? The strong man's heart waxed for an instant very weak and faint as it answered Yea.

For himself there would be left another brief bout

at sword-play, like those of old times, and then a long sleep. He had had enow of French alliances, enow of their fair faces and fair words. He couched his first lance under the old Red Cross, and he would die under it after all. His mind was soon made up. Leaning over the chapellan's shoulder, he bade the other indite as follows:

My LORD CONSTABLE:—I thank, as is most due, for your gracious proffers both yourself, and the puissant king whom you serve; nevertheless, I may not accept them, neither render myself to your bidding. In England I was born and bred; for many a year I took King Edward's pay, and from the hand of the Prince, his son, received I the accolade: wherefore it comporteth not with mine honor to bear arms against him now. So I purpose to maintain myself here to the uttermost of my poor power, and when that is spent to betake myself to God's mercy, expecting none from man.

RALPH BRAKESPEARE.

Given at our castle of Hacquemont this
Martinmas Eve.

This missive Ralph himself placed in the hands of the French knight, who, with all formal courtesy, presently took his leave.

By this time, as may be imagined, all in the castle were astir; and, as he paced back through the courtyard, not a few peered anxiously in their lord's face, striving to discern therein some sign from which they might draw augury as to the nature of the message brought thither, and the answer thereto. But that face told no tales, and, as none dared to question the chapellan—who, indeed, was bound to secrecy—the household were fain to devour their curiosity as best they might. As for Ralph himself, he was possessed now with the calm sense of rest of one who, having been tossed about hither and thither on a sea of doubt, anchors at last on a firm resolve. His brow bore no trace either of anger or pain when he joined Odille in her chamber, and his voice was quite steady while he said his say. It was brief enough. He told her that he had been summoned to Poictiers, there to render homage and accept service under the Constable, with promise of renewal of his fief; but certain conditions were attached thereto with which he could not in honor comply without some debate, unless compelled thereto by force of arms. It was possible Hacquemont might be beleaguered ere long. He doubted not to obtain fair terms of surrender to such siege with small danger to life or limb of any therein; but, for many reasons, Odille and her wardens were best elsewhere for the present, so he had determined they should leave early on the morrow for Bordeaux, under sufficient escort, headed by Gualtier de Marsan and Lanyon.

Now the Lady Odille, though perchance too weak to be quite sincere, was a pure, pious woman, and, after her own light, did her duty; but she had hard work to repress a thrill of guilty pleasure as she listened, and could not keep back the treacherous flush that mounted even to her smooth, white forehead. Nevertheless she did contrive, in duteous phrase, to set forth her willingness to bide with her husband, and share his perils to the last; nay, she even prayed, with some urgency, that she might not be driven from his side. Years and years after she remembered how sadly Ralph smiled as he answered, stroking the braids of her dark, smooth hair with his broad palm—

"Nay, nay, sweetheart, think not to change my resolve. It is best so, trust me. 'Tis a long journey for thee, specially since thou hast been of late seldom in saddle; but I think thou art stronger than thou fanciest, and in Bordeaux thou wilt be tenderly cared for. In these troublous times, with so many *routiers* abroad, even convents are scarce safe quarters, else would I house thee with the Abbess thy kinswoman. Bid thy tiring-women make ready their mails. An' thou wilt be guided by me, thou wilt keep thy chamber, and take what rest thou canst before morning. Be not wakeful to watch for me. It may be late ere I lie down to sleep; there is much to order within doors and without."

So Ralph departed, leaving his wife in a bewilderment of wonder, self-reproach, and fear; in which were mingled—as was aforesaid—some throbs of sinful, guilty joy, which at last relieved itself in a passionate burst of weeping.

By this time Lanyon had returned, and was presently summoned to his lord's presence. As the eyes of the two men met, Ralph knew that it would be vain to dissemble here. Without any preamble, he told the other the contents of the Constable's letter.

"What thinkest I answered—ha?"

"Not words of peace, I wot," the esquire returned bluntly. "Marry, had the Frenchman come yestereven your lordship might have pondered longer over the matter; but men indite not courtly periods bearing such a brow as was thine when we parted. Perchance it is as well."

"It is best," Ralph said, setting his lips. "If thou

canst guess at what chafed my humor to-day, breathe it not even to thyself, I charge thee. Now hearken diligently. This is what thou must do."

Lanyon received with mute attention all the directions concerning the escort, whereof he was to have the chief charge. When all was ended he advanced, and with his wonted slow deliberation kneeled down, resting both hands on Brakespeare's knee.

"My lord Sir Ralph," he said, "I have followed you faithfully, and performed your bidding—whether for good or evil—for hard on thirty years; receiving my wages duly, but never having once craved favor at your hands—albeit, if I mistake not, it hath been my luck more than once to stand betwixt you and death. Lo, now I crave—not as a right, but humbly, on bended knee—that you will suffer me to bide here with you, and take my chance with yourself under shield, rather than send me forth on duty for which any minion page might suffice—ay, even such a gay, damoret as yon Gualtier de Marsan."

Ralph gripped his squire's shoulder hard; if his words were rough, his eyes were kind even to tenderness.

"Rise up, fool," he said. "Art not grown wiser since—near a score of years agone—thou didst cumber me with scruples in this very chamber? Thou hast spoken sooth: through thy long true service thou hast had little guerdon beyond thy full share of hard blows —God wot I begrudge not this now. I swear by mine honor that I have no mind thou shouldst be absent when work is a-doing here. When thou hast bestowed thy lady safe at Bordeaux, and delivered a certain letter, thou mayst return as quickly as thou wilt, and spare not for the spoiling of horseflesh. If the Constable be the hawk men bespeak him, he needs must circle ere he swoop. Nay, should we be beset ere thy return, their lines will surely be drawn on the hither side of the secret issue. 'Twill be easy to worm thy way through the brushwood; and one within shall listen night and day for thy knock. Art thou content?"

Lanyon almost laughed aloud as he sprang lightsomely to his feet.

"Yea, more than content! I thank your lordship heartily; dolt indeed was I to have mistrusted your good-will. Now will I about the ordering of this gear instantly, an' ye would give me the roll of such as are to ride forth to-morrow."

"That is soon done," Brakespeare replied, and he proceeded to check off from the roll of the garrison near a score of names—including nearly all the special retainers, young and old, who had been bred in the actual house-service of Hacquemont. "'Twill not weaken us much to lose these," Ralph muttered, as he finished his task, "and be we ever so well victualed, we need feed no useless mouths."

The esquire nodded his head assentingly with a surly smile.

"I am glad to see your lordship hath not set down my gossip Gilles; 'twere hard measure indeed to rack his creaking joints in saddle. Though he hath few teeth left, I will warrant him to show sport yet if he fight from his kennel."

All that afternoon Ralph spent in directing necessary

preparations within and without the walls, including the repairs for all warlike engines, and laying down lines for new. He had scant appetite at supper, yet he forced himself to take some food and drink. Then after a brief visit to Odille's apartment, and seeing that she had betaken herself to rest, he shut himself up alone in the presence-chamber. He had another task to perform before he thought of sleep.

Hard in more ways than one. Ralph Brakespeare, even in early youth, had possessed but poor clerkly skill, and even this, through long disuse, had grown rusty; so that it became a toil to scrawl the hieroglyphic that stood for his signature. Yet now he had to write certain lines that he dared indite to none, and which yet must be made plain enough to be read some day. In all great sorrows and agonies—even in the tortures of the damned, if Dante saw aright—something of the grotesque mingles. If one's heart were in the work, there would be no fitter subject for caricature than a face blurred and deformed by weeping. Many would scarce have refrained a smile, had they watched the painful effort that it cost the Free Companion to form character after character with his stiff, unpractised fingers. His brows ached and throbbed from very weariness, long before the work was complete, but it was done at last, and the letter, rendered from the Norman French, ran thus:

DEAR LADY AND WIFE:—When first thine honorable father, now at rest, unfolded to me his designs concerning us twain, I did earnestly object mine own unworthiness—saying that one of my nurture and training, to say naught of my years, was no fitting mate for so delicate a dame. When my lord waxed urgent, and would in nowise be gainsaid, I required of him a promise that on thine inclinations should be put no force; binding myself to accept denial in all patience and humility. So I departed on my journey, hoping no more for favorable answer at my return than for any other bounteous miracle. When I came hither, my good lord straightly affirmed, that, having not at all strained his authority or unduly swayed thy will, he had found thee nothing loth—but rather well-disposed toward such espousal. On thus relying; I spake, and was answered. The error was grievous doubtless, yet sure I am it was not wrought wittingly. Wherefore I pray thee lay not heavy blame either on thy father's memory or mine; for when thou shall peruse these words, I shall be even as he. Much hath been made clear to me since this forenoon, when I chanced to overhear converse betwixt thee and the Sieur de Marsan—not of aforethought, as thou wilt well believe, did I play the spy. I sat a-musing in the tourelle by which ye two halted, and the first words so struck my spirits, that for awhile I was like one in a trance, who with eyes and ears open cannot stir finger. Some bitter truths I heard, yet I heard also that Messire Gualtier under sore temptation—how sore, dear, none know better than I—hath borne himself in chaste and loyal fashion; neither failing in reverence due to thee, nor contriving against mine honor. Wherefore I hold him blameless, and I here aver that, if at fitting season thou shouldst deign to grace him with thine hand, ye need never be kept apart for conscience sake or mine: in proof whereof I commit thee to that esquire's escort tomorrow without doubt or fear.

For me, my time must needs be short—Du Guesclin, the Constable, underlieth my cartel, and he will answer it ere long perchance in his proper person. I purpose to hold this place *à l'outrance*, and when it shall be forced, to take no quarter, so I am like to trouble thee no more. The good merchant, who will deliver thee this letter—in whom also my lord thy father greatly trusted—hath moneys enow to provide for thine honorable maintenance till—either as widow or wife— thou art brought back hither.

Ma douce amie, for thy duteous kindness, which hath made my life of late blessed beyond my deserts, may God requite thee, and keep thee ever in his holy guard. And so I bid thee heartily farewell. Thy loving husband and true servitor till death, RALPH BRAKESPEARE.

The letter was duly addressed and sealed, and then wrapped in an outer square of parchment; in the withinside of which the knight made shift to trace a few more lines with his stiff, cramped fingers. After adding the superscription he closed the packet, carefully thrusting it into the breast of his doublet.

This was so long a-doing that it was past midnight when he sought his sleeping-chamber. Despite his great weight and size, the Free Companion could tread lightly as a girl when he chose, and he entered so softly that Odille's slumbers were not broken. She looked exceeding fair—fairer, Ralph thought, than he had ever seen her, and with her head nestling on her arm, while the rich dark hair half shaded one flushed cheek. There was a half-smile on her lips, though a tear or two, clinging to her long eyelashes, showed that her dreams had not been joyous. Setting down the lamp he carried, and still treading very softly, Ralph drew nearer and nearer till he knelt down by the couch, and so remained—resting his chin on his clasped hand, gazing on his wife's face with terrible earnestness in his eyes. Under such a steadfast gaze sleepers are said often to wake, but Odille never even stirred uneasily; for any sign of life he showed beyond the gleaming of his haggard eyes her husband might have been one of the figures that kneel under the canopies of tombs.

In that strange fashion was passed the very last night that those two would ever spend together. At length gray light stole in through the ill-closed window-curtains; as Ralph arose shaking himself, with something like a groan, Odille awoke. Even as she did so her husband's lips were laid lightly on her brow.

"It is full time to rise, *belle amie*. Thou seest I am afoot already. Loth though I be to part with thee, even for a brief season, I would fain see thee in saddle. Thou hast a long journey before thee, and the days shorten fast."

Just then, by one of those vague impulses in which surely some prescience mingles, Odille's heart was drawn nearer to her husband than it had ever been, with a remorseful tenderness. Her arm stole round his neck, as she whispered—

"Blessed St. Ursula! How pale thou art! If this parting irks thee so, why dost send me forth? Trust me, I too am loth to go; yet of a surety we shall meet soon."

"It is but the dawn-light," he said, "that maketh me look wan, and a little weariness beside; seek not to turn me from my purpose, sweetheart. All is ordered wisely, and fear not: we shall meet—in God's good time."

The cheery tones waxed very solemn in the utterance of those last words: in after years Odille knew right well why.

By this time all the household was astir, and during the bustle of departure those two were not alone again together. The pack-horse stood loaded, and most of the escort were already mustered in the courtyard as

Sir Ralph drew Lanyon aside and gave into his charge the sealed packet, with all direction as to its safe delivery.

"Thou mayst tell Sir John Felton how it stands with us here," he went on carelessly. "We fought side by side at Poictiers; and I did him a shrewd turn when I dragged him from under his destrere in the mellay. 'Tis a chance if he remembers this; moreover, his own hands are too full to send help so far afield, even for a stake better worth saving than an old Freebooter's bones. Be watchful and wary, after thy fashion, and trust me, I will keep faith with thee."

As the knight turned away he came face to face with De Marsan. The esquire's countenance was more downcast than usual, and very pale—save for a scarlet spot on either cheek bone. In all his movements there was a nervous, feverish haste; and under the other's steady eyes his own sank, if they did not quail.

"Fare thou well for the nonce, Messire Gaultier," Brakespeare said; "many things may happen ere thou and I foregather again. Lo! I deliver to thy keeping the most precious thing I own, feeling well assured that thou wilt quit thyself of the trust worthily, as thou hast done heretofore—at cost of how much soever of thine own peril or pain."

And he held out his hand, which the other took, and —answering never a word—saluted reverently, with lips that struck cold like a corpse. Just then the Lady Odille came down with her maidens, busked for the journey. The courtyard was full to overflowing; for not only the escort, but all the garrison not on actual duty were gathered there; but Ralph took his wife in his arms before them all, and held her for some seconds closely embraced. Then he kissed her on her forehead, and on her eyes, from which tears were streaming. His countenance was so calm that never an one there—not even the woman pressed against his heart, guessed how near that heart was to breaking. Then he lifted her lightly into the saddle, settling her riding-skirt deftly and carefully—as he used to do in the old hawking days—and still keeping silence took the bridle of the jennet and led it forth through the arch of the barbican, and over the outer drawbridge. There he stopped and kissed his wife once more—this time only on the left hand, that hung listlessly down, saying softly, "God be with thee, sweetheart"—and so let her pass on.

Then the escort filed out two abreast, Lanyon and three others spurring to the front as soon as they were past the drawbridge to form an advanced guard, De Marsan bringing up the extreme rear. At the turning of the descent, where it plunged into the woodland, the Lady Odille turned in her saddle and looked back. She saw dimly, through tears, her husband fixed statue-like on the very same spot where she had left him—just within the square shadow cast forward by the barbican wall. She waved her kerchief twice or thrice, but her adieu was seemingly unnoticed; for there came back no answering sign. Many times thereafter—in night or day dreams—the lady saw that stately martial figure, with crossed arms and head slightly bent as though in thought or in sorrow; but in life or substance she saw him never more.

CHAPTER XLV.

HAD it been Ralph Brakespeare's wont to fret or make moan over what was past and gone, there would have been scant leisure for such follies just now. But it was not in his nature so to abase himself, and when he had once faced his sorrow he no more thought of letting it overmaster him than of yielding without drawing sword to any foe in flesh and blood. The next three days were very busy ones at Hacquemont. There was the victualing of the castle to be provided for, walls to be prepared as thoroughly as haste would permit, stones and bolts to be provided for the great engines, with a store of lighter missiles for the hand artillery. All these matters the Free Companion directed with unwearying care; not seldom himself doffing doublet, and giving example to his artificers, where there was special need for strength or skill.

So each night came more quickly than might have been looked for, and he lay down too tired to dream. Toward the evening of the third day, when all things were ready, Sir Ralph mustered his entire garrison in the courtyard, and thus bespoke them:

"Good friends and followers, it behooves ye to know how matters stand with us here; for I will take no man's service by fraud or cozenage, neither shall any risk life or liberty farther for me, unless by his own free-will. I have been summoned—as some of ye may have partly guessed—to render homage to the French king, and to serve under the banner of the Lord du Guesclin, his Constable. Now this—wherefore, it boots not to explain—suits in nowise with my humor; rather am I minded to hold this castle to the uttermost against any force, great or small, that may come to beleaguer it. But I constrain none to abye with me, in a strait well-nigh desperate; for of rescue or relief there is, I confess, but scant hope. So I hereby give license to each and every one of you now to depart, receiving full wages up to this very hour; and such as it shall please thus to go forth I assoilzie of any cowardice or treachery. Most here were bred and born in France, even as I was bred and born in Merry England yonder, and shame it were to my knighthood if I enforced—yea, or overpersuaded—such to bear arms against their natural suzerain. Furthermore I needs must avow that, for mine own self, I purpose to take no quarter, albeit when I am sped I doubt not that the Lord du Guesclin, or whosoever holdeth command in his stead, will grant to any one who shall require it fair terms of surrender. Now let any speak, or hereafter hold their peace; for whoso bideth with me, from this night forth must needs bide to the end."

All left in Hacquemont were, as hath been aforesaid, picked men; chosen by an eye that seldom erred in scanning the points of a soldier. Yet it was scarce to be expected but that some two or three would have availed themselves readily of a proffer so frank and timely. It was only fair to reckon that the old *routiers*, who had gone through fire and water beyond Alps with the famous Free Companion, should stand by him to the last—for even those masterful thieves were not exempt from a rude, wild code of honor—but there were others there, who, had they listened to the voice of prudence or even the prompting of natural affection, would surely have left the stranger to fight out his rash battle alone; but never a man gave token of such purpose by word or sign—nay, the brows of some grew dark and overcast, as if they liked not the choice set before them. A murmur ran through the crowd, not hard to interpret, and at the last, one bolder and readier of tongue than his fellows spoke out:

"My lord, if this be no jest, we pray you to prove your followers no farther. We have ever been bounteously entreated by you; not in the matters of wage alone, but with kindness not to be paid in coin. Should any leave you in such a strait—ay, were it mine own brother that stands here, I should never break bread with him thereafter, nor give him water to slake his thirst; and so say we all."

For the first time since he began to be lonely, Ralph Brakespeare smiled.

"It is no jest," he said, "but bitter earnest; yet be it as ye will, and I thank ye heartily."

Then waving his hand in sign of dismissal, the knight went up into the keep. Save when he went his wonted round of the sentinels, he exchanged no other word with any that evening.

The fourth day passed quietly enough at Hacquemont. So also did the fifth, up to the afternoon, when two of the mounted scouts came in, bringing tidings that from the summit of a hill some five leagues distant, they had caught sight of a clump of spears, followed by a large body of footmen, and what the scouts took to be a long battering-train, marching eastward, in the act of crossing the Vezere to the southeast of Coutrances.

Ralph received the news with perfect coolness.

"Then we shall not see them before to-morrow at noon, at the earliest," he answered. "The Constable, or whosoever may be his lieutenant, will scarce adventure his artillery over our rough roads under darkness. They will camp near Bergerac to-night." But he muttered within himself as he turned away, "I would honest Will Lanyon were back. 'Twill break the poor knave's heart if he be caught by the way, and 'tis a chance if he stumble not on some of their scurriers unawares."

The knight was sitting over a solitary meal an hour or two after sundown, eating and drinking rather mechanically, when the sound of a bugle without the barbican made him start—not in any wonder or alarm, but with pleasure. He knew this call well enough; and, settling himself in his chair again, drained a beaker with deeper relish than he had felt of late, muttering—

"So the old fox hath slipped the hunters, and found his way home."

A few minutes later Lanyon stood in his lord's presence; and, after making his reverence, waited to be spoken to.

"Thou art welcome back, Will," the knight said. "Thy scruples were idle, as thou seest. How did my dear lady and wife compass her journey? Thou didst not, I trust, press forward beyond her strength."

"The Lady Odille bore her journey bravely," the

esquire answered, "and she was well enough in body, albeit somewhat sad in spirit, when I took my leave. She charged me to bear to your worship her loving duty; and to entreat that, for her sake, you would not rashly risk your person. Also I delivered the packet to Messire Bartelot, for the which I hold his receipt. He, too, commended himself humbly to your lordship, and would have had me lodge with him that night; but after our cattle were refreshed, I cared not to tarry longer, and so we turned bridle, and rode homeward under the moon."

"How sayest thou 'we?'" the other asked hastily. "Comest thou then not back alone?"

The esquire shifted from one foot to the other a little uneasily.

"Not altogether alone," he grumbled I——" He stopped, looking back over his shoulder." Glancing in the same direction, Brakespeare saw framed in the dark doorway leading to the stair the white face of Gualtier de Marsan, who stood there bareheaded, with his helmet in his hand. The Free Companion frowned in surprise or displeasure: nevertheless he beckoned the other to approach.

"How cometh this about, Messire Gaultier? Didst thou not comprehend it was thy duty to watch over the safety of my Lady Odille, and do her bidding as heretofore, till thou wert relieved of the trust?"

The esquire advanced, till he stood close to the dais, looking his lord full in the face; and this time his eyes did not quail.

"Noble seigneur," he said, "I crave your pardon humbly if I have gainsaid your wishes or misconceived mine own duty. After my poor judgment I did right, and as alone it would beseem my father's son. The gracious Lady Odille, even from her childhood, hath been watched and ministered unto by true honest folk —not by *faitours* and cowards. Foulest of such should I have been had I tarried yonder, discharging page's office, whilst you were in deadly peril; for my fellow-esquire here could not make but half confession when I questioned him straightly: so when I had seen the Lady Odille and her household safely bestowed, I joined myself to him forthwith and we rode back together. If it be your pleasure to send me forth again, I will depart instantly; but in such case I swear by the most Holy Trinity that not to the morning light will I outlive such shame."

"Questioning!" Lanyon grumbled; "marry, if questioning were all! Well, I must bear the blame of bewraying my lord's confidence. I wax soft-hearted so I wax old: years agone I had not been thus beguiled."

"I blame neither of ye overmuch," Brakespeare answered, his countenance clearing. "Yea indeed, Gualtier, for once thou wert right in following thy conscience rather than thy mere duty. Mayhap, when thou art old, thou wilt remember these words of mine. Go now, and disarm and refresh yourselves speedily; ye must have made good speed on your homeward ride."

"Such speed," Lanyon retorted, "that my stout destrere is utterly foundered, I fear; and his is scarce in better case. But 'tis partly your lordship's fault; you bade me not spare horseflesh."

"Tush!" Brakespeare answered, "thou art excused,

mon vieux routier. What matters horseflesh to such as are cooped within four walls? There will be more destreres in the stalls than men to back them before all is done here. Get thee gone now. I will speak with thee anon."

About ten of the clock on the following morning the scouts returned again, and reported the head of the French column to be scarce more than a league distant; and an hour or so later a clump of spears—in the midst of which was borne the guidon of a knight-banneret—filed out of the woodland on to the narrow plateau. From the midst of these, so soon as they had halted, a herald rode out, and—having thrice sounded his trumpet—cried aloud that Sir Olivier de Clisson desired to hold parley with the Seigneur of Hacquemont.

When Sir Ralph Brakespeare showed himself on the battlements of the barbican, which he did almost instantly, the leader of the party beneath stretched forth his right hand ungantleted. Under this knight's raised vizor might be discerned one of those dark, rough-hewn faces that, in repose, are wont to look something stolid or stern; but when lighted up are far from forbidding. His voice was very clear and sonorous, though marked with a strong provincial accent.

"Valiant sir," he began, "I am charged by my lord the Constable, to entreat you to consider whether ye will not repent yourself while there yet is time of the message ye sent him but lately; and for mine own part—though I am little apt to show favor to thy countrymen—I do earnestly back this his prayer. I would have you know that there followeth me such an armament—fully provided with all matters necessary for siege—as ye may not hope long to withstand. Those of your party in Bordeaux and thereabouts have enow to do to hold their own, without sending succor to any; and, unless rescue arrive in force far superior to mine own, I stir not from before this castle till it be rendered. Once more I renew the fair proffer set down in my lord Constable's letter—yourself could hardly crave more gracious one. Had ye been for these years past King Edward's soldier and liegeman, instead of warring—with high renown, as I must needs confess—all these years, for your own hand, ye were not bound in honor to hold this place against such odds. Furthermore, under your pleasure, it were better surely to abate somewhat of prejudice rather than expose the fair and gentle lady whom ye wedded to the perils and hardships of siege, albeit at our hand she need fear naught. So I beseech you, give me now your last answer—being well aware that if ye continue stubborn ye need look for no farther mercy or grace."

Without pause or hesitation Sir Ralph Brakespeare made answer. "Sir Olivier de Clisson, I cannot choose but thank the lord Constable, and yourself to boot, for your kindly proffers—of the which, nevertheless, I may in nowise avail myself. To what I have written I hold. As for the lady whereof ye spake, though she might safely—come the worst—rely on your courtesy, she need not be beholden to it as yet; for she is safely bestowed, far out of harm's way—far, I trow, beyond the sound of French trumpets. There are no women or weaklings within these walls, but only men-at-arms, with whom ye may deal as ye list—when ye have the power. So set on, and spare not, when ye will; and God befend the right!"

Clisson shut his vizor, and drew on his gantlet, muttering as he turned away, "His blood be on his own head. 'Tis a shrewd pity, too. A hardy knight, I warrant him, and never yet saw I Free Lance who bore himself so stoutly."

Even while the parley was proceeding, more and more spears had come gleaming up through the woodland: but before the plateau on the summit grew crowded, De Clisson ordered his trumpets to sound the halt, while, with two or three others, he took survey.

The castle of Hacquemont, as hath been aforesaid, crowned an eminence steep and rocky in most parts, though not exceeding high. Round such a place it was not easy to draw regular siege lines; and—except on one side—there was no space broad or level enough for the working of all ordinary battering-engines. But it was not for naught that the Breton captain had already become famous in this especial line of warfare. He was endowed with the quick eye and mechanical instinct of a born engineer, and made light of obstacles that would have puzzled others; while he could use to the uttermost the faintest vantage of ground. Within an hour many axes were ringing in the woodland, and tree after tree came tumbling down before the sturdy pioneers. Others cleared away the brushwood binding it as it was felled into fagots and bundles. This work had a double object—the clearing of the ground for the maneuvers of attack, and the providing of huts and booths to shelter man and beast, and so deftly was it performed that when night closed in the little hill was almost bare, and nearly all the besieging force was housed in some sort of fashion, though only the knights and their esquires lodged in tents or pavilions. The French had marched some distance that day, and De Clisson was too wise a captain to overtax the strength of his soldiers. Though the moon was bright, he deferred the heavy task of bringing up his battering-engines and bombards till the morrow, and remained quiet through the night—only keeping under arms a force sufficient to guard against surprise or sally.

Early on the morrow there came to De Clisson's tent three of his knights, and the chiefest worthy—Sir Yvon de Laconnet by name—thus bespoke him:

"Noble sir, we entreat you to consider that it will scarce redound to your honor, or ours, to lie long before so mean a castle—which must needs be poorly garrisoned—when towns and fortresses—such as Civerolles, Becherel, Niort, Sancerre, Brest and Mortaigne have gone down quickly before your arm: wherefore we beseech you that, before sitting down here with all your battering-train, you will give us license to try open assault. The ditch is not deep, and may easily be filled, so as to give holding-ground for the ladders: an' we have leave to advance our banners, we doubt not to give good account of the castle ere noon."

Sir Olivier pondered awhile. He was by no means so confident as to the chance of open assault, but—himself a born Breton—he knew well with what stubborn intractable characters he had to deal, and felt that it was better to risk somewhat than to provoke discontent among his subalterns. So, rather sullenly and ungraciously, he gave the required permission, insisting only on prompt obedience—should he think fit to sound the recall. Up to this time very few of the defenders had shown themselves on the towers or battlements. Every now and then the figure of a knight in bright steel armor and a plain helmet, bearing no crest or plume, might be seen passing along the walls, or leaning forth to watch the preparations below. Partly from his great size and stature, partly from his bearing, the besiegers soon came to recognize Sir Ralph Brakespeare, and many had tales to tell, more or less wild or improbable, as they pointed out to their fellows the terrible Free Companion.

About nine of the clock the French trumpets sounded, and their storming parties, under the several pennons of Yvon de Laconnet, Alain de Beaumanoir and Geoffrey de Kerimel—the knights who had sought and obtained of their leader that perilous honor—marched up the hill to the assault in echelon order, choosing for the point of attack the northwest angle of the castle walls, where the plateau was wide enough to allow one company at least to form on level ground. In the front rank, a few places in advance of the column, came the pavisors, bearing long triangular shields, intended to shelter the crossbowmen, while by aid of windlass and lever they bent the ponderous arbalest or discharged the quarrel; then came the crossbowmen— harnessed after their fashion in steel salade shoulder and thigh plates, and thick, wide-sleeved haqueton; then the more completely equipped mounted archers, who only on such occasions fought afoot; lastly, the knights and esquires in full armor of plate and mail. In the rear of each division marched pioneers and pavylers, some bearing scaling ladders; others, fascines and rude hurdles for filling up the ditch.

Even now, when the assault was imminent, there seemed little stir within the castle wall, only at rare intervals a helmet showed itself at a crenelle, and withdrew again speedily. But it might have been noticed that just here the dark beams that betokened the presence of trebuchet and petrary were most frequent; as if the captain of the besieged had known of a certainty where the first assault would be made. On the very verge of the moat the pavisors were planted; and from behind these the arbalestriers made ready to sweep the battlements with their quarrels. The men-at-arms halted while those who bore the fascines advanced on either flank, and began to construct a sort of causeway athwart the moat, which here was but moderately deep, and scarce half full of water.

This work went on steadily, and still the garrison within made no hostile sign; only, ever and anon, the knight in bright armor leaned forth from a certain crenelle, and watched the progress of things below. On each of these occasions Ralph Brakespeare was the mark of many quarrels, but these—though they rattled on helmet, gorgering, and breastplate—glanced off, scarcely dinting the steel. That plain harness, whereon was neither graving, boss nor damascene, was a very masterpiece of the armorer's art, and even in Milan was worth a banneret's ransom.

So Sir Yvon de Laconnet, under whose pennon was ranged the leading company of stormers, was fain to wait patiently till the causeway was completed; much marveling in himself at the strange supineness of those within, and half suspecting stratagem. At length the fascines were level with the bank, and when the hurdles were laid thereon, there was foundation firm enough not only to support the assailants but to give fair foothold for their scaling-ladders. Then, without farther delay—crying aloud " St. Yves Laconnet "— the men-at-arms threw themselves on the causeway, four abreast, bearing the ladders in their midst; while the arbalestriers tarried still on the bank, to cover the assault with their artillery. As the head of the column touched the castle wall, a voice from above—distinctly audible as though the air had been deathly still, instead of filled with the rising of battle, spoke these two words—

"*Laissez aller!*"

And a huge mass of stones, like a crag toppling slowly over the battlements, fell into the very midst of the front rank, crushing Sir Yvon de Laconnet into a shapeless mass, and sorely maiming two others. This was only the forerunner of a storm of missiles of all weights and sizes that for several minutes hailed down without pity or stay. Now it was seen wherefore the wary Free Companion had suffered the causeway to be made without hindrance. Each one of his engines had been leveled with cool deliberation, and—as at short distance a stone, bullet, or beam could be shot to a hair's-breadth—not one of them missed its mark, or wasted itself on a spot already swept by one of its fellows. The carnage wrought in brief space was marvelous. It was wrought, too, with scarce any loss to the defenders, who could discharge their engines with very moderate danger to their own persons, from bolt or quarrel. When the storm of missiles began to slacken, the causeway was cumbered with corpses, and writhing bodies; while in the ditch on either side wallowed those who had been thrust from above in the turmoil, or had cast themselves off in their agony or fear. Several of these last contrived to struggle to the farther bank, and were drawn out by their comrades, but more—some even unwounded—were smothered, under the weight of their harness, in the water and ooze.

A crueller repulse, or one likelier to discourage those who came up in support, could scarce be imagined, but Geoffrey de Kerimel, who led the second division, was a Breton to the backbone, endowed with more than his fair share of the surly obstinacy that makes better soldiers and more dangerous rebels than mere dashing valor. Hastily, as though fearful that the trumpets in the rear, sounding recall, might balk him of his purpose, he gave the word to advance. The second division came on, much as the first had done, saving that they could not keep close order, and were fain to make their way as best they could across the causeway, thrusting aside the corpses with scant ceremony, and not always pausing to make distinction betwixt the dead and the dying. But as De Laconnet's crossbowmen still lined the moat-bank, those attached to De Kerimel's company were not required for like duty. So laying down their ponderous crennequins, they drew their short swords and prepared to support the men-at-arms to the best of their power.

The second company were exposed to no such peril

as the first, for reason good. The cumbrous wall-engines then in use, when once discharged, could not be brought to bear again without some time and trouble; so that the garrison were not able to offer any serious resistance to the rearing of the scaling-ladders. Two of them were set up abreast, each in a notch of a crenelle, and were soon crowded with stormers swarming up eagerly. The right hand party was led by Sir Geoffrey de Kerimel in person; the other by a strong and valiant esquire—Manoel Cassouan by name. As Sir Geoffrey's head rose on the level of the battlements he came face to face with the knight in bright armor, wearing his vizor down, and in his right hand swaying carelessly a great steel mace, as if he had no present intention to strike.

"Valiant sir," the Englishman said coolly, " whose title I know not, for I mind not before to have seen your pennon, doth it please you to yield yourself my prisoner, 'rescue or no rescue?' For I hold you now at such vantage that in no other wise may you carry your life away."

The Breton laughed hoarsely in his helmet, and, with no other answer, mounted two more rungs, brandishing his *epée d'armes*. Sir Ralph Brakespeare —for the speaker was none other—laughed too, and as the other strove to thrust himself through the crenelle, his mace descended, crushing in helmet and brain-pan like egg-shells, so that Geoffrey de Kerimel fell back without a stagger—carrying with him headlong the two who stood next upon the ladder.

Others swarmed up a pace, but never an one of these fairly gained footing within the battlements; for there stood the Free Companion, swaying his mace as a smith sways his fore-hammer—only that instead of the blithe clink of the anvil each blow was followed by a ghastly dull crash. Against the weapon, aided by advantage of height and ground, neither skill of fence nor harness of proof could avail. The fatal crenelle was all splashed with blood-gouts, till a foul, dark streamlet oozed therefrom, and trickled down the wall. At last the attack wavered and slackened; there was no longer press and throng at the ladder foot, for even the stubborn Bretons began to doubt whether it were their bounden duty to front—not peril slow but seemingly certain death.

The stormers on the other ladder, if they encountered no single champion of such terrible prowess, met with a very stout resistance, and could barely hold their own. There Gualtier de Marsan led the defenders, and did his devoir right gallantly, dealing such strokes as could scarce have been expected in one of his slender frame, not long since raised up from sore sickness. Before they had exchanged half a dozen blows his sword-point had found passage through Manoel de Cassouan's gorget, and hurled him backward with a mortal wound. For some minutes fierce foining went on, with glaive and battle-ax and shortened spear. While the fight was at its hottest there came up Lanyon, from another part of the walls whither he had been sent by his lord. For a brief space the old esquire stood aside, looking on with a kind of grim approval, but not seeking to take any part therein. At last he pushed his way to the front, and touched the shoulder of De Marsan, who had that second hurled back another adversary.

"Cover my head while I stoop, Messire Gualtier," he said, "and I will show thee a trick worth the seeing, if my sinews have not grown slack through idlesse."

Even while he spoke, Lanyon leaned forward and grasped the ladder, the topmost rungs of which were just then clear—for the rearmost assailants had been somewhat thrown into confusion by their comrade's fall. Then he braced his knees firmly against either side of the deep crenelle, till his body formed a sort of *arquebouton*, and thrust forward with his whole strength. The strain was so great that one might have seen the brawny muscles start out under the *cuir-bouilli* covering the back of his legs and thighs; but, little by little, ladder began to yield, till one tremendous jerk sent it headlong backward into the moat with all its freight.

A sound betwixt a shriek and groan came up from below, echoed by Lanyon's surly chuckle as he picked himself out of the embrasure, where in that last effort he had fallen prone; and the assault was over, the right-hand storming-party were already wavering in their attack, and the disaster of their fellows turned wavering into instant retreat. All scrambled across the causeway, or struggled out of the moat as quickly as they might, leaving behind their dead and wounded. Even had the trumpets not sounded sharply the recall, it is more than doubtful if Alain de Beaumanoir would have found enough to have followed him in a third essay.

CHAPTER XLVI.

VERY wroth was Sir Olivier de Clisson as he watched the failure of the first assault, though he knew not as yet the full extent of the disaster, and he chafed yet more bitterly over the second repulse; but when he heard of Yvon de Laconnet's miserable end, and of Geoffrey de Kerimel's death, his anger was turned into a great sorrow—for he had loved both of them well. He smote upon his breast with his clenched hand as he said aloud—

"Now may God pardon me, in that for mere vainglory I suffered my judgment to be overruled, and set on a needless hazard the lives of two valiant knights and many a good man-at-arms. Lo! here I make vow that if ever I win back to Rennes, there shall be said in the cathedral church a hundred masses each for the souls of Sir Yvon de Laconnet and Sir Geoffrey de Kerimel; neither will I put harness from off my back till they be here avenged. It is well we came amply furnished with engines and bombards: we will have yon wretched castle, if we pluck it down stone by stone."

Nevertheless De Clisson first bade his trumpets sound a parley, and sent forward his own body-squire, to pray for leave to take up their dead and wounded without molestation. This was granted readily. When the corpses were brought in, several besides Geoffrey de Kerimel's bore the same manner of death-wound—a wound evidently inflicted by a single downright blow that crashed steel and bone together—and some of the bluff Bretons glanced at each other rather ruefully, as they gathered round to look on the Free Companion's handwriting.

It was but natural that those withinside should triumph somewhat in their complete success; which had been achieved, too, at the cost of not a single life, but only a few sharp flesh-wounds.

Long speeches were not in Brakespeare's way at any time. He made no set oration to his garrison, but for each and every one he had a kindly or cheery word. The rawest recruit there—and some there were who had never before seen a blow struck in anger—felt that he had not periled his life for naught in serving such a captain.

The rest of that day passed quietly enough; for De Clisson set all his mind to the bringing up of his battering-train, and to the construction of those movable pent-houses called *chats-faux*, which in all regular sieges were then employed to protect the miners and pioneers. For the last purpose he used partly some of the trees just felled, partly beams taken from some deserted houses hard by; for the country folk had fled at the first news of the Bretons' approach, not guessing in what humor they would come. Nevertheless, De Clisson forbade his soldiers to plunder, or treat any that they should meet otherwise than as friends; and would allow only such matters to be taken as were absolutely necessary for the sustenance of his troops, or the requirements of his engineers. Night fell before all things were in order, for it was slow and toilsome work dragging up bombards, trebuchet and mangonel over the steep, rocky ground; so both besiegers and besieged lay quiet till the morning.

When it was barely light the siege opened in earnest, and soon it became evident on which side lay the advantage. Setting aside their bombards, the French had brought with them engines infinitely more powerful than any to be found at Hacquemont; for some of these last were of very antique make, and others had been hastily constructed of unseasoned wood, though with no mean skill. So the besiegers were enabled to do infinite damage, keeping just without the range of the missiles from within. De Clisson had great skill and practise in this line of warfare. Instead of dividing his battering-train, and attacking at divers points, be brought its full force to bear at once on one—the weakest point—that where the fruitless assault had been made; for there the plateau was broadest, and afforded most space for the working of his engines, and there was the longest space of curtain-wall betwixt the barbican and the nearest tower. The stone whereof Hacquemont was built, though of fairly durable quality, was neither granite nor limestone, and had waxed rotten under the rain and frost and winds of two centuries or more. Before the bombards and other artillery had played on it for an hour, there were shrewd gashes in the curtain-wall, and more than one of the battlements had toppled down into the moat. That same moat, too, soon ceased to be an efficient defense; for the *chats-faux* worked up slowly and surely to the very verge, and under their shelter worked the miners— filling up the ditch before them, not with a frail causeway of fascines, but with solid earth, on which, if need were, even one of those great siege-towers called *belfrois* could be rolled forward in safety. It was all in vain that the besieged bent trebuchet, petrary and mangonel against those solid pent-houses, for the heaviest missiles harmed nothing worse than planks and hide; neither could they work their engines in comparative safety as before; for the fire of all manner of artillery from without was so heavy and well directed, that by noon several of the Hacquemont men had been slain outright, and many more been sorely hurt by splinters of stone.

Brakespeare owned to himself, at length, that his followers were risking life and limb to little purpose; so he bade them get under cover. Thenceforward the French artillery played on unanswered; neither did the miners meet with any hindrance, while step by step they crept forward under their *chats-faux*, till they reached the castle wall itself, and fell to work there with mattock and pick. Then the fire from the bombards and battering-engines ceased, perforce, for there was danger of hurting their own men—either by the rebound of missiles or by a shot leveled too low. They were not suffered long to work in peace. Instantly that there was respite from the French artillery, the garrison gathered to their posts again; and soon a huge cantle of the battlements, already loosened by the enemy's fire, thundered down on the top of the largest *chat-faux*. The solid planks and beams cracked like straws under the weight, and scarce one of the miners thereunder escaped without maiming or mortal hurt. Quicklime and blazing pitch too came pouring down amain, so that the pent-houses were often in a blaze, which could not be extinguished without running the gantlet of the arbalests and mangonels ranged along the walls. Nevertheless, the French worked on stubbornly; and by sundown, by one means or another, there was a breach effected in the curtain-wall—nearly, if not quite, practicable. Then De Clisson sounded the recall. He knew that, sooner or later, the game must be in his own hands, and he chose—having made one false move already—to win it now by rule. He withdrew his *chats-faux*—indeed they were so shattered and charred as to be of little farther service—and returned to his encampment, leaving only on the plateau sufficient force to guard his battering-train from any chance of sally. He bade his troops rest and refresh themselves as best they might, for there would be sharp work to do on the morrow. But he himself, according to his vow, ate and drank in his helmet, and lay down in full harness.

The temper of the besieged was, as might be imagined, very different to what it had been on the evening before. There had been no brisk hand-to-hand work to warm their blood, only the same wearisome roar and whistle of the artillery without, the same crash and crumble of stone around their ears, the same rattle of pick and mattock under their feet. Many a man there thought within himself that night they were indeed fighting utterly without hope; yet never an one murmured or looked sad or sullenly on his captain when he came among them; and never a man, sorely hurt, flinched from due share of watch and ward. It was very late when Sir Ralph Brakespeare and Lanyon encountered in the courtyard, near the doorway of the keep.

"Follow me up hither, Will," the knight said. "I bade them bring up a stoup of Auxerre and any viands that are to hand into the presence-chamber. I have eaten naught save a manchet to-day; and thou, I wot, hast scarce fared better. Starving is sheer folly, with such work as we have before us to-morrow."

The esquire followed, seemingly nothing loth; and they found both wine and meat set out above.

"Sit thou down over agaisnt me," Ralph said. Then, seeing the other hesitated, he smiled. "Nay, the time is something short for ceremony; besides, thou and I have eaten and drunken together some few times since we emptied thy wallet by the spring under Westerham Down."

Lanyon complied without more ado, and there was silence, while the two made play with cup and platter, like the valiant trenchermen they were.

"How old art thou, Will?" the knight asked at length, suddenly.

The esquire looked up with rather a puzzled expression.

"Good faith, my lord, 'tis some time since I cared to keep just account of my years; yet I should reckon them two or three over fifty."

"Ay; art thou so much mine elder?" Ralph replied, "truly I had not thought it. Well, each of us in our fifty years, more or less, have had a busy time—if not a blithe—busier, I wot, than haps to most who die at fourscore and ten."

"Yea so, my lord," the esquire assented, "even if we

have done now with both work and play. Howbeit I see not why this should be so, unless ye be still resolved to surrender on no terms, how fair soever."

The knight shook his head.

"It would matter little," he said, "whether I changed my purpose or no. Thou and I will never more ride forth together; this I know of a surety."

So rising, he came round till he stood behind Lanyon's chair and began to speak—resting one hand on the other's shoulder.

"I am not given to superstition, and I hold the reading of dreams to be an old wife's trade; nevertheless I am assured that I have gotten my warrant. Yesternight I lay down, as thou knowest, in the middle watch, and slept presently, after the brisk day's work. Then I dreamed this dream:

"I walked my rounds, as it seemed to me, on the walls yonder—at what hour I cannot say: it surely was not night, for the light of the Frenchman's camp-fires glimmered all palely; yet never, even under storm, have I seen the day so murkily overcast. Moreover, the air was so heavy that I felt choking in my bascinet, and was fain to lay it by. As I walked on thus, bareheaded, and came to the northwest battlements—whereof scarce one is now upstanding—there advanced to meet me one whom I saw instantly to be none of our own sentinels. It was a knight in fair rich armor, wearing a crested helmet with its vizor down, and a surcoat much longer than those now in fashion. I challenged as he drew near, demanding to be informed of his name, and whether he came as friend or foe. He answered in a low voice, but marvelously clear—

"'We are not strangers altogether, though we met but once, and that long time ago. When thou hast looked on my face thou wilt judge in what guise I come.'

"As he raised his vizor I drew back in a great wonder, and—I will confess it—in some fear. Truly I had looked on that face before; ay, Will, and so hast thou. It was on the evening when, up yonder among the dunes I ran my first course with grinded spears. It was Loys de Chastelnaye, and no other. As we stood together in the dusky light I saw the gold chevrons glimmer on his surcoat. I knew it was a spirit I was talking with, yet I felt fear no longer."

"'Good my lord,' I said, 'I trust well ye come not as mine enemy, for I wot of no reason why there should still be feud betwixt us. In fair fight ye were sped, much to my sorrow; neither have I since willingly wrought aught against the peace of you or yours.'

"He smiled upon me, even as he smiled on that same evening when we washed the blood from his lips, and gave him to drink of water.

"'Thou hast rightly judged,' he answered. 'In all amity I am here to render thee one good office in payment for many; for had I lived I could not have served this House of Hacquemont so wightly as thou hast done, and well thou knowest wherefore I love all who bear that name. Lo, now, I warn thee that within three days at the farthest thou wilt be even as I, wherefore make thy peace with God as best thou canst, and fear not. There hath been much intercession made for thee of late by one whose prayers may something avail.'

"Even whilst he spake the dusk behind him seemed to lighten; and, though I saw none approach, I was 'ware of a woman in bright white robes, standing close beside us. I knew it was the *damoiselle* Marguerite, before she lifted her veil, and before I heard her voice. Will, thou mindest how rarely sweet it was long ago—it hath sevenfold the music now. Thus she bespoke me:

"Yea, I also say "Fear not:" for every ill that burdeneth thy soul since my cross was plucked from thy neck, thou hast, in one shape or other, done penance; and within these days past—forasmuch as under sharp trial thy heart waxed not hard—thou hast won much on Heaven's mercy. Against the wrong thou mayst have done to others, there shall be set, I well trust, that thou hast wrought for the weal of me and mine. I kissed thee once in sign of friendship; lo, now, here in my dear lord's presence, I kiss thee as a sister, lovingly.'

"With a right joyful heart, I swear to thee, I knelt down before and she laid her lips here on my brow, but they felt so deadly cold that I started and awoke."

The esquire had listened, sitting stock-still, and when he spoke, after a minute or two, he neither turned his head nor looked up.

"And, my lord, is this your dream? was there no word of me?"

"I have told thee all," Brakespeare replied, "letter for letter, and well I wis I have forgotten naught."

Lanyon glanced up in his master's face with a quaint humor on his own.

"Truly, I was overbold," he grumbled, "to think that knight or high-born dame, whether in flesh or spirit, would concern themselves greatly as to what would befall a battered old *routier*. Under your leave I will prophesy for mine own self. Your worship may remember certain words of mine when your hand rested on my shoulder—even as to-day awhile ago, only that we were far out in the deep sea. 'Whether ye sink or swim,' I said, 'I am minded to keep your company.' So say I now: which founders first is but small matter."

Just then the door at the lower end of the presence-chamber opened, and Gualtier de Marsan came in to inquire his lord's farther orders for the night. Ralph looked kindly on the esquire, and half pityingly too, for the other's face was very wan and weary.

"I have no more work for thee to-night. De Clisson is too wary a captain to attempt the breach darkling, so we must needs have rest to dawn. I am minded to take repose, and I counsel thee, Gualtier, to do likewise: thy strength is somewhat minished by sickness, and I fear me it hath been overtaxed already. Trust me, I was not so busy but that I marked how gallantly thou didst bear thyself before Bullhead here," he smote Lanyon on the shoulder, "played his old sleight with the scaling-ladder. So rest you well while you may."

There was an eager, wistful look in De Marsan's eyes, and it seemed as though he would have spoken; but if he had any such thought, the presence of the other esquire restrained him. With a low obeisance he turned and left the presence-chamber.

That interruption, brief as it was, had broke the thread of the previous discourse, and the knight and squire spoke no more together, save on mere matters of duty, that night. Each understood the other thoroughly well, and was content to let things bide.

CHAPTER XLVII.

THE chapellan of Hacquemont was still at his post. It had been at first intended that he should go forth with Odille and her escort, but the old priest prayed so earnestly to be suffered to remain that he at last prevailed; indeed it was not likely—unless by some unlucky accident—that harm would befall him. While it was yet dark Ralph confessed himself and heard mass in the castle chapel. Many in the garrison besides Lanyon and De Marsan did likewise, albeit one of the spearmen who had come from over Alps was heard to mutter discontentedly in his beard, " that their captain's brains must be wool-gathering. In the merry old days he would have found time for no such mummeries." But this was not altogether so. The Free Companion from boyhood upward had ever been rather a foe than a friend to frock and cowl; he had once lain actually under the Church's ban, and for many years had been something more than irregular in observance of devotion; but he had never thought blasphemously or even lightly in his heart of the faith of his forefathers, and now, looking death calmly in the face, he was minded to meet it, not like a Pagan, but like a Chrisom, though sinful man.

The breach in the northwestern walls was, as has been aforesaid, nearly, if not quite, practicable when on the previous evening the French artillery slackened fire, and during the night the besieged made no attempt to repair it. Sir Ralph Brakespeare knew better than to exhaust his men's strength in fruitless toil. Even if hewn stones and skilled masons had been at hand, their work would not have stood an hour when the bombards and great battering-engines were again brought to bear thereon. So all preparations against assault were made within side the breach, out of sight of the besiegers.

Soon after dawn the French were astir: but contrary to the expectation of all in Hacquemont no present attempt was made to storm. The night had brought counsel to Olivier de Clisson, and he was little likely now to be led into error—either by his own impatience or the rashness of others. More lives had been lost already before this worthless fortress than had been spent in the capture of strong and wealthy towns, and the Breton leader determined within himself that he would use to the uttermost all his mechanical advantages rather than shed another drop of blood in hair-brained emprise: so once again the huge battering-engines began to play, all directed at one spot—the face of the breach. The missiles were so concentrated and so deftly aimed that the gap was not greatly widened; but the heaps of disjointed masonry grew lower and flatter, till they became almost level—literally pounded to powder under the pitiless fire, and the ascent from without seemed hardly more difficult and steep than that of a rough mountain road; or, at the worst, the dry bed of a mountain torrent.

About ten of the clock De Clisson owned to himself that naught could be gained by farther delay; so he bade his artillery cease and all things be made ready for assault. Hitherto the garrison had kept carefully under cover—some in the keep itself, some in the towers on either side of the northwest curtain-wall; in the which, though somewhat shaken and damaged, there was still found sufficient shelter—but the instant the fire of the enemy's artillery abated a trumpet within the castle sounded the "assembly." The Free Companion knew right well what that lull and stillness after the tempest portended, and mustered his men instantly to meet the assault.

The time was so short, and the breach so open, that little could be done to hinder the advance of the stormers; yet something the garrison attempted by their leader's orders—strewing here and there planks slippery with oil, and driving into every available crevice sharpened stakes or truncheons of lances, so as to make a kind of rude stockade. Throughout the siege the Red Cross of St. George had floated from the keep; but now, on either of the two towers flanking the breach, was planted a pennon. On the one was blazoned a *rouge dragon*, the device of Hacquemont; the other—it had not been aired for many a day—bore the device of two splintered lances, crossed, on a sable field.

The French advanced eight abreast, their order resembling that of a modern column of subdivision, shouting the war-cries of their different leaders. In the front rank marched Sir Alain de Beaumanoir, who claimed that honor in right of having been forbidden to try his fortune in the first assault. Next to him came Sir Tristan de la Roye, a very valiant Breton knight; who, in the last campaigns under the Constable, had acquired great renown; Sir Olivier de Clisson himself was a little to the rearward. All the withinside of the breach was lined with armed men; how deep they stood could not be discerned from without. In the center of these stood Sir Ralph Brakespeare, swaying the mace that had done such terrible service on the first day of the siege; at either shoulder were his two esquires.

The ill-fortune of his brothers-in-arms seemed to cling to Alain de Beaumanoir. He and his next followers were much hindered by the slippery planks and sharp truncheons of the stockade, and while the knight recovered himself from a stumble a stone hurled from the battlements above struck him down with a severe though not a mortal wound. But Tristan de la Roye and the rest pressed on undismayed; sparing neither themselves nor their fallen comrades, who they pushed aside, or trampled on rudely. The stakes were all soon broken, and the oiled planks grew rough with blood and dust. So, ere long, besiegers and besieged came fairly hand to hand. The last-named were helped by firmer footing and vantage of ground; for the upward slope of the ruins was still somewhat steep, and at the crown of the breach there was a kind of rampart of disjoined stones and fragments of masonry—not much more than knee-high, but still no light impediment with a determined enemy beyond. Then there ensued a combat both obstinate and cruel. Spears were almost useless in the close mellay, and all the work was done with mace, glaive and gisarme. Mere weight of numbers in their rear would have kept the foremost assailants from retreating, had they been so minded; but the stubborn Breton blood was fairly roused; never a man of them flinched, though one after another dropped in his tracks, and never a foot of ground was gained.

If from without the shots went up lustily of "Clisson! Clisson!" and "St. Yves Bretagne!" no less lustily rang the answer from within—"Hacquemont! Hacquemont! St. George Guienne!" Though the defenders too were falling fast, the gaps were filled as soon as made. In that front rank Ralph Brakespeare and his two esquires—all the three as yet unhurt—bore up the brunt of the battle. Sir Tristande la Roye himself was down, choking in his blood—a dexterous stroke, dealt by Gaultier de Marsan, had cloven through his camail, just beneath the fastening of his helmet—and the press was so great that his esquires could not win from their lord breathing-space, or even drag him from under trampling feet. Even while the din was at its height, a clear imperious voice made itself heard ever and anon—

"*Bretagne! Bretagne! Hardis mes gars; point ne tresbuschez!*"

And that voice came nearer and nearer, till Olivier de Clisson himself stood in the forefront of his men—almost within arm's length of Ralph Brakespeare.

Then there came a lull in the fray; for, as though by tacit consent, the meaner combatants on either side drew back a little, most lowering their weapons as those two famous champions were set face to face. So far as could be judged through their heavy plate armor they seemed very fairly matched—the Breton might have been some two inches lower in stature, but his breadth of shoulder and depth of chest were marvelous, and even on that unsteady footing (for every stone was slippery now with blood) his brawny limbs bore him up like a tower. Save during the brief parley from the barbican those two had never met, and the vizors of both were closely locked now; nevertheless through instinct, or that freemasonry which exists only among men of their peculiar stamp, each guessed at once to whom he was opposed and made himself ready accordingly.

Sir Olivier de Clisson carried only his great *epée d'armes*. Seeing this, the Free Companion cast down beside him his dripping mace, and bared his own blade.

The Breton bowed his head, as if acknowledging a courtesy, then " *à nous deux*," he said between his teeth, and the duel began.

There was no fear of foul play from the followers of either champion; for the rules of chivalry were so well understood and so rigidly enforced in those days, that the meanest who rode under knight's pennon knew better than to infringe them. The strength and skill of the combatants were so evenly poised, and both were such rare masters of their weapon, that for awhile no great damage was done. Blows that seemed as if they must needs have been deadly were either warded altogether or so turned that they fell slantwise; but as the fierce delight of battle overmastered them, they grew less careful to guard, and more eager to strike. Red drops oozed through two or three gaps in De Clisson's armor of proof, and his blade had bitten deep more than once through the joints of the other's

Milan harness. Still they smote on without let or stay, till it was almost a miracle how mortal sinews could support such a strain—unrefreshed by a second's breathing-space. None that looked on that passage of arms had ever seen the like, and De Clisson himself, in after days, was wont to quote as the most notable feat of his famous life his having held his own so long. It was ended at length in this wise: The Breton, in fetching a desperate stroke, over-reached himself, and stumbled slightly forward; before he could recover himself, the Free Companion's blade descended in full swing on the crest of the other's helmet. The edge was sorely notched and blunted, nevertheless it clove sheer through the outer plate, and crushed steel *coiffe* down on the brain-pan so that Olivier de Clisson dropped as one dead—blood streaming from nose and mouth through his vizor bars.

The Free Companion made no attempt to follow up his victory; he dropped his *epée d'armes*—in that last blow it had been so injured as to be well-nigh useless—and catching up his mace, again stood ready for the attack. Howbeit none of the assailants offered to advance, till two Breton squires had raised their lord's body from the spot to which it had rolled, and borne it to the rear. It was a stricken hour before the remedies of the camp-leech conquered the obstinate swoon, and it was days before the swimming left Olivier de Clisson's brain, or that his hand was steady enough to couch lance.

That the Bretons were for the moment greatly discomfited by their captain's fall may not be doubted; but the panic lasted not long, nor was there any lack of leaders. So the attack was renewed more savagely than ever; as if another disgrace were to be atoned for. Mortal thews and sinews are not iron and stone, and bulwarks of bolted granite go down often enough before the incessant lashing of the surge. It was only natural that the small defending force should at length be thrust back by the mere weight of the living torrent hurled against their front. Every inch of ground cost lives, yet, step by step, the Hacquemont men were borne back from the breach into the courtyard, in the midst of which rose the keep. Just then Ralph drew back a pace or two out of the mellay, and said some words in an undertone to one of his Italian veterans, who had been fighting close to his shoulder. When the tide of battle fairly turned, and the day looked utterly desperate, the five *soudards* had thrust foward and closed round their captain: just as you may see the old hounds pressing to the front when the pack breaks from scent to view. The *routier* nodded his head without speaking, and forcing his way backward through the press, entered the tower on the right. Thence, in a miuute or so, he emerged, carrying Brakespeare's own pennon, with which he disappeared into the keep.

When the space grew broader—so that the assailants could bring their weight and numbers better to bear—it soon became apparent how fearfully the garrison was overmatched; yet they were too well trained and too ably maneuvered to make a disorderly retreat; and still presented so strong a front that there was no chance of their being surrounded as they fell back slowly on the open doorway of their last stronghold.

The Bretons pressed on more and more furiously, incited partly by the confidence of success, partly by the desire of cutting off their enemies from the keep—or, at least, of entering it with them pellmell; for if the door were once shut and barred, there would still remain the storming of the steep narrow stair. Nevertheless the men of Hacquement made good their retreat, disappearing one after another through the low dark arch, till Brakespeare himself, who was hindermost of all, stood within a fathom of the threshold.

No; not quite the hindermost.

Ralph had cleared a half-circle in front with a *moulinet* of his terrible weapon, and his foot was planted for the backward spring that would have carried him within the doorway, when he saw something that changed his purpose. Throughout the mellay—both at the breach and in the courtyard—Lanyon had been almost side by side with his lord, fighting in his own dogged fashion, and taking no heed of divers flesh-wounds and bruises that would have gone near to disable many. He was right well aware that it behooved to gain a moment's leisure to bar the door in the face of the assailants; so when the Bretons made their last fierce charge, he hurled himself right in the teeth of their left flank—knowing that oftentimes the sudden onslaught even of a single man will for a second or two hold several in check. He never doubted but he should be able to fight his way back over the brief space that divided him from the keep; and this, perchance, he might have done, had not one of his sollerets slipped on a stone, so that he fell forward on his face right under the feet of his enemies. The esquire's prowess that day had made him a marked man. He was scarcely down when some half-dozen were upon him, hacking and hewing with glaive and battle-ax, like woodmen ribing the trunk and limbs of a tough felled oak.

This was the sight that checked the Free Companion in the act of his backward spring.

The passions of those who, from youth upward, have made fighting their trade, are not easily stirred by mere change of blows, howsoever hard; .up to this time—save, perchance, for a brief space during his combat with De Clisson—Ralph had kept himself perfectly calm and cool. But now the blood surged hotly through his veins, and mounted to his eyes. Only once before in all his life had the real Bersekyr fit possessed him, and then, as now, it was at Hacquemont. He gnashed his teeth as he swore that " dead or alive, his old comrade should be with him to the last," and plunged headlong into the press, striking such blows as made all that he had heretofore dealt seem but boy's play; and shouting the war-cry—disused now for many a day—" Brakespeare! Brakespeare! " Some two or three of the Bretons—brained before they were well aware—fell athwart Lanyon as he lay prone; the others recoiled, fairly appalled, crying out " Sorcery," or that " the Fiend in man's shape was among them." Before this panic passed, the Free Companion had lifted his esquire in his arms, and borne him into the tower, the door of which was instantly barred behind him.

Without staggering or faltering, the knight carried his burden up into the presence-chamber, where all who survived of the garrison were gathered together, and sat down on the ledge of the dais, supporting Lanyon's head on his knee.

"Unhelm him, one of ye—he must have air."

As Ralph spoke he threw back his iron vizor. The esquire's armor was hacked almost to fragments; there was scarce a hand's-breadth of body or limbs ungashed, and one deep sword-wound under the left arm-pit would have sufficed to let life out had there been none other. His cheeks were too strongly tanned altogether to lose their color, but the brown was flecked and streaked with ashen gray, and the lips were already contracting, so that the strong white teeth showed betwixt. Nevertheless, after a minute or so, there came a stir in the lower limbs and a gurgle in the throat; then Lanyon opened his eyes. Those eyes were not so dim and hazy but that they saw at once who leaned over him, and whose hand held his own fast. For a second the dying man's glance wandered aside, to where one of his comrades stood holding the black pennon, once so famous among the Free Lances; then it rested again on his master's face and dwelt there.

"Farewell till our next meeting, old friend," the knight said quietly, "and God requite thy true service better than I have done."

Then his lips began to work, and those who stood by heard a ghastly semblance of the surly chuckle, which showed that, after his own stolid fashion, he was relishing a jest. Then he gasped out these words one by one:

"Messire—Ralph—I—founder—first—despite—the

dream." The last syllables mingled with the death-rattle.

A few seconds later Brakespeare loosed very geutly the clasp of the corpse's fingers.

"Draw him aside, so that he be not trampled on," the knight said, as he rose. His face had settled down again and bore no sign of grief or pain, or even of the heat of battle; and in the same measured voice in which he had once before made brief oration to his garrison, he thus bespoke them:

"Good friends and followers, while we have brief breathing-space—for the door below will yield to naught less than engine or *bellier*—take counsel, I pray you, for your own safety. Hardily, thus far, have ye stood at my back; I render you hearty thanks therefor; but I now discharge each and every one of you from such duty—nay, I earnestly urge that ye will risk your lives no farther. Too many lie dead without there already; to such as remain the French will surely show fair quarter. I am under a vow to fight here *à l'outrance* but none such binds any of ye; wherefore I counsel you to ascend to the platform up yonder and make what terms ye will for your own selves with them below, leaving me here to do as seemeth me good—only let French hands, and none of yours, pluck down St. George's banner. And so shall ye be free of all shame or blood-guiltiness in sight both of God and man."

The thing may sound incredible nowadays, but in those times—whether for good or evil—men acted not by our standard and rule. Among those who listened to the Free Companion there was neither dispute nor doubt. They cried out with one accord praying their captain to forbear such words, for that they all were ready to stand by him to the death. Brakespeare, as he thought, had well-nigh done with earthly vanities, yet his heart swelled with soldierly pride at this last proof of his power, and his cheek flushed a little as he bowed his head, saying simply—

"It is well."

Then he beckoned to the esquire De Marsan, who, all this while, had stood somewhat apart.

"Reach me down, I pray thee," he said, "yon *epée d'armes* that hangs behind thee on the wall." Having unsheathed the weapon, the knight went on speaking:

"Messire Gualtier, when on the morrow after Poictiers Prince Edward gave me right to wear gold spurs, I was a poorer man than thou art—ay, and nameless to boot—yet had I not merited the grace so well as thou, within these last days, hath done. Kneel down, then; there is much blood on this hand of mine, yet naught that should disable it from bestowing accolade; and for this purpose I use the sword long worn worthily by Philippe of Hacquemont, thy good lord and mine."

Drawing his breath so hard that it sounded like a sob, the esquire knelt reverently down, and Ralph laid the blade on his shoulder, saying—

"Rise, Sir Gualtier de Marsan. Be brave and fortunate."

As the new-made knight gained his feet the eyes of the two men met in a long steadfast gaze, and a great weight was lifted from Gualtier's soul; for he knew then of a surety that Odille's husband was aware of and had forgiven all.

The Fortunes of a Free Lance.

"I have one thing more to do," the Free Companion said. "Bring hither my pennon." When it was brought he looked on the *banderolle* attentively, turning it over and over. Then he wrenched it off the staff and tore it into shreds between his strong fingers as if it had been made of tissue. The bitter significance of the action escaped none who stood by; and, with hearts sad, if not sinking, they waited for what was to follow.

All this while the besiegers had not been idle. When the door was first closed some few smote on it with mace and curtal-ax, but it was too strongly plated to yield to such puny weapons, so they were fain to wait for battering-ram. There was no lack of such things in their camp, and ere long there was brought a beam of about the thickness of a small ship's mast, heavily shod with iron, and furnished throughout its length with rope beckets. A score of archers, standing ten on either side, laid hold of these, and with their full strength swung the ram against the door. The first blow fell just as the last thread of the pennon fluttered down at Brakespeare's feet, and stroke followed stroke till the door was fairly forced from its hinges and came clattering in. Now the lowermost stair of the keep did not wind like the upper one, but came straight up into the presence-chamber. Yet it was both steep and narrow, so that the storming it could be no light matter; but the Bretons had waxed furious under repulse, and their leaders had spared neither reproaches nor gibes while they waited without. If the foremost had hesitated to enter, they would have been thrust forward by their fellows; so the stairway was

was soon full, and echoing with the clash of steel. The assailants, both within and without the tower, shouted their war-cries aloud; but the defenders answered never a word—they fought not the less savagely because they fought mute. It skills not to relate the incidents of that last passage of arms, which differed little from many that had gone before. It is sufficient to say that after the foining had gone on for ten minutes or more, Ralph Brakespeare and Gualtier de Marsan, though both sorely wounded, still stood where they had first taken post—on the fourth step below the stair-head.

Despite of this the event could not long have been doubtful. Sir Guiscard de Keroualles, of whom mention before has been made, was a very wary veteran. Casting his eyes around as he stood in the courtyard, he soon devised a fresh mode of attack. The scaling-ladders that were tall enough for the battlements were useless here, but two of these, bound together, reached easily the top of the keep. Sir Guiscard himself mounted first, and many others followed unopposed, till the platform at the summit was crowded. Then the Bretons, who by their captain's order had hitherto kept silence, raised a great shout, and poured down the upper stairway, and through the open door at the upper end of the presence-chamber, so that before the Hacquemont men were well aware, they found themselves taken in the rear. There was a rush back from the stair-head instantly. Brakespeare and De Marsan, unsupported from behind, were borne back, perforce, by the mere weight in their front; so the mellay recoiled to the body of the hall. This lasted not long. The sturdiest of the garrison saw that fighting on against such odds was mere self-slaughter, so cries of "surrender" went up all round, and one after another cast down his weapon. Two men only neither cried for quarter nor ceased to smite—Brakespeare and De Marsan. But Gualtier was weak with loss of blood, and his sword-arm utterly weary, so he was soon borne down and lay in a swoon on the flag-stones. Yet was not the fray quite ended, nor Hacquemont quite won; for in the center of the hall there still was turmoil and clash of steel, and medley of voices—some crying out to "slay," and some, but these were few, to "spare" —and in that mid-eddy Ralph Brakespeare's mace still rose and fell. Twice he was beaten to his knee, and twice he rose again—hurling back his assailants as a brave bull, though a-dying, shakes off the ban-dogs. But, during the second struggle, the fastenings of his helmet burst, and when his bare head rose again half a span above the sea of helmets, the crisp, grizzled brown hair was red-wet. He swept his left hand across his brow, for the blood well-nigh blinded him, and whirled his mace round once more. His arm seemed not a whit less strong and dexterous than when, with one blow, it brained Geoffrey de Kerimel; and once again the assailants drew back from its sweep, so that for a second or two the Free Companion stood almost solitary in their midst, reared to his full height, and with a great bright light in his steadfast eyes. It was a strange sight, that struck most there either with wonder, pity, or fear, and something like a hush ensued; but almost immediately this was broken by a hoarse voice, crying—

"*Sous au sorcellier!*"

And a savage-looking archer stepped out of the throng in the knight's rear, and smote on his bare head with his gisarme.

Without a moan or a struggle, Ralph Brakespeare pitched forward—dead before his forehead touched the flagstones.

When De Clisson heard what had been done, he was very ill-pleased thereat, for he averred that he had rather than a thousand golden crowns have taken the Free Companion alive, sith he had not slain him with his own hand. And very rueful waxed the knight's countenance as he looked at the gaps in his muster-roll, and counted up the cost of the siege; for the booty found in Hacquemont hardly amounted to a month's pay of a hundred spearmen, and the castle itself, as a fortalice, was scarce worth the winning. So De Clisson departed, leaving behind a force sufficient to guard and repair the place, letting the old garrison go where they would—first binding them by oath not to bear arms against France. With him, too, went Gualtier de Marsan, but not as a prisoner; for the new-made knight, having satisfied his honor and discharged his duty as esquire, was not minded to persist in bearing arms against his natural sovereign. So he became liegeman of France again, and by dint of good service found favor both with King and Constable.

When the news of what had been done at Hacquemont came to Bordeaux, and the ancient merchant who had the packet in charge delivered to the Lady Odille her husband's letter, the widow's mourning for many days after was real. It was embittered, too, by some sharp twinges of remorse, and for awhile she thought that nothing would fill the void of the true unselfish love that she had never valued till now. Nevertheless, two years later, when Gualtier de Marsan urged his suit, she listened readily; and, during the brief peace of Bruges, they were married, and the intercession of De Guesclin easily obtained for Odille's husband the investiture of all the fiefs of Hacquemont.

There, for many years, those two dwelt very happy in a grave quiet way, for old times were never quite forgotten—and children grew up around them, who listened eagerly to the story of the puissant champion who once saved Hacquemont with his single arm; and afterward, by his desperate defense, made it famous through France.

Over Ralph Brakespeare's grave in the castle chapel was laid a fair marble slab; whereon were graved a name, a date, and an escutcheon. The escutcheon bore —not the arms of Hacquemont, but a device better fitted to the life, the fortunes, and the death of the strong soldier, who early in life cut himself adrift from kith and kin, and struggled onward as a nameless man —the device of

Two splintered lances, crossed, on a sable field.

THE END.

A FEW OF
GROSSET & DUNLAP'S
Great Books at Little Prices
NEW, CLEVER, ENTERTAINING.

GRET: The Story of a Pagan. By Beatrice Mantle. Illustrated by C. M. Relyea.

The wild free life of an Oregon lumber camp furnishes the setting for this strong original story. Gret is the daughter of the camp and is utterly content with the wild life—until love comes. A fine book, unmarred by convention.

OLD CHESTER TALES. By Margaret Deland. Illustrated by Howard Pyle.

A vivid yet delicate portrayal of characters in an old New England town. Dr. Lavendar's fine, kindly wisdom is brought to bear upon the lives of all, permeating the whole volume like the pungent odor of pine, healthful and life giving. "Old Chester Tales" will surely be among the books that abide.

THE MEMOIRS OF A BABY. By Josephine Daskam. Illustrated by F. Y. Cory.

The dawning intelligence of the baby was grappled with by its great aunt, an elderly maiden, whose book knowledge of babies was something at which even the infant himself winked. A delicious bit of humor.

REBECCA MARY. By Annie Hamilton Donnell. Illustrated by Elizabeth Shippen Green.

The heart tragedies of this little girl with no one near to share them, are told with a delicate art, a keen appreciation of the needs of the childish heart and a humorous knowledge of the workings of the childish mind.

THE FLY ON THE WHEEL. By Katherine Cecil Thurston. Frontispiece by Harrison Fisher.

An Irish story of real power, perfect in development and showing a true conception of the spirited Hibernian character as displayed in the tragic as well as the tender phases of life.

THE MAN FROM BRODNEY'S. By George Barr McCutcheon. Illustrated by Harrison Fisher.

An island in the South Sea is the setting for this entertaining tale, and an all-conquering hero and a beautiful princess figure in a most complicated plot. One of Mr. McCutcheon's best books.

TOLD BY UNCLE REMUS. By Joel Chandler Harris. Illustrated by A. B. Frost, J. M. Conde and Frank Verbeck.

Again Uncle Remus enters the fields of childhood, and leads another little boy to that non-locatable land called "Brer Rabbit's Laughing Place," and again the quaint animals spring into active life and play their parts, for the edification of a small but appreciative audience.

THE CLIMBER. By E. F. Benson. With frontispiece.

An unsparing analysis of an ambitious woman's soul—a woman who believed that in social supremacy she would find happiness, and who finds instead the utter despair of one who has chosen the things that pass away.

LYNCH'S DAUGHTER. By Leonard Merrick. Illustrated by Geo. Brehm.

A story of to-day, telling how a rich girl acquires ideals of beautiful and simple living, and of men and love, quite apart from the teachings of her father, "Old Man Lynch" of Wall St. True to life, clever in treatment.

GROSSET & DUNLAP, 526 WEST 26th ST., NEW YORK

GROSSET & DUNLAP'S
DRAMATIZED NOVELS
A Few that are Making Theatrical History

MARY JANE'S PA. By Norman Way. Illustrated with scenes from the play.

Delightful, irresponsible "Mary Jane's Pa" awakes one morning to find himself famous, and, genius being ill adapted to domestic joys, he wanders from home to work out his own unique destiny. One of the most humorous bits of recent fiction.

CHERUB DEVINE. By Sewell Ford.

"Cherub," a good hearted but not over refined young man is brought in touch with the aristocracy. Of sprightly wit, he is sometimes a merciless analyst, but he proves in the end that manhood counts for more than ancient lineage by winning the love of the fairest girl in the flock.

A WOMAN'S WAY. By Charles Somerville. Illustrated with scenes from the play.

A story in which a woman's wit and self-sacrificing love save her husband from the toils of an adventuress, and change an apparently tragic situation into one of delicious comedy.

THE CLIMAX. By George C. Jenks.

With ambition luring her on, a young choir soprano leaves the little village where she was born and the limited audience of St. Jude's to train for the opera in New York. She leaves love behind her and meets love more ardent but not more sincere in her new environment. How she works, how she studies, how she suffers, are vividly portrayed.

A FOOL THERE WAS. By Porter Emerson Browne. Illustrated by Edmund Magrath and W. W. Fawcett.

A relentless portrayal of the career of a man who comes under the influence of a beautiful but evil woman; how she lures him on and on, how he struggles, falls and rises, only to fall again into her net, make a story of unflinching realism.

THE SQUAW MAN. By Julie Opp Faversham and Edwin Milton Royle. Illustrated with scenes from the play.

A glowing story, rapid in action, bright in dialogue with a fine courageous hero and a beautiful English heroine.

THE GIRL IN WAITING. By Archibald Eyre. Illustrated with scenes from the play.

A droll little comedy of misunderstandings, told with a light touch, a venturesome spirit and an eye for human oddities.

THE SCARLET PIMPERNEL. By Baroness Orczy. Illustrated with scenes from the play.

A realistic story of the days of the French Revolution, abounding in dramatic incident, with a young English soldier of fortune, daring, mysterious as the hero,

GROSSET & DUNLAP, 526 WEST 26th ST., NEW YORK